W9-ALJ-047

MAGILL'S SURVEY OF AMERICAN LITERATURE

MAGILL'S SURVEY OF AMERICAN LITERATURE

Volume 3

Hawthorne–Lurie

Edited by

FRANK N. MAGILL

Marshall Cavendish Corporation

New York • London • Toronto • Sydney • Singapore

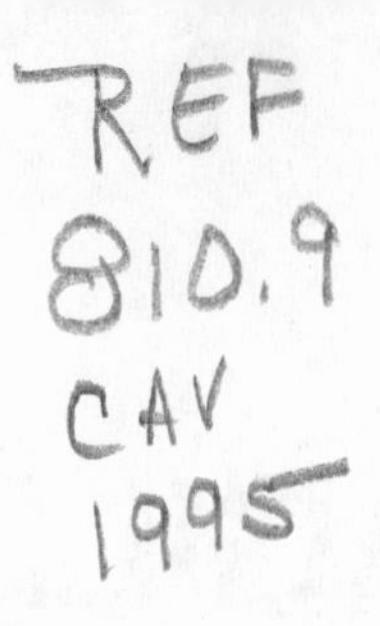

Published By
Marshall Cavendish Corporation
2415 Jerusalem Avenue
P.O. Box 587
North Bellmore, New York 11710
United States of America

∞ The paper used in these volumes conforms to the American National Standard for Permanence of Paper for Printed Library Materials, Z39.48-1984.

Library of Congress Cataloging-in-Publication Data

Magill's survey of American literature. Edited by Frank N. Magill.
p. cm.
Includes bibliographical references and index.
1. American literature—Dictionaries. 2. American literature—Bio-bibliography. 3. Authors, American—Biography—Dictionaries. I. Magill, Frank Northen, 1907.
PS21.M34 1991
810.9'0003—dc20
ISBN 1-85435-437-X (set) 91-28113
ISBN 1-85435-440-X (volume 3) CIP

Second Printing

PRINTED IN THE UNITED STATES OF AMERICA

CONTENTS

page

Hawthorne, Nathaniel 837
H. D. 852
Heinlein, Robert A. 863
Heller, Joseph 878
Hellman, Lillian 886
Hemingway, Ernest 897
Herbert, Frank 913
Hinton, S. E. 921
Howells, William Dean 932
Hughes, Langston 943
Hurston, Zora Neale 955

Irving, John 967
Irving, Washington 980

James, Henry 989
Jeffers, Robinson 1003
Jewett, Sarah Orne 1016

Keillor, Garrison 1028
Kennedy, William 1039
Kerouac, Jack 1050
Kesey, Ken 1059
King, Stephen 1067
Kingston, Maxine Hong 1082
Knowles, John 1095

L'Amour, Louis 1103
Lee, Harper 1113
Le Guin, Ursula K. 1120
Lewis, Sinclair 1129
London, Jack 1142
Longfellow, Henry Wadsworth 1155
Lowell, Robert 1166
Lurie, Alison 1178

Glossary XLIII
List of Authors LVII

MAGILL'S SURVEY OF AMERICAN LITERATURE

NATHANIEL HAWTHORNE

Born: Salem, Massachusetts
July 4, 1804

Died: Plymouth, New Hampshire
May 19, 1864

Principal Literary Achievement

The first American fiction writer to achieve international fame, Hawthorne demonstrated how moving literature dealing with serious philosophical issues could be developed from the comparatively crude early American civilization.

Biography

Nathaniel Hawthorne was the descendant of Puritan colonists responsible for the persecution of people accused of witchcraft during the seventeenth century. His sense of guilt over the superstitious cruelty of his ancestors is reflected in much of his writing. His father, a sea captain, died when Nathaniel was only four years old. The fact that he grew up without a male role model and was surrounded by adoring female relatives helps to account for his personality, which has been consistently described by biographers as shy, inhibited, narcissistic, and introverted. Ironically, he was an exceptionally handsome young man who was much sought after by the young ladies.

With his widowed mother and his two sisters, he had to live on the charity of relatives and resented his status as a poor relation in an enterprising Yankee society which revered the almighty dollar. This, too, helps to explain his solitary and independent nature. Most of the towns in Massachusetts were small and still surrounded by virgin forests. As a boy, Hawthorne loved to go hunting and fishing by himself; the wilderness of North America exerted its own influence over the imaginative boy, which lasted the rest of his life and can be seen in his stories and novels. He attended Bowdoin College in Maine but was not an outstanding student. He read only what interested him, tending to skip over the rest. After graduation, he considered the conventional careers that were open to him and rejected them all. "I do not want to be a doctor and live by men's diseases, nor a minister to live by their sins, nor a lawyer to live by their quarrels," he wrote to his mother. "So, I don't see that there is anything left for me but to be an author."

Hawthorne's life was, in a sense, uneventful; it was mainly devoted to literature.

For more than twelve years after graduating from Bowdoin, he spent most of his days and nights in a room in his mother's home, patiently writing pages and pages of manuscripts, many of which he burned. In addition to experimenting with stories and essays, he began keeping a journal in which he jotted down random impressions, a practice he pursued throughout his life. His published notebooks make up many volumes. He used his notebooks the way many painters use sketchbooks: to collect little details for incorporation into his finished productions. He was also developing his own style and trying to discover what kinds of characters, incidents, and themes he might write about. It was a difficult task for a writer in Hawthorne's time and place, because there was virtually nothing to emulate in contemporary American fiction. The popular fiction writers of his day were all Europeans. Americans were far more interested in the charms of an older culture than in the prosaic facts of their own. One of the most successful writers of the day was the Scottish poet, novelist, historian, and biographer Sir Walter Scott, whose novels *Ivanhoe* (1819) and *Quentin Durward* (1824) are best known to modern readers. Scott wrote about lords and ladies in castles and manor houses; he could draw on centuries of history and legend for material. By comparison, Hawthorne—in the raw, new civilization of North America—was at a tremendous competitive disadvantage. Nevertheless, he persisted in studying the history of New England and struggling to find subject matter for his fiction in the people and places of his native land.

In 1828, Hawthorne published *Fanshawe: A Tale*, a romantic novel he had started writing in college. He was not at all satisfied with his work and did not publish another novel for almost a quarter of a century. During that time he produced short pieces, which were published in various New England magazines. Finally, in 1837, he published a collection of his short pieces under the title *Twice-Told Tales*, a book which is regarded as a classic of world literature. The stories and sketches in this volume are unmistakably American; they also bear the stamp of Hawthorne's genius, which was characterized by strength of imagination and a painstaking attention to small detail. The book was warmly reviewed by Hawthorne's former college classmate Henry Wadsworth Longfellow, who was to become the most famous American poet of his day.

In 1839, Hawthorne was appointed weigher and gauger at Boston Custom House; he wrote amusingly of this experience in the introduction to *The Scarlet Letter* (1850). He was not happy with this sinecure and resigned in 1841 in order to join the socialist community of Brook Farm. There he became acquainted with some of the most important thinkers of his day, including the philosopher Ralph Waldo Emerson, and the naturalist Henry David Thoreau, author of the autobiographical masterpiece *Walden* (1854). He was strongly influenced by their doctrine of Transcendentalism, which is characterized by a belief in the importance of intuition rather than reason in arriving at truth. Hawthorne was too much of a "loner" to fit into the socialist community, however, and left after eight months. He believed that man had to be reformed from within rather than being reformed by the imposition of new social arrangements. The twentieth century failure of socialism in Russia and Eastern Europe suggests that Hawthorne was not only correct but was also far in advance of his time.

Shortly after leaving Brook Farm, he married Sophia Amelia Peabody. This began the happiest period of his life. They had three children, and the love and responsibility of family life had a humanizing effect on him; however, he also had the burden of supporting four other persons on the uncertain income of a writer.

It was not until the publication of his novel *The Scarlet Letter* in 1850 that Hawthorne became a well-known writer. The next year he published his second great novel, *The House of the Seven Gables,* along with a book of stories for children called *A Wonder-Book for Boys and Girls.* (Hawthorne contributed greatly to the development of a literature for children, which was virtually nonexistent before his time.) All these works brought him fame and money. He was one of the few American fiction writers of his time who made a financial success of this profession.

In 1853, Hawthorne's good friend of college days, Franklin Pierce, became President of the United States and appointed Hawthorne to be American Consul at Liverpool. Hawthorne and his family spent the next seven years in Europe, and Hawthorne published two books based on his European experiences: *The Marble Faun* (1860), a novel based on Italian history, and *Our Old Home* (1863), a collection of essays about England.

Hawthorne returned to the United States in 1860 and lived in Concord, Massachusetts, near such famous figures as Longfellow and Emerson. Upon his death in 1864, he was widely eulogized as one of America's foremost men of letters.

Analysis

Although Hawthorne is still required reading in many American literature courses in high schools and colleges, he is not especially popular with young readers. American fiction has changed greatly since his time. Popular twentieth century novelists such as Ernest Hemingway, F. Scott Fitzgerald, and J. D. Salinger make Hawthorne seem sententious and tedious, like some elderly relative who dominates the dinner-table conversation. Hawthorne's style, once considered elegant and aristocratic, now seems artificial and needlessly complicated, the pernicious effect of the study of Latin. He is weak in dramatic construction; he avoids confrontations where confrontations seem obviously called for, as in the case of Arthur Dimmesdale and Roger Chillingworth at the conclusion of *The Scarlet Letter.*

Hawthorne has no qualms about stopping his narrative to present long descriptions of trees, flowers, streams, clouds, sunsets, houses, streets, pedestrians, and so forth. He lived at a time when photography was in its infancy and there was no way of reproducing photographs in books or magazines. (One of the principal characters in *The House of the Seven Gables* earns his living by making "daguerreotypes," a primitive form of black-and-white photography.) Readers of Hawthorne's time enjoyed verbal descriptions of beautiful landscapes or picturesque towns and cities; it was the only means they had of "seeing" them. Modern readers, who are saturated with television, motion pictures, and reproductions of color photographs on glossy paper, have lost the ability to appreciate such detailed verbal descriptions and have a tendency to skip over them in order to get on with the story.

Hawthorne's characters agonize over moral problems. They often seem impossibly noble or impossibly sinister to readers who are accustomed to more subtle characterization in fiction. Probably the feature that does the most to "date" Hawthorne's stories and novels is his old-fashioned dialogue. In his day, the novels of Sir Walter Scott were the rage both in England and the United States. Hawthorne devoured Scott's novels in his youth, and it can be seen from the most casual comparison that Hawthorne's and Scott's characters talk in the same overblown fashion, full of courtly phrases, noble sentiments, polysyllabic words, and carefully balanced sentences. Mark Twain, the great American novelist, short story writer, and humorist, sounded the death knell for this kind of writing—at least in the United States—by producing novels such as *The Adventures of Huckleberry Finn* (1884), in which the characters talk like real people and are actuated by credible human motivations.

This being the case, why do English teachers continue to assign Hawthorne's short stories and novels as required reading in American literature courses? Hawthorne is important as the founding father of genuine American literature—as opposed to the transplanted English literature that flourished on the North American continent before his time. Hawthorne can also be regarded as one of the creators of the modern short story, a literary form that has been described as America's unique contribution to world literature. He is important because of the influence he had on his successors, particularly in terms of theme and subject matter. He was the first American fiction writer to portray the color and drama in ordinary American life, so later writers such as Sherwood Anderson, Theodore Dreiser, Sinclair Lewis, and William Faulkner—in fact, all succeeding American writers—are deeply indebted to him. Through his dedication to his craft, he showed his successors how to be American writers and not English men of letters living in exile. In practical terms, Hawthorne proved to American writers that they could compete with the more sophisticated English writers for the dollars readers paid for books. His works might be called an artistic declaration of independence.

In the long run, Hawthorne may be regarded as an important writer primarily because of his interest in human psychology and his explorations—daring at the time—of the dark side of human consciousness. Prior to Hawthorne, the function of literature was considered to be to elevate the human spirit. In the words of Henry James (an American writer who moved to England and became a British subject), what most appealed to Hawthorne's imagination was "the old secret of mankind in general . . . the secret that we are really not by any means so good as a well-regulated society requires us to appear." According to the founder of psychoanalysis, Sigmund Freud, civilization requires men to suppress and deny their aggressive and sexual impulses, which leads to inner conflict, guilt, and in some individuals to neurosis and psychosis. This is the area of human consciousness that Hawthorne was exploring before Freud was even born. He approached it in a guarded way; that is why his works are so full of allegory and symbolism. Modern men of letters such as horror writer Stephen King have no such qualms. Hawthorne lived and died before the English naturalist Charles Darwin published his theory, now generally accepted, that the human race is descended from an apelike animal. Most people of Hawthorne's time believed that man had been created by God and was more like the angels than the lower animals. This belief compelled them to deny the animal passions that were seething inside them; however, they could secretly recognize their portraits in such Hawthorne stories as "Young Goodman Brown" (1835) and "The Minister's Black Veil" (1836). In his refined and genteel way, Hawthorne opened up a whole new world of human experience for his literary heirs to explore. His example led to a literature that was more honest in discussing human emotions and motivations. This hypersensitive, reclusive man had a remarkable strength of character which enabled him to carve out a new literature for a new nation.

MY KINSMAN, MAJOR MOLINEAUX

First published: 1832
Type of work: Short story

A penniless country youth searches colonial Boston for an influential kinsman, but discovers that the kinsman is being banished in disgrace.

Although on the surface "My Kinsman, Major Molineaux" appears to be a simple story, it offers much information about Hawthorne's experience, attitudes, interests, and artistic aims. This ability to suggest a wealth of meaning in compressed form is a sure sign of genius. The moral of the story is that no one should look to others to help him: He must learn to look out for himself. This message is expressed in philosophical terms by Hawthorne's friend and mentor, the Transcendental philosopher Ralph Waldo Emerson, in his famous essay "Self-Reliance" (1841). Hawthorne's early experiences as a poor relation living on the charity of his own "kinsmen" had taught him the bitterness of dependency. The story also shows Hawthorne's interest in early American history, which he studied assiduously during his "silent years" of self-imprisonment from 1825 to 1837 and used as subject matter for much of his fiction. It also shows the power of his imagination. "Mr. Hawthorne's distinctive trait," wrote Edgar Allan Poe, a contemporary writer of great imaginative talent himself, "is invention, creation, imagination, originality—a trait which, in the literature of fiction, is positively worth all the rest." In "My Kinsman, Major Molineaux," Hawthorne performs the difficult feat of re-creating a colonial city of a century before his time, complete with streets, houses, shops, sounds, smells, and a variety of inhabitants. It is this sensation of being transported backward in time that holds the greatest interest for the reader.

Another feature of this story, to be seen again and again in Hawthorne's later work, is his sardonic, tongue-in-cheek humor, which mercifully brightens some of his grim subject matter. Although Hawthorne seems greatly concerned with matters of religion and morality, he deliberately took a more sophisticated and intellectual approach to these matters than was the case with his Puritan ancestors.

Hawthorne's technical skill as a prose writer, which he polished during his years of seclusion after graduating from college, is clearly evident. He uses light and darkness as did the great painters Caravaggio and Rembrandt Van Rijn, who called their technique "chiaroscuro." The story consists of a succession of night scenes feebly lighted by candles and lanterns or flickering fireplaces glimpsed through windows and doorways. The feeling of darkness is maintained until the climax in order to provide a vivid contrast when the protagonist's proud and influential kinsman Major Molineaux is seen in the midst of a horrible parade with all his pain and humiliation pitilessly revealed to the world by the light of all the blazing torches. The brightness of the parade symbolizes the young hero's sudden enlightenment.

Finally, the story touches on what was Hawthorne's favorite idea: that everyone, no matter how dignified and righteous he may appear, has a dark side to his nature which is hidden from the world like the dark side of the moon. Hawthorne does not reveal why Major Molineaux has been tarred and feathered by the townspeople, but their behavior indicates that he has well deserved it.

YOUNG GOODMAN BROWN

First published: 1835
Type of work: Short story

A young man sneaks off to the forest to witness a devil-worshiping orgy and is shocked to find many respected citizens in attendance.

"Young Goodman Brown" is a perfect example of Hawthorne's favorite theme that human nature is full of hidden wickedness. The young hero's journey in the story is symbolic of one's journey through life, in which each individual gradually loses his or her naïveté and innocence as a result of exposure to greed, lust, envy, perversion, and the other sins of humanity. The crowning blow to Brown's naïve conception of the world comes when he discovers that his own meek and innocent wife Faith is one of the celebrants at this Walpurgis Night orgy. As is often the case, Hawthorne treats his theme with a tongue-in-cheek humor which arises mainly from the contrast between people's real characters and the false faces they present to the world. The humor is vital to this story; the reader is enticed along the forest pathway by an illusion of frivolity and comes to realize the full horror intended only after finishing the last page.

Stories such as this entitle Hawthorne to be considered one of the principal founders of the modern short story, a form of literature in which American authors have excelled. The essence of a modern short story, as defined by Edgar Allan Poe in a newspaper review of Hawthorne's *Twice Told Tales*, is that every detail contributes to a single effect. Prior to Hawthorne's time, short stories tended to be episodic and loosely structured, often resembling essays. The single effect produced by a modern short story can be produced by the overall mood, as is often the case in the stories of the Russian writer Anton Chekhov, or mainly by a surprising or shocking ending, as is usually the case in the stories of the French writer Guy de Maupassant and the American writer O. Henry. In "My Kinsman, Major Molineaux," the effect of terror and dismay is produced by the surprise ending. In "Young Goodman Brown," the effect of horror and disillusionment spiced with sardonic humor is produced by the overall mood.

Hawthorne writes about witches and devils like a man who does not really believe in such grotesque creatures but appreciates them as colorful and dramatic symbols of humanity's hidden guilt and fear. Some of his stories are not unlike modern horror films which evoke laughter from the audience along with shivers and shrieks. This indicates a sophisticated modern attitude which was characteristic of many of his European and American contemporaries who were trying to reconcile traditional beliefs with modern scientific knowledge.

WAKEFIELD

First published: 1835
Type of work: Short story

On a mere whim, a middle-aged man leaves his wife and lives by himself for twenty years within one block of his home in busy London.

"Wakefield" has an unusual form: It is part story and part essay. The author does not try to conceal his presence, as is usually done by fiction writers for the sake of achieving greater verisimilitude, but actually invites the reader to participate with him in creating the story and deducing a moral. Instead of aiming at suspense, Hawthorne gives the whole plot away in one sentence: "The man, under pretence of going on a journey, took lodgings in the next street to his own house, and there, unheard of by his wife or friends, and without the shadow of a reason for such self-banishment, dwelt upwards of twenty years." The form resembles a musical composition in which the theme is stated at the beginning and then embellished with variations until it is recapitulated at the end. The story is a masterpiece: It demonstrates Hawthorne's imagination and artistic skill. It also has a haunting effect, like a beautiful but elusive melody.

"Wakefield" is not only a psychological study but also a sociological study. How is it possible for a man to be swallowed up so completely by a big city that he is able to live undetected for twenty years within one block of his wife's residence and never bump into any of the friends who believe him to be dead? That he would wish to do it at all is strange enough, but the fact that this story is regarded as one of Hawthorne's finest creations shows that many readers are able to identify with Wakefield. Hawthorne is talking about the loneliness and alienation of modern life, one of his favorite themes. Civilization was becoming more and more complex, and the individual was gradually being swallowed up. He does not say how Wakefield managed to live for twenty years without any income, but presumably he would have transferred funds to a different bank account under an assumed name. In earlier times it would have been impossible for most people to survive without interacting with others; however, one of the features of modern civilization is that each individual tends to be a separate and interchangeable component of an enormously complex social machine.

In addition, the story reflects Hawthorne's personal loneliness and addiction to solitude, which remained with him even after he was married and had fathered three children. Many of the people who knew him best, such as Ralph Waldo Emerson, described him as cold and aloof. Only Hawthorne's devoted wife Sophie seemed to understand her husband's true nature, which was shy, sensitive, and idealistic. Hawthorne's, and his character Wakefield's, sense of being totally isolated while surrounded by thousands of people may have been relatively unusual in the first half of the nineteenth century, but it is commonplace today. It is one of the reasons there is so much alcoholism and drug abuse. The ability to capture such important social themes in literature is an unmistakable sign of genius and an indication of why Hawthorne's works are valuable to modern readers.

THE MINISTER'S BLACK VEIL

First published: 1836
Type of work: Short story

A minister who feels overwhelmed by guilty impulses hides his face behind a veil for the rest of his life, to the consternation of his parishioners.

In "The Minister's Black Veil," Hawthorne plays another variation on his favorite theme that mankind is universally afflicted with the Seven Deadly Sins of pride, covetousness, lust, envy, gluttony, anger, and sloth. Like all Hawthorne's short stories, it displays the author's vivid imagination. It also shows exceptional artistry. Whereas in "Young Goodman Brown" Hawthorne tears off people's masks and exposes their real faces, in "The Minister's Black Veil" he hides the face of a single character and thereby creates the impression that the exposed faces of all the other characters are actually masked.

"The Minister's Black Veil" lacks the relieving humor of stories such as "Wakefield," "Young Goodman Brown," and "My Kinsman, Major Molineaux." Consequently, the single effect it produces by its overall mood is unremittingly grim and unpleasant. It is hard to sympathize with any man who would choose to wear a black veil all of his life, even to bed, and it is certainly easy to understand why his horrified fiancée would decide to reject him. The story is interesting mainly because the minister is an obvious precursor of the Reverend Arthur Dimmesdale in Hawthorne's most famous work, the novel *The Scarlet Letter.*

THE OLD MANSE

First published: 1846
Type of work: Essay

In this peaceful description of his life in an old house in Concord, Hawthorne includes brief descriptions of neighbors Emerson and Thoreau.

"The Old Manse" is an example of the kind of short pieces that Hawthorne published in collections of short stories although they were not stories but sketches or essays. Other notable examples of such rambling descriptive pieces, which Hawthorne loved to write, are "The Toll Bridge" and "Rills from the Town Pump" in his *Twice-Told Tales.* As Edgar Allan Poe pointed out in his famous review of that book, these nonfiction pieces are characterized by a feeling that Poe called "repose." They are almost the opposite of short stories, in that nothing dramatic ever happens in them. Modern editors frequently refer to such works as "mood pieces." There is no conflict; they do not have much of a point and do not build to any sort of climax. Consequently, they are now only popular with literary connoisseurs and not with the modern reader conditioned to expect thrills and titillation in his reading matter.

"The Old Manse" was published as an introduction to a collection of Hawthorne's short pieces entitled *Mosses from an Old Manse* (1846), which contained such excellent short stories as "The Birthmark" and "Rappaccini's Daughter." Although "The Old Manse" is not a short story at all, it does evoke a mood of rustic peace and domestic bliss. It also contains interesting thumbnail descriptions of his famous neighbors Emerson and Thoreau. In this introduction, Hawthorne describes his contented life with his wife and children in a big house in Concord, Massachusetts, which had formerly been the home of Emerson. It was called The Old Manse and has been preserved for posterity as a national monument.

THE SCARLET LETTER

First published: 1850
Type of work: Novel

In Puritan times, a young woman is condemned to wear the embroidered letter "A" (for adultery) over her breast for having an illegitimate baby.

The Scarlet Letter was Hawthorne's most successful work and is still regarded as his masterpiece. The entire novel is built on the five simple words contained in one of the Ten Commandments: "Thou shalt not commit adultery." The fact that Hawthorne was able to base such a long work on such a simple premise is an indication of genius. The great Russian writer Leo Tolstoy did much the same thing in his novel

Anna Karenina (1875-1877) some quarter of a century later, and no doubt he was influenced by Hawthorne's example. Another prominent Russian writer, Anton Chekhov, in "The Lady with a Pet Dog" (1899), emulated Hawthorne's very modern treatment of the psychological turmoil arising from adultery. Theodore Dreiser's novel, *An American Tragedy* (1925), deals with a similar theme.

Most people in Hawthorne's day had orthodox notions of religion, based on the Bible. They thought of God as a bearded super-patriarch living up above the clouds who was somehow able to see everything that was happening on Earth and was keeping a record of everyone's sins with the intention of punishing them in the afterlife. Hawthorne and his intellectual contemporaries no longer believed in heaven and hell, or angels and devils, because modern science was rapidly undermining the authority of the Bible. Yet this did not by any means imply that Hawthorne rejected traditional morality. He realized that it was the basis of civilization and wanted to place morality on a foundation of reason. *The Scarlet Letter* shows people being punished for their sins in the here and now through the operation of natural cause and effect. Arthur Dimmesdale is punished by his own feelings of guilt, remorse, and shame. Long before the time of Sigmund Freud, Hawthorne showed how mental problems create physical ailments. Dimmesdale eventually dies of guilt, although his mind is relieved by his public confession.

Hawthorne's novel was a financial success. No doubt it was popular because it dealt with sexual matters, although in a heavily veiled manner. Much has been made of Hawthorne's use of symbolism; however, it may be that he employed it mainly because he was not able to describe certain things more explicitly. For example, the sin of adultery means sexual intercourse between a married person and a partner other than the lawful spouse. It was utterly impossible for Hawthorne to depict this graphically in his day; his book would never even have been published if he had touched on such material. His solution was ingenious: Hester Prynne gives birth to a little girl who is living proof of the sin. So Pearl, her daughter, is a symbol of the act of adultery. Hawthorne also calls Pearl "a living hieroglyphic," which simply means that as she gets older it should be possible to "read" her father's identity from studying her facial features. Thus she is not only a symbol of adultery and a symbol of guilt but also a symbol of Dimmesdale's craven fear of exposure.

The scarlet letter "A" which Hester is condemned to wear over her breast is of course another symbol of unlawful sexual intercourse. In a sense it might be described as a fetish: an object that arouses sexual desire, or at least sexual thoughts. It functions as a "stimulus" (in the terminology of behavioral psychologists): Each time the scarlet letter is mentioned, the reader gets a subliminal mental image of a naked man and woman engaged in sexual intercourse. Modern readers accustomed to explicit descriptions of sexuality would hardly find Hawthorne's novel titillating, but the mere suggestion of unsanctioned sexual intercourse—or, indeed, any sexual behavior at all—was daring for Hawthorne's time.

Like the minister's black veil in the story of that name, Hester Prynne's scarlet letter has a dual nature. It is a continuing accusation directed at all the members of the community: It suggests that all of them should be wearing their own letters over their breasts, although not all of them would wear the same letter. The fact that Hester's letter "A" is ornate, like the letters in a book from which a child learns the alphabet, and the fact that her little daughter is constantly touching it and trying to understand its meaning, suggest that there is a whole alphabet of sins that could be attached to the gowns and shirt fronts of the other citizens. Dimmesdale himself deserves more than one letter: He could wear a "C" for cowardice, an "H" for hypocrisy, or an "L" for lying. The novel implicitly refers to the famous incident in the New Testament in which a woman who had been caught in the act of adultery was brought before Jesus and he was asked if it was permissible to stone her to death as prescribed by Mosaic law. Jesus replied: "He that is without sin among you, let him first cast a stone at her." Everyone in the mob withdrew in silent admission of his own hidden guilt.

Hawthorne created the character of Roger Chillingworth because he needed an antagonist to move the plot along. One of Hawthorne's weaknesses as a fiction writer was that he tended to lavish his attention on visual elements such as descriptions of landscapes and to avoid heated interactions between his characters. This weakness is attributable to his own shy and passive character. The only sins he himself committed were probably committed in his imagination. Static plots with heavy emphasis on visual description might suffice for short works, but a full-length novel needed an ongoing conflict to retain reader interest. Chillingworth's behavior is strange; why does he not kill Dimmesdale, for example, if he feels so outraged? If not that, he could denounce him to the whole community, which might even be worse. It is only because of Chillingworth's odd notion of revenge that the novel is able to move forward to its conclusion. It is hard to see exactly what he is trying to accomplish by his sadistic treatment of Dimmesdale; although he is indispensable to the plot, he is the least believable of all the characters. This seems like an artistic flaw in the novel, yet Hawthorne is masterful in demonstrating how human sins are not punished in some hypothetical afterlife but in the here and now through the suffering they bring. A sensitive man such as Arthur Dimmesdale must suffer for the suffering he causes others, and an insensitive man such as Roger Chillingworth blinds himself to the harm he causes and is self-condemned to go through life as a blind man.

THE HOUSE OF THE SEVEN GABLES

First published: 1851
Type of work: Novel

A man who builds a house on land obtained through perjury incurs a family curse which brings misfortune for the next two hundred years.

The House of the Seven Gables is based upon another of the Ten Commandments: "Thou shalt not bear false witness against thy neighbor." To illustrate his thesis,

Hawthorne drew upon another verse from the book of Exodus, which reads in part: "I the Lord thy God am a jealous God, visiting the iniquity of the fathers upon the children unto the third and fourth generation of them that hate me." What Hawthorne chose to do was considerably more difficult than what he had done in *The Scarlet Letter*, a story which covered a time span of less than ten years. In *The House of the Seven Gables*, he was trying to show how Old Maule's curse afflicted his false accuser and all his descendants for two centuries. He was not entirely successful, but it was a gallant effort. Henry James says of this novel:

> [I]t has always seemed to me more like a prologue to a great novel than a great novel itself. I think this is partly owing to the fact that the subject, the donnée, as the French say, of the story, does not quite fill it out, and that we get at the same time an impression of certain complicated purposes on the author's part, which seem to reach beyond it.

To deal with all the descendants of the greedy and malicious Colonel Pyncheon over a period of two hundred years would require several thick volumes. Hawthorne attempted to cope with this artistic problem by dramatizing the plight of the last few descendants and referring to the others in expository flashbacks. As James suggests, however, this does not give satisfactory proof of his proposition that a curse could affect every member of a family for such a long period of time.

In *The Scarlet Letter* it is quite easy to see how the sin of adultery can be "punished" through natural laws. The minister succumbs to passion and then feels guilty when he is forced to witness the suffering he has caused. The biggest question raised by the story of *The House of the Seven Gables*, on the other hand, is whether a house can carry a curse for two hundred years, and, if so, how. Furthermore, if Matthew Maule had the power to invoke such a curse, then Colonel Pyncheon was not bearing false witness when he caused him to be hanged for witchcraft.

William Faulkner was obviously influenced by this novel. Many of Faulkner's works deal with the theme of how entire Southern families were cursed for the sin of exploiting black slaves. In his famous novel *The Sound and the Fury* (1929), he shows the degeneration of an old Southern family in a manner echoing the degeneration of the Pyncheon family in *The House of the Seven Gables.* In Faulkner's long story "The Bear" (1942), the protagonist gives up title to the land he inherited from his slave-owning ancestors to get rid of the curse he feels he inherited along with it. Faulkner's treatment of the theme of succeeding generations being visited with the iniquity of their forefathers seems more plausible than Hawthorne's; it is easy to see how white aristocrats would be forced to perpetuate their unjust treatment of blacks in order to maintain their status. Each generation would be morally weakened by the parasitical dependence on exploited labor and at the same time forced to see the visible results of their sins in the debasement of the people they exploited.

In *The House of the Seven Gables*, however, Hawthorne does not adequately illustrate the mechanism by which Colonel Pyncheon's sin is passed on to his descendants. If a man makes a fortune through wicked business practices and then leaves the money to his son when he dies, is it necessary that his son will be injured by the money, or is it possible that the son will enjoy the money and live a happy life? It is a moot question. In *The Beautiful and Damned* (1922), a novel by another famous American writer, F. Scott Fitzgerald, the hero expects to inherit the bulk of an estate valued at around 100 million dollars that was accumulated by his grandfather through ruthless business dealings. The hero becomes a drunken wastrel because he feels no need to do anything for himself. This seems entirely plausible; the reader can readily understand the psychological process by which this result would come about (and in fact it was exactly what happened to many so-called "playboys" of Fitzgerald's generation). In chapter 20, Hawthorne writes, "Old Maule's prophecy was probably founded on a knowledge of this physical predisposition in the Pyncheon race" [that is, the predisposition to have strokes]. Here Hawthorne is deliberately trying to show a rational, non-supernatural explanation for the apparent punishments inflicted for mortal sins. Like the great English epic poet John Milton, one of his favorite authors, Hawthorne is trying "to justify [or rationalize] the ways of God to man." Since he is dealing with dozens of descendants over two centuries, however, he is not as convincing as with Arthur Dimmesdale and Hester Prynne, his "Adam and Eve," in *The Scarlet Letter.*

The House of the Seven Gables, like *The Scarlet Letter*, is a series of finely executed tableaux. One of the finest of these, as well as one of the most unusual and most characteristic of Hawthorne, is chapter 18, entitled, "Governor Pyncheon." Hawthorne wrote for a more leisurely world in which one day was pretty much the same as the next and people rarely traveled more than a few miles from their homes; his writing must be read slowly and savored. Chapter 18 describes a dead man sitting in a chair. He died of a stroke, another apparent victim of Maule's curse. His watch, which he was holding in his hand at the time of his death, is still ticking, and Hawthorne describes that ticking, the only sound to be heard in the room. Hawthorne loved such details. He describes the changing patterns of light inside the room as the sun moves from east to west.

> Meanwhile the twilight is glooming upward out of the corners of the room. The shadows of the tall furniture grow deeper, and at first become more definite; then, spreading wider, they lose their distinctness of outline in the dark, gray tide of oblivion, as it were, that creeps slowly over the various objects, and the one human figure sitting in the midst of them.

He speculates on where the dead man might have been expected and what some people might be thinking of his unexplained absence. The dead man was going to be nominated for governor that very day: it was to have been the crowning moment of his externally honorable but secretly vicious career. The moonlight comes in the window, and still the dead man sits there. Hawthorne imagines the ghosts of Pyncheon's ancestors coming out of the shadows to stalk the room, along with the ghost of Matthew Maule, the wronged man who originally placed a curse on the house of the seven gables. The modern reader who tries to skip over or race through such long descriptive passages is missing the very best that Hawthorne has to offer: the use of his powerful imagination to create finely detailed word pictures. These images bring a vanished world back to life, so that the reader can step through the picture frame and enter the town of Salem as it existed in the first half of the eighteenth century.

It is worth repeating that Hawthorne was not personally as obsessed with guilt as his stories and novels might suggest. According to his great admirer Henry James,

> Nothing is more curious and interesting than this almost exclusively *imported* character of the sense of sin in Hawthorne's mind; it seems to exist there merely for an artistic or literary purpose. . . . What pleased him in such subjects was their picturesqueness, their rich duskiness of colour, their chiaroscuro; but they were not the expression of a hopeless, or even a predominantly melancholy, feeling about the human soul.

Summary

Although Hawthorne seems preoccupied with sin and guilt, he was far from being a fire-and-brimstone preacher. He believed that God is a spirit pervading all creation and that human failings are punished by natural processes. He did not believe in heaven and hell except as they symbolize the happiness or suffering that people produce through their own actions. Hawthorne's ghosts and demons are merely psychological symbols with interesting dramatic and artistic potentialities. This shy, hypersensitive writer had an iron will which enabled him to endure loneliness, discouragement, and financial hardship for the sake of his art. His life and work set a lasting example for American writers.

Bibliography

Howells, William Dean. "Hawthorne's Hester Prynne." In *Heroines of Fiction*. Vol. 1. New York: Harper, 1901.

James, Henry. *Hawthorne.* London: Macmillan, 1967.

Lawrence, D. H. "Hawthorne's Blithedale Romance." In *Studies in Classic American Literature.* New York: Viking Press, 1968.

____________. "Nathaniel Hawthorne and *The Scarlet Letter.*" In *Studies in Classic American Literature.* New York: Viking Press, 1968.

Martin, Terence. *Nathaniel Hawthorne.* Rev. ed. New York: Chelsea House, 1981.

Poe, Edgar Allan. "Hawthorne's Twice-Told Tales." In *Selections from the Critical Writings of Edgar Allan Poe.* New York: Gordian Press, 1981.

Van Doren, Mark. *Nathaniel Hawthorne.* New York: Viking Press, 1957.

Woodberry, George E. *Nathaniel Hawthorne.* New York: Chelsea House, 1981.

Bill Delaney

H. D.

Born: Bethlehem, Pennsylvania
September 10, 1886
Died: Zurich, Switzerland
September 28, 1961

Principal Literary Achievement

The exemplary poet of the Imagist movement in the twentieth century's second decade, H. D. is also considered the "poet's poet" for her meticulously crafted and myth-inspired epic verse written during the twenty-year period from the early years of World War II to her death twenty years later.

Biography

Hilda Doolittle, or H. D., was born September 10, 1886, in Bethlehem, Pennsylvania. Her upbringing encouraged her fascination with mysteries, especially mysteries of worlds that lie beyond the ken of the naked eye. Her astronomer father, Professor Eric Doolittle, explored the universe, and so would her older half-brother, Eric. The Doolittles moved in 1895 to Philadelphia, where, at the University of Pennsylvania, her father became the director of the university's Flower Astronomical Observatory. The American poet William Carlos Williams, who became friends with Hilda when he was a medical student at the university, later described H. D.'s father as "a tall gaunt man who seldom even at table focused upon anything nearer, literally, than the moon."

Hilda's mother, Helen Wolle, was teaching music and painting at a Bethlehem seminary when she met Professor Doolittle, a recent widower. H. D. was reared with her mother's sensitivity to the arts and was introduced to the mysteries of her mother's spiritual world, the Moravian religion. Bethlehem itself had been christened in 1741 by Count Zinzendorf, who, offering a retreat from religious persecution in Germany, was one of the founders of the Moravian church in the United States. The Moravians encouraged individual interpretation of scripture as an approach to salvation and truth and stressed a strong faith in the healing power of love, and particularly in redemption through the love of Christ.

H. D. attended Bryn Mawr College in 1904, withdrawing in 1906 for health reasons. She completed her education at home by studying Greek and Latin and the mysterious worlds of the ancients. She shared this love of the classics and her interests in writing with Ezra Pound, the American poet, who was just starting his liter-

ary career and was studying Romance languages at the University of Pennsylvania; she and Pound became engaged to be married. All friends at this time, H. D., Ezra Pound, and William Carlos Williams would later become three main forces in twentieth century literature.

Through Ezra Pound's encouragement, H. D. went to London in 1911. Pound, already in London since 1908, had been active in its literary and artistic circles, befriending young writers, such as Ford Madox Ford, T. E. Hulme, F. S. Flint, and T. S. Eliot, and the already established W. B. Yeats. Joining the activity, H. D. became known for her short, crisp verse; her "Priapus" (1913, later retitled "Orchard") and "Hermes of the Ways" (1913) were published in *Poetry* magazine; other poems were published in the *Little Review* and *The Egoist*.

It was at that time that Pound gave her the pseudonym and epithet "H. D., Imagiste," from which he promoted the poetic movement of Imagism—poetry that presents "no slither," but a clear-cut image that presents "an intellectual and emotional complex in an instant of time." Some of H. D.'s poems were included in 1914 in *Des Imagistes: An Anthology.*

In 1913, her engagement with Pound broken for some time, H. D. married Richard Aldington, a British writer also active in the Imagist enthusiasm. During the early years of her marriage and through the years of World War I, H. D.'s poetic popularity rose. Her poems increasingly appeared in literary magazines and anthologies. She published her collection *Sea Garden* (1916) and her translation of Euripides' *Choruses from Iphigeneia in Aulis* (1916), and she became the assistant editor of *The Egoist*, for which she also wrote reviews.

The time was personally traumatic, however; in 1915, H. D.'s first child was stillborn. Her life with Aldington was unsettling; he enlisted in the army in 1916 and was sent to France in 1918. Her personal and literary life was enriched and complicated with a relationship with the British writer D. H. Lawrence, whom she first met in 1914. H. D.'s younger brother was killed in the war, her father dying shortly after of the shock. After the war, her marriage was all but legally over. Pregnant, ill with double pneumonia, and near a nervous breakdown, H. D. gave birth to a daughter, Perdita.

H. D.'s physical and psychological recovery and Perdita's care were made possible by the English novelist Winifred Ellerman (her pseudonym was Bryher), daughter of a wealthy shipping-line owner, Sir John Ellerman. With Bryher, H. D. and Perdita took up residence in Switzerland and traveled to Greece in 1920 as part of H. D.'s convalescence.

In the period between the two world wars, H. D. pursued varied interests. She translated the ancients, particularly Euripides; she reviewed films, and even made one, *Borderline* (1930), with Bryher, Kenneth Macpherson, and Paul Robeson; and published verse collections, *Heliodora and Other Poems* (1924) and *Red Roses for Bronze* (1931). The greater percentage of H. D.'s writing during this time, however, was autobiographical fiction—full-length novels, *Palimpsest* (1926) and "Her" (published as *HERmione* in 1981), *Hedylus* (1928), and shorter works of novelette or short-story length, *Kora and Ka* (1934) and *Mira-Mare* (1934). Often set in ancient Egypt or classical Greece, the stories' characters are weakly veiled personas of H. D. herself and those close to her. The style is stream of consciousness: The narratives blend characters' freely associated thoughts and memories, time and place, past and present, dream and reality.

H. D.'s interest in dreams, the psychology of the mind, and her own psychological health led her in March of 1933 to Vienna to undergo psychoanalysis with its founder, Sigmund Freud. Freud was then seventy-seven years old, at the end of his prestigious and controversial career. Freud helped her, she wrote, to "take stock of her modest possessions" and "steer her course" through her troubles. Her *Tribute to Freud* was published in 1956. In 1974, an expanded version of the book was published that included "Advent," the journal that she kept during her first sessions.

H. D. had survived the personal and cultural devastation of World War I, and she feared the approach of World War II. She returned to London and responded to the challenge through an intense period of writing. She returned to writing poetry, poetry that many consider to be her best—*The Walls Do Not Fall* (1944), *Tribute to the Angels* (1945), and *The Flowering of the Rod* (1946), later published together as *Trilogy* (1973). These three works of epic length, developing a complex of themes within the context of the war, are markedly different from H. D.'s earlier verse.

H. D. lived in Switzerland during most of the 1950's, troubled by a weakening bone condition, compounded by abdominal surgery and a broken hip. She returned to the United States briefly in 1960 to receive the Award of Merit medal for poetry of the American Academy of Arts and Letters, the first woman to have been awarded this prize. Her last poem *Hermetic Definition* (1972), written mostly while bedridden and completed seven months before her death, is a final testament to H. D.'s great ability to overcome a challenge, respond to poetic inspiration, and sustain intense poetic mediation and wonderfully crafted verse in epic form. H. D. died of a stroke on September 28, 1961, in Zurich, Switzerland.

Analysis

Mysteries fascinated H. D.—the mysteries of life, of the mind, of civilization, of the past, of language—and she re-created in her writings those mysteries and her delight in discovering them. One can approach her work in the same spirit, piecing together the clues she weaves from the many disciplines and civilizations that have attempted to explain the world—her father's world of astronomy, medieval alchemy and astrology, her mother's Moravian religion, and Egyptian, Greek, and Roman mythology.

A central model for H. D.'s imagination was the palimpsest—the title, in fact, of her first novel. A palimpsest, a parchment or manuscript that was used in civilization's earliest writing, was erased to make room for more writing. Often the palimpsest, like a common chalkboard, was imperfectly erased, and the original writing was still visible along with subsequent writing. The palimpsest, then, simultaneously represents several different moments in time, with the past often peering into the present. In modern terms, time and place are relative, or all one; as one of her characters in *Palimpsest* reflects, "the present and the actual past and the future were (Einstein was right) one. All planes were going, on, on, on together and the same laws of hospitality held on all levels of life. Going on and on and on."

H. D.'s poetry and fiction is very seldom chronologically developed. Time and place and identities overlap. In "The Gift" (1969), H. D. explores the parallels between London, 1941, and Bethlehem, Pennsylvania, 1741, and her own childhood years. Civilizations and myths can compose the same palimpsest; the sun god, Helios, may appear in twentieth century London in the guise of a poet. H. D. sees the Egyptian god, Thoth, the inventor of writing and god of wisdom, the Greek god Hermes, and the Roman Mercury as one and the same.

The palimpsest is also the model for H. D.'s imagination, for the mind and memory, where all merges as one. Everything in the mind may seem in disorder, as three layers of a palimpsest viewed at once, but if one searches long enough, patterns will be revealed and a sense of order restored—in the mind or in the world. H. D. often likened her own self to the mythical Egyptian goddess Isis, searching the world to recover the scattered limbs of her murdered brother Osiris.

Much of the character of H. D.'s writing is cerebral and psychological, as it explores universal patterns to be found in the mind and memory. H. D. linked herself, as artist, with ancient scribes and visionaries and with modern psychologists. "Religion, art, and medicine, through the latter ages, became separated," she wrote in *Tribute to Freud*. She foresaw "these three working together, to form a new vehicle of expression or a new form of thinking or of living." By exploring the memory—individual memory and civilization's memory—the poet is within reach of the healing powers that priests and psychoanalysts provide through enabling one to understand oneself as well as the world.

Poetry's resource is language, and readers of H. D. will find that much of her work also explores the possibilities of language, discovering patterns in sound and meaning: "For example:/ Osiris equates O-sir-is or O-Sire-is;/ Osiris,/ the star Sirius," she writes in *The Walls Do Not Fall*. In *Tribute to the Angels*, the word *mer*, French for sea, undergoes a metamorphosis, or parthenogenesis, giving birth to Mary: "mer, mere, mère, mater, Maia, Mary,/ Star of the Sea,/ Mother." Mere is unmixed or pure; *mère* is French for mother; *mater*, Latin for mother; Maia, the loveliest of the Pleiades, is the mother of Hermes by Zeus; and Mary, mother of Christ.

H. D. freely associates words and ideas, as she does deities and places, civilizations and cultures. Her writing delights in the duality of language, what words reveal and what they conceal, and it re-creates a sense of discovery or imminent discovery. H. D.'s writing, her style and philosophy, and one's experience when reading her prose or verse can be summed up by Julia Ashton, her self-portrait in the novel *Bid Me to Live* (1960):

> If you look at a word long enough, this peculiar twist, its magic angle, would lead somewhere, like that Phoenician track, trod by the old traders. She was a trader in gold, the old gold, the myrrh of the dead spirit. She was bargaining with each word. She brooded over each word, as if to hatch it.

OREAD

First published: 1914
Type of work: Poem

The voice of the poem invokes the forces of nature, delighting in its energy.

"Oread" well represents H. D.'s early lyrical verse and the Imagist movement of poetry early in the twentieth century:

> Whirl up, sea—
> whirl your pointed pines,
> splash your great pines
> on our rocks,
> hurl your green over us,
> cover us with your pools of fir.

Terse and compact, the poem crisply conveys the natural forces at work, or called upon to work, by the series of active verbs and imperatives—"whirl," "splash," "hurl," and "cover." The hard-hitting lines stress a sense of urgency for nature to fulfill this request.

Ezra Pound's assessment of H. D.'s poetry best sums up "Oread" and the ideal verse he saw distinguishing the new American poetry for the century: "objective—no slither; direct—no excessive use of adjective, no metaphors that won't permit examination. It's straight talk, straight as the Greek!"

THE GARDEN

First published: 1915
Type of work: Poem

An appeal is made to the wind to bring relief from intense summer heat.

"The Garden," sometimes entitled "Heat," relates a mundane request of a type that many people commonly make relating to the seasons. One wishes—or prays—for rain as well as for a breath of fresh air. In this poem, however, H. D. elevates the request into a poetic occasion, one that provides readers a focus for intense contemplation.

As in "Oread" and many of her poems, the poet opens with an address or appeal—to nature, to a deity, to another person, or to herself. "O wind, rend open the heat,/ cut apart the heat,/ rend it to tatters." The poetic voice makes the immediate request in pounding, aggressive, and compact lines and follows with a number of direct assertions—fruit cannot even fall in heat this intense, the poem states. The compression of the poem itself seems to reinforce the close air and the poem's concluding plea to the wind: "Cut the heat—/ plough through it,/ turning it on either side/ of your path."

TRILOGY

First published: *The Walls Do Not Fall*, 1944; *Tribute to the Angels*, 1945; *The Flowering of the Rod*, 1946; as *Trilogy*, 1973

Type of work: Poem

In the midst of the worldwide destruction of World War II, universal questions concerning civilization's survival, art and religion, and personal salvation are explored.

The Walls Do Not Fall opens in confusion: "An incident here and there,/ and rails gone (for guns)/ from your (and my) old town square." The setting is London. Bombing raids during World War II were called "incidents" by the government and press, and iron railings were taken as scrap to make weapons. Yet the setting is also Karnak, Egypt, in 1923, when the tomb of Tutankhamen is opened; hieroglyphs—"bee, chick and hare"—decorate the temple and perhaps contain a prophecy. H. D. finds that war-torn London and time-worn Luxor are part of the same pattern; the traditional fog and mist of London mix with the musty air of the temple ruins. This mirroring of place is only one example of her "search for historical parallels,/ research into psychic affinities." H. D., or the voice of this work, then muses, "we passed the flame: we wonder/ what saved us? what for?" After surviving World War I and, so far, the incessant bombing of London in World War II, it would seem a natural question for any survivor to ask oneself. H. D. explores the answer to this question.

Determining to whom the poet is addressing this question—other than to herself—will also provide the answer as to the purpose of the poet's survival. H. D. addresses or invokes a divine Presence throughout the poem, the Presence perhaps the spiritual savior. As London and Karnak merge, so do the personages Ra, Osiris, and "*Amen*." Ra, the great sun god of the Egyptians, is equated with Osiris. As king of Egypt, Osiris taught his people, who were sunk into barbarity, the blessings of civilization. Murdered and dismembered by his brother, Set, who scattered his parts across the earth, Osiris was restored by Isis. Osiris in this poem is then equated with *Amen*, the Theban fertility god, who in turn the Egyptians later identified with Ra. All are defined as "healers, helpers/ of the One, *Amen*, All-father."

The poem also pays homage to female deities, to a composite all-mother. Astarte, the Phoenician goddess of fertility and love, is also the Egyptian Isis. Isis is also, by bringing Osiris back to life, mother. Astarte and Isis, therefore, are identified here with "Love, the Creator,// the original great-mother."

These divine personages all relate to universal myths and patterns of rebirth and resurrection, death and rebirth. By invoking these myths, H. D. offers one answer to the question as to why the survivors of the war have been saved. She envisions the war in her midst as fulfilling this universal pattern of civilization; she "explains symbols of the past/ in to-day's imagery." In the closing of the poem, the dominating myth is of Osiris and Isis: "Osiris,/ the star Sirius,/ relates resurrection myth/ and resurrection reality/ through the ages."

To answer the opening question of "what for" and why "us," the poem undertakes a defense of poetry. H. D. claims that poets are like the ancient scribes; "we are the same lot." Poets find the answers to combat the evils of the world and carry the keys to the mysteries: "we are the keepers of the secret,/ the carriers, the spinners/ of the rare intangible thread/ that binds all humanity/ to ancient wisdom."

In short, H. D. defends the old adage that the pen is mightier than the sword. Despite the devastation created by the weapons of war, words are immortal, and "we take them with us/ beyond death." She puts the sword in its place by lecturing that without language, "you would not have been, O Sword,/ without idea and the Word's mediation." She admonishes the sword to remember that "your Triumph, however exultant,/ must one day be over,/ *in the beginning/ was the Word*." There is a triumph in this poem. The poet has affirmed that civilization can endure the worst, and the spiritual foundation on which she bases this claim has held up—the walls do not fall. Yet the triumph is tempered; London and the poet are still in the dark. How the historical pattern will be colored in is still left to be discovered: "we are voyagers, discoverers/ of the not-known,/ the unrecorded;/ we have no map;/ possibly we will reach haven,/ heaven."

Tribute to the Angels begins where *The Walls Do Not Fall* leaves off, quoting for its epigraph ". . . possibly we will reach haven,/ heaven.": This possibility seems a certitude in this poem, as it soon stages a celebration of love and rebirth. H. D. wrote this poem in the last two weeks of May, 1944, an optimistic time during the war. It was spring, a time for rebirth, the season itself manifesting the certain ascent from the hell of war: "surely never, never/ was a spring more bountiful/ than this; never, never/ was a season more beautiful."

The tribute of the poem is to the guardian angels that H. D. imagines having "saved us" during the devastation. The angels, the seven unnamed angels from the gospels of Saint John, H. D. christens throughout this poetic series with angelic names from Christian and pre-Christian beliefs; all stand for goodness, healing, strength, resurrection, righteousness, light, and life. Her praise and the angels' names, ending in "-el," ring throughout—Gabriel, Azrael, Raphael, Uriel, Annael, Michael, Zadkiel—as jubilant church bells in Venice, the city named for Venus, goddess of Love. Signs of love, fertility, and rebirth abound. The bells become lilies, spiritually pollinating the city: "the whole city . . ./ will be covered with gold pollen shaken/ from the bell-towers, lilies plundered/ with the weight of massive bees."

Unlike the blacked-out London of *The Walls Do Not Fall*, its darkness broken only by fire bombs, the imagery of *Tribute to the Angels* is whiteness and light, natural and divine, day and night: "glowed the star Hesperus,/ white, far and luminous,// Phosphorus at sun-rise,/ Hesperus at sun-set." Dominating the celebration is a mothering or nurturing presence that embodies this whiteness. She is "*white as snow,/ so as no fuller on earth/ can white them*." Identified as Our Lady, she is another H. D. composite of several female deities—of the pre-Christian *Bona Dea*, the Byzantine Santa Sophia, the Holy Spirit, Venus, and Mary. Our Lady "brings the Book of Life, obviously."

The key sign of renewed life in the poem, the best evidence that certainly "we" will reach heaven, is the flowering of life from death; a charred tree bursts into flower. The poet sees this as no mystery to ponder and no hieroglyph to be interpreted as in the first section: "this is no rune nor riddle." Although surely taking credit for the pun on the word "ruin," H. D. assures the reader that this sign is "no trick of the pen." Instead of the ashes one would expect to find, there is "but a cluster of garden-pinks/ or a face like a Christmas-rose." With this affirmation, the poem ends with a ceremonious chant:

This is the flowering of the rod,
this is the flowering of the burnt-out wood,
where, Zadkiel, we pause to give
thanks that we rise again from death and live.

The third poem of the trilogy, *The Flowering of the Rod*, follows the pattern of taking the last lines of the previous poem for its epigraph (". . . *pause to give/ thanks that we rise again from death and live*"), perhaps to establish a sense of continuity between the poems in the trilogy. *The Flowering of the Rod*, however, soon makes a clear departure from the previous two works. Since the heralding of peace in *Tribute to the Angels*, the D-Day invasion of Europe brought back the war's devastation in full force: "for even now,/ the terrible banner/ darkens the bridge-head."

H. D. has had enough of it. The voice of the poem states that she already proved, in *The Walls Do Not Fall*, that she could stand up against the pressures of the war; the poet will now "leave the smouldering cities." She also states that she gave all that she could in her celebration of love in *Tribute to the Angels*, but perhaps her emotions were as mistaken as her prediction for peace: "alas, it was pity, rather than love, we gave;/ now having given all, let us leave all."

H. D. wants to move on—no more arguing, no more standing around and staring, as she characterizes the approaches of the previous two poems, respectively. The direction this poem takes—its theme, imagery, and story line—was perhaps suggested by the time of year. She begins writing on December 18, 1944, a week before Christmas. The poem leaves destruction and pity "and mount[s] higher/ to love—to resurrection," the resurrection of Christ. H. D. is perhaps most comfortable with this theme and in this setting, for it brings her home to Bethlehem—biblical Bethlehem and Bethlehem, Pennsylvania, christened in 1741 by her Moravian church—two hundred years before World War II. At the center of the Moravian worship was redemption through the love of Christ.

After reinforcing, then, the opening poetic apology with a series of sections that underline the poet's "insistent calling," the poem makes a "bee-line" to two stories—Mary Magdalene washing Christ's feet and Kaspar, one of the three Magi, bringing his jar of myrrh to the Nativity. The two narratives cross paths as the poem stages a scene in which Mary and Kaspar meet. During this meeting, Mary, in a typical H. D. transformation, mystically merges with myrrh: "I am Mary—O, there are Marys a-plenty,/ (though I am Mara, bitter) I shall be Mary-myrrh."

Mary, myrrh, or both bring about Kaspar's revelation, a half-second trance in which he sees a seed of myrrh burst open and bloom, opening "petal by petal, a circle." The opening flower reveals to Kaspar "the whole scope and plan/ of our and his civilization on this,/ his and our earth, before Adam.// . . . it was small and intimate,/ Paradise/ before Eve . . ."

The style as much as the content of *The Flowering of the Rod* differs from the previous two poems. A controlled poetic voice has replaced the agitated and elegaic voice of *The Walls Do Not Fall* and the exuberant one of *Tribute to the Angels.* The biblical events are understated, without drama and pomp, and the poetic narrative is often colloquial. Mary is introduced by the statement that she "was naturally reviled for having left home/ and not caring for house-work." Whenever Christ meets with His disciples, there is "always a crowd hanging about outside." The style in this poem allows for humor. Simon, the host, wishes to "avoid a scene" when Mary lets down her hair to prepare to wash Christ's feet, a scene that Kaspar knows "rarely happens, perhaps once/ in a little over two thousand years."

H. D. describes these events in Christ's life mundanely, but the mundane and the mysterious come together in some of the finest verse in the poem. The end is now the beginning—the birth of Christ. Mary, mother of Christ, holds her child in her arms as she speaks to Kaspar, who has modestly proffered his gift of myrrh:

> But she spoke so he looked at her,
> she was shy and simple and young;
>
> she said, Sir, it is a most beautiful fragrance,
> as of all flowering things together;
>
> but Kaspar knew the seal of the jar was unbroken.
> he did not know whether she knew
>
> the fragrance came from the bundle of myrrh
> she held in her arms.

Summary

H. D. has often been conveniently packaged as a lyrical poet and her influence limited to her contributions during the Imagist movement early in the century. Yet just as her early friends and associates did, H. D. went well beyond the lyric, experimenting with other forms, exploring universal themes within the classical tradition of epic verse, and developing an idiosyncratic style that would itself influence the next generation of poets.

Throughout H. D.'s work, from early to late years, runs a strong independent temperament and high seriousness. The driving force in her work is the intent to bring together the best of what culture and civilization have created and from it to create anew. In this quest, nothing is excluded except the unsatisfactory.

Bibliography

Creeley, Robert. "Robert Creeley in Conversation with Charles Tomlinson." *Review* 10 (January, 1964): 24-35.

Friedman, Susan Stanford. *Psyche Reborn: The Emergence of H. D.* Bloomington: Indiana University Press, 1981.

Gregory, Horace. Review of "The Walls Do Not Fall." *Sewanee Review* 52 (Autumn, 1944): 585-586.

Jarrell, Randall. "Verse Chronicle." Review of *Tribute to the Angels. The Nation* 161 (December 29, 1945): 741-742.

Kreymborg, Alfred. "A Challenge to Mammon." Review of *Tribute to the Angels. Saturday Review of Literature* 28 (December 29, 1945): 11.

Kunitz, Stanley. "A Tale of a Jar." Review of *The Flowering of the Rod. Poetry* 70 (April, 1947): 36-42.

Levertov, Denise. "H. D.: An Appreciation." *Poetry* 100 (June, 1962): 182-186.

Robinson, Janice S. *H. D.: The Life and Work of an American Poet*. Boston: Houghton-Mifflin, 1982.

Watts, Harold H. "H. D. and the Age of Myth." In *Hound and Quarry.* London: Routledge and Kegan Paul, 1953.

Steven P. Schultz

ROBERT A. HEINLEIN

Born: Butler, Missouri
July 7, 1907
Died: Carmel, California
May 8, 1988

Principal Literary Achievement

Known as "the dean of science fiction," Heinlein has been the most popular science fiction author ever since the "golden age" of the 1930's.

Biography

Robert Anson Heinlein was born in Butler, Missouri, on July 7, 1907, the son of Rex Ivar and Bam Lyle Heinlein. He was the third of seven children. Graduated from Kansas City Central High School in 1924, Heinlein enrolled at a branch campus of the University of Missouri near his home. His dream, however, was to follow his older brother Rex into the U.S. Naval Academy at Annapolis. Soliciting some fifty letters of recommendation in his behalf, Heinlein won an appointment to the academy in 1925. Commissioned with the Navy class of 1929, Lieutenant Robert Heinlein would serve only five years (as gunnery officer on several ships, including the first modern aircraft carrier, the U.S.S. *Lexington*) before a diagnosis of tuberculosis gave him a mandatory medical discharge in 1934.

For the next five years, Heinlein would try many occupations before becoming a writer. Pursuing graduate studies in physics at the University of California at Los Angeles, he also dabbled in architecture, mining, real estate, and state politics in Colorado and California. None of these ventures paid off, and Heinlein found himself in 1939, at the age of thirty-two, broke, with a mortgage, and virtually unemployable. A short story contest in the science fiction magazine *Thrilling Wonder Stories* offered a fifty-dollar prize. Tempted by the prize, Heinlein wrote his first story "Life Line," and sold it to the top science fiction magazine, *Astounding Science-Fiction*, for twenty dollars more than the contest prize.

The editor of *Astounding Science-Fiction*, the influential John Campbell, liked the story and wanted more. Thus, quite by accident, and against his will, Heinlein became a writer. By 1941, Heinlein was supplying one-fifth of the contents of the magazine—he produced so much that Campbell insisted on publishing half of Heinlein's stories under a pseudonym, Anson MacDonald. Heinlein was also the most popular writer in the magazine: He tied with "MacDonald" (that is, with himself) for first place in the readers' polls.

When Japan bombed Pearl Harbor, Heinlein immediately reported to the Navy for wartime service. He was assigned to the U.S. Naval Air Experimental Station at Mustin Field in Philadelphia. Two other science fiction writers trained by John Campbell were also there: Isaac Asimov and L. Sprague de Camp. Heinlein tested new plastic materials for aircraft and, with de Camp, developed the first pressure suits. One chemist and test engineer he met at Mustin Field would become a lifelong companion: Lt. Virginia Gerstenfeld, who became Mrs. Heinlein in 1948.

Although Heinlein would not write any fiction during the war, a backlog of Heinlein stories continued to appear through 1942, establishing what John Campbell called a "future history" series. Campbell had noticed that many of Heinlein's stories had interrelated details, and that they all implied a coherent view of developments in the coming centuries. Many writers imitated this "future history" approach to science fiction, but it was Heinlein's invention.

After the war, Heinlein returned to writing, determined to sell science fiction outside the pulp magazines. He did so in three significant ways. In 1947, he became the first science fiction writer to write for mass-market magazines, publishing "Space Jockey" in *The Saturday Evening Post*. Second, in the same year, he was asked by Scribner's to write a juvenile novel for hardcover publication—a rare occurrence in those days, when science fiction was almost always restricted to paperback books.

Heinlein, according to the contract with Scribner's, produced a novel a year over the next decade: *Rocketship Galileo* (1947), *Space Cadet* (1948), *Red Planet: A Colonial Boy on Mars* (1949), *Farmer in the Sky* (1950), *Between Planets* (1951), *The Rolling Stones* (1952), *Starman Jones* (1953), *The Star Beast* (1954), *Tunnel in the Sky* (1955), *Time for the Stars* (1956), *Citizen of the Galaxy* (1957), and *Have Space Suit—Will Travel* (1958). These novels, written for high school readers, are often considered Heinlein's best works. A third way in which Heinlein brought science fiction into the mainstream was with the 1950 film *Destination Moon*. Based on Heinlein's script, this was the first Hollywood science fiction film to attempt to create sets, actions, and dialogue that were scientifically accurate.

In 1955, the World Science Fiction Convention, a fan group, began giving an annual award (called a "Hugo") for the year's best science fiction. Heinlein had been the group's guest of honor in 1941, and in 1956 his novel *Double Star* (1956) received a Hugo. He would win again in 1960 for *Starship Troopers* (1959), 1962 for *Stranger in a Strange Land* (1961), and 1967 for *The Moon Is a Harsh Mistress* (1966). The Science Fiction Writers of America, who give an equivalent award (the "Nebula"), never gave one to a Heinlein novel, but in 1975 they gave Heinlein their first "Grand Master" award for lifetime achievement in science fiction.

Heinlein's second Hugo winner, *Stranger in a Strange Land*, became the first work of science fiction to make *The New York Times* best-seller list. He would make the list again with *Time Enough for Love* (1973), *The Number of the Beast* (1980), *Job: A Comedy of Justice* (1984), and *The Cat Who Walks Through Walls* (1985).

Heinlein suffered a near stroke in 1978. A year later, he testified before the House Committee on Science and Technology, pointing out that the technology that had helped save his life, and the lives of countless others, came from space research. A weak heart did not keep Heinlein from publishing regularly through the 1980's. His last novel, *To Sail Beyond the Sunset* (1987), appeared on his eightieth birthday. On May 8, 1988, Heinlein died of heart failure. He was cremated, and his ashes were scattered at sea with full military honors.

Analysis

The hard science underlying Robert Heinlein's fiction is more that of the engineer than of the researcher or theoretical scientist. Many science fiction writers show the gadgets and institutions of a possible future; Heinlein shows how they work. It is his skill in integrating scientific explanation with the dialogue and plot of his stories that makes him one of the foremost science fiction writers.

Paradoxically, however, this "hard science," nuts-and-bolts science fiction writer introduced the term "speculative fiction" as a wider-ranging name for his field, in order to include nonscientific fantasy. In his own fiction, Heinlein bridges the gap between pure science and pure fantasy by offering the incredible "magic" of fantasy fiction but providing plausible scientific explanations. For example, one finds a fire-breathing dragon in *Glory Road* (1963), yet when the hero laments the reek of the flammable ketones in the dragon's breath, the reader must admit that it is possible to ignite the by-products of digestion. Further, in *The Number of the Beast*, one encounters denizens of the Land of Oz and other fictional characters, but their "real" existence is attributed to the nature of infinity. Although Heinlein's purpose in that novel is satirical, he makes it clear that a ship which can travel through space and time can follow an infinite number of time lines, making all worlds accessible.

As popular as Heinlein is, some readers have criticized what they have perceived as a didactic or moralizing tone. Some readers reject Heinlein on these grounds for being too "preachy"; others embrace him as their spiritual father for the same quality. Whatever the reader's reaction, definite moral values are implicit in virtually every Heinlein novel. Yet even morality is given a scientific basis. In *Starship Troopers*, Heinlein presented "the first scientific theory of morals," which he articulated in his own voice in a 1973 lecture at Annapolis, later published in his collection *Expanded Universe* (1980). Defining moral behavior as "behavior that tends toward survival," Heinlein makes it an aspect of evolution:

> Evolution is a process that never stops. Baboons who fail to exhibit moral behavior do not survive; they wind up as meat for leopards. Every baboon generation has to pass this examination in moral behavior; those who bilge it don't have progeny.

Placing the welfare of one's tribe before one's own is moral behavior, but it also ensures the survival of the tribe, even at the cost of the individual's life.

The emphasis on moral teaching in Heinlein's fiction is appropriate for his juvenile series for Scribner's (1947-1958). Each of the novels has a young protagonist who learns an important lesson about growing up, usually related to his responsibility to other people. In *Space Cadet*, for example, an early exploration of themes developed in *Starship Troopers*, recruits in the Space Academy learn diplomacy in making contact with another race on Venus. In *Between Planets*, a youth with dual planetary citizenship must choose sides in a war between Venus colonials and Earth. In *Starman Jones*, a boy who rises to the top in the spaceman's hierarchy has to decide whether to reveal the lie that helped get him there.

In all the juvenile novels, a vital decision made by the young hero, usually affecting the fate of a great number of people, is the turning point of the plot. The decision invariably marks the first step toward adulthood for the protagonist. Adulthood, in Heinlein's moral framework outlined above, consists in making decisions based on the good of the group rather than one's own personal needs. The group may be as small as the family unit, as in *The Rolling Stones*, in which an interplanetary freighter is run by an adventurous family, or *Farmer in the Sky*, in which a teenaged boy battles to save his family's homestead on Jupiter's moon Ganymede. At the other extreme, the group for whom the protagonists of *The Star Beast* and *Have Space Suit—Will Travel* sacrifice is the entire human race.

Although Heinlein has a reputation for moral conservatism on civic issues, he has been accused of (or praised for) expressing liberal views of sex and religion. In terms of religion, the charge is unjust: the ethic usually presented in his fiction is simply religious tolerance. In fact, what is remarkable about Heinlein's view of the future is that religions will not be snuffed by the advance of science, but will take on many new forms. The Martian-reared protagonist of *Stranger in a Strange Land* becomes the messiah for a new sect and invests it with Martian religious ideas. The hero of *Job: A Comedy of Justice* is a fundamentalist minister who falls in love with a Scandinavian woman who worships the Norse gods.

Even Heinlein's supposedly licentious treatment of sex in his fiction is a direct result of his "future history" approach—projecting the realities, both scientific and social, of the possible worlds to come. In *The Moon Is a Harsh Mistress*, Heinlein explains line and clan marriages that exist on the moon, where women are scarce and are shared among several husbands. In *Time Enough for Love*, every imaginable family and sexual arrangement is described over Lazarus Long's thousand-year lifespan; the same aspects of his mother's long life are explored in Heinlein's last novel. Yet, although Heinlein wrote increasingly about sex after 1961, he was never explicit in wording or description.

RED PLANET

First published: 1949
Type of work: Novel

A young man, with the help of his Martian "pet," thwarts a plot against the Martian colonists.

The third of Heinlein's juvenile novels, *Red Planet* was his first story to describe the Martian culture he would return to in *Stranger in a Strange Land*. The main Martian character, however, is not the adult biped described in that book, but a bouncy, spherical nymph named Willis. Willis is kept as a pet by a human colonist named Jim Marlowe, who is unaware that Willis belongs to the same race as the tall, silent, dominant species who built the ancient Martian cities.

As the story begins, Jim and his friend, Frank Sutton, enter college at Lowell Academy (Heinlein's tribute to the nineteenth century astronomer Percival Lowell). Jim goes against the wishes of his parents—and, as it turns out, the rules of the college—by bringing his "pet," Willis, to school. Willis is a Martian roundhead, a hairy sphere about the size of a billiard ball, who can imitate any sound and has learned enough English to converse with Jim and his friends. More important, his familiarity with the adult Martians makes Willis an intercessor on behalf of the Earth colonists.

When the college authorities confiscate Willis, Jim faces a dilemma. He was reared to respect authority, yet in this case he believes that the authority is wrong. Furthermore, Willis' abilities as a sort of Martian tape recorder reveal to Jim a plot by the Earth company that runs the colony to cancel the migration, thereby forcing the colonists to face the deadly Martian winter—and making room for more immigrants (and greater profit for the company). The colonists, warned by Jim and backed by the Martian elders whom Jim and Frank befriend through the mischievous Willis, storm the company offices and force the bureaucrats to reinstate the migration.

The "revolution" of the colonists is a larger version of the coming-of-age theme in Jim's character. Just as Jim learns in the course of the novel to make mature decisions for himself, away from his parents, so the colony itself must become independent from its earthly "parent." There is even a further variation on the theme in the character of Willis: Willis is a "nymph," an earlier stage in development from the mysterious Martian elders Jim and Frank meet. Willis will metamorphose into an adult Martian; Jim will become an independent, mature man; the colony will become an independent political entity.

The science in *Red Planet* is outdated, yet the novel illustrates Heinlein's contention that science fiction is not ruined when science catches up with it. "Updating can't save a poor story," he said in *Expanded Universe*, "and it isn't necessary for a good one. All of H. G. Wells' SF stories are hopelessly dated . . . and they remain the *best*, the most gripping science fiction stories to be found anywhere." The premise of a southern-hemisphere Martian colony farming by the water melted from the ice cap each spring (a seasonal phenomenon observed by telescope) fell apart when satellite analysis revealed the poles to be frozen carbon dioxide, not frozen water.

Nevertheless, the basic picture of a colony dependent on Earth remains valid. Whoever establishes a colony on Mars, whether governments or private corporations, or some combination, the colonies will at first be client states, tied to Earth economically and politically. The pioneers will find that many decisions affecting their welfare will be made by people on Earth.

Another bit of science in *Red Planet* illustrates Heinlein's confidence in technology's ability to help humans survive in hostile environments. Many science fiction writers have been reluctant to base future colonies on Mars because of the scarcity of oxygen in its atmosphere. Yet Heinlein points out that there almost certainly is oxygen on Mars—not in the atmosphere, but in oxide compounds in the soil. Jim's father in *Red Planet* is involved in a massive project to release the oxygen locked in the Martian soil and pump it into the air, making Mars more friendly to humans. Human beings will survive in space, Heinlein insists, not only by adapting to harsh environments, but also by adapting the environments themselves.

The minor conflict that opens the story—Jim's reluctance to give up Willis—returns at the end as a difficult reality Jim must face in coming of age. In negotiations with the Martians, it becomes necessary for Jim to return Willis to his own people so that he can metamorphose into an adult Martian. The novel ends at that turning point, but Willis' projected physical transformation is a reflection of Jim's less tangible passage into manhood, which is in turn a reflection of the colony's coming-of-age. Doc MacRae, the colony's physician and Jim's friend and mentor, comments on Jim's loss of Willis in the closing lines of the book: "He'll get over it. Probably he'll find another bouncer and teach him English and call him Willis, too. Then he'll grow up and not make pets of bouncers." MacRae is one of many mentor types in Heinlein's juveniles, though the type appears in his adult fiction also. He is an adult who represents the values of the adult society yet sympathizes with the boys. Jim and Frank talk with Doc more freely than with their parents.

Red Planet is a classic initiation or coming-of-age story. Jack Williamson, Heinlein's friend and fellow writer, considered it the first artistic success of the Scribner's juvenile series. Teenagers can readily identify with the protagonist, Jim Marlowe, but the most memorable character is the scene-stealing Martian nymph Willis, who is one of the most enjoyable and fully realized alien characters in science fiction. "Here, for the first time," says Williamson, "Heinlein is making the most of his aliens." Willis alone would make the book worth reading.

CITIZEN OF THE GALAXY

First published: 1957
Type of work: Novel

A boy who begins life as a slave inherits a fortune and works to crush the interplanetary slave trade.

The Scribner's juvenile series took a giant leap in a new direction with *Citizen of the Galaxy.* Though the protagonist is indeed a boy who comes of age in the novel, the point of view is much more adult (it was the only one of the juveniles to be serialized in *Astounding Science Fiction*), and the locale, for the first time in the series, is outside the solar system. The world in which Thorby, the main character, grows up is much darker than any previously seen in Heinlein's fiction. The reader first sees him in the dirty, decadent, savage streets of the spaceport Jubbulpore. Thorby had been kidnapped and sold into slavery; when the story opens, he is on the auction block again, so thin and scarred that no one but a dirty beggar offers to buy him.

The beggar, Baslim the Cripple, is one of Heinlein's most fascinating characters. Though a beggar, he and the hole in which he lives have unexpected resources. He turns out to be a secret agent of the Exotic Corps, an interplanetary police force combating slavery. Baslim begins to train Thorby in his trade, without telling the boy about the "X-Corps," but he is killed by powerful enemies before Thorby can learn his trade.

Following Baslim's orders, given to him under hypnosis before Baslim's death, Thorby seeks out Captain Krausa of the spaceship *Sisu*. Krausa adopts him into "The Free Traders," a race of space gypsies who travel the galaxy buying and selling. Thorby adapts to this strange new culture with the help of an anthropologist traveling with the ship, who explains the ways of these people who spend their entire lives in a city-sized ship, the *Sisu*. Just when Thorby gets accustomed to the nomadic life, however, he finally discovers where he came from before he was kidnapped, and he is returned "home"—to Earth. Even more, he discovers that he is "Rudbek of Rudbek," heir to a vast fortune, and head of an international conglomerate that makes him the most powerful individual on Earth. Ironically, his company is behind the very slave trade which victimized him.

Yet this is not a rags-to-riches cliché, and the story is not over. Wealth isolates Thorby, and powerful men who know more about the treachery of international trade attempt to keep him from finding out too much about his own company—about shady operations such as the slave trade, for example. Thorby fights back, with the help of a pretty girl who seems intent on marrying him. They win, but Thorby is not ready for a family. Instead, he marries the service, enlisting in Baslim's Exotic Corps to continue the fight against intergalactic slavery.

The key to understanding the major theme of *Citizen of the Galaxy*, and of the juvenile series as a whole, is in the title. Each stage of the plot is concerned with various aspects of citizenship: the relationship of the individual to society. As a slave, Thorby is not a citizen, so society is an enemy. It is impossible to engender any sense of duty toward society in a boy when that society denies his value as a person. Baslim not only frees Thorby legally but also gives him the personal dignity necessary to become a citizen.

At this stage, however, Thorby's sense of duty does not extend beyond Baslim. In the *Sisu*, however, he is adopted into a family and learns to feel a loyalty to the entire ship. When he discovers that he is a galactic citizen, however, with records on Earth, he becomes a citizen in the moral sense: He discovers, at the end of the novel, his responsibility to his entire race. He devotes his life to ending slavery.

The science in *Citizen of the Galaxy* is not the nuts-and-bolts explanation of gadgets and planets found in the earlier novels. Here the science is anthropology, the study of how people get along together. Much of the technical explanation is given by the anthropologist Thorby meets on board the *Sisu*, Dr. Margaret Mader (a near anagram of the name of twentieth century anthropologist Margaret Mead). She teaches Thorby a version of Heinlein's moral Darwinism—that rules of social behavior are necessary to the survival of the species and cannot be ignored. "Few things are good or evil in themselves," she tells him. "But things that are right or wrong according to their culture, really *are* so."

The rule under discussion at that point is the law of exogamy—a rule that requires marrying outside the tribe. Dr. Mader explains that such a rule is necessary, not only to avoid inbreeding, but also "because a ship is too small to be a stable culture." Therefore, no trader may marry anyone from his or her own ship, even if there is no blood relationship between them.

Psychology is another social science explored in the novel. Thorby's emotional scars from his years as a slave and as a triple orphan (first losing his natural parents, then "Pop" Baslim, then his adoptive father, Captain Krausa) make him a psychological risk for the Exotic Corps. Baslim begins Thorby's psychiatric healing with hypnotherapy shortly after he adopts Thorby. The disruption of losing Baslim, however, and being thrust into an unfamiliar culture unsettle Thorby until Captain Krausa officially adopts him in a solemn public ceremony.

Yet when the Exotic Corps discovers Thorby's identity as a missing person from Earth, and Captain Krausa sends him back where he "belongs," Thorby feels abandoned again. Thus, like many men from broken homes who come of age, he finds an artificial family in the military. By joining Baslim's own service, the Exotic Corps, Thorby feels he is returning home. In fact, he tells the recruiter he wants to be "adopted" by the Corps. When the recruiter corrects him, saying "Enlisted," Thorby simply responds, "Whatever the word is." To him, membership in the Corps is adoption, whatever the terminology.

STARSHIP TROOPERS

First published: 1959
Type of work: Novel

A young recruit in the space navy learns the values of citizenship as he fights in Earth's first intergalactic war.

In addition to winning for Heinlein his first Hugo award, *Starship Troopers* put an end to the Scribner's juvenile series. Heinlein wrote it for the series, but Scribner's rejected it. That rejection was the beginning of years of controversy over *Starship Troopers.*

Many readers, and a majority of academic critics, objected to the overt militarism of the book. Despite the Hugo, science fiction fans at conventions in 1960 distanced themselves from the book's philosophy; a youth-oriented radio talk show on WMCA in New York even devoted its October 23, 1960, broadcast to a critique of *Starship*

Troopers and its philosophy. There had been military settings in the juvenile series before: *Space Cadet* describes an interplanetary military; the protagonist of *Between Planets* joins a militia on Venus; *Citizen of the Galaxy* ends with its hero enlisting in the Exotic Corps. What is different about this novel is that it describes a society in which government service of some sort (though not always infantry) is an absolute requirement for full citizenship.

This system, often distorted by critics into a fascist nightmare, is what caused the controversy—and guaranteed sales. It is described through the experiences of the narrator, Juan ("Johnny") Rico, who enlists in the Mobile Infantry and tells of his training. Much of the story is interrupted by his flashbacks to a high school civics course on history and moral philosophy. Mandatory for all high school students in the society Heinlein depicts, this course teaches the moral imperative of citizenship: placing society's welfare before one's own. The course must be taught by a veteran of government service, who has by that service proved this moral imperative.

The flashbacks do not interrupt the flow of the narrative, for the points discussed in the classes are always germane to what is happening to Johnny in boot camp. Furthermore, Johnny's instructor of the class, Jean V. Dubois, is very much like his drill instructor, Ship's Sergeant Charles Zim. Indeed, it turns out that Dubois, whom Johnny is shocked to discover was a lieutenant colonel in the M. I., was a battle comrade of Sergeant Zim.

Both Dubois and Zim are mentor characters, a familiar type in Heinlein's fiction—especially in the juvenile series for which *Starship Troopers* was originally written. They are distanced from Johnny a bit more than usual in the juveniles by the institutional respect necessary in high school and in the military. Nevertheless, these characters give Johnny the moral and intellectual guidance that he cannot get from his parents.

Following the pattern of the coming-of-age story in the other juveniles, this book depicts Johnny Rico's maturing process as a function of his independent decision making. His first independent choice is the enlistment itself. Johnny's father, a successful businessman, scorns the military and denounces the history and moral philosophy course as a shameless recruiting device for government service. His mother, a domineering, overly protective woman, weeps at the news of his enlistment and refuses to see him off.

Johnny's breach with his parents is healed, paradoxically, by the completion of his "breaking away." Halfway through the novel he receives a letter of reconciliation from his mother, though she reveals that his father will still not allow his name to be mentioned. When his mother is killed by an alien attack on Earth, however, Johnny's father sees the wisdom of Johnny's decision to enlist and joins the M. I. himself. In the final chapter the reader sees Johnny's father as a platoon sergeant in "Rico's Roughnecks," Johnny's first command as an officer. Father and son fight side by side.

It may be argued that the powered suit described in *Starship Troopers* is the true hero of the book. It is perhaps the best example of Heinlein's skill at scientific explanation, and of his "engineering" approach to science fiction. There are tidbits of description and explanation throughout the book, but chapter 7 is virtually all a treatise on the p-suit. The science behind it is the principal of negative feedback, which Johnny describes as a nontechnical expert. Any muscular movement of a soldier wearing a p-suit is picked up by sensors in the suit and amplified by its hardware, turning every p-suited soldier into a superman.

The delivery system for p-suited M. I. is described in almost as much detail in the opening chapter. The M. I. are also known as "cap troopers." The "cap" is short for "capsule," the metal egg in which the M. I. soldier is dropped from a space ship onto the surface of a planet. The metal skin burns off in the atmosphere, and the cap trooper lands by parachute and suit jets—an interplanetary version of today's para-trooper.

In *Expanded Universe*, Heinlein categorized the four most common criticisms of *Starship Troopers* and the society it depicts and defended his novel against each of them. The first, an objection to a requirement that only veterans could vote, is based on a popular misunderstanding of the word "veteran." In *Starship Troopers*, as in common usage, the word does not necessarily mean "military veteran." The book makes clear that most veterans are what would be called former civil servants.

To the second objection, that the system traps people in government service indefinitely, Heinlein specifies that any enlistee can resign at any time, except soldiers in combat. The third objection, especially pointed during the Vietnam War, is a repugnance for conscription. There is no conscription in the novel, however, and Heinlein also objected to the draft. The final criticism, that the novel and its society are militaristic, is somewhat imprecise. Since no member of the military is allowed to vote, the government is not a military one. *Starship Troopers* does glorify the military, however, and that fact delighted Heinlein.

STRANGER IN A STRANGE LAND

First published: 1961
Type of work: Novel

A human born on Mars is reared by Martians and returned to Earth, where he finds human ways strange.

Though *Stranger in a Strange Land* is the publisher's title for this novel (Heinlein called it *The Heretic* or *The Man from Mars*), it expresses some of the subtleties of the title character. The "Stranger" is Valentine Michael Smith, and the "Strange Land" is human culture, for though he is human, Smith was reared by Martians, the same inscrutable race described in *Red Planet* and *Podkayne of Mars.*

Probably Heinlein's most critically acclaimed book, it is usually most praised for messages that Heinlein did not intend. Depicting a society in the near future revelling in lax sexual mores and yearning for a new religion, *Stranger* was misunderstood as celebrating those aspects of contemporary culture. Hence, the novel became a cult classic on college campuses through the 1960's and 1970's, read both in and out of class. Though easily refuted, the rumor that *Stranger in a Strange Land* influenced the mass-murderer Charles Manson still persists in science fiction circles: It is even reported as "fact" in some reference works.

The appeal of the book is in the character of Smith himself: more Martian than man, he has psychic and physical powers beyond those of most humans, and he trains his friends to develop those powers. The artificial "family" that Smith attracts appealed to the communal nature of the 1960's counterculture (and led to the spurious connection with Manson.) The head of the family is not Smith, who is a young man throughout the long novel, but one of Heinlein's most fascinating creations, Jubal Harshaw.

Harshaw is one of Heinlein's perennial mentor characters, an attorney, M.D., scientist, and popular author, who has amassed enough of a fortune to isolate himself from the rest of the world. When Smith is brought to Earth from Mars, where he was born when his parents made the first expedition there, the government keeps him in seclusion. When a young nurse "rescues" Smith (or "Mike," as his friends begin calling him), Harshaw offers them both protection from overzealous government thugs.

What makes Mike an effective point-of-view character is the common science fiction technique of defamiliarization. By presenting common aspects of his reader's society as unfamiliar (as they would be to a human reared on Mars), Heinlein is able to bring readers to question the basic presuppositions of their culture. Tolerance of new ways of thinking, necessary for any technological or cultural advance, is the result Heinlein desires. One vehicle for conveying the idea of tolerance is the minor character Duke, a handyman employed by Jubal Harshaw. Duke is revulsed by Mike's "inhuman" ideas, and he says so bluntly. Jubal, though he is fond of Duke, will not tolerate intolerance and offers an ultimatum: accept Mike as he is or leave Jubal's employ. Duke stays and becomes one of Mike's closest friends.

Since much of the book's thrust is social, not scientific, there is little of Heinlein's famous scientific explanation. What little there is, however, is interesting: When Mike first comes to Earth, he has to be kept in a hydraulic bed to protect him from the strain of Earth's gravity—two and a half times that of Mars. The bed, described in detail, is what is now known as a "water bed." Heinlein had invented it when hospitalized for tuberculosis after his discharge from the Navy, but he never patented it. The first commercial versions were made from Heinlein's specifications, but the patent courts ruled the invention to be in the public domain.

Of psychology and sociology, on the other hand, there is much in this book. Heinlein's attempt to produce a truly alien psychology—with the ironic twist of placing it in a biologically human frame—is a masterpiece of the genre. It introduced the word "grok," which became a catch phrase in the 1960's counterculture. The novel's hesitation in translating this word shows Heinlein's understanding of the intimate connection between language and thought. Much of Mike's Martian philosophy/psychology/theology cannot be expressed in English. Consequently, Jubal orders his "family" to learn Martian.

The meaning of "grok," as it slowly unfolds in the course of the book, is manifold. While it seems to have no English equivalent, some approximations are offered: "to understand, "to cherish," "to become one with." Its implications seem to be metaphysical: When one enters the essence of a thing, one "groks" it. The ceremony by which this term is introduced is a Martian "Water Sharing." This invention of Heinlein's, referred to also in *Red Planet* and *Podkayne of Mars* (the Martians of *Double Star* are totally different), is akin to the Christian eucharist. By sharing water—sipping water from the same source—two individuals become one. One is expected to perform any duty for a "water brother"—even to die.

It is not wide-eyed innocent Valentine Michael Smith, but the cynical huckster Jubal Harshaw who suggests making a religion out of the water ceremony. His motives are not pious, but mercenary: He rightly observes that religion is big business in his corrupt culture. The curious relationship of Smith and Harshaw modulates Harshaw's position as a mentor character. Though Smith's primary importance to the people on Earth lies in what he can teach them, and though he brings the ancient wisdom of a culture much older and more advanced than anything on Earth, he turns to Jubal to learn about his human heritage. Still, Jubal learns as much from him as he does from Jubal.

The structure of the novel is a function of Mike's learning process. Many critics have observed that this most "adult" of Heinlein's novels fits the pattern of his juvenile series. It is divided into five parts, all of whose titles describe Mike's maturing process: "His Maculate Origin," "His Preposterous Heritage," "His Eccentric Education," "His Scandalous Career," and "His Happy Destiny." The book's structure has often been criticized as episodic and aimless, but Heinlein revealed in *Expanded Universe* that this is the only novel he ever outlined before writing. Every piece fits in this novel, which won for Heinlein his second Hugo award and his first appearance on the New York Times best-seller list.

THE MOON IS A HARSH MISTRESS

First published: 1966
Type of work: Novel

The moon's main computer develops a personality and helps the moon colonists in a revolution against absentee landlords on Earth.

Heinlein received his fourth and final Hugo award for *The Moon Is a Harsh Mistress.* Though it is a masterpiece in every way—scientific background, plot construction, setting, characterization—it is usually remembered for the brilliant characterization of "Mike," the supercomputer that develops a personality. Though Mike receives the most attention, all the major figures are among Heinlein's most completely realized characters. Mike's first friend, the computer technician Manuel Garcia O'Kelly ("Mannie"), is the narrator of the novel. Born free, but son of criminals transported to the moon when it was a prison colony, Mannie shows the cautious independence of an ex-con in a repressive system.

Mannie's narration itself is a stylistic masterpiece, for Heinlein has created, as he does in no other novel, a version of the streamlined language a moon colonist (or "Loony" as they proudly call themselves) might speak in the year 2076. Since, as Professor Leon Stover observes in his book-length study of Heinlein, there is little stylistic play in Heinlein's fiction, it is worth looking closely at his only stylistic experiment in *The Moon Is a Harsh Mistress.* It is a fair extrapolation of what might someday be spoken on the moon, as it amalgamates Russian, Chinese, and Australian and American English. Since all four nations are likely colonizers of the moon, one should not expect pure English among the settlers.

Even the English is mutated. Articles are used rarely, perhaps under the influence of Russian, and personal pronouns are often dropped when they appear as subjects. The expletive "there" is dropped in the phrase "there is": In the opening paragraph of the novel, Mannie observes, "I see also is to be mass meeting tonight." Many other words are dropped at random if they can be supplied by context. Thus, one finds Mannie saying, "Won't worry about what can't help," and asking, "Matters whether you get answer in microsecond rather than millisecond as long as correct?"

Mike's only two other friends are a tall, beautiful, blonde woman, Wyoming Knott, and Mannie's old mentor, Professor Bernardo de la Paz. The professor is a typical Heinlein mentor character, yet his seemingly Marxist politics have puzzled critics who had typed Heinlein as a right-wing fanatic. A close study of the political theory laid out by the professor in chapter 6, however, will help the reader to square it with Heinlein's theory of citizenship discussed above. The professor places the welfare of society above his own, which is Heinlein's definition of patriotism, yet does not identify his current corrupt government with "society." Wyoming Knott, or "Wyoh," is a feminist and political activist, well-read in revolutionary political theory, but from Mannie's point of view naïve about the real world. The second human being Mike meets as a self-aware personality, Wyoh immediately helps him to create a female persona, "Michelle," to become *her* computer friend.

Mike's personality is the main attraction of the novel, as well as one of Heinlein's most masterful technological creations. The theory of artificial intelligence in *The Moon Is a Harsh Mistress*, written long before AI was a common term in computer science, is proposed by Mannie in the opening chapter. Mike was designed to draw conclusions on limited data, an inductive method foreign to computers but very human. On top of that, other computer systems were linked to him as the lunar complex grew, until he had more circuits than the human brain. This large number of connections, Mannie guesses, is what made Mike "come alive":

> Somewhere along evolutionary chain from macromolecule to human brain self-awareness crept in. Psychologists assert it happens automatically whenever brain acquires certain very high number of associational paths. Can't see it matters whether paths are protein or platinum.

Whether or not Mannie's theory is correct—and he admits in the epilogue that it remains only a theory—Mike is as human as most Loonies, and is as scornful of the moon's dependence on Earth.

Another bit of scientific background in the novel is an exercise in interplanetary ballistics, worked out (quite accurately) only a few years before the first moon landing. The Loonies, though exploited by Earth, are reluctant to rebel because of Earth's superior firepower. When someone laments, "What can we do? Throw rocks?" Mike suggests exactly that. Since the moon rides on the "top" of Earth's "gravity well," it is simple to catapult large pieces of lunar rock. If directed to enter Earth's atmosphere obliquely, the rocks can hit with enough impact to cause an explosion, like striking sparks on flint. Since Mike had been Luna's ballistic computer, it is an easy task for him: The Loonies win their independence by throwing rocks.

It is no accident that Heinlein gives so specific a date for the setting of this novel—something he rarely did. The Loonies declare their revolution on July 4, 2076—on the tricentennial of American independence. This date, chosen by Professor de la Paz (with his devotion to political history), highlights a connection Heinlein made consistently in his fiction between the spirit of independence that forged the American nation and that same spirit in the future colonizers of space. Almost twenty years earlier, Heinlein had explored the theme in *Red Planet*, wherein Martian colonists fight for independence from Earth. Recognizing that the pioneer spirit is flagging in the land of his birth, Heinlein urges readers, through his fiction, to see that they need to recapture it if they want to participate in the bonanza of outer space.

Summary

The most popular science fiction writer of science fiction's golden age, Robert A. Heinlein was a master at merging scientific explanation (the "engineer's-eye-view") and fast-paced adventure. Controversial because of his supposed right-wing philosophy, Heinlein is still widely read even by those who oppose those views. His novels consistently reflect a moral position on citizenship, stressing the individual's duties toward the family, nation, and human race.

Bibliography

Franklin, H. Bruce. *Robert A. Heinlein: America as Science Fiction*. New York: Oxford University Press, 1980.

Olander, Joseph D., and Martin H. Greenberg, eds. *Robert A. Heinlein*. New York: Taplinger, 1977.

Slusser, George Edgar. *Stranger in His Own Land*. San Bernardino, Calif.: Borgo Press, 1976.

Stover, Leon. *Robert A. Heinlein*. Boston: G. K. Hall, 1987.

John R. Holmes

JOSEPH HELLER

Born: Brooklyn, New York
May 1, 1923

Principal Literary Achievement

Heller was the first of the postmodern writers to use "black humor" in a successful long novel, *Catch-22*, which has remained one of the most popular novels of the post-World War II era.

Biography

Joseph Heller was born and reared in Brooklyn, New York. At the age of nineteen, he enlisted in the United States Army Air Force and was first trained as an armorer, later transferring to cadet school and graduating as a second lieutenant. Sent to Italy, he flew sixty missions as a bombardier. He was discharged as a first lieutenant.

After the war, Heller returned to the United States and resumed his education, attending the University of Southern California; he was graduated from New York University in 1948. He was married to Shirley Held in 1945; he and his wife had two children. That marriage ended in divorce, and in 1987 he married Valerie Humphries. Heller received an M.A. degree from Columbia University in 1949 and spent the next year as a Fulbright scholar at the University of Oxford before teaching for two years at Pennsylvania State University.

Heller left the academic world in 1952 and spent the next decade working for *Time* and *Look* magazines as an editor and for *McCall's* as an advertising promotion man. During those years he sold some short fiction to *Esquire* and *The Atlantic Monthly* and began work on his first novel, *Catch-22*, which was published in 1961. While the novel did not receive unanimously favorable reviews, it was highly popular from the beginning and retained its popularity for a long time; in the first ten years after its publication, *Catch-22* sold 7 million copies in various editions, added a new term to the language, and was made into a successful motion picture in 1970.

After the publication of *Catch-22*, Heller resumed a part-time academic career as a teacher of creative writing at Yale University and at the University of Pennsylvania. During the 1960's, he also wrote scripts for television, wrote the antiwar play *We Bombed in New Haven* (1968), and worked on dramatic adaptations of parts of *Catch-22*. Between 1971 and 1975, he was distinguished visiting writer at the City University of New York.

Heller's second novel was a long time in the writing, leading to rumors that he

had written himself out on the first. When it appeared, *Something Happened* (1974) was a shock to critics who had expected a second novel similar to *Catch-22*. Some critics responded harshly, feeling that *Something Happened* was tedious and unexciting; others saw the book as a brilliant exercise in suspenseful character portrayal and as a daring departure from the style and techniques of *Catch-22*. The new book was not a popular success.

Heller's later novels include the more conventional satirical story of a young man on the make, *Good as Gold* (1979), and a return to the spirit of *Catch-22* in *God Knows* (1984), a wild explanation by the biblical King David of his life and experiences, told in a hip modern style and punctuated with frequent references to events long after David's time. *Picture This* (1988) is less a novel than an unusual speculation on history; starting from Rembrandt van Rijn's famous painting *Aristotle Contemplating a Bust of Homer*, it provides ironic commentary on the Greece of Aristotle's time, on Rembrandt's life, artistic practice, and finances, and on value in the world of art.

Late in 1981, Heller contracted Guillain-Barre syndrome, a disease that attacks the nerves and that causes increasing paralysis and can be fatal. He was hospitalized for several months as a result but eventually recovered fully. His only work of nonfiction, *No Laughing Matter* (1986), written with Speed Vogel, is an account of that experience.

Analysis

Joseph Heller was one of the pioneers among the novelists of the 1960's who attempted to end the long reign of realism as the dominant force in American fiction. These writers, who also included Thomas Pynchon, John Barth, Robert Coover, Bruce Jay Friedman, and others, rejected what they regarded as solemn and often dull attempts to use fiction to portray the lives of everyday characters. The generation just prior to theirs, which included Norman Mailer, James Jones, William Styron, and Saul Bellow, had emerged from World War II writing novels about experiences very much like their own, using the established methods of realism: accurate description of ordinary events, plots based on logic and avoiding coincidences, and characters neither heroic nor truly tragic that readers would recognize as similar to people they might have known.

The new generation, emerging in the early 1960's, believed that the novelist should start from the premise that fiction should acknowledge that it cannot be real and cannot successfully imitate reality. By its methods, fiction should call attention to its real nature, which is the creation of an imaginary world that may comment on the real world and reflect some of its qualities but that is not an imitation of it. Because many of the early efforts of these writers portrayed violent and sometimes brutal events in wildly humorous terms, their fiction was at first called "black humor." Later, it was given the name "fabulation," suggesting that these writers were creating fabulous works, fables rather than realistic fictions. More recently, the term "metafiction" has been popularized, suggesting that these authors go beyond the bounds of traditional fiction in their novels. The term "absurdist" has also been used to describe this kind of fiction, suggesting both the absurd quality of what goes on in the novels and the absurd nature of the world the authors observe around them.

One aspect of the new fiction was the abandonment by the writers of the implication that they were simply reporters, or that the author was only a disembodied voice telling about real events. The role of the author as the creator of the fiction and manipulator of the characters was to be clear, as was the fact that the world in which the characters moved was not intended to be the world in which real human beings existed. In one novel, for example, writer Gilbert Sorrentino used the names of characters who had appeared in minor roles in James Joyce's modern classic, *Ulysses* (1922); they had been wandering in a kind of limbo, waiting for another writer to use them in a different novel. In other novels, Pynchon and Heller in particular gave characters names that were intentionally improbable and humorous: Benny Profane, Jessica Swanlake, Mike Fallopian, Major Major Major, Chief White Halfoat, Milo Minderbinder.

Joseph Heller's *Catch-22* was an immediate success when it was published in 1961, especially among young people, although some reviewers found it childish and exaggerated. The major contributions made by Heller to the new mode in fiction include the absence of a conventional plot or narrative sequence in the novel. Chapters in *Catch-22* are named for characters, although the title character of a chapter may not in fact even be the center of attention. The chief indications of the passage of time are the steady increase in the number of missions the men must fly to complete their hitches and references to crucial events, such as the Great Bologna Raid or the death of Snowden.

Heller was also among the first to portray war and its violence from an absurdly comic perspective. Earlier writers had occasionally shown war as grimly comic in its grotesque moments, but none treated war consistently as the subject for jokes and wild horseplay, as Heller does. The point he was making in *Catch-22* was that his characters had only two choices: They could talk and behave in ways that amused or distracted them or they could go crazy. In either case, they were likely to be killed, but one choice would allow them to retain some semblance of sanity as long as they lived. A number of writers who have produced novels about the Korean or Vietnam wars have followed Heller's lead in this regard.

Heller's later fiction is less successful in its attempts to be experimental and innovative. *Something Happened* is an unusual effort to convey meaning in a circuitous fashion, as the narrator and central character, Bob Slocum, tries to come to grips with a crucial event in his life; for a long time, the event itself remains hidden from the reader. *Something Happened* is a fascinating experiment, which lacks some of the vigor and most of the social criticism of *Catch-22*. After writing a conventional novel, *Good as Gold*, Heller later tried to return to the manner of his first novel in *God Knows*, his rewriting of biblical history. *Picture This* is in its own way highly unconventional, but it does not really pretend to be fiction.

CATCH-22

First published: 1961
Type of work: Novel

The flyers in a World War II bombing squadron battle the absurdity of war as well as their nominal enemies, the Germans.

The events on the tiny Mediterranean island of Pianola, where Heller's characters are stationed, are often grotesque exaggerations of events in the larger society. There is a Great Loyalty Oath Crusade, when the entrepreneur Milo Minderbinder, supply officer of the group, tries to insist that all the officers and men sign loyalty oaths before they can eat in the group's mess halls. Other actions are simply inexplicable, as with the reluctant officer who refuses to see anyone during office hours. Still others are grim, such as the "soldier in white" who is placed in the hospital ward with other officers, completely encased in plaster; he never moves or speaks, and after a couple of days he is declared dead.

Heller's central character, Yossarian, is fond of confusing other characters with apparently crazy but logical views of events, and he frequently undertakes bizarre actions—for example, sitting in a tree naked during the funeral of one of the flyers. It becomes clear, however, that for Yossarian and his buddies—other flyers, such as Orr and Dunbar—jokes and unusual behavior are the only ways to retain something like sanity. Their commanders are even crazier than they are, their missions become increasingly hazardous, and their fellow fliers die, one by one or in groups.

Yossarian is the most rebellious character in *Catch-22*, willing to try any way of circumventing authority and retaining his individuality. He argues that he is a unique victim because the people he drops bombs on are trying to kill him. When the logical Clevinger responds by pointing out that the Germans are trying to kill everyone, Yossarian says simply that that does not matter to him if he is killed. As the novel progresses, it becomes clear that all the men, in fact, are dying: Doc Daneeka, Kraft, Coombs, Kid Sampson, McWatt, Chief White Halfoat. In a single raid, Dobbs, Havemeyer, and Nately are killed, as is the most insane of all, Hungry Joe. Some simply disappear. Others die in horrible accidents, as Kid Sampson does: Swimming at the beach with others, he jumps up from a raft just as McWatt swoops low in his plane to salute his friends. Sampson is cut in half by the propeller, and McWatt, in his horror, deliberately flies his plane into a mountain.

There are frequent references throughout *Catch-22* to the death of Snowden, a gunner on one of the planes. Only at the very end is the secret of Snowden's death revealed, when Yossarian's witnessing of the event is recorded in terrible detail, and he understands its full meaning: Man is no more than physical matter, and once the life spirit is gone, what is left is only garbage. This understanding first encourages Yossarian to accept the bargain offered by the evil colonels, Corn and Cathcart: He can escape further missions if he will like them and speak well of them. The same understanding, however, eventually leads Yossarian to refuse the offer and try to escape the way his friend Orr has, by rowing a raft through the Mediterranean, out the Straits of Gibraltar, and around to the North Sea and eventually to sanctuary in neutral Sweden. It is an impossible idea, but it is the only one left to him.

The novel's title refers to a trick that is always available to the colonels and generals. In any offer they make to the flyers, whether to limit the number of required missions or to improve conditions at the base, there is a single catch, "Catch-22," which in effect enables the leaders to do anything they want. They can break any promise they have made or introduce new regulations simply by citing Catch-22.

The world that Heller creates is absurd to such an extent that the grimness of what is going on is often cloaked by the foolishness of the action, as in the Great Loyalty Oath Crusade or in Milo Minderbinder's attempt to corner the global market on cotton followed by his desperate attempt to get rid of all the cotton he has acquired, even trying to get the men to accept it as candy. Yet the references to death are everywhere, and the number of deaths piles up. Yossarian's walk through Rome at the end, seeing all the horrors of the world in which he lives, punctuates all the foolishness with a dark period. He finally must decide to do something, even if it is only to resign from the war machine and try any means to find his way to freedom.

SOMETHING HAPPENED

First published: 1974
Type of work: Novel

An ordinary man struggles to deal with the banality and absurdity of his marriage, his family, and his job.

Bob Slocum talks endlessly and compulsively. He talks about the people with whom he works; he talks about each member of his family; he talks about the women in his life. When he is not talking to other characters, in long stretches of rapid-fire dialogue, he is talking to himself about what he fears, what he wishes he had done, and what he hopes for (but not very hard). His talk reveals that he is a bully with his daughter, son, and wife, but also that he loves them, knows what they fear, and wishes he could remove the causes of those fears. Yet he cannot bring himself to name the members of his family. His wife is called that, his son and daughter are never called by name. The only family member he ever names is his youngest, Derek, a boy with Down's syndrome who is an embarrassment to all the other members of the family. They know they should love and cherish the helpless child, but they would be happier if he were not there and if the series of unpleasant women hired to look after him could be dispensed with. Still, Slocum and his wife cannot bring themselves to institutionalize the child, so he is always present.

A major achievement of *Something Happened* is Heller's ability to sustain interest in and even a degree of sympathy for Slocum, who is in many ways a despicable individual. He lies, frequently and easily. Told by an executive that he is being considered to replace the head of another division in the corporation where he works, he lies to the man and to his own boss. At work he is a toady, obsequiously playing up to anyone he fears, even as he enjoys instilling fear in those below him. At home, he manipulates his family, especially his wife and daughter. He relishes his superiority to them in one-upmanship, playing verbal games with them which he knows will humiliate them and make them hate and fear him. He hates the fact that they cannot seem to deal with their own lives: His wife thinks that she is losing her attractiveness; his daughter thinks that she is fat and ugly, and he hates them for feeling that way. At the same time, he feels sorry for them and wishes he could make them more confident. His thoughts often turn to physical violence, which he never actually commits.

Slocum is most tender about his son, a boy of nine who is experiencing all the fears and horrors that his father had at the same age. He hates gym class and Bob Slocum tries to ease his way by talking to the dim-witted gym teacher, Forgione. The boy hates speaking to groups, reflecting Slocum's wish to speak successfully at his company's annual meetings and his fear that he will not be allowed to speak (and that he will make a mess of things if he is). Slocum is haunted by the fear that something will happen to the boy and he will be unable to help in time.

Much of the time, Slocum is thinking about women. He plans continuously to figure out ways to get younger women to go to bed with him; he reminisces about the lovemaking of the early years of his courtship and marriage. He returns compulsively to memories of a young woman he met when working at his first job, a woman he might have made love to but did not. He regrets bitterly what he considers his failure and wishes he could meet the woman again—although he has known for several years that she has died, a suicide. His memory of her makes his recent conquests among the young women he meets at work or while traveling seem silly; once he has seduced a woman, he has no desire to see her again.

Heller sustains interest in this character in part because he keeps revealing new depths of his soul, and in part because there is an atmosphere of fear and horror underlying all Slocum's ramblings. "Something must have happened to me sometime," he says on the first page of the novel, and that something is not revealed until the very end. Then, the real horror becomes clear. Slocum's son, the one person he loves unreservedly, was injured in an automobile accident. He bled profusely from superficial wounds but was not seriously injured. He died, however, when Slocum, trying to comfort him, held him too closely and suffocated him. In a brief epilogue it is clear that Slocum has gone on with his life. He has been promoted; he plays more golf, a game he hates; he inspires fear in more of his fellow employees. No one knows that he was responsible for his son's death.

Something Happened does not have the fierce wit or the absurd humor of *Catch-22*. It deals much more clearly with ordinary people and everyday lives, and it takes the risk of boring the reader with Slocum's unstoppable voice. In the end, however, it has a powerful emotional effect. As a portrait of a damned and suffering individual, it has few rivals in recent fiction.

Summary

Joseph Heller has experimented with fictional and semifictional forms throughout his career. His gift for the wildly comic and grotesque, however, found its fullest expression in his first novel, and *Catch-22* remains his major claim to a place in the front rank of contemporary novelists. *Catch-22* exposed the absurdities of twentieth century warfare and bureaucracy through the use of black humor, and it was an immensely influential book throughout the turbulent 1960's.

Bibliography

Aldridge, John W. *The American Novel and the Way We Live Now.* New York: Oxford University Press, 1982.

Gelb, Barbara. "Catching Joseph Heller." *The New York Times Magazine*, March 4, 1979, p. 15.

LeClair, Thomas. "Joseph Heller, *Something Happened*, and the Art of Excess." *Studies in American Fiction* 9 (Autumn, 1981): 245-260.

Martine, James L., ed. *American Novelists.* Detroit: Gale Research, 1986.

Merrill, Robert. "The Structure and Meaning of *Catch-22*." *Studies in American Fiction* 14 (Autumn, 1986): 139-152.

Plimpton, George, ed. *Writers at Work: The Paris Review Interviews.* 5th ser. New York: Penguin Books, 1981.

Richter, David H. *Fable's End: Completeness and Closure in Rhetorical Fiction*. Chicago: University of Chicago Press, 1975.

John M. Muste

LILLIAN HELLMAN

Born: New Orleans, Louisiana
June 20, 1905
Died: Martha's Vineyard, Massachusetts
June 30, 1984

Principal Literary Achievement

Hellman achieved distinction in two separate careers—first as a renowned playwright of the Broadway stage and then as a deft, elegant autobiographer.

Biography

Lillian Hellman was born in New Orleans, Louisiana, the only child of Max and Julia Hellman. She was spoiled as a child, and she doted on her philandering father. Her childhood was divided between New Orleans and New York; she spent half the year in each city as her father, a traveling salesman, made his living after having failed in business in her native city. Reared also by her father's two sisters, who owned a boardinghouse in New Orleans, Hellman got to know a variety of human types that would later people her plays and memoirs.

Hellman had an inclination to write at an early age, but she was not certain where her talent lay. Attempts to write fiction came to very little, and she spent most of her twenties working at odd jobs in publishing, the theater, and films. Married to short-story writer and playwright Arthur Kober, Hellman was able to soak up the atmosphere of the theater, but somehow it did not occur to her to write plays. Not until she met and began to live with Dashiell Hammett, the famous detective writer, did she begin to show the melodramatic flair that would make her first produced play, *The Children's Hour* (1934), an enormous Broadway success.

Soon in demand as a screenwriter as well, Hellman developed a reputation as an outspoken woman, radical in her politics and daring in her love affairs. In the 1930's and early 1940's, she divided her time between New York and Hollywood and traveled extensively abroad, including important trips to the Soviet Union in 1937 and during World War II. Except for the failure of her second play, *Days to Come* (1936), Hellman produced one hit play after another, from *The Little Foxes* (1939) to *Watch on the Rhine* (1941) to *The Searching Wind* (1944) to *Another Part of the Forest* (1946)—all of which were made into motion pictures.

Although she would write two other successful plays, *The Autumn Garden* (1951) and *Toys in the Attic* (1960), and several adaptations of other writers' work for the

stage, it gradually became clear to her that her interest and ability to write for the theater were waning. Similarly, offers to write motion pictures after the 1940's were infrequent—in part because Hellman had become blacklisted as a leftist writer.

Hellman turned to teaching shortly after the death of Dashiell Hammett in 1961 and held several appointments at Harvard and Yale universities, the University of California at Berkeley, and other colleges while developing a new career as an autobiographer. The publication of her first memoir, *An Unfinished Woman* (1969), received rave reviews praising her spare, elliptical style and her tough, truthful character. Hellman followed this success with *Pentimento* (1973), considered by many critics even better than *An Unfinished Woman* in its series of character portraits that read like the finest short fiction. Hellman was lauded by feminists for her independence, although a few had reservations about what they deemed to be her subservient attitude toward Hammett. Much in demand as a public speaker and teacher, and prominent in the political protests of the 1960's and 1970's against social injustice and government tyranny, Hellman became a kind of institution and role model for young people, especially women.

The first signs of fissures in Hellman's seemingly impregnable reputation came with the publication of *Scoundrel Time* (1976), her memoir of the McCarthy period, in which she recounted her testimony before the House Committee on Un-American Activities and attacked liberals for not having done more to oppose the witchhunt for Communists. Initial reviews were favorable, but then a barrage of attacks on the book and on Hellman's character began to dominate the press; critics found fault with her interpretation of the period, which made her seem more heroic than others who testified before Congress and lost their jobs and, in some cases, their careers.

Hellman was unrepentant and largely unresponsive when the attacks broadened to suggest that much in her memoirs was fabricated, including "Julia," the story of the noble anti-Fascist whom Hellman had helped to smuggle money out of Germany to support Adolf Hitler's opponents. In failing health in her last years, Hellman remained a revered figure in the theater, with many successful revivals of her plays and with her memoirs still avidly read if not accorded quite the high favor of their initial reception.

Analysis

A very strong sense of morality pervades both Hellman's plays and her memoirs. Melodrama suits her as a literary form because it stresses the conflict of good and evil. Clashing personalities, rather than development of individual character, spark her sense of drama. In *The Children's Hour*, two blameless schoolteachers are accused of lesbianism by a malevolent, spoiled child whom they have tried to discipline. In *The Little Foxes*, the greed of the members of a single family, competing among themselves in the post-Civil War South, is what motivates their actions. In *Watch on the Rhine*, the selfless heroism of Kurt Muller is set against the irremediable evil of the Fascism he fights. It is no accident, therefore, that Hellman should also be attracted to historical figures, such as Joan of Arc in *The Lark* (1955), who oppose the status quo and search for a sense of moral authority. That play reveals just how much Hellman trusts individuals rather than the state.

If Hellman were merely a melodramatist, however, her work would not remain in such high standing. If her characters do not develop to any great extent, they are the products of acute psychological perceptions. Kurt Muller, for example, with his broken hands, is a vulnerable, frightened hero, forced to kill for his cause with a melancholy determination and an absolute lack of self-righteousness that make him interesting in himself and not merely a symbol of the good. Although some of his dialogue verges on the sentimental, Hellman's command of diction and her use of understatement keep the message of the play from becoming heavy-handed.

Hellman's first phase as a playwright (from 1934 to 1951) is also her most melodramatic period, in which she concentrates on externals—brilliant evocations of the South in *The Little Foxes* and *Another Part of the Forest*, of the growth of Fascism and its appeasement in the period between the two world wars in *The Searching Wind*, of the struggle between labor and capital in a small Ohio town in *Days to Come.* Her motion-picture scripts—such as *Dead End* (1937)—evoke the heroism of the common man and the corruption of the Establishment.

Hellman's later plays and her memoirs probe her characters' motivations and her own, as if her argument shifts somewhat from a confrontation with society to an engagement with herself. In *The Autumn Garden*, a group of middle-aged characters gradually confront their sense of failure, the unfulfilled dreams of their youth, upon the return of Nick Dennery, an old friend who tries to relive the past; Nick wants to pretend that he is still the same man who set off to conquer the world, leaving his sweetheart behind. Each character's romantic notions about his or her life are deftly, even gently, demolished in a play that reflects Hellman's increasing concern with a form of novelistic, inner-directed drama inspired by Russian playwright and writer Anton Chekhov and a move away from the social realism of Norwegian playwright Henrik Ibsen that informed her earlier plays.

Hellman edited a collection of Chekhov's letters in her remaining period as a playwright, and the plot of her final original play, *Toys in the Attic*, is clearly modeled on Chekhov's *Tri sestry* (1901; *Three Sisters*, 1920). In Hellman's play, two sisters are devoted to their hapless brother Julian. Sacrificing everything for him, they are not prepared when he returns home with a windfall and proposes to change their lives, lavishing gifts upon them and buying them tickets for the trip they have always said they wanted. Like Chekhov's sisters, Hellman's actually have no intention of leaving home or of changing the illusions on which their lives have been built.

Both *The Autumn Garden* and *Toys in the Attic* are memory plays. They are about their characters' romanticizing of the past and their inability to accept the present on its own terms or to see what they have really made of their own lives. Gradually, certain of Hellman's characters in these plays do admit to the fact that they have been living a lie—creating a pleasing fiction of their lives. Such moments of self-revelation are rare in Hellman's earlier plays, although Martha Dobie's shocked recognition in *The Children's Hour* that there might be some basis to the accusation that she has harbored lesbian tendencies suggests that from the start of her career Hellman was working toward a way of combining her gift for melodrama with a complex sense of human psychology.

When Hellman turned to the memoir form, she drew upon certain elements of her plays. She admits in *Pentimento* that the family in *The Little Foxes* is based on her mother's relatives, and clearly the two sisters in *Toys in the Attic* are versions of the two aunts who helped to rear Hellman in New Orleans. Even in the memoirs, Hellman's forte is not narrative; *An Unfinished Woman*, for example, is disjointed. Hellman makes little attempt to write a chronological, well-developed autobiography. Rather, she tends to fasten on key incidents in her life—parts of her childhood, a trip to Spain—to evoke her temperament and her times. In fact, the last three chapters of *An Unfinished Woman* are character portraits of important people in her life. Hellman turned her next memoir, *Pentimento,* into a collection of portraits. Where *Scoundrel Time* is weakest is precisely in her attempt to write a narrative of the Cold War years; she makes grave errors of fact, and her usual gift for incisive character portrayal distorts the historical record.

Quite aside from faults of style or fact, however, Hellman's memoirs are a permanent contribution to American literature, for she provides the record and the testament of a writer and activist who always remained her own person. Her depictions of Dorothy Parker, Dashiell Hammett, and members of her family, and of Hollywood, the Soviet Union, and other places she visited and the home she built are masterpieces in the genre of the memoir, balancing a sense of past and present and providing a feeling for how she created her career that is likely to ensure the continuing relevance of her work.

THE CHILDREN'S HOUR

First published: 1934
Type of work: Play

Accused of being lesbians, two teachers lose their school; one of them commits suicide in the awful suspicion that she may have harbored illicit feelings.

The Children's Hour was a shocking play for its time. It was based on an actual incident in nineteenth century Scotland, in which a pupil accused her schoolteachers of lesbianism. The word itself is never spoken in *The Children's Hour,* but the mere hint of it—the innuendo that there is something "unnatural" going on between Martha Dobie and Karen Wright—is enough to damn them in the eyes of their community. Mary, the child who levels the charge against her teachers, has been spoiled by her grandmother and has learned early how to manipulate adults. Her doting grandmother is shocked by Mary's allegations and takes it upon herself to withdraw Mary from the school and to advise other parents to do the same.

It is the power of the lie, of a child's tenacious unwillingness to speak the truth even when it means the ruin of several lives, that accounts for the enormous power of the play. Mary is mean, plain evil, a point Hellman makes shrewdly in scenes that show how Mary intimidates a schoolmate into lying to support her charge against the teachers. Hellman works her audience's emotions into a fine sense of outrage at how a big lie is capable of gripping a society's imagination. Not a political play in itself, *The Children's Hour* nevertheless has political implications, since it exposes the way mass psychology can be manipulated to serve falsehood. Realizing the importance of this theme, Hellman directed a revival of the play during the McCarthy period, when she believed that many Americans were being victimized by the lie that they were Communists disloyal to the United States.

Many critics have puzzled over the play's third act, in which Martha Dobie, suspecting that she has had lesbian feelings for Karen, commits suicide. She does so partly out of guilt, for Karen's engagement to Joseph Cardin has been broken and Martha believes that she has destroyed her dear friend's life. Hellman's point seems to be that Martha's outrage at the charge against her has blinded her to what may be the true nature of her feelings. Her belated self-realization—when she no longer has the energy or the will to fight the charge—is then all the more devastating to her. In her memoirs, Hellman admits that she is not sure whether she ever got the third act of the play "right." On the other hand, the play does seem enriched by the fact that from the perspective of the third act, Mary becomes a character not only of great evil but of great intuitiveness in picking out precisely that element of Karen's and Martha's friendship which the two women themselves had never carefully examined.

The Children's Hour should not be taken as a play about lesbianism itself—a point that Hellman made herself by changing the plot of the play in a film adaptation entitled *These Three* (1935). In the film, Martha is accused of an illicit affair with Karen's fiancé, Joseph Cardin. Nearly as powerful as the play, *These Three* proves that even without the controversial element of lesbianism, Hellman's major theme about the power of a big lie remains intact.

The Children's Hour was an enormous success on Broadway—it ran longer than any other Hellman play—and no doubt its sensational aspects helped make it a hit. It retains an important place in the canon of classic American plays, and it has been revived repeatedly in recent years.

WATCH ON THE RHINE

First produced: 1941 (first published, 1941)
Type of work: Play

Kurt Muller, an anti-Fascist refugee in the home of his American wife's mother, is forced to kill an informer and return to Europe.

Watch on the Rhine was written and produced before the United States' entry into World War II. Concerned about the spread of Fascism across Europe and certain that sooner or later the United States would have to confront the menace of Hitler and Benito Mussolini, Hellman had gone to Spain to express her solidarity with the constituted government that tried to resist its overthrow by Fascist leader Francisco Franco. Bitterly disappointed at her country's failure to help Spain or to oppose Fascism, Hellman wrote *Watch on the Rhine* as a warning to a naïve and complacent America.

The play is set in the Washington, D.C., home of Fanny Farrelly, a socially prominent widow. She has frowned on the marriage of her daughter Sara to Kurt Muller and on Sara's years in Europe. When Sara decides to return home with her family, however, Fanny is delighted at the opportunity to repair the breach with her daughter. At first, there is some awkwardness, for Fanny does not understand what Sara and Kurt have been doing in Europe, and she acts rather in the manner of the grande dame who has always had her way and rarely had her opinions challenged. Gradually, however, Kurt's sincere, modest manner wins her over. Kurt does not quarrel, but he is perceptive and pointed in defense of his years as an underground anti-Fascist. Wisely, Hellman employs Sara to conduct the argument with her mother, to point out that Fanny has been nonchalant and innocent about the evil that surrounds her.

Fanny has in her home another foreign guest, Teck, a penurious Rumanian nobleman who plots to inform on Kurt to the German embassy. By winning the favor of the Germans, Teck hopes to prosper. When Kurt realizes his danger, he kills Teck. Finally realizing what is at stake, and accepting her complicity in harboring Teck and her part in his murder, Fanny allows Kurt time to escape to Europe, where he will continue the anti-Fascist struggle.

One of Hellman's most successful plays, *Watch on the Rhine* both castigated Americans for their blindness to the evil that was about to envelop them and praised them for ultimately having the sense to oppose Fascism. Fanny, for all her faults, is a deeply moral character, willing to admit her grave mistake in misjudging Kurt and estranging herself from Sara and willing to assume her role in the reprehensible yet necessary actions required to eradicate evil. The complex characterization of Kurt is what makes the moral earnestness of the play palatable. He is courteous (never forgetting that he is a guest in the Farrelly home), shrewd (eschewing any fervor that might put off the ill-informed Americans), and self-deprecating (he does not make large claims for what he can do but simply states what he believes he has to do). Kurt is brave because of his convictions; he is also vulnerable and appealing because of his concern for his wife and children and for the morality of his own acts. He cannot be sure that by killing he will not become like the Fascists, but not to act—to allow Teck to inform on him—is to put in jeopardy not only his family but also the lives of his colleagues.

By setting *Watch on the Rhine* in an American home, Hellman provided Americans with a very concrete, domestic sense of how the war in Europe would affect their lives. The United States could not isolate itself from world events—indeed, by its know-nothing attitudes, the country helped to perpetuate evil. Yet at the same time, the play implies that it is not too late to rectify things.

AN UNFINISHED WOMAN

First published: 1969
Type of work: Memoir

A provocative account of Hellman's childhood, her years in Hollywood, and her friendships with Dashiell Hammett, Dorothy Parker, and others.

An Unfinished Woman had a ravishing impact on its first readers. Hellman wrote engagingly about her childhood in New Orleans and New York, of her handsome, philandering father, of her dizzy but warmhearted mother, and of her shrewd and compassionate aunts. It was all very dramatic—Hellman's jump from her favorite tree (breaking her nose) when she discovered that her father was seeing another woman, her running away from home and being surprised by her first period, her confused first years in Hollywood as a reader of scripts (and her later ambivalent relationship with film mogul Samuel Goldwyn), the stormy affair with Dashiell Hammett, and many other incidents revealed a fiery, independent, comic, and defiant personality.

As Hellman notes in *An Unfinished Woman*, she did not intend to be the bookkeeper of her life—that is, relating in strict chronological fashion every period and incident in her career. She would, rather, trust to her memory to evoke the crucial events and characters. She devotes, for example, whole chapters to Dorothy Parker and Dashiell Hammett, since her friendships with them spanned much of her adult life. The structures of these chapters are built around the personalities she describes and not on any consistent time sequence. Indeed, Hellman is not willing to vouch for her dates; she stresses that she is remembering and reshaping the events that have remained important to her. In her chapter on Spain, for example, she does not try to reconstruct a narrative of her brief visit during the Civil War. Rather, she presents extracts from her diary, vivid reports of what it felt like to move around the country, gauging the people's moods and responding to their curiosity about America.

Several reviewers noted how little space Hellman gives to the theater in her first memoir. She shows virtually no interest in detailing what happened backstage, how she came to write her plays, or the social lives of actors, playwrights, and producers. Although she includes a chapter about the theater in *Pentimento*, *An Unfinished Woman* accurately reflects her lack of concern or enjoyment of the business of the theater. Her plays were written in isolation; she rarely revised them in production and did not like the process of collaboration. This was also true, she points out in *An Unfinished Woman*, in Hollywood, where, except for her first assignment as a screenwriter, she worked alone—a remarkable privilege in an industry known for employing teams of writers to work on one screenplay.

The title of Hellman's first memoir implies that the significance of her life, the meaning of its key events, had not settled in her mind. At several points, she confesses her inability to come to a conclusion, and the memoir itself ends with the word "however." The idea that she was "unfinished" and still in the process of discovering herself held great appeal for her readers, and she was urged by several reviewers to write another memoir. She obliged them by producing *Pentimento*, a collection of character portraits that in style and structure picked up directly from the last three chapters of *An Unfinished Woman*.

PENTIMENTO

First published: 1973
Type of work: Memoir

Hellman's second work of autobiography is organized around a collection of portraits of important people in her life.

With chapters on the theater, on key events in her relationship with Dashiell Hammett, Julia, and others, Hellman perfects the form of the short memoir. *An Unfinished Woman* had made sporadic references to the unreliability of memory and to how, over time, the imagination works over the past, transforming it into emblems of the self. By choosing the painter's term "pentimento" as a title, Hellman stresses how important it is for her readers to see that she is writing from the point of view of the present and is "repenting"—that is, changing in words the scenes she remembers, finding a deeper meaning in them, and setting them in a new context—much as a painter may paint over a scene or a figure on a canvas, having changed his or her mind about how it should be depicted.

Two of Hellman's character portraits, "Bethe" and "Willy," are about relatives whose stories help Hellman focus on her own development. Bethe has come to America from Germany, destined to be the bride in an arranged marriage, but she leaves her feckless husband for a passionate affair with another man, an Italian with underworld connections. Although Bethe's behavior is condemned by Hellman's family, Hellman's two aunts never quite abandon Bethe, and Hellman depicts herself as an adolescent who is fascinated by Bethe's sexuality and her willingness to sacrifice everything for the man she loves. Not so much a celebration of romantic love as it is confirmation of a woman's right to live as she likes, "Bethe" is clearly emblematic of Hellman's own life—of her leaving her husband for Hammett and her willingness to cope with her family's disapproval.

Similarly, Willy, Hellman's extravagant and sexually attractive uncle, represents the type of man she would often be drawn toward in later life. Willy is a venture capitalist, an independent operator who never quite fits in with his wife's wealthy family. He is a man who makes and loses his fortune several times, a man with mistresses and hearty appetites, who almost persuades a grown-up Hellman to accompany him on one of his expeditions abroad. His generosity and flair make him an enviable alternative to the gross competitiveness of her mother's family, who have made Hellman feel small—especially after her father's failure in business.

Undoubtedly, the most riveting story in *Pentimento* is "Julia." She is Hellman's darling childhood friend, the political activist from a wealthy family who spurns an easy life, earns a medical degree at the University of Oxford and (studying with Sigmund Freud in Vienna) becomes involved in the anti-Fascist movement. Julia is beautiful, courageous, and uncompromising—in short, everything that Hellman deems heroic and attractive in an individual. Not seeing herself as a heroine, Hellman nevertheless allows herself to be coaxed by Julia into a scheme of transporting money across Germany for the anti-Fascist forces.

It is a moving story. Hellman admits at its beginning that her memory is perfectly capable of playing her false, but she says that in the case of Julia she is absolutely confident of what she remembers. As the most compelling part of *Pentimento*, it is not surprising that "Julia" became a motion picture (in 1977), with Vanessa Redgrave as the stalwart Julia and Jane Fonda as Hellman. The remarkable friendship between two women, the hazards of their meeting in Germany, and Hellman's later desperate attempt to find Julia's child after the war make for a highly charged narrative of intrigue and romance that lends itself well to the screen.

As do other parts of Hellman's memoirs, "Julia" has internal inconsistencies and improbabilities. Critics have pointed out discrepancies in dates and have been unable to verify the basic facts of Hellman's purportedly true story. In the very title of the book, Hellman seems to imply that there is as much art as there is fact in her narrative, but because of the way she romanticized her own part in history, it was perhaps inevitable that her critics should seek to diminish her influence.

Summary

Lillian Hellman's place in the American theater is secure. *The Children's Hour, The Little Foxes, Another Part of the Forest, The Autumn Garden*, and *Toys in the Attic* reflect an astute moral intelligence and a vividness of characterization that will ensure the continuing revival of her major work.

Hellman also contributed an elegance of style to the memoir form; her depictions of events and portraits of friends in her life, although admitted by Hellman to contain factual inaccuracies, captivated readers.

Bibliography

Adler, Jacob H. *Lillian Hellman*. Austin, Tex.: Steck-Vaughn, 1969.

Dick, Bernard F. *Hellman in Hollywood*. Teaneck, N.J.: Fairleigh Dickinson University Press, 1982.

Falk, Doris. *Lillian Hellman*. New York: Frederick Ungar, 1978.

Holmin, Lorena Ross. *The Dramatic Works of Lillian Hellman*. Stockholm: Almqvist & Wiksell, 1973.

Lederer, Katherine. *Lillian Hellman*. Boston: Twayne, 1979.

Moody, Richard. *Lillian Hellman*. New York: Pegasus, 1972.

Newman, Robert. *The Cold War Romance of Lillian Hellman and John Melby.* Chapel Hill: University of North Carolina Press, 1989.

Rollyson, Carl. *Lillian Hellman: Her Legend and Her Legacy.* New York: St. Martin's Press, 1988.

Triesch, Manfred. *The Lillian Hellman Collection at the University of Texas.* Austin: University of Texas Press, 1967.

Wright, William. *Lillian Hellman: The Image, the Woman.* New York: Simon & Schuster, 1986.

Carl Rollyson

ERNEST HEMINGWAY

Born: Oak Park, Illinois
July 21, 1899
Died: Ketchum, Idaho
July 2, 1961

Principal Literary Achievement

Considered a master of terse, direct expression, Hemingway, the 1954 Nobel laureate in literature, had a profound stylistic impact upon most of the major authors who followed him, even though his own output was not huge.

Biography

Ernest Miller Hemingway was born into an affluent family in the Chicago suburb of Oak Park, Illinois, on July 21, 1899, the eldest of six children. The father, Clarence Edmond, was a physician. His mother, the former Grace Hall, kept an attractive house at 439 North Oak Park Avenue, her father's dwelling, into which her husband moved and lived until her father's death in 1905. Grace exposed her son to the arts by taking him to museums in Chicago and by having him take piano lessons. Hemingway, as both son and writer, frequently rebelled against her puritanical values.

As a student at Oak Park High School, from which he was graduated in 1917, Hemingway contributed to the school newspaper and other publications. Upon graduation, Hemingway realized that he would soon be in some way drawn into World War I. His first job, as a reporter for the Kansas City *Star*, was cut short when, after being rejected for military service because of weak eyesight, he enlisted as an ambulance driver for the Red Cross early in 1918 and was sent to Italy.

On July 8, 1918, Hemingway, who served with some heroism, was wounded by mortar fire at Fossalta di Piave. Hospitalized for an extended period, he formed a liaison with a nurse. When he returned to the United States, the dashing, dark-haired Hemingway was considered a conquering hero and was in great demand to speak before civic groups about his war experience. He was lionized for his heroism.

After recuperating at his family's summer home in Michigan, Hemingway became a reporter for the Toronto *Star* and *Star Weekly*, which sent him to Europe as a foreign correspondent in 1921, shortly after his marriage to Hadley Richardson. They settled in Paris, where they met many of the foremost contributors to Europe's avant-garde artistic scene. Among his Parisian associates Hemingway numbered Sherwood Anderson, Ford Madox Ford, James Joyce, Ezra Pound, and—perhaps most

significant—Gertrude Stein. It was from her that he learned the elements of literary style that were later to affect his writing most directly.

Hemingway began to write short stories and, in 1923, published *Three Stories and Ten Poems* in Paris, followed the next year by *In Our Time*, a collection of short stories, which was republished in 1925 in the United States. By then, Hemingway was beginning to move away from reporting and full time into his career.

In 1926, he published *The Torrents of Spring* and his renowned novel of the lost generation, *The Sun Also Rises*, with Charles Scribner's Sons in New York, who remained his publisher for all but one of his later books. *The Sun Also Rises* established Hemingway's early reputation, although real commercial success evaded him for another two years until *A Farewell to Arms* appeared in 1929. In both books, he did what he always did best: wrote about men under pressure responding to it in a way that he defined as courageous. For Hemingway, courage came from showing grace under pressure.

Men Without Women appeared in 1927, the year in which Hemingway divorced Hadley and married Pauline Pfeiffer. In 1928, Hemingway decided to return to the United States. He and Pauline used their house in Key West, Florida, as their base until 1939, although their stays there were interrupted by frequent travel, particularly from 1936 to 1938, when Hemingway went to Spain to cover the Spanish Civil War for the North American Newspaper Alliance.

The Key West years were productive ones for Hemingway. He was happy there and began his extensive adventures as a sport fisherman in the Gulf of Mexico, much more elaborate excursions than his cherished childhood fishing and hunting trips with his father in northern Michigan. At about this time, Hemingway, who had experienced the running of the bulls at Pamplona, began to develop his lifelong interest in bullfighting. His book on the subject, *Death in the Afternoon*, appeared in 1932, his first book to depart from the war theme that had come for many to define his writing; his major concern, however, is still grace under pressure.

Ever seeking new adventures, Hemingway took his first African safari in 1933 and 1934; during these travels he also revisited Spain and France. His *Green Hills of Africa*, published in 1935, resulted from this first of his many African ventures. Back in Key West after the Spanish War ended in 1938, Hemingway was restless, and in 1939, he bought his *Finca Vigía* outside Havana and moved there.

Hemingway's obsession with adventure and with proving his masculinity—clear motivations for many of his more daring adventures—made him difficult to live with; in 1940, Pauline divorced him. In the same year, *For Whom the Bell Tolls* was published, and Hemingway married newswoman Martha Gellhorn, several years his senior, whom he regarded subconsciously as a mother figure, as he probably did all his wives. His resentment of his own mother usually came in his marriages to be directed against the wife/mothers he chose to marry.

With the entry of the United States into World War II, Hemingway again went to Europe as a war correspondent. He participated in the Normandy invasion, hatched a personal scheme to liberate Paris, and attached himself to the Fourth Infantry

Division somewhat against the will of its officers. When he returned to Cuba during the war, he became a self-appointed anti-submarine operative, sailing into the ocean on his yacht to spot enemy submarines and disable any he encountered. The U.S. government was embarrassed by Hemingway's unsolicited help. His literary production declined during this period, and his drinking was out of control. When Martha Gellhorn divorced him in 1944, he quickly married Mary Welsh, who remained his wife until, seeking the same solution to his problems that his father had earlier, he committed suicide in 1961.

Hemingway's artistic end seemed imminent in 1950 when his novel *Across the River and into the Trees* was poorly received by critics and the public alike; however, he rallied from that defeat and, in 1952, published one of his most popular stories, the novella *The Old Man and the Sea*. About a year after the book was published, Hemingway survived two airplane crashes in Africa. Reported dead, he eventually charged out of the bush with a bottle of whiskey in his hand. In 1954, he was awarded the Nobel Prize in Literature, but, because of his injuries, could not attend the awards ceremony. His citation, although the Nobel Prize is for the full body of one's literary work, specifically cited *The Old Man and the Sea* as exemplifying what the award seeks to honor in literature.

When Cuba fell to Fidel Castro in 1959, Hemingway bought his final residence, a house in Ketchum, Idaho. He moved there in 1959, the same year in which he began treatments for depression and various physical ills at the Mayo Clinic in Rochester, Minnesota. His despondence over his declining health and over his inability to write as well as he once did led him to end his life on July 2, 1961, by putting a twelve-gauge shotgun into his mouth and pulling the trigger.

Analysis

During Ernest Hemingway's formative years, his mother tried to civilize her offspring. His father, on the other hand, exposed the boy to such masculine activities as hunting, fishing, and living in the woods during those periods when he could take time away from his medical practice to be with his family at its summer home near Petosky, Michigan. Hemingway, never a large man, endured an adolescence of viewing the world from the perspective of someone five feet, four inches tall. This early perspective eventually made itself felt in his work.

Beginning to write long before the graphic arts had coined the term "minimalist," Hemingway was an early minimalist in his writing. He learned part of the minimalist lesson during his years as a newspaper reporter. He learned, also, during that period the importance of close, accurate observation. As anyone who has studied journalism knows, journalistic writing is direct, unencumbered, and accessible. Journalists write short sentences that they incorporate into short paragraphs. Their vocabulary is simple, their syntax not obscure.

During his apprenticeship as a writer, Hemingway was a journalist—but not merely a journalist. He was a journalist living in post-World War I Paris, certainly the preferred gathering place of avant-garde artists and intellectuals of that age. Besides living at the geographical center of European—and therefore, worldwide—intellectual and artistic ferment, Hemingway was a part of an inner circle of challenging artists.

Ezra Pound, newly emerged from his Imagist and vorticist stages in poetry, was working on his *Cantos*, which he began to publish in 1930 and published periodically for the next ten years. Pound was also encouraging and guiding the young T. S. Eliot, who dwelt just across the English Channel in London, as he wrote *The Waste Land* (1922), the poem that came to define modernism in poetry. Ford Madox Ford was turning his efforts to recording in novels and short stories much he had experienced in the war. Sherwood Anderson, goaded by Gertrude Stein, was discovering metaphors for the whole of human existence in his close examination of lives of the people whose houses fronted on the main street of his native Winesburg, Ohio.

Around Gertrude Stein grew a circle of artists bent on redefining art as it was then known. Pablo Picasso had passed from expressionism to Impressionism and was emerging as a cubist, accomplishing with paint what others would come to work toward achieving with words. Henri Matisse was rediscovering color and using it in ways and in forms that alarmed the public and set an aesthetic revolution going in the minds of artists. Fortunately for Hemingway, he soon became a favored guest at 27 rue des Fleures, where the redoubtable Gertrude Stein lived with Alice B. Toklas, her companion, who talked with the wives while Stein picked the brains of their creative husbands. Such was the intellectual milieu in which Hemingway found himself as a youth not quite twenty-five. He was a reporter, and the pressure of that job assured his fluency in writing. The writing he did on his own was less voluminous than the writing he was paid to do.

Hemingway set for himself the task of writing about a thousand words a day, or about three typed pages. He did not consider his work done, however, until he had revised that thousand words down to about three hundred. His sentences were short. His words were simple. His constructions were uncomplicated, his prose electrified. He assured himself of its electricity by reading what he wrote each day to his wife. When she got goose bumps from what he read her, he knew that he was on target.

Hemingway was a consciously masculine writer. His protagonists, with the possible exception of Jake Barnes in *The Sun Also Rises*, were men engaged in extreme external conflicts, be it the solitary conflict of Santiago in *The Old Man and the Sea* as he tried to beach his fish after a three-day struggle or that of the bullfighter in *Death in the Afternoon*, the adventurers in *The Green Hills of Africa*, his autobiographical character, Frederic Henry, in *A Farewell to Arms*, or Robert Jordan, who fought with the Spanish loyalists in *For Whom the Bell Tolls.*

In nearly everything he wrote, Hemingway depicted courage as he defined the word: grace under pressure. He was fearful lest he not be considered courageous himself, and he rankled when William Faulkner, who was awarded the Nobel Prize in Literature four years before Hemingway received it in 1954, was quoted in an interview as suggesting that Hemingway was lacking in courage—an astute observation on Faulkner's part. Hemingway learned much about literary style, especially about depicting human speech authentically, from Stein. He, in turn, became a stylistic model for such modern writers as James Jones, Nelson Algren, and Norman Mailer. Perhaps no other twentieth century American author has been the spiritual progenitor to as many notable literary offspring.

Whereas William Faulkner examined his native Mississippi microscopically in his work, Ernest Hemingway bolted from the environment in which he had grown up. His major work explores foreign cultures in one way or another. If his cast of characters is American, as it often is, these characters live out their roles in foreign, usually hostile, environments. Moving people away from all that is most familiar to them heightens the pressure under which they must perform, and that is clearly a part of Hemingway's technique. Even Santiago in *The Old Man and the Sea*, although he is adrift in his fishing skiff in the waters off his native land, finds himself alone in a huge, hostile environment.

This book is, however, different from most of the others. In it Hemingway is more mellow than he has been in any of his earlier work. He is still tough, but the old man survives, and although the sharks that close in on his boat strip the flesh from his prized catch, he has the satisfaction of having prevailed in the struggle. It is this book that tipped the balance in favor of Hemingway's winning the Nobel Prize. His earlier work had not been affirmative enough to reflect the Nobel Foundation's guidelines. *The Old Man and the Sea*, although it does not retreat from Hemingway's basic themes, ends on a note of subdued triumph.

THE SUN ALSO RISES

First published: 1926
Type of work: Novel

In post-World War I Europe, a group of expatriates wanders about the Basque country trying to find meaning in life.

Hemingway's characters in *The Sun Also Rises* are much like the people with whom he came into daily contact in the Paris of the early 1920's. A large group of expatriates, labeled by Gertrude Stein "the lost generation," lived by their wits, by what jobs they could find, or by handouts from home. So it is with the characters in Hemingway's first novel.

The story revolves around two Americans—Jake Barnes, a newspaperman whose war injury has made him impotent, and Robert Cohn, who boxed well enough at Princeton University that he became the university's middleweight boxing champ. Cohn, the son of a wealthy Jewish family, married when he left college and lived combatively with his wife until she left him for someone else. Then he drifted to California and salved his post-marital wounds by founding an avant-garde review and settling in with Frances Clyne as his mistress.

Cohn and Frances are living in Paris when Jake first meets him shortly after the armistice. Cohn has come to Paris to work on his first novel. He has a social life that includes his writing but that compartmentalizes his two other principal activities, boxing and tennis. Cohn's friendships do not spill over onto one another. His boxing friends are his boxing friends. They know neither his tennis friends nor his friends who read and write. Cohn's life is neatly arranged.

Jake is in love with a British war widow, Lady Brett Ashley, but his impotence makes marriage unthinkable for them. Jake sublimates by listening to his friends complain while he sits in bars drinking enormously. When this life begins to wear on him, Jake escapes to the Pyrenees and luxuriates in the trout fishing the fast-moving streams in the Basque country provide or he goes to Spain for the bullfights, of which he is an aficionado.

One dismal night, Jake takes a prostitute to the Café Napolitain for a drink and conversation. They go on to have dinner at a restaurant on the Left Bank, where they happen upon Robert Cohn and Frances, as well as some of Jake's other friends. In the course of the evening, Lady Brett comes in, trailing young swains behind her. It is soon evident that Robert Cohn is much taken by her. Lady Brett rebuffs Robert, refusing to join him for dinner, saying that she has a date with Jake. They leave together. They avoid any mention of Jake's emasculating injury, but it is clearly on both their minds, setting up the tension necessary to the story.

Cohn later asks Jake questions about Lady Brett. He also sends Frances conveniently to England, against her will. Jake's friend Bill Gorton is about to arrive by steamship from the States. Robert Cohn and Lady Brett go off to San Sebastian in the Basque country after Brett convinces Robert that he needs a change.

Jake decides to take his visitor to Spain for trout fishing and to see the running of the bulls and the bullfights at Pamplona. The plot thickens when Brett's former fiancé, Michael Campbell, arrives in Paris from Britain. He and Brett have arranged to meet Jake and Bill in Pamplona for the bullfights. This leaves Robert Cohn in San Sebastian by himself. Never one to fade quietly into the background, Cohn joins the party in Bayonne. Then they all are to meet in Pamplona for the bullfight. When Bill and Jake get to Bayonne, Cohn is waiting for them.

They continue to Pamplona, and the next morning Bill and Jake take the bus to Burgette, riding on top of it, sharing their wine with the Basque peasants who ride with them. This is one of the most colorful and memorable scenes in the book, one in which Hemingway captures and depicts local color with such an astounding veracity that many people, having read *The Sun Also Rises*, have gone to the Basque country to try to relive some of what Hemingway depicted in it, including this bus ride.

The three men finally get to Pamplona, where Mike and Brett are staying. It is apparent that Robert Cohn is not welcome, and Mike Campbell does little to disguise his annoyance. Finally, however, the festivities are sufficient to distract their attention from their rivalry. The bullfight is magnificent. The torero, Pedro Romero, is brilliant, and Lady Brett, never one to linger long over any one man, falls in love with him even before she meets him. Soon after she meets him, she takes him to her room.

Jake and Bill, meanwhile, are drinking heavily. Jake tells the drunken Cohn that Brett has gone off with the torero, and Cohn strikes his two companions, knocking them both to the floor. He soon apologizes and breaks down in tears. He is totally confused by Brett and decides to leave for Paris the next day. He is not to depart without having his satisfaction, however, so he bursts in upon Brett and her new conquest. He beats Romero badly, but not enough to keep him from performing magnificently in the next day's bullfight. The party disperses, and Jake lands in San Sebastian alone. Brett sends him a telegram asking that he come to her in Madrid, where she also is alone and without any money. She has decided to go back to Mike because they have similar backgrounds. She and Jake ride around Madrid in a taxi, while Brett fantasizes about how good it could have been for the two of them had Jake not been injured in the war.

Hemingway has depicted the pointless, purposeless wandering of the lost generation. He has captured their ennui and their dislocatedness. In a way, Robert Cohn's striking out at people is the manifestation of what Jake might be doing over his anger at having been wounded in the way he was. Jake, however, has accepted the inevitable and has learned to live with what he cannot change.

A FAREWELL TO ARMS

First published: 1929
Type of work: Novel

A tragic story of a young, injured ambulance driver and the nurse he falls in love with during the war in Italy.

Frederic Henry, the protagonist in *A Farewell to Arms*, is a young American in Italy serving, as Hemingway did, as an ambulance driver during World War I. He meets Catherine Barkley, newly arrived with a group of British nurses who are to set up a hospital near the front. Frederic likes Catherine, whom he visits as often as he can between ambulance trips to evacuate the wounded.

Catherine, who has recently lost her fiancé in the war, is vulnerable. Probably she feels more emotion for Frederic than he feels for her. He is about to leave for the front, where an assault is being mounted. She gives him a Saint Anthony medal, but it does not assure him the protection she hopes it will. A mortar shell explodes above Frederic's dugout and he is wounded, much as Hemingway himself had been. He is evacuated to a hospital in Milan.

Frederic is not the perfect patient. He keeps wine under his bed and drinks as much of it as he can get away with. By the time Catherine comes to the hospital to see him, it is he who is vulnerable, and he realizes that he is in love with her. She stays with him through the surgery that his wounds necessitate; he has a happy recuperation, which Catherine nurses him through. They find restaurants that are off Milan's beaten path and take carriage rides into the surrounding countryside. Catherine often comes to Frederic's hospital room at night. He already knows that she is pregnant from a hotel-room encounter before he left for the front.

Frederic repairs quickly, and by October, a few months after he was first injured, he is ready to go on convalescent leave with Catherine in tow. His plans are scuttled, however, when he develops jaundice, a condition the head nurse blames on his surreptitious drinking, accusing him of doing this to avoid further service at the front. When Frederic returns to his post, his unit is ordered to take its ambulances and equipment south to the Po valley. The Allies, hard pressed by Austrian shelling and by the knowledge that German reinforcements are joining the Austrians, are pessimistic and disheartened. Hemingway shows the unglorious aspects of war in realistic detail.

Hard pressed by the enemy, the Americans retreat, Frederic driving an ambulance south along roads cluttered with evacuees. Rain is falling and the whole plain along which the retreat is taking place becomes a quagmire. Frederic, with two Italian sergeants he has picked up, begins to drive across open country, hoping to reach Udine at the Austrian border by that route. When his ambulance becomes stuck in the mud, Frederic tries to get the Italians to help him extricate it, but they want to flee. Frederic shoots one of them, wounding him. An Italian corpsman finishes the sergeant off, putting a bullet into his head. Life is cheap when people are under this sort of pressure.

When Frederic and his friends set out on foot for Udine, they see German motorcycles ahead of them. Chaos reigns as officers pull off their insignias and people try to flee in every direction. Those whom the Germans capture are given kangaroo trials and are summarily executed. Frederic is detained, and his fate seems sealed. Under cover of night, however, he escapes and jumps into a river, where he holds onto a log. He crosses the plain on foot until he can hop a freight train for Milan, where he tries to find Catherine. Learning that the contingent of British nurses has been sent to Stresa, and now dressed in civilian clothing, he makes his way to Stresa for his reunion with Catherine. Learning that the authorities plan to arrest him for desertion, Frederic borrows a rowboat, and he and Catherine use it to row all night to neutral Switzerland, where they are arrested but soon released, their passports being in order and Frederic's pockets bulging with money.

They wait out the fall in Montreux in the Swiss mountains, living happily in a small inn as Catherine's pregnancy advances. Their situation is idyllic. When it is finally time for Catherine to deliver the baby, she has a difficult time. The baby is stillborn. Frederic, exhausted, goes out for something to eat, and when he returns, he learns that Catherine has suffered a hemorrhage. He rushes to her and stays at her side, but she dies. He walks back to his hotel room in the rain.

In this novel, Hemingway has written a tragic love story, but beyond that he has written an antiwar book, one that shows the irrationality of the kind of combat into which Frederic was drawn. The glamour and heroism of war tarnish quickly in the face of the realities that Frederic encounters in combat. The enemy would annihilate him; that is what war is about. Shockingly, Frederic himself is brutalized by the war.

He shoots an ally who will not do his bidding.

The love story around which the book revolves has been compared with that of *Romeo and Juliet*, to which it bears the affinity of having an unhappy outcome that results not from any weakness within the characters themselves but from circumstances over which they have no control. They are pawns in a large chess game that they neither understand nor can control.

FOR WHOM THE BELL TOLLS

First published: 1940
Type of work: Novel

This novel tells about three days in the life of an American teacher helping the Spanish Loyalists in their fight against the Fascists.

In this novel, Hemingway clearly demonstrates what the title, taken from a John Donne poem, promises. The essence of the poem from which the title is drawn is that when anyone dies, all humankind is involved—everyone dies a little. Hemingway, himself a correspondent in Spain during its civil war, uses his novel to show that a small skirmish confined to a single nation affects the entire world and cannot be dismissed as something local.

Robert Jordan, the protagonist, is an American teacher who is in Spain to fight with the Loyalists. The book chronicles three crucial days in his life and in the lives of the Loyalists he is there to help. Jordan's mission is to destroy a bridge that is a vital link for the Fascists. He has had considerable demolition experience in the past, but this is the most intricate job he has undertaken. It must be timed precisely, and to orchestrate the demolition, he must enlist the aid of a band of Loyalist guerrillas, working through their leader, Pablo.

Pablo is not dependable, although his wife, Pilar, is. Pablo drinks too much and is weak. Pilar is outspoken, vulgar, direct, and dependable. Jordan knows he can depend upon her, but he is less sure of her husband. Jordan needs to concentrate on how the bridge is constructed so that he can plan his demolition as effectively as possible. He is holed up in a cave with Pablo and Pilar along with members of their band. Among those in the cave is Maria, a young girl who has been ravaged by the Fascists. They have humiliated her every way they could, and Jordan, hearing of this, is so morally indignant that killing them becomes in his mind a moral act.

Another inhabitant of the cave is Anselmo, an old man who can be depended upon to do what he is told, even if it means killing, to which he is basically opposed. Jordan likes the guerrillas; he respects their stand against Fascist oppression. He understands their motives, which are less ideological than his, and he sympathizes with their lot. During Jordan's first night in the guerrilla camp, Maria makes her way into his sleeping bag, and they have a night of blissful sex. He promises Maria that he will marry her some day, although he fears what lies ahead. He deplores his fear because he realizes that it weakens anyone who is out to accomplish a dangerous mission.

His plans now quite well plotted out, Jordan discovers the night before his intricate mission is to be carried out that Pablo has defected, stealing his explosives and detonators. The next day, a repentant Pablo returns, but without the detonators; Jordan knows that the bridge must now be blown up with hand grenades, a much more dangerous and a much less effective way to accomplish the end of destroying this vital link.

Jordan has little choice but to forgive Pablo, because he needs him. He devises an alternate plan for the demolition, one that must be orchestrated precisely. His work is to begin when Loyalist forces begin bombing the Fascist stronghold. Anselmo, who hates to kill, must kill the sentry so that the Loyalists can position themselves to explode their grenades.

All goes as planned, but in the melee, Anselmo is struck by flying metal and killed. Jordan, realizing that had they been able to use detonators Anselmo would be alive, has to restrain his urge to kill Pablo. His emotions are high, but so are the stakes in the game he is playing, so he must control himself. He still needs Pablo.

In order to escape, Jordan and his party must cross a road that is within firing range of the Fascists: Those who cross will be fully exposed. The first pair to cross the road will probably escape, because the enemy will not yet have been alerted, but after the first crossing, the others will be in grave danger. Ironically, Jordan must send Pablo first, because Pablo knows the road. He insists that Maria go with Pablo when they leave. The two make the crossing without incident. Then Jordan sends Pilar and two other guerrillas who have been involved in the mission after them. They succeed in reaching safety. Only Jordan remains to make the run to safety. He rides his horse onto the road, and gunfire rings out. The horse, injured gravely, falls and crushes Jordan's leg. The others steal out and pull him to safety, but it is apparent that he is too badly injured to travel.

Maria wants to stay with Jordan, but he will not hear of this. He talks with her, saying that while she is alive, a bit of him will live, suggesting possibly that she is carrying his child. Finally, the guerrillas and Maria must leave. Jordan is left alone with his submachine gun. He reflects on why he is in this situation, convincing himself that what he has done was right and necessary. His faith in the common people remains undiminished as a Fascist officer, who essentially holds Jordan's death warrant, approaches.

For Whom the Bell Tolls was, at that point in his career, Hemingway's most articulate statement of what he thought people must do under pressure. It is significant that Robert Jordan fights in a conflict to which he has no real obligation—he is neither Spanish nor an impoverished peasant; that is the essence of what the title means. In Hemingway's view, no human can overlook the plight of other human beings, and people find their highest nobility in defending the ideals in which they believe.

THE OLD MAN AND THE SEA

First published: 1952
Type of work: Novella

This allegorical story is about an old fisherman down on his luck who hooks the largest marlin ever caught in the waters he fishes.

The Old Man and the Sea is in many ways Hemingway's most controlled piece of writing. Short and direct, it is the story of Santiago, who essentially is alone throughout the story. The beguiling boy who usually assists him has been ordered by his father not to do so after Santiago goes for forty days without a catch. Manolin still comes to see the old man, but he no longer sails with him.

The story opens on the eighty-fourth day since Santiago has caught anything. He survives on the food that Manolin buys him from the money he steals or begs from tourists. Manolin also makes sure that Santiago has bait. As they eat their meager repast, Santiago and Manolin reminisce about happier days, remembering good catches and Joe DiMaggio and other pleasant things from their past.

That night, Santiago dreams of tigers rather than of his wife, now some time dead. He wakes to set out for his eighty-fifth day of fruitless fishing. Fishing is all he knows, so he has no choice. The details of the morning and of the sea are flawlessly presented. Hemingway transports his readers to Santiago's small boat. Through Santiago's eyes they see the man-of-war birds flying over a school of dolphin leaping in the air to snag flying fishes. They are moving faster than Santiago can go, so there is no hope that he will change his luck by catching a dolphin.

As the morning wears on, Santiago hooks one small fish. He is encouraged by this tiny triumph, taking it as a sign that his luck might be changing. His baited line is deep below the surface, a full hundred fathoms down. He waits. The sun beats down hotly upon him as it inches toward its zenith. Then, around noon, something takes the bait. Santiago knows from the feel of the line that he has hooked a big fish.

Rather than coming to the surface, the hooked fish tows Santiago's boat in a northwesterly direction, continuing this action into the night. Santiago braces himself for a night of struggle, drawing the line across his shoulder. He eats small pieces of the raw tuna he had caught earlier. At a sudden jerk on the line, Santiago's right hand is gashed across the palm. His fingers cramp. He waits for the sun to warm him.

The next morning, Santiago sees his marlin for the first time. It leaps in the air, and Santiago knows the dimensions of the contest in which he is engaged. He has never seen a larger fish. As the day wears on and the sun beats down, Santiago is hard pressed to stay awake. He hallucinates, recalling ways in which he has shown his strength in the past. He husbands his water supply carefully, not knowing how long he will be at sea.

Before sunset, he hooks a small dolphin and two flying fish that will sustain him for a while. When night falls, he sleeps fitfully, the lines secured around him. The marlin has a spurt of action and pulls the line through Santiago's hands, again lacerating them—giving him his stigmata, if one wishes to pursue a Christian interpretation, as some critics have. As the night wears on, the marlin tires. By midmorning, Santiago is able to draw the fish to the skiff and secure it to the side. He fantasizes about his triumphant return to the Havana harbor, dreaming of having made his fortune by catching this fabulous fish. It is then that the Mako sharks begin circling, lunging in to tear flesh from the noble marlin. Santiago is no match for them.

By the time he gets to the harbor long after sunset, little is left of his catch. He disembarks, seeing that only the backbone and tail of the marlin remain. He carries his mast and sails on his shoulders, stumbling in exhaustion as he goes, reminiscent of Christ carrying his cross to Calvary. Other fishermen surround the skiff the next day, marveling at the eighteen-foot length of Santiago's catch, even though all its flesh has been torn off. Unfeeling tourists going into a restaurant see the remains and wonder what they are, having no idea of their meaning. Santiago sleeps much of the day away, dreaming of lions.

In many ways, *The Old Man and the Sea* marks the culmination of Hemingway's creative endeavors. The book, reflecting Hemingway's consistent use of everyday language and avoidance of abstraction, is at once realistic and impressionistic. Although it is filled with symbolism, the symbols are neither heavy-handed nor artificial. Over and above these strengths, Hemingway in this novella is in greater control of the unities of time, place, and character than he is in any of the other works except *For Whom the Bell Tolls.* His small cast of participants—essentially Santiago and Manolin, with very little even of the latter—allows him to explore deeply the recesses of a man's inner being with no distraction from other human influences.

Obviously influenced significantly by Herman Melville's *Moby Dick* (1851), Hemingway's small classic makes its impact in quite a different way. Hemingway, as has been noted earlier, might be called a minimalist. In calling him that, however, one should probably qualify the statement further to indicate that in his minimalism, Hemingway becomes an essentialist. He is in search of essences, much as the ancient Greek philosophers were. In *The Old Man and the Sea*, he gets in touch with the quintessence of human existence. Santiago, a humble fisherman, is a genuine hero, responding with grace to the pressures upon him and emerging victorious in ways that few protagonists in modern literature have.

NOW I LAY ME

First published: 1927
Type of work: Short story

An early biographical story in the Nick Adams sequence.

This early story in a sequence that features Nick Adams as the protagonist takes place in northern Italy during World War I. Nick Adams, like Hemingway, has been wounded and is convalescing at the hospital in Milan. Among the problems he encounters is his inability to sleep. He engages in all sorts of ploys to overcome this condition, but nothing he does helps him sleep. In his restless, wakeful state at night, Nick tosses and turns, mulling over many of life's profoundest questions. He has been face to face with death. He has given up his youth in that moment when his life might well have ended on a battlefield in an alien land. He is not sure that his sanity is fully intact.

The last third of the story is given over to commonplace dialogue, to a conversation Nick has with John, another wounded soldier convalescing as Nick is. As the two talk, one is reminded of the banality of the dialogue in Gertrude Stein's *Three Lives* (1909), a book in which Stein sought to capture the cadences of the actual speech of working-class women. Such speech, when faithfully recorded, is repetitious, tedious, and boring, as is much of the dialogue in this story.

This is not a weakness, however. Hemingway uses this technique to capture the tedium, the commonplaceness of life, which, aside from those rare moments of heroic action that elicit outstanding individual performance, is a pretty flat affair.

In their conversation, John is trying to persuade Nick to marry. Nick's reflections throughout the story, however, make it clear to the reader that Nick has many questions to be answered before marriage is a viable solution for him. He and John live on two vastly different planes, and what John suggests for Nick is what would work in John's world rather than in Nick's.

This story in part is about the inability of human beings to communicate effectively with each other. Background, upbringing, personal predilections—all of these stand between what is being communicated and what is being received. On one level, a large part of Hemingway's writing is concerned with this problem, and it is reflection on it that kept Hemingway writing, that kept him ever trying to find the way to connect the perceptions of two people into a single, unified, mutually agreed-upon message.

A CLEAN WELL-LIGHTED PLACE

First published: 1933
Type of work: Short story

A restrained story in which setting is central to the meaning.

One of Hemingway's most frequently reproduced and read short stories is "A Clean Well-Lighted Place," a quite amazing tour de force in that it is largely a story of setting rather than character or action. Only five pages long, "A Clean Well-Lighted Place" takes place late at night in a small Spanish restaurant. The only customer, an old man, attempted suicide a week earlier.

The two waiters, a young one and an older one, talk about the customer. The young waiter wants to close the place and put the old man out. The older waiter thinks they should not, but the young waiter prevails. The older waiter reflects on the difference between a well-lighted establishment such as his and a dark, smoky bodega, and in doing so touches on many of life's deeper mysteries.

In the most dramatic incident in this restrained story, the old waiter recites the Lord's Prayer, but in doing so, he substitutes the Spanish word *nada* (nothingness) for all the significant nouns and verbs in the prayer. In writing this passage, Hemingway captured much of the nihilistic sentiment that was abroad in the 1920's and 1930's and that T. S. Eliot had reflected earlier in *The Waste Land* and two years after that in "The Hollow Men." The story does not really move toward anything, but its directionlessness, reminiscent of the directionlessness of the lost generation as reflected in *The Sun Also Rises*, is perhaps a human condition.

"A Clean Well-Lighted Place" is another minimalist piece of writing that moves toward essentialism. It has the same sort of careful control of theme, style, character, and setting that Hemingway later achieved so successfully in *The Old Man and the Sea*.

THE SNOWS OF KILAMANJARO

First published: 1936
Type of work: Short story

The story of a writer dying in Africa.

Reminiscent of Ambrose Bierce's "An Occurrence at Owl Creek Bridge" (1891), "The Snows of Kilamanjaro" tells of a writer, Harry, who faces almost immediate death in Africa from gangrene. A rescue plane is to fly in and rescue him, but the prognosis is grave. In the story, the great, white, hovering plane arrives, sparkling in the bright sun.

The fact is that the plane does not arrive. What the reader is told is Harry's final dream. His wife comes into the bedroom and finds him dead. The story is important in the Hemingway canon because, like *A Farewell to Arms* and other of his works, it contrasts the mountain (purity) to the plain (corruption). Harry spends the last afternoon of his life quarrelling with his wife. Like the protagonist in Henry James's "The Middle Years," written in 1882, Harry bemoans the fact that he has wasted his talent. Harry, the supreme egoist, is morally bankrupt. The gangrene in his rotting leg is no worse than the spiritual gangrene that has rotted his soul.

In his prefatory paragraph, Hemingway describes and situates Kenya's Mt. Kilamanjaro—at 19,710 feet the highest mountain in Africa. He reveals that close to its summit is the desiccated, frozen carcass of a leopard, whose presence at that altitude is a mystery. In sharp contrast to the pure, cold mountaintop and noble leopard are the overheated plain below and the hyena that emits almost human cries at the moment of Harry's death, awakening Helen, Harry's wife, who finds her husband dead.

Hemingway places Harry on an acme artistically but shows him being devoured by those for whom he writes—or, perhaps, like the hyena in Hemingway's *The Green Hills of Africa*, he is self-devouring. Certainly like Belmonte, the bullfighter in *The Sun Also Rises*, he is exceptionally talented but appalled by his audience, represented in the story by Helen and by the hyena, both of whom weep at Harry's death. The sustained metaphor of the mountaintop/leopard and the plain/hyena presents the sharp, controlled contrasts that make "The Snows of Kilamanjaro" one of Hemingway's most artistically successful stories.

Summary

Like many writers, Ernest Hemingway was a man of many contradictions and of a very convoluted nature. A master stylist, he identified with common people and captured them in their speech patterns, faithfully depicted in his pages. His personal and political philosophy have much to do with proving oneself. Life to Hemingway was a battle to be fought valiantly, as Santiago fought the marlin in *The Old Man and the Sea*. Perhaps for Hemingway there are no victors, only people who display grace under pressure.

Bibliography

Baker, Carlos. *Ernest Hemingway: A Life Story.* New York: Charles Scribner's Sons, 1969.

Griffin, Peter. *Along with Youth: Hemingway, the Early Years.* New York: Oxford University Press, 1985.

Lee, Robert A. *Ernest Hemingway: New Critical Essays.* Totowa, N.J.: Barnes & Noble Books, 1983.

Lynn, Kenneth S. *Hemingway: The Life and the Work.* New York: Simon & Schuster, 1987.

Meyers, Jeffrey. *Hemingway: A Biography.* New York: Harper & Row, 1985.

R. Baird Shuman

FRANK HERBERT

Born: Tacoma, Washington
October 8, 1920
Died: Madison, Wisconsin
February 11, 1986

Principal Literary Achievement

Critical and popular acclaim earned by his novel *Dune* made Herbert one of the most popular and influential science fiction authors of all time.

Biography

Frank Herbert grew up during the Depression era in a family which practiced economy but never lacked food or shelter, even when his father was unemployed. Life in Washington state, where he grew up on a farm, helped catch and smoke salmon, jack-lighted deer with his father to supplement their domestic meat supply, and apprenticed as a skin-diver with an uncle who was introducing Japanese methods of oyster farming to the area, was—according to Herbert—a rich experience.

By the age of eight, he knew he wanted to be a writer. In his teens, he was already known to his contemporaries as an accomplished story-teller, thus following in the footsteps of his paternal grandmother, who could not read but commanded a great store of folk songs. Her songs and her Appalachian dialect introduced young Herbert both to oral literature and to the wide variation in human language.

In his high school years, Herbert was an avid reader and an enthusiastic member of the school newspaper staff. He substituted during the summer for vacationing reporters on the *Tacoma Ledger*. At nineteen, he was graduated from high school and began his journalistic career as a reporter for the *Glendale Star.*

In 1940, he married Flora Parkinson, with whom he had a daughter, Penny. He enlisted in the Navy in 1941 but was released on a medical discharge shortly thereafter. In 1945, his first short story, "The Survival of the Cunning," appeared in *Esquire.* In the same year, Herbert moved to Seattle and took a job with the *Seattle Post-Intelligencer.* For instruction in writing fiction, he attended classes for a year at the University of Washington, where he met Beverly Stuart. His first marriage had been short-lived, but his marriage to Beverly in 1946 lasted until her death in 1984 and produced two sons, Brian and Bruce.

Herbert made a conscious decision to write science fiction, because he saw it as a field with fewer literary restrictions and therefore greater artistic and imaginative

freedom. In 1952, his first science-fiction story, "Looking for Something," appeared in *Startling Stories*, and in 1956 he published his first science-fiction novel, *Dragon of the Sea* (later retitled *Under Pressure*).

Herbert worked on a number of West Coast newspapers until he joined the *San Francisco Examiner* in 1959, where he was a writer and editor until 1969. His wife—to whom he referred as his "best critic"—supported his writing ambitions by working as an advertising copywriter so that he could take leave from his job as a journalist from time to time, and concentrate on his writing and on being a "househusband." During these years, he published science-fiction novels: *The Green Brain* (1966), *Destination: Void* (1966), *The Eyes of Heisenberg* (1966), *The Heaven Makers* (1968), *The Santaroga Barrier* (1968), and *Dune* (1965) and *Dune Messiah* (1969).

By 1969, Herbert's career as a science-fiction writer allowed him to stop working as a full-time journalist. He moved back to Washington, where he continued writing, also working as an education writer on the *Seattle Post-Intelligencer* before leaving journalism completely in 1972. Professionally, he became a full-time writer, but in fact he also spent much of his time and energy on a six-acre farm, where he and his wife undertook to create a model of an ecologically sound and energy self-sufficient operation. They used solar panels, methane gas recovered from chicken manure, and an electricity-generating windmill which was built and patented by Herbert himself. They produced great quantities of chicken meat and a surplus of vegetables, and they grew their own wine grapes.

Writing continuously, tending this version of "Ecotopia," and caring for his wife in her battle with cancer, Herbert rarely appeared in public, or even very far from his farm. Now and then, he lectured at the University of Washington. In 1980, Herbert and his family began spending half of the year in a new home on Maui, and Herbert devoted much of his time to nursing his wife until her death in 1984. Shortly after he married Teresa Shackleford, his former representative at Putnam, he was diagnosed as having pancreatic cancer. He worked until his death, with a lap-top computer, while receiving experimental treatment at the University of Wisconsin. In 1986, the year of his death, his collaborative novel with his son, Brian—*Man of Two Worlds*—was published.

Analysis

In 1965, thirteen years after publication of his first science-fiction short story and nine years after the publication of the mildly futuristic *Dragon of the Sea* (*Under Pressure*), Herbert wrote his second science fiction novel: *Dune*. His work thereafter reflects these extreme opposites in that it can be divided—without reference to any particular time in his creative life—into three categories: "Earth-bound" novels, novels set far from Earth in space and time, and novels which take Earth as one setting in a distant future.

The Earth-bound novels tend to analyze a single aspect of human psychology or social organization. *Under Pressure*, which alone among his works has consistently received critical acclaim equal to that accorded *Dune*, is considered one of the finest of submarine tales. It even inspired fan mail from men who had served in submarines. The other novels of this group are viewed as more typical of science-fiction tales with a message: ecology (*The Green Brain*), runaway science and technology (*The White Plague*, 1982), and the possibility—and dangers—of a communal mind (*Hellstrom's Hive*, 1973, and *The Santaroga Barrier*).

The novels which deal with Earth in the distant future or in another reality are inclined to use this perspective as a vehicle for parody or satire through which Herbert pokes fun at science-fiction genres such as the futuristic detective story (*Whipping Star*, 1970), comments wryly on an aspect of society, such as the use and abuse of the law (*The Dosadi Experiment*, 1977), or toys with the reader's preconceptions of the hostile and superior alien (*Man of Two Worlds*).

The novels which describe worlds far removed from the here and now are composed almost exclusively of his two novel cycles—one centering on the planet Pandora, and the other on the planet Arrakis, otherwise known as Dune.

The Pandora cycle begins with *Destination: Void*, the tale of clones sent into space on a ship programmed to fail and thus to challenge them to "wake up" and become fully conscious individuals, asserting their own personalities and intellects in finding the solution to this deadly problem. While this book was written by Herbert alone, the other three were written in collaboration with Bill Ransom: *The Jesus Incident* (1979), *The Lazarus Effect* (1983), and *The Ascension Factor* (1989). *Destination: Void*, which is characterized by dialogues and interior monologues, is praised by supporters of Herbert's dialogic style for its philosophical and psychological exploration of consciousness and sanity, and it is decried by detractors of that style as tedious. The succeeding three novels are more recognizably science-fiction adventure tales which, however, also comment upon the nature of being human by tracing the development of new strains of humanity on the planet Pandora.

THE DUNE SERIES

First published: *Dune*, 1965; *Dune Messiah*, 1969, *Children of Dune*, 1976; *God Emperor of Dune*, 1981; *Heretics of Dune*, 1984; *Chapterhouse: Dune*, 1985

Type of work: Novels

A generations-long saga of humanity struggling to balance free will and fatalism, with probing analyses of messianism, fanaticism, ecology, technology, and the nature of history, myth, and language.

Herbert's position as a preeminent science-fiction author who transcended the perceived bounds of his craft and enticed a large new audience to the genre—especially from college campuses—clearly rests upon *Dune* and its sequels. The power of this fictional world and its peoples to capture the imaginations of readers has been much analyzed, and there are many aspects and strands to the evaluations.

Dune and its successors are rich in historical analogies. In the feudal political setting which suggests that social conflict is a Darwinian necessity—ruthlessly clearing away the old to introduce the new—the reader encounters a complex balance of powers which resembles a futuristic version of the later Holy Roman Empire: the Emperor and his Sardaukar (janissary-like shock troops); the CHOAM Company, which monopolizes the spice trade (as the British East India Company once monopolized trade in India); the Landsraad or Great Houses (like Imperial Electors); the Guild, which uses the prescient qualities of spice to monopolize all shipping (like the Hansa and other trade alliances); the Ixians, who control all the non-biological aspects of technology; the Tleilaxu, who have the secret of biological regeneration; and the all-female Bene Gesserit, whose use of spice gives each member access to the memories and personalities of those who have gone before her—a kind of drug-induced, encyclopedic knowledge of past events, and a vivid example of Herbert's technique of playing internal against external dialogue.

The Bene Gesserit is said to have been modeled on Herbert's ten maternal aunts, but it also reflects the role of the medieval Church in its self-imposed task of guiding and bettering humanity. The Order's close-knit organization and strict discipline and Leto II's characterization of its "rhetorical despotism" recalls one of the most successful of Catholic orders—the Jesuits, who were responsible for some of Herbert's early education.

To some, *Dune* is above all an ecological novel, and there is some support for this view. As a reporter, Herbert covered efforts to understand the development and spread of sand dunes on the Pacific Coast, and, as a consultant to Pakistan for the Lincoln Foundation, he studied the unusual characteristics of water management there and helped project a land-use and redistribution policy. He describes in great detail the delicate natural balance on Arrakis: the desert which covers the entire planet, the hidden but crucial role of the so-called "sand-trout" in the life cycle, the giant sandworms which live only in this desert, and the drug called "mélange" or "spice," which also occurs nowhere else. It becomes clear that the spice is a by-product of the gigantic sandworms. Without the sand, the worms would die; without the worms, the sand might succumb to vegetation; without both of them, the most valued substance in the known universe—seen by some readers as a symbol for the twentieth century's need and greed for petroleum—would cease to exist. The transformation of Arrakis into an arable planet is planned in *Dune* by the Fremen leader, Liet-Kynes. This change is actually brought about by Leto II in the fourth novel, *God Emperor of Dune*, and the problem of dwindling mélange supplies is not solved until the sixth novel, *Chapterhouse, Dune.*

The Fremen who live in the most remote areas of Arrakis are a vividly drawn example of human adaptation to severe conditions. Their air-traps to catch, condense, and store the moisture in the air parallel the catch-basins employed in and around the Sahara. Their still-suits—technical marvels that preserve and re-use all of the body's moisture—are covered by loose garments similar to those worn by Bedouins to insulate the body from harsh sun and oppressive heat. Their ability to travel by riding the great sandworms is similar to the Berbers' use of the camel to establish trade routes through the Sahara.

If ecology is the ever-present background of *Dune*, the heroic figure dominates the foreground. As originally conceived, *Dune* was to be a fictional treatment of the social/political/military upheavals caused by the periodic appearances of messianic figures in human history. Herbert's preface to *Heretics of Dune* notes that parts of the two novels that followed *Dune*—*Dune Messiah* and *Children of Dune*—were written during the composition of *Dune*, so they are, at least to some extent, part of a continuing consideration of the hero.

In *Dune*, Paul Atreides is revealed as the charismatic leader the universe has awaited. Although unwillingly, he causes the Fremen jihad, which transforms the known universe. The swashbuckling hero of *Dune* then becomes the blind Preacher of *Children of Dune*, who cries out like the Old Testament prophet against the decadent society which has deified him after his apparent death. Focus shifts to his sister, Alia—the "virgin-harlot"—who has assumed control of the empire and has been corrupted by power and by an excessive use of mélange, and to his twin children who are "pre-born," that is, prescient and telepathic even in the womb. Some readers complain that *Dune Messiah* and *Children of Dune* are anticlimactic and unsatisfying. Others find that Herbert has made a telling statement about putting too much trust in charismatic leaders.

The wild strain which appears in Paul Atreides can be traced through the series; at least one central character in each novel is of the Atreides bloodline and is responsible for decisive events. The significance of this bloodline is enhanced by the family name in a novel cycle which uses many words and names to evoke historical parallels: jihad, Zensunni (selecting one word each from Islam and Buddhism), Sha-Nama (the actual title of the Persian Book of Kings), the Orange Catholic Bible (a committee-made religious document), Bedwine (reminiscent of Bedouin), Carthag (city of the evil Harkonnens), and even an Atreides named Darwi (perhaps to remind the reader of Darwin).

The family name, Atreides, evokes the ancient royal house headed by Agamemnon, who sacrificed his daughter in order to wage the Trojan War and was assassinated by his wife and avenged by his son. In *Children of Dune*, the tie is made explicit when Leto II and Ghanima acknowledge Agamemnon as an ancestor and their father, Paul, speaks of the "curse" on their house.

It is the Atreides line which has been prepared for generations by the genetic manipulators of the Bene Gesserit in order to produce the messianic figure predicted in the myths which the order has planted on various worlds. The Bene Gesserit also runs through the whole series, contributing crucial characters, practicing a behind-the-scenes manipulation of events that produces mixed results, and providing a focus for the implied discussion of drug use and "drug cultures." As the Guild cannot do without its spice if it is to navigate, so the Bene Gesserit cannot forego the spice which initiates each member with the so-called Agony and opens the access to previous lives. As becomes obvious in *God Emperor of Dune*, the loss of mélange will force humanity back toward a complete reliance on technology. That reliance had been broken long before the action of *Dune* in a "jihad" which eliminated computers and ushered in the era of the Mentat—a human being trained to be, at need, the equivalent of a computer.

While the Bene Gesserit struggle to survive under the benevolent repression of Leto II, and to recover the mélange supplies thereafter, they are challenged by a more worldly version of themselves, returning from a long scattering of peoples which followed Leto's reign. Their rivals had no spice at all, so they have developed an adrenaline-based substitute. The comparison of spice to this new drug is a non-judgmental version of the comparison drawn in the 1970's and 1980's between natural consciousness-expanding drugs used by some religious groups and the newer "designer drugs." The pejorative term used for the Bene Gesserit—witches—and for their rivals—whores—reassert the medieval Mary/Eve dichotomy of the female seen in Alia: half divine or magical, half earthly and sinful. This motif of apparent misogyny is deceptively offset by a different kind of sexist perspective, when Leto II explains his all-female guards by stating that single-sex men's groups are much more prone toward adolescence, homosexuality, cultism, and sadism, and that women's religion "runs deeper."

The final binding figure in the series is that of Duncan Idaho, faithful retainer of Duke Leto Atreides, who dies defending Paul and his mother in *Dune*. His dead flesh is used by the Tleilaxu to create a ghola (a clone of sorts made from dead flesh, and perhaps named with the Golem of Jewish legend in mind). Gholas of Idaho appear in all the many generations of the Dune cycle, and each one must—like the clones of *Destination: Void*—win his way to true consciousness and humanity. The pain of awakening in each successive Idaho ghola is in ironic contrast to its creators. The Tleilaxan government—a fanatic group which thinks in terms of believers and "powindah," or infidels—has renewed itself through the ages by the same technique. In *Heretics of Dune*, this mindless perpetuation of dogma is set in sharp relief by the agony the Idaho ghola undergoes to achieve its consciousness. At the end of *Chapterhouse: Dune*, it is this Idaho ghola and an Atreides Bene Gesserit who escape entirely from the world of *Dune* to start anew.

Summary

Frank Herbert's *Dune*—refused by a multitude of publishers—became one of the most popular books of its time. The Dune series is compared by some enthusiasts to J. R. R. Tolkien's trilogy *The Lord of the Rings* (1955) in its creation of a dazzlingly detailed world in which great forces clash, great personalities and organizations rise and fall, and much is said by analogy about the contemporary world and its values. Depending upon the reader's predilections, it is possible to find a metaphor for a variety of historical and contemporary situations. Humanity survives and prevails, but—unlike in Tolkien's work—no philosophy or system dominates. Dynamic balance persists.

Bibliography

Aldiss, Brian W. *Billion Year Spree: The True History of Science Fiction*. New York: Schocken Books, 1974.

McNelly, Willis E. *The Dune Encyclopedia*. New York: Berkley, 1984.

O'Reilly, Timothy. *Frank Herbert*. New York: Frederick Ungar, 1981.

Parkinson, Robert C. "*Dune*—An Unfinished Tetralogy." *Extrapolation* 13 (December, 1971): 16-24.

Touponce, William F. *Frank Herbert*. Boston: Twayne, 1988.

James L. Hodge

S. E. HINTON

Born: Tulsa, Oklahoma
July 22, 1948

Principal Literary Achievement

S. E. Hinton has contributed novels to the young adult genre that she herself is credited with helping to initiate in 1967 with *The Outsiders.*

Biography

For a writer who has sold millions of copies of her novels, S. E. (Susan Eloise) Hinton carries a very brief and unassuming biography. She was born and has spent most of her life in Tulsa, Oklahoma, which is also the setting for her fiction. In her junior year of high school, her father died of cancer; that same year, at the age of seventeen, she completed the manuscript for *The Outsiders* (1967). She enrolled in the University of Tulsa in 1966, and the novel was published in her freshman year. She was graduated in 1970 with a degree in education. She and her husband, David Inhofe, live in Tulsa, where their son, Nicholas David, was born in 1983.

While Hinton has given several interviews, she remains a private and rather shadowy figure. The myths that have grown up about her—that she was herself a gang member like the young "greasers" she depicts so graphically in *The Outsiders,* for example—are probably more a tribute to her novels: Her young fans get so involved in her work that they imagine more about her than can be true. Her private life has remained just that, and she has gained the most publicity by involving herself in two of the film productions of her novels: She was present on the set of Francis Ford Coppola's *The Outsiders* in 1983 (she plays a minor part as a nurse in the film), and she wrote the screenplay for Coppola's film version of *Rumble Fish* (the novel was published in 1975) later that year.

S. E. Hinton has produced a novel approximately every four years since *The Outsiders*; by the time she was thirty-one, she had four major young adult works under her belt and was considered by many critics and teachers to be one of the most important figures in the development of the young adult novel. In July of 1988, she was awarded the first YASD/SLJ Author Achievement Award, given by the Young Adult Services Division of the American Library Association and *School Library Journal*, for novels that provide young adults "a window through which they can view their world and which [can] help them to grow and to understand themselves and their role in society."

Analysis

In April of 1967, Viking Press published S. E. Hinton's *The Outsiders*, and its appearance marked the start of what has since become known as young adult, or YA, literature. Prior to that date, literature for adolescents comprised leftover children's literature (such as Kate Douglas Wiggin's *Rebecca of Sunnybrook Farm*, 1903) or adult novels that had been adopted by younger readers (such as Harper Lee's 1960 *To Kill a Mockingbird*). The few works which were aimed specifically at the youth market (the novels of John Tunis or Maureen Daly) were simplistic and moralistic, even to adolescent readers.

In 1967 all that changed, and a new genre was born, thanks in large part to S. E. Hinton. Since that date, the genre of young adult fiction has developed into a major cultural force, and publishers regularly deploy editors and even whole divisions to work in the teenage market. What marks this genre, and what distinguishes it from the "juvenile" literary forms that existed prior to 1967, is that young adult literature talks to adolescents realistically about matters that concern them, in language that is their own. The novels of Robert Cormier, M. E. Kerr, Paul Zindel, Richard Peck, and dozens of other young adult writers cover experiences that were banned from adolescent literature before the 1960's but that are on the minds of teenagers nevertheless—including sex, death, and divorce. At times, young adult novels can be romantic and melodramatic, but the most significant young adult books are noteworthy for what has been called their "new realism," for their attempts to render adolescent experience as it is really lived by teenagers. Sickness, alcoholism, single-parent families—these and other problems have become the focus of the genre.

S. E. Hinton has been an important part of this movement from the very beginning. In fact, her career has paralleled the development of the genre, and about every four years she has added another work to it: After *The Outsiders* in 1967, *That Was Then, This Is Now* was published in 1971, *Rumble Fish* in 1975, *Tex* in 1979, and *Taming the Star Runner*—after a gap of nine years (her son was born in 1983)—in 1988. More than 10 million copies of these novels have been printed since 1967, and popular films of the first four have been viewed by many millions more; Hinton's work has been at the center of any discussion of the young adult genre.

It has been argued that Hinton's own development as a writer has been disappointing; readers may find that her fourth and fifth novels, for example, differ only slightly from her earliest ones. Rather than expanding into new literary directions, she has attempted to perfect her basic story and story-telling technique. Put more positively, her literary career has been based on a limited, although successful, formula: Her protagonists are all white male adolescents, and at the center of each of her novels is the story of a special relationship between two of them, usually brothers. She has been accused of sexism, and her female characters are indeed decidedly weaker than her male heroes. As in much young adult fiction, adult characters play minor roles in Hinton's novels, and they tend to be weak and ineffective. The young males learn about life from themselves, or through the intense, often violent interactions with one another.

Her first four novels are all first-person narratives in which a young boy narrates his adventures with other males. While all the novels are set in Tulsa (or an urban/rural area much like it), there is also a very generalized quality to the novels: They could be anywhere, or nowhere, for there are very few historical references to date or place her works. In a sense, this happens because Hinton is writing a contemporary form of the medieval allegory, in which the focus is on characters wrestling with moral or ethical problems. There is much violence in the novels, some romance (but no sex), and sanitized language that few parents would find offensive. (For this reason, it seems odd that her novels, and especially the first, *The Outsiders*, should have been banned in a number of communities; the cause may have been the shock of the realistic descriptions of gang "rumbles.") Her plots are loose or episodic and often melodramatic; clearly her focus, and her strength, is her characterization, and it is her characters that readers remember: Ponyboy Curtis (*The Outsiders*), Bryon Douglas (*That Was Then, This Is Now*), and Tex. She generally, and especially in these first-person narrators, creates characters that are interesting and believable, and adolescents, as well as others, read her novels avidly and identify quickly with the tough but sensitive people she creates.

THE OUTSIDERS

First published: 1967
Type of work: Novel

Fourteen-year-old Ponyboy Curtis narrates the story of his coming of age in a world of gangs and gang violence.

When S. E. Hinton published *The Outsiders* in 1967, she used her initials so that readers would think she was a man. It was assumed by publishers, in that pre-young adult era, that readers would not believe that a woman could write realistically about the urban street world that Hinton's first novel depicts. It is a sign of how far the genre has evolved since 1967 that *The Outsiders* seems so tame today.

The novel is set in a small southwestern city (similar to Tulsa), but in some ways it could be any city in the United States, for the novel is vague and dreamy in form. There are few adults, and the world of *The Outsiders* is divided into wealthy "Socs" (short for "socials") and "greasers," the tough gang members who dress in their early-1960's uniform of long hair, blue jeans, and tee-shirts. The three Curtis brothers—Darry, the oldest, Soda, the middle, and Ponyboy, the narrator—live together and have taken care of one another since their parents were killed in an automobile accident some years before. Surrounding the Curtises are other teenagers who share greaser values and the Curtis hospitality.

The action in this short novel is, as in most young adult fiction, simple and straightforward and covers only a few days. After an argument with his older brother, Ponyboy and his friend Johnny run to a nearby park, where they are attacked by a carload of Socs, angry at the greasers for picking up their girls earlier that evening. In the fight, Johnny stabs and kills Bob, the Soc leader, and Johnny and Ponyboy are forced to flee the city, with the help of Dally Winston, the toughest greaser in the novel. Later, in a fire in the church where they are hiding out, Dally, Johnny, and Ponyboy manage to rescue trapped children and become heroes. The death of Bob leads to a major "rumble," however, and the greasers defeat the Socs in this violent finale. Johnny dies of his wounds from the fire; Dally goes wild, robs a grocery store, and is gunned down by the police.

In the brief denouement, Pony thinks of the hundreds of greasers like himself who are misunderstood and decides that someone should tell their story: "[M]aybe people would understand then and wouldn't be so quick to judge a boy by the amount of hair oil he wore." He picks up a pen and begins the theme for his English class that will become *The Outsiders*: "When I stepped out into the bright sunlight from the darkness of the movie house. . . ."

The major theme of the novel is the story of Ponyboy's successful initiation: He has survived the rumble, worked out his relationship with his brother Darry, and, in spite of the deaths of two friends, is a better and stronger person by novel's end. Pony's initiation also has a number of subthemes. The first is what could be called the brotherhood theme. Loyalty is a cardinal gang rule, and the rumble at the end of the novel is only a particularly violent and ritualistic enactment of this value. Dally dies, in fact, because he became a loner and broke away from his supportive greaser gang.

Working with this brotherhood idea is the more important theme of eliminating prejudice. The greasers and Socs of the novel represent two clear socioeconomic groups in this world, and their ignorance and hatred of one another are what lead to the class warfare. Differences are created by social class, Hinton says, but underneath these superficial differences are people who share more than what separates them. As Ponyboy discovers, the sunset can be seen equally well from both sides of town.

Yet how can the characters recognize this "family of man" that they all share? One obvious answer is in being sensitive to and tolerant of the world around them and breaking down the prejudice and ignorance that keep them from this recognition. In their sanctuary, Johnny and Ponyboy share Robert Frost's poem "Nothing Gold Can Stay," and later, in his dying note to Ponyboy, Johnny says that Frost

> "meant you're gold when you're a kid, like green. When you're a kid everything's new, dawn. . . . Like the way you dig sunsets, Pony. . . . There's still lots of good in the world."

The good exists if one can retain one's childlike innocence and capacity for wonder. Ponyboy begins the novel in response to Johnny's counsel; his sensitivity and intelligence lead him to try to tell the story of the greasers and the Socs, and what links them.

There are a number of literary allusions for a work this short: Aside from the Frost poem, there are references to Charles Dickens' *Great Expectations* (1860-1861) and to Margaret Mitchell's *Gone with the Wind* (1936). The novel also contains a very literary three-part structure (city, country escape, city) reminiscent of Mark Twain's *The Adventures of Huckleberry Finn* (1884). Other literary echoes include *Romeo and Juliet* (c.1595) and *West Side Story* (1957). A deceptively simple story, *The Outsiders* is a fairly complex novel and one with a number of thematic strains and literary devices.

When director Francis Ford Coppola made the film of *The Outsiders* in 1983, he took the same respectful attitude toward the work as the adolescents from Fresno, California, who had written urging him to translate the book to film, and the film plays like an adolescent fantasy. There is a vagueness to both novel and film that one usually finds only in the world of romance: Characters are two-dimensional and play out preordained roles, setting is generalized and abstract, there is no sense of historical time (the story is taking place in the early 1960's, readers guess, but mostly from the clothing), and the plot essentially consists of a series of ritualistic set pieces.

The novel, like the film, has been extremely popular with teenagers—probably because it was one of the first young adult books to deal with social classes as teenagers actually view them. Written when Hinton was only seventeen, *The Outsiders* was the first novel to deal sympathetically with "greasers," to describe adolescent outsiders not as hoodlums or juvenile delinquents but as normal young people locked into class roles and conflicts. The freshness of its young author's vision explains much of the book's popularity.

THAT WAS THEN, THIS IS NOW

First published: 1971
Type of work: Novel

In his passage from childhood innocence to adult maturity, Bryon Douglas learns about the high cost of friendship.

In many ways, *That Was Then, This Is Now* is a sequel to *The Outsiders*, for the setting in this second S. E. Hinton novel is similar, and some of the same characters appear. It is a few years later, however, and the concerns in this adolescent world have changed.

Mark Jennings, fifteen, has been living with Bryon Douglas, the sixteen-year-old narrator of the novel, and his mother since Mark's parents killed each other in a drunken fight seven years before. Mark and Bryon are as close as brothers—and perhaps too close. As the novel unravels, it becomes apparent that Mark has been dealing drugs, and it is those drugs that permanently damage M&M, the brother of Bryon's girlfriend, Cathy Carlson. Bryon grows in the course of the novel, especially in his relationship with Cathy, but Mark does not. When Bryon discovers the truth about Mark, he turns him over to the police, and the younger boy is given five years in the state reformatory.

Bryon does not even have the consolation of Cathy, however; feeling guilty over what he has done to Mark, Bryon pushes her away, and she is going with an older Ponyboy Curtis at novel's end. The novel thus concludes on a sad and somber note: Bryon wishes that he were a kid again, "when I had all the answers." He has left the security of childhood, but he has paid a high price for his growth to maturity, and he has lost his two best friends in the process. There are, he has learned, few easy answers to life's tough questions.

While characterization in *That Was Then, This Is Now* may be somewhat unsophisticated, character development certainly is not; there is a definite, if gradual, growth that is missing in Hinton's first novel. Bryon grows to be able to care about people outside his family: Cathy, M&M, and others. Caring does not guarantee happiness, Hinton implies—"Nothing can wear you out like caring about people," Mark complains at one point—but it is the only full way to live. The novel ends on a depressing note, uncharacteristic for such an early young adult novel but a realistic sign of things to come in the genre.

In a very real sense, *That Was Then, This Is Now* is an extension of the themes of *The Outsiders.* Readers learn the limitations to the lessons of loyalty, for example: Loyalty to the gang was simpler in the first novel, but here loyalty is conditioned by time and place, and a character may be forced to turn in a brother if he violates the law.

The world of *That Was Then, This Is Now,* in short, is broader and more complex than that of *The Outsiders,* yet S. E. Hinton is even more programmatic in this second book. She clearly has messages she wishes to send to young readers: about the dangers of drugs (both taking and dealing them), about the limits of group loyalty, and about the complexity of the real social world. If Hinton tends to be more realistic in her downbeat conclusion here, the lessons along the way seem much more didactic.

At the same time, the style of the second novel seems looser than the first. Bryon's narrative voice does not have the same compelling conviction as does Ponyboy's in *The Outsiders.* Hinton seems to know—and to like—Ponyboy better, and Bryon's slangy adolescent voice is often vague. Setting, as in the original, is generalized; profanity and sexual activity are again both missing. Literary language, on the other hand, as in most of S. E. Hinton's work, is quite effective; Mark, for example, is consistently characterized through the novel's imagery as a lion. *That Was Then, This Is Now* does not have the spark of Hinton's first novel. The author at age twenty-one had lost a certain freshness she had at seventeen and had not yet been able to replace it with sufficient knowledge or experience. *That Was Then, This Is Now* has several important themes and good character development, but it lacks the force and vitality of *The Outsiders.*

RUMBLE FISH

First published: 1975
Type of work: Novel

Rusty-James learns about the world from his older brother, Motorcycle Boy, until the latter is killed.

Rumble Fish contains many elements of the successful Hinton formula, in which a young male protagonist narrates the story of his often violent experiences during a crucial period of growing up. There are few adults or women who intrude on this romantic male stage, where the protagonist—like his reader—learns a number of important lessons about the world and his role in it. The names of the characters hint at the novel's allegorical mode: "Rusty-James" and "Motorcycle Boy," respectively, the narrator and the older brother who gives the narrator his lessons. The distinction of *Rumble Fish* is the intensity of its negative message.

If anything, *Rumble Fish* is more violent and action-packed than Hinton's earlier novels, for it includes a number of gang battles, from the early fight between Rusty-James and Biff Wilcox to Motorcycle Boy's violent death. Rusty-James is stabbed in that first rumble but is patched up by Motorcycle Boy at home, where the reader discovers that their mother has escaped to California and the two boys live with their alcoholic father. Time after time in the novel, Rusty-James has similar violent encounters, only to be saved by Motorcycle Boy, who appears out of nowhere, like a knight from a medieval romance. Motorcycle Boy is not able in the end to save himself, however: Trying to free the "rumble fish" of the title by taking them from the pet store where they are sold and pouring them into the river, he is shot and killed by police. Rusty-James is taken to a reformatory. Six years later, Rusty-James encounters his friend Steve from this period on a beach in Southern California. It is clear that Steve would like to reconnect with Rusty-James, but the narrator has no such illusions:

> I waved back. I wasn't going to see him. I wasn't going to meet him for dinner, or anything else. I figured if I didn't see him, I'd start forgetting again. But it's been taking me longer than I thought it would.

What Rusty-James has been trying to forget, apparently, is the death of Motorcycle Boy and the memories of that painful period.

What makes *Rumble Fish* different from earlier Hinton stories is the darkness of this vision. Here is no happy ending, as in *The Outsiders*, and no bittersweet lesson about growing up, as in *That Was Then, This Is Now.* What readers find instead is a novel about the impossibility of escaping the past, or one's own biological destiny, and the finality of ending alone.

Also different is the mode of the novel: *Rumble Fish* has a dreamy, almost mythic mood to it. (Francis Ford Coppola's film version of the novel captured this quality perfectly, in its mixed use of color and black-and-white photography.) The character of Motorcycle Boy is more romantic, and thus less realistic, than any previous character in Hinton's novels. The mixed critical reaction to the novel—much stronger than to earlier Hinton novels—indicates this difficulty. Many critics of young adult fiction had trouble dealing with a work that was so much darker and more somber and stylistically moodier.

TEX

First published: 1979
Type of work: Novel

Through his struggles with and against his brother Mason, Tex McCormick grows into his world and himself.

In many ways, *Tex* is the most successful fulfillment of the Hinton formula. The novel avoids the pitfalls of the earlier romantic versions of the Hinton story, and it succeeds where Hinton is best: in characterization and in relevant themes.

The standard Hinton elements are here, but they coalesce as they never have before. Tex and Mason McCormick have almost been abandoned by their father, who is following the rodeo circuit, and Mason has developed an ulcer taking care of Tex, being a star athlete, and working to get into college. He is even forced to sell Tex's horse, Negrito, when the two boys run out of money. The action is fast-paced: Tex and his friend Johnny are constantly getting into trouble, Tex and Johnny's sister Jamie develop a budding romance, and Mason's friend Lem is dealing drugs. In the multiple climaxes, Tex saves Mason's life when a hitchhiker pulls a gun on them. When Tex accompanies Lem on a drug deal, however, he himself is shot by one of the customers and ends up in the hospital. In the novel's denouement, Tex discovers who his real father is, and the various strands of this novel are neatly resolved.

Tex works because readers are carried along by the story and because the major characters are believable and sympathetic. The ideas in the novel work as well. Again there is the theme of "outsiders"—orphans, abandoned children, and loners. The resolution is much more satisfactory than it was in *Rumble Fish* (where readers last saw Motorcycle Boy dead and Rusty-James sitting alone on the California beach): Tex gains a new father (at least his name) and a new sense of family, works out his problems with his brother, and begins a romance. The conclusion is not without worries: "Love ought to be a real simple thing," Tex complains in the end. "Animals don't complicate it, but with humans it gets so mixed up it's hard to know what you feel, much less how to say it."

Tex has the most mature ending of the four Hinton novels and an affirmative ending for its youthful readers. Tex does not end up dead, in jail, or alone. In spite of the strikes against him (both from his environment and from within himself), he manages to survive and succeed.

TAMING THE STAR RUNNER

First published: 1988
Type of work: Novel

Stranded on an isolated Oklahoma horse ranch, Travis Harris manages to fall in love, become a novelist, and save a friend.

In *Taming the Star Runner*, Hinton tries a different approach to telling her story: She abandons her first-person narration for a third-person point of view. The intensity which had earlier carried readers along in the voices of Ponyboy Curtis or Tex is replaced by the distance of the author's perspective.

Travis Harris has been sent to his uncle's Oklahoma horse ranch because his mother is afraid that he will eventually kill his stepfather, Stan. There are other reasons for getting Travis out of the violent urban world that so resembles earlier Hinton novels, and this past will catch up with him before he finishes the novel. Travis is like many Hinton characters: a loner, conscious of the impression he makes, and always trying to be "cool." He has considerable time in the first half of the novel to work on this image, for his uncle Ken's horse ranch is isolated, and Travis is too young to drive. His uncle ignores Travis most of the time, because he has his own problems trying to fight his wife Teresa for custody of their son Christopher. Travis spends time around the barn that Ken has leased to eighteen-year-old Casey Kencaide for her riding school, begins to work for her, and gets more and more involved in the world of training and showing horses.

In true Hinton fashion, the action in the novel, and especially in its second half, is fast-paced: There are riding competitions, a thunderstorm during which the Star Runner of the title breaks free, and scenes in which Travis must deal with his old friend Joe from the city, who is involved in murder. Some of the thematic strands are quite strong, especially Travis' developing relationships with Casey and Ken. *Taming the Star Runner* is certainly the most "adult" of Hinton's five novels: Drugs and alcohol figure in realistic ways, the language is stronger, and the sexual theme is more mature.

Hinton's primary strength, characterization, is weakened in *Taming the Star Runner* by her choice of a third-person point of view. While readers have no trouble accepting *The Outsiders*' Ponyboy Curtis as a writer, it is more difficult to believe the same of Travis Harris, who, at fifteen, has written a novel that he sells in the course of *Taming the Star Runner.* He simply looks and sounds too much like the "sleazy punk" that both readers and other characters see from the outside. As his uncle says, "Sorry, kid, you haven't given me the impression you could write a complex sentence." Or, as Ms. Carmichael, his editor, remarks on first meeting

Travis, "I couldn't believe you had written that book. Your speaking style is so different from the way you write." It is almost impossible for readers to accept a character who speaks as Travis does ("You can fix up the spelling, huh?" he asks Ms. Carmichael in that first meeting) as a novelist. If Travis Harris had narrated his own story, the plot manipulations and the melodramatic aspects of the novel would have been less obvious.

Summary

A popular "young adult" novelist, S. E. Hinton reuses many elements throughout her novels. Few parents appear in her novels, and the protagonists are often searching for substitutes, which they find in slightly older males; the focus is primarily on young men bonding with one another. Her plots are action-packed, and the central character usually narrates the story of his emerging self and conflicting loyalties. Both the strengths and weaknesses of the young adult genre are apparent in Hinton's work. She has created a unique first-person voice that invites readers to share the story.

Bibliography

Daly, Jay. *Presenting S. E. Hinton*. Boston: Twayne, 1989.

Donelson, Kenneth L., and Alleen Pace Nilsen. *Literature for Today's Young Adults.* 3d ed. Glenview, Ill.: Scott, Foresman, 1989.

Mills, Randall K. "The Novels of S. E. Hinton: Springboard to Personal Growth for Adolescents." *Adolescence* 22 (Fall, 1987): 641-46.

Stanek, Lou Willett. *A Teacher's Guide to the Paperback Editions of the Novels of S. E. Hinton*. New York: Dell, 1975.

David Peck

WILLIAM DEAN HOWELLS

Born: Martins Ferry, Ohio
March 1, 1837
Died: New York, New York
May 11, 1920

Principal Literary Achievement

Known as "the dean of American letters," Howells is largely responsible for the dominance of the realistic school of writing in modern American literature.

Biography

William Dean Howells was born at Martins Ferry, in Belmont County, Ohio, on March 1, 1837, the second child of William Cooper Howells and Mary Dean Howells. When Howells was three, the family moved to Hamilton, Ohio, where Howells' father operated a printing business and published a newspaper, the *Intelligencer.* In 1849, his father's business failed and the family moved to Dayton, Ohio.

The move to Dayton brought to a close Howells' formal education. At the age of seven, he had begun helping his father by setting type and delivering papers, and as the family's financial condition worsened both Howells and his older brother were forced to drop out of school. Although he always regretted that he had not been able to attend school, Howells believed that his association with the printing trade, and the fact that his father read to the family whenever possible, made up in part for his lack of formal education.

The Dayton business failed in 1850 and the family moved to Greene County, Ohio. While Howells' father and brother attempted to revive an old paper mill, the Howells family lived in a log cabin on a stream near the town of Xenia. Years later, Howells wrote about the experience in *My Year in a Log Cabin* (1893). When efforts to revive the paper mill failed, the family moved to Columbus. While the family was in Columbus, Howells worked as a compositor for the *Ohio State Journal*. In 1852, Howells' father became editor of the Ashtabula, Ohio, *Sentinel*. Six months later, Mr. Howells moved the paper to Jefferson, Ohio.

Howells' first poem, "Old Winter, Loose Thy Hold On Us," was published in 1851, but his writing career had begun while he was setting type for the Ashtabula *Sentinel*. Along with the regular news, Howells inserted his own sketches, stories,

and poems. His published prose also included one serial romance. By 1855, Howells was contributing to several Ohio newspapers, and in 1857 he was offered a position as a subordinate editor for the Cincinnati *Gazette.* After a year in Cincinnati, Howells was offered a position on the *Ohio State Journal* staff, and before the end of 1859, he had become that newspaper's unofficial literary editor. Howells' first book, *Poems of Two Friends,* was published in 1860 (the other friend was John James Piatt). Howells' poems were also being printed in *The Atlantic Monthly,* the *Saturday Press,* and the Cincinnati *Dial*. Samples of his poetry appeared in *Poets and Poetry of the West* (1860).

During the 1860 presidential campaign, the publishers of the *Ohio State Journal* printed a three-hundred-page campaign book, *Lives and Speeches of Abraham Lincoln and Hannibal Hamlin*. Howells' contribution was an essay on Lincoln. Howells used his share of the profits from the book to go on a tour of New England and Canadian factories. His tour developed into a literary pilgrimage of New England. His later account of the trip became the opening chapter of *Literary Friends and Acquaintances* (1900).

In 1861, at the beginning of the Civil War, Howells became United States consul to Venice. A year later he married Elinor Gertrude Mead, whom he had met in Columbus before leaving for Europe. When the war ended, Howells returned to the United States, determined to find full-time employment as a writer. Like Bartley Hubbard, who appears in both *A Modern Instance* (1882) and *The Rise of Silas Lapham* (1885), Howells went to New York determined to find enough free-lance work to support his family until he could secure permanent, full-time employment. After working briefly for *The Nation*, Howells became assistant editor of *The Atlantic Monthly.* He became editor-in-chief in 1871 and remained with the magazine until 1881.

During his stay in Italy, Howells had continued to write, and his first prose work, *Venetian Life,* was published in 1866. The Italian experience exerted a strong influence on Howells; it resulted in three travel books and a series of essays on Italian poets. Howells also wrote four international novels about Americans in Italy: *A Foregone Conclusion* (1875), *The Lady of the Aroostook* (1879), *A Fearful Responsibility* (1881), and *Indian Summer* (1886). Howells left *The Atlantic Monthly* in 1881 and reached the peak of his power as novelist and critic in the decade which followed. It was during this period that he published what many consider his most representative novels: *A Modern Instance, Indian Summer, The Rise of Silas Lapham*, *Annie Kilburn* (1889), and *A Hazard of New Fortunes* (1890).

After 1890, Howells' power as a writer gradually declined. *A Hazard of New Fortunes* was followed by many novels on a smaller scale, but only two of them, *The Landlord at Lion's Head* (1897) and *The Leatherwood God* (1916), compare with the novels of the 1880's. Howells' most significant production during this period was his series of literary recollections and reminiscences. Some of his most important works on literary criticism were also produced during this period. In 1900, Howells assumed responsibility for "The Editor's Easy Chair," a column appearing in *Harper's Monthly*, and he continued writing the column until his death at the age of eighty-three.

Analysis

As a writer, an editor, and a literary critic, William Dean Howells led the revolt against nineteenth century sentimentality in fiction, and he was largely responsible for the dominance of the realistic school of writing in twentieth century American literature.

Although strongly influenced by Russian realistic writers, Howells' initial interest in realism was the result of his reaction to the excessive sentimentalism which characterized the popular romanticistic novels of his day—the kind of literature referred to as "Slop, Silly Slop" in *The Rise of Silas Lapham*. Howells disliked this kind of writing for several reasons. In the first place, he felt that it failed to serve any practical purpose. Capitalizing on what he called the "cheap and meretricious," this sentimental fiction stirred the emotions but provided little, if any, intellectual stimulus. As a social activist, Howells considered this a major flaw. The novel, the supreme literary form, should be intellectually stimulating. As a convert to socialism who was sensitive to the social and economic problems of his time, Howells was convinced that through fidelity to truth the realistic novelist could sow seeds which eventually would result in significant changes not only in the lives of individual readers but in the nation as a whole as well. Ultimately, the concept that the novel has this indirect, slow-moving power became one of the prime tenets of Howells' literary theory. Whatever else he might have been attempting in his novels, each one was in some way designed to sow seeds which, he hoped, would sprout and grow and be harvested in the reader's experience. In Howells' opinion, the realistic novel could be a prime factor in the initiation of needed social change.

Howells also objected to sentimental fiction because readers formed erroneous ideas about life as a result of having read it. Since the writers of popular fiction were not committed to presenting life as it really is, readers were encouraged to entertain false hopes, or were prompted to act in a manner which resulted in strained relationships. In his novels, Howells' characters frequently attribute the problems they face to the unrealistic ideas others have picked up from the novelists. In *A Modern Instance*, for example, Ben Halleck, who is attempting to understand Marcia Hubbard says, "Isn't there a theory that women forgive injuries, but never ignominies?" Atherton, the lawyer, replies that while this is what the novelists teach, experience makes him doubt their skill as prophets.

The use of Atherton to express one of his own opinions is characteristic of Howells as a novelist. In the realistic novel, Howells held, the writer should supply everything the reader needs to get the picture, but the writer himself should not intrude. In his own novels, he avoids intrusion through the use of chorus characters. As in ancient Greek dramas, these chorus characters provide commentary on issues raised in the novels. In Howells' major novels, certain individuals appear from time to time to debate moral or philosophical issues in Howells' place. Characters such as Atherton in *A Modern Instance*, Sewell in *The Rise of Silas Lapham*, the Reverend Mr. Waters in *Indian Summer*, and the March couple in *A Hazard of New Fortunes* allow Howells to be present but invisible.

One of the problems Howells faced as a pioneer in the field of realistic literature was the conservatism of the literary establishment. In *Criticism and Fiction* (1891), Howells observed that new authors were judged by comparisons with recognized authors and not by their fidelity to their own experiences. As a result, young writers who imitate the way they have heard men talk are made to feel unworthy by the "stupid people" who want the characters in modern novels to talk like those in William Shakespeare's plays. Writers are trained to take out the "life-likeness" and put in the "book-likeness."

For the most part, Howells was successful in putting "life-likeness" into his novels. His carefully conceived characters, whose speech echoes the language of the street, work well together in credible actions and settings. Taken as a whole, Howells' novels provide the modern reader with a panoramic view of the life and manners of a whole social group and era. In the opinion of some critics, however, Howells' view is too panoramic. It has been observed that his careful documentation often bogs down, primarily because of his conviction that nothing in life is insignificant. This all-inclusiveness has prompted Howells' critics to suggest that he is capable of making a literary mountain out of a commonplace molehill. While they grudgingly admit that Howells is true to realist's commitment to writing nothing he has not heard or seen, they often add that Howells has seen and heard nothing worth telling—but feels a compulsion to tell it anyway.

Another criticism of Howells is that his novels often lack a discernible plot or end rather inconclusively, leaving a number of dangling loose ends. While this criticism has a certain validity, it should be noted that Howells was more interested in a realistic portrayal of life than he was in a carefully worked out plot. As a realist, Howells could not avoid the fact that life moves at a slower pace than that demanded by a plot. In addition, life often raises more questions than it answers. Because of his commitment to realism, Howells often found himself dealing with situations which, if he maintained his realistic approach, could not be resolved. If his novels ended inconclusively, or with some loose ends here and there, this happened because he was forced to confess, as Atherton confesses at the end of *A Modern Instance*, "I don't know."

A MODERN INSTANCE

First published: 1882
Type of work: Novel

Two years after being abandoned, a young woman travels to Indiana to contest her self-indulgent husband's unfounded petition for divorce.

A Modern Instance, the first complete treatment of divorce in a serious American novel, was the most intense study of American society that Howells had done up to this point in his writing career.

The novel's principal concern is with the relationship of motive and action of justice. In the novel, Howells uses the divorce theme to portray the widening cultural divisions in American society, and in this way, *A Modern Instance* anticipates many of Howells' later novels in both its style and preoccupations. Old and new, rural and urban, life in the West and life in the East, and traditional orthodoxy and modern intellectual skepticism are compared in a series of contrasts which reveal Howells' concern with the social and economic problems of his time. Characteristically, minor characters are used as a chorus to discuss, debate, and analyze issues and questions raised as the story develops.

There is a touch of irony in Howells' choice of a title, which is taken from the description, in Shakespeare's *As You Like It*, of the well-fed justice who is "[F]ull of wise saws and modern instances." The modern instance is the marriage and divorce of Marcia Gaylor and Bartley Hubbard, characters who also appear in *The Rise of Silas Lapham* (1885), and the novel deals primarily with the question of justice. The "wise saws" in this modern instance are the answers various characters in the novel give to the question, "If judgment must be based on any human activity (such as divorce), should the judgment be based on the motive which prompted the action or on the consequences of the activity?"

One of the first "wise saws" appears early in the novel, when Bartley wounds his printer, Henry Bird, and then attempts to excuse his action. The doctor treating Henry's concussion responds, "Intentions have very little to do with physical effects." Later in the novel, as Marcia Hubbard's party travels to Indiana to contest Bartley Hubbard's divorce petition, Squire Gaylord tells Ben Halleck that the group is traveling to Indiana solely in the interest of preventing a great wrong. His argument is that men act and the consequences follow inevitably. "We've got nothing to do with their motive," he tells Ben Halleck.

Back in New York, Eustace Atherton and his wife, Clara, are also discussing the relationship of cause and effect to the Hubbard divorce. Atherton is of the opinion that whatever her intentions, Marcia Gaylord set in motion a series of events leading to an inevitable conclusion when she eloped with Bartley Hubbard. Atherton points out that Bartley and Marcia in some way are responsible for what is taking place in Indiana. "In some sort," he says, "they chose misery for themselves. . . . In the long run their fate must be a just one." Clara responds that she cannot see any justice in what has happened to Marcia because she does not "believe any woman ever meant better by her husband than she did." Atherton's response echoes the response of the doctor: "Oh, the meaning doesn't count. It's our deeds that judge us."

One of the criticisms of Howells is that his novels often end inconclusively. In this instance, the criticism may be justified, because Howells does not answer the questions he has raised in *A Modern Instance.* This may be, however, because Howells came to the conclusion that there are no correct answers. It is impossible to say, for example, whether Bartley Hubbard's death at Whited Sepulchre, Arizona, was the "penalty or consequences . . . of all that had gone before." As Howells notes in an uncharacteristic artistic intrusion at the end of the novel, the choice between penalty and consequences depends on how "we choose to consider it." That choice, as the name of the Arizona town suggests, may be based on a willingness to be the one to cast the first stone.

THE RISE OF SILAS LAPHAM

First published: 1885
Type of work: Novel

After achieving success without due concern for the morality of his methods, a self-reliant Boston paint manufacturer, through financial disaster, "rises" to a new standard of ethical behavior.

In *The Rise of Silas Lapham*, which is set in Boston, Howells tells of the collapse and fall of the financial empire of rustic Vermont entrepreneur Silas Lapham. The title is ironic, for the "rise" with which Howells is primarily concerned is Lapham's moral resurrection. This rise takes place when Lapham's business fails as a result of his decision to abandon the elastic and self-serving business codes which have been instrumental in his financial rise.

There are, in effect, two plots developing simultaneously in *The Rise of Silas Lapham*. In addition to the main plot, which follows Lapham's financial rise and fall, there is a subplot involving a triangle composed of Irene and Penelope Lapham and Tom Corey. In both the main plot and the subplot, the conflicts or dilemmas faced by those involved are resolved through the application of an "economy of pain" formula. This formula is introduced by the Reverend Sewell, one of the novel's chorus characters. According to Sewell's formula, conflict must be resolved by a choice of action which limits the pain inherent in the action to the fewest number of individuals. Lapham's moral rise may be directly attributed to his acceptance of this formula, for the choice he makes in the end is one which will limit the pain associated with his decision to himself and a few other individuals.

The Rise of Silas Lapham is a comparatively (for Howells) short novel, and Howells achieved this brevity through the use of symbols which reinforce or give emotional dimension to some deeper meaning already incorporated within the framework of the novel's narrative. For example, Howells uses two references to holes to suggest subtly that providence has played a role in both of Lapham's rises. His financial rise began after his father discovered the raw materials for the Lapham paint "in a hole made by a tree blowing down." Lapham's subsequent moral rise also involves a hole. Refusing to take credit for his own moral reformation, Lapham says, at the end of the novel, "Seems sometimes as if it was a hole opened for me, and I crept out of it."

Howells most dramatic use of symbolism to reinforce an already apparent meaning may be found at the climax of the novel when Lapham, after pacing the floor all night, decides on a course of action which is morally sound, but which will ruin him financially. Mrs. Howells, unable to help, sits upstairs listening to her husband's restless footsteps in the room below. As dawn breaks, Mrs. Lapham is reminded of a biblical quotation, which becomes, in effect, a symbol or metaphor of the entire course of Lapham's rise and fall. Like Jacob, Silas Lapham wrestles "until the breaking of the day," and, also like Jacob, the all-night struggle marked a turning point in Lapham's life. Although ruined financially, he is morally whole, and his transformation can be seen in his response to the Reverend Sewell's question as to whether Lapham has any regrets about what he has done. Lapham says that "if the thing was to do over again, right in the same way, I guess I would have to do it."

INDIAN SUMMER

First published: 1886
Type of work: Novel

After a brief engagement to a girl half his age, a retired newspaperman marries the former best friend of a girl to whom he had been engaged as a young man.

Indian Summer, Howells' last international novel, was written after Howells and his family revisited Italy after his resignation from *The Atlantic Monthly.* The novel's title and tone reflect the nostalgic mood the visit produced in Howells. Set in Italy against a background of scenes taken from Howells' *Tuscan Cities* (1885), *Indian Summer* is the story of middle-aged bachelor Theodore Colville's romantic involvement with two women, one his own age and the other much younger. The principal theme of the book is the January and May romance between Colville and the younger woman, Imogene Graham, but a number of the themes which preoccupy Howells in his other fiction also appear in the novel. The relationship between motive and consequences, for example, is touched on as Colville and the Reverend Waters, a chorus character, discuss the moral implications involved in Colville's involvement with Imogene. Waters concludes: "In the moral world we are responsible only for the wrong that we intend." Howells' principal preoccupation, however, is with the dangers of sentimentalism, particularly the kind gleaned from popular novels. This danger is emphasized as the romance between Colville and Imogene Graham develops. Imogene, who is under the spell of the sentimental novels, suffers from the illusion that the ideas she had derived from poems and novels can be applied to the real situations. Imagining that she has a mission with regard to Colville, who has experienced a shattered love affair, Imogene puts herself into the role of the self-sacrificing heroine who would make up to Colville the wrong done by another woman. Colville, flattered by Imogene's attention, allows himself to be pleasantly deceived into thinking Imogene actually loves him. He even begins to talk like the characters in sentimental novels. Only a fortuitous—or providential—accident prevents normally commonsensical Colville from making the mistake of going through with his marriage to Imogene. The near miss, in effect, is Howells' way of showing the dangers of sentimentalism, which can even soften the hard head of a man such as Theodore Colville.

Indian Summer is a short novel which follows Howells' formula of placing a few carefully conceived characters in a credible situation and allowing them to work out the action dramatically, with the least amount of intrusion by the author. The tone is mellow, mildly satirical, and decidedly anti-sentimental. As in his other novels, Howells' skill as a novelist is demonstrated by his use of natural symbolism to represent Colville's ambivalent feelings about Italy and the United States. Characteristically, Howells also uses contrasts at key points to enrich the theme of Indian summer. Age, weather, the seasons, and history are contrasted, but much of the novel's effect depends upon international contrasts. The "white Italian moonlight," the "mild Italian spring," and the ancient landscape with "history written all over it" are contrasted with a newer, more blustery, less autumnal America.

The title, the tone, the mellow contrasts, and the atmosphere of the most pleasant of seasons all belie the fact that Howells has an ulterior motive. As he thought the best fiction should, *Indian Summer* has the power to show things past and not seen and to encourage reflection and introspection. That this kind of critical self-evaluation is necessary is reflected in the Reverend Waters' observation that people are "a long time learning to act with common-sense or even common sanity in what are called matters of affection."

A HAZARD OF NEW FORTUNES

First published: 1890
Type of work: Novel

At a considerable risk to his family's security, a Boston insurance agent relocates in New York City to edit a magazine established by a newly rich midwesterner.

Using the execution of Chicago's Haymarket anarchists, the Brooklyn trolley-car strike of 1889, and the legendary greed of the Gilded Age as backdrops, *A Hazard of New Fortunes* follows the struggles of fifteen major characters to establish a national magazine in New York City. These major characters, along with a substantial cast of minor ones, become a microcosm for Howells' indictment of the American scramble for success.

In order to manage all the materials involved in this, his longest novel, Howells divided the book into five parts. In parts 1, 2, and 3, the characters involved with the magazine, *Every Other Week*, are introduced, and the process of interweaving their lives begins. Howells develops his characters through dramatic contrasts. The socialite Margaret Vance is contrasted with the rustic Dryfoos daughters, the newly rich entrepreneur and speculator Jacob Dryfoos is contrasted with his passive son Conrad, and the unreconstructed Confederate Colonel Woodburn is contrasted with the German revolutionary Lindau.

In the third part, the principal conflict underlying the story is introduced when Basil March, anticipating his first meeting with newly rich Jacob Dryfoos, experiences a "disagreeable feeling of being owned and of being about to be inspected by his proprietor." The conflict latent in this type of employer-employee relationship erupts in the fourth part when March resigns as editor after Dryfoos demands that March's friend Lindau be fired. At the end of the novel, the scene shifts to the New York streetcar street riot to show that the Dryfoos-March conflict is a microcosm of the conflicts inherent in American society as a whole.

While Howells' primary preoccupation in *A Hazard of New Fortunes* is this employer-employee conflict, several of the themes found in his other novels also surface. Howells is still interested in the relationship between determinism and chance, as he was in *A Modern Instance* and *The Rise of Silas Lapham*. Early in the novel, for example, before March accepts the editor's position, Fulkerson argues that the role of editor has been predetermined by March. "You ain't an insurance man by nature," Fulkerson says. "You're a natural-born literary man; and you've been going against the grain." The idea of "going against the grain" is also examined by Dryfoos, after his son's death. He says that he had not stopped his son from being a preacher, even though he thought he had. "I reckon," he muses, "if a child has got any particular bent, it was given to him." Trying to "bend" the child some other way is "goin' against the grain."

At the end of the novel, during a discussion of Conrad Dryfoos' apparently pointless death, Basil March echoes Dryfoos' statement that it "ain't any use" to attempt to change what has already been determined. Conrad's death, March says, "was forecast from the beginning of time, and was entirely an effect of his coming into the world."

Howells, however, is not completely comfortable with a determinism that is, as Mrs. March points out, fatalism. Chance and cause and effect, two topics considered in other Howells novels, must also be considered. Chance, for example, has been involved in March's entry "by accident" into the insurance business. It was by chance that he met Fulkerson on the Quebec ferry and discussed his interests in literature. Chance was also behind the "crazy fortuities" and "heterogenous forces" which cooperated in the production of the first issue of *Every Other Week* and made March feel as if the whole thing were a waking dream.

Cause and effect and human volition must also be considered, and it is interesting to note that, for all its other preoccupations, *A Hazard of New Fortunes* ends, as many of Howells' novels end, in an open-ended discussion of the relationship between motive (or intention), consequences, and justice. Discussing Margaret Vance's complicity in the death of Conrad Dryfoos, Basil March tells his wife that Margaret "did nothing wrong." In his opinion, even if Margaret was "unwittingly" instrumental in causing Conrad's death, motive or consequence might mitigate her guilt. Mrs. March seems to agree, but the novel ends with her uncertain "But still—."

Summary

As an editor and a literary critic, William Dean Howells exerted a profound influence on the course of American literature. Even so, his place in literature rests ultimately on his work as a novelist. Writing in a style which H. L. Mencken called "a new harmony of the old, old words" and following the principles Howells himself laid down in numerous works on the craft of writing realistic fiction, he created a body of literature that provides the best insights into and most penetrating analyses of the social and economic structure of the United States in the second half of the nineteenth century. While much of what Howells wrote is marked by somewhat archaic preoccupations, the serious reader may still discover in Howells the kind of novels which, in Howells' words, can "charm the mind and win the heart."

Bibliography

Carrington, George C., and Ildikó Carrington. *Plots and Characters in the Fiction of William Dean Howells.* Hamden, Conn.: Archon Books, 1967.

Carter, Everett. *Howells and the Age of Realism*. Hamden, Conn.: Archon Books, 1966.

Eschholz, Paul A., ed. *Critics on William Dean Howells.* Coral Gables, Fla.: University of Miami Press, 1975.

Gibson, William M. *William D. Howells.* Minneapolis: University of Minnesota Press, 1967.

Kirk, Clara M., and Rudolph Kirk. *William Dean Howells.* New York: Twayne, 1962.

McMurray, William. *The Literary Realism of William Dean Howells.* Carbondale: Southern Illinois University Press, 1967.

Chandice M. Johnson, Jr.

LANGSTON HUGHES

Born: Joplin, Missouri
February 1, 1902
Died: New York, New York
May 22, 1967

Principal Literary Achievement

A key figure in the Harlem Renaissance of the 1920's and 1930's and an influential figure in the Black Arts movement until his death, Hughes was an American poet, short story writer, novelist, and playwright.

Biography

James Mercer Langston Hughes was born in Joplin, Missouri, on February 1, 1902, to James Nathaniel and Carrie Mercer Langston Hughes. In 1903, Langston's father, angered and frustrated by a series of events, including the all-white Oklahoma examining board's refusal to let him take the bar examination, left the United States for Mexico, where he prospered and eventually sent money for the support of his son. Hughes says in his first autobiography, *The Big Sea* (1940), that he hated his father, that his father was interested only in making money, and that his father was contemptuous of blacks, Mexicans, and anyone who was poor. Langston's mother, who refused to accompany his father to Mexico, was unable to find work, despite her year of college at the University of Kansas. Consequently, she moved from city to city, sometimes taking Langston with her. Although she did not work as a domestic, she worked at poorly paid clerical jobs that provided insufficient income to support her and her child. Mostly, Langston lived with his grandmother in Lawrence, Kansas, for almost nine years, until her death in 1912.

Upon his grandmother's death, Hughes was sent to live with family friends, Uncle and Auntie Reed, key figures in his often-anthologized essay "Salvation," excerpted from *The Big Sea*. Uncle and Auntie Reed, while they provided Hughes with a sense of family and with regular meals, were much more zealously religious than Hughes's family. In "Salvation," Hughes recounts the loss of his faith when he felt abandoned by Jesus, who did not come to save him during the revival at Auntie Reed's church. Hughes, who was almost thirteen at the time, pretended that he had seen Jesus, and he says he cried in bed that night because he had deceived everybody in the church.

In 1914, Langston's mother remarried, and in 1916, Langston joined his mother and stepfather, Homer Clark, in Cleveland, where Clark was then a steelworker.

Clark shifted jobs frequently, and often the family was financially insecure or impoverished. Nevertheless, the four years Hughes spent at Central High School were productive in introducing him to music, poetry, and art. Throughout his school years, Hughes was an avid reader, and he was influenced particularly by Carl Sandburg's poetry.

In 1921, when Hughes arrived as a student at Columbia University, he learned that the school had an unstated policy not to house black students. Though the university's authorities reluctantly assigned Hughes a room, the event set the tone for the one year that Hughes spent there. Hughes continued his formal education in 1926 when he enrolled at Lincoln University in Pennsylvania. During his university years, he published *The Weary Blues* (1926), *Fire* (1926), and *Fine Clothes to the Jew* (1927). He was graduated from Lincoln University in 1929.

As an adult, Langston Hughes, like his mother, was a drifter, rarely staying in one place long enough to establish roots. In 1923, Hughes began his world travel with a trip to Africa, a journey that he recounts in *The Big Sea*. He says, ironically, that Africa was the only place in the world that he was called a white man. He later visited numerous countries, including The Netherlands, Italy, France, the Soviet Union, Spain, Japan, and China. Through his travels, Hughes met a number of other well-known writers; among them were Theodore Dreiser, Vachel Lindsay, Zora Neale Hurston, Ernest Hemingway, Richard Wright, Lillian Hellman, André Malraux, and Pablo Neruda. Few writers have had such expansive world travel combined with such a rich exposure to other writers. This complex combination of experiences is evident in his second autobiography, *I Wonder as I Wander* (1956). Hughes once remarked to black American writer Richard Wright that six months in one place was long enough to make life complicated. Despite Hughes's rootlessness, he published seventeen volumes of poetry, two novels, seven collections of short stories, and twenty-six plays. He also edited anthologies, published historical works, and translated the works of other writers, especially poets.

In 1927 in New York, Hughes met Charlotte Mason, his patron until the winter of 1930, when they had a philosophical falling out regarding their views of the place of black artists. Shortly after this break, Hughes also broke with Zora Neale Hurston (another artist funded by Mason), who had submitted a play written by her and Hughes to her agent without consulting Hughes.

Although several sources credit Hughes as the first black American writer to support himself with his writing, his life-style was by no means luxurious. In the 1930's, Hughes sent most of his earnings to his mother, who had breast cancer. His father, with whom Hughes had a falling out in 1922, died in Mexico in 1934. Hughes learned of the death too late to attend the funeral, and he had been left out of his father's will. He supported his mother until her death in 1938.

Though some reports of Hughes's death say he died in New York City's Polyclinic Hospital, where he was treated as an indigent until the hospital orderly recognized him, Arnold Rampersad in *The Life of Langston Hughes* debunks that story. Hughes did, in fact, register in the hospital as James L. Hughes, and only one chart listed him as James Langston Hughes. His secretary, Raoul Abdul, however, kept in constant touch with Hughes until his death. Hughes requested that none of his friends except writer Arna Bontemps be informed of his hospitalization. Hughes's ill health could not be kept secret, so Hughes received several calls and even a few uninvited visitors while he was hospitalized.

Hughes's memorial service was a fitting end to his adventurous life. Approximately 275 friends were invited to what was, first and foremost, a concert by blues and jazz pianist Randy Weston, ending with Hughes's "Do Nothing Till You Hear From Me." Arna Bontemps read several of Hughes's poems about death. Later in the day, a small group of mourners gathered at Ferncliff Crematory in Hartsdale, New York, joined hands, bowed their heads, and recited "The Negro Speaks of Rivers" as Hughes's body was rolled toward the flames.

Analysis

Langston Hughes, whose writing career spanned more than half a century, was diverse in his themes, which included connectedness, transitoriness, racism, integration, poverty, myth, history, and universal freedom. Particularly unique to his work was his integration of his writing with blues and jazz. He wrote operettas, and many of his poems were set to music.

Although Hughes, like most writers, objected to reducing authors to labels, such as "black" or "woman" or "American," his name is inevitably linked to the Harlem Renaissance of the 1920's and 1930's; this movement, centered in New York City, marked an awakening of black American artists. In addition, many of Hughes's books, such as *A Negro Looks at Soviet Central Asia* (1934), *Famous American Negroes* (1954), *Famous Negro Music Makers* (1955), *The First Book of Negroes* (1952), and *Famous Negro Heroes of America* (1958), focus on race. His own ancestry was a combination of black, white, and American Indian. Among numerous anthologies edited by Hughes are collections of black American poets and short story writers. For example, Alice Walker's first short story was published in Hughes's *The Best Short Stories by Negro Writers* (1967). Still, Hughes's point about labels is well taken; writers create their art from what they know, and Hughes believed his writing would illuminate truths about all humanity.

Despite Hughes's diversity, he is primarily known for his poetry and short stories rather than for his plays, novels, anthologies, or translations. One of his most popular books, *The Negro Mother and Other Dramatic Recitations* (1931), was written specifically to reach "the hearts of the people." In a letter written October 13, 1931, to William Pickens, Hughes says:

> I have felt that much of our [black artists'] poetry has been aimed at the heads of the high-brows, rather than at the hearts of the people. And we all know that most Negro books published by white publishers are advertised and sold largely to white readers, and little or no effort is made to reach the great masses of the colored people.
>
> I have written "THE NEGRO MOTHER" with the hope that my own people will like it, and will buy it.

Hughes succeeded. The public bought and liked *The Negro Mother.*

As Hughes's friend Arna Bontemps acknowledged in a preface to Donald C. Dickinson's *A Bio-bibliography of Langston Hughes* (1972), Hughes, because he earned his living by writing, had to be diverse and had to write books that would sell. Naturally, the quality of the work varies. Criticism of Hughes's work, however, is not especially helpful in determining which writing is his strongest. As Hughes himself realized, most of the early critics were middle-class white men whose views were restricted by their own expectations. Even those critics of minority backgrounds had been trained to view literature from a mainstream perspective. Predictably, Hughes's works attacking white views were poorly received by critics, as were works aimed at the "hearts of the people." Readers of Langston Hughes are well advised to go to Hughes's writing and to form their own views of it.

Hughes's poetry and short stories are set among real people, mostly black Americans, mostly poor people. Typical of such characters is Jesse B. Simple, a black laborer, who is the central figure of a weekly column that Hughes wrote for the *New York Post*. Simple has an estranged wife, a party-loving woman friend, a curious landlady, a third-floor apartment, and tired feet that he claims tell the story of his life. He cares about people and justice and integrity; even in his bitter moments, he is saved from becoming maudlin by a sort of innocent humor. For example, in "Simple Prays a Prayer," he becomes embittered by the insensitivity of American white society and concludes, "I hope He [God] smites white folks down!" Yet he adds, "I hope he lets Mrs. Roosevelt alone."

Hughes say in his introduction to *The Best of Simple* (1961), that people tell him they have known his characters. Hughes agrees. Some of the stories are retellings of his experiences during his world travel, but all have a universal quality of shared human experience in Harlem. Consistently, Hughes's writing, like Jesse B. Simple, is honest and unpretentious.

HOME

First published: 1934
Type of work: Short story

Roy Williams, a young black musician returning home from performing in Europe to his small Southern hometown, is lynched by white racists.

"Home," first published in *Esquire* magazine in 1934, juxtaposes the sensitivity of a young, black classical violinist and jazz musician returning home ill from Europe against the unconcealed racism of his small Southern hometown. Hughes subtly puts the story in a historical context by telling the reader that the musician, Roy Williams, landed in New York "on the day that Hoover drove the veterans out of Washington."

Williams arrives home, formally dressed, and becomes aware that he is home when he hears the racial slurs of the white men at the train station. He is warmly received by his mother, Sister Williams, who organizes a fund-raising concert at the black church which she attends. Predictably, the fifty-cent seats at the front of the church are occupied by whites and the twenty-five-cent seats in back are occupied by blacks. Art does not, as Hughes points out often in his writing, integrate people socially.

After the concert, Williams meets a woman in the audience who has caught his eye, a white woman wearing a cheap coat and a red hat, someone who seems to understand the classical music he played. She is Miss Reese, an aging music teacher in the local white high school. Miss Reese invites Williams to perform at the white high school, after which their respect for each other deepens.

Williams becomes increasingly ill and has difficulty sleeping, so he goes on late-night walks, on which he is sometimes formally dressed. On one such evening, he meets Miss Reese stepping out of a drug store. He bows to her in greeting and extends his hand just as a group of "white young ruffians with red-necks" comes out of the movie theater. When they see him reaching toward a white woman, they attack him. (Among the group of attackers, Williams thinks he recognizes his white childhood playmate, Charlie Mumford.) After beating Williams, the mob drags him to the woods, where they strip him and leave his body hanging there all night, "like a violin for the wind to play." One of Williams' last thoughts is that he knows that now he will never get home to his mother.

Though the image of respect between the two musicians offers a lingering redemptive image, Hughes makes it clear that art can neither transform the mob nor protect the artist from racism. The story, anthologized in *The Ways of White Folks* (1934), deals honestly with the futility of a black artist trying to survive in such an environment.

The theme of the inequitable distribution of wealth also pervades "Home." Williams recalls the prostitutes in Austria and Germany, young women trying to get enough money to feed themselves and their parents. He feels heartsick at the wealth he sees squandered in the nightclubs where he performs. He thinks of home as a place where poverty is not so bad. Yet, when Williams lands in New York, he finds most of his old friends—musicians and actors—unemployed, hungry, and begging for handouts. Even though Williams' mother offers him "real food" when he arrives home, he cannot eat. The poverty Williams finds at home is linked to racism, and his mother's food cannot cure that illness.

"Home," divided into six sections, contains many allusions to jazz and classical music. The dialogue is rhythmic and poetic, and section 3 reads more like poetry than prose. Section 4 begins with a concert program. The final section is cacophonous, as the mob destroys Williams. Still, Hughes says that the roaring voices and scuffing feet of the lynch mob are "split by the moonlight into a thousand notes like a Beethoven sonata." The final allusion to Beethoven's "Moonlight Sonata" speaks to something enduring, perhaps the same vision in the final lines of Hughes's "The Negro Mother" (1931):

Oh, my dark children, may my dreams and my prayers
Impel you forever up the great stairs—
For I will be with you till no white brother
Dares keep down the children of the Negro mother.

THE BLUES I'M PLAYING

First published: 1934
Type of work: Short story

Oceola Jones, a black jazz and classical pianist, is forced by her white patron to choose between love and art.

"The Blues I'm Playing," first published in *Esquire* magazine (1934), is anthologized in Hughes's collection of fourteen short stories, *The Ways of White Folks.* This story, like the others in the collection, depicts the racial attitudes that surface when whites and blacks interact. The central character, Oceola Jones, is a young black music teacher, herself a gifted jazz and classical musician with insufficient time and money to pursue her art. Mrs. Dora Ellsworth, an aging, wealthy, childless widow, is kind and generous, but she cannot discern great art. Nevertheless, she wants to help young artists pursue their art. Ormond Hunter, a music critic, forwards Oceola Jones to Ellsworth and assures Ellsworth that Jones is talented. He is correct.

Fascinated by Jones's talent and blackness, Mrs. Ellsworth pours money and energy into Oceola Jones's musical training. Jones is the only black person Ellsworth has known. While Ellsworth loves to hear Jones play classical music, Ellsworth increasingly dislikes the jazz and blues, which in her view represent Oceola's unsublimated soul.

Mrs. Ellsworth, learning through Ormond Hunter that the man staying with Oceola does not pay rent, suggests that Oceola move out of the small apartment, but Oceola refuses because she has promised the man, Pete, that he can stay with her until fall, when he will enroll in medical school. Ellsworth is pleased when Pete goes to medical school and leaves Oceola to her music. Jones's musical career progresses to Ellsworth's satisfaction until Pete is graduated. Then, to Mrs. Ellsworth's chagrin, Oceola and Pete make plans to marry. Oceola argues that music and sexuality and children are not incompatible. Mrs. Ellsworth believes they are.

In the final scene of the story, the conflict culminates in Mrs. Ellsworth's music room, a luxurious room adorned with lilies in priceless Persian vases. Jones has come to play for Ellsworth one final time before Ellsworth leaves for Europe. Both understand that their relationship has come to an end. Oceola begins by playing classical music. Gradually, Mrs. Ellsworth begins talking aloud to herself and admonishing Jones's choice to marry. In response, Oceola shifts to jazz and finally to heavy blues music that makes the lilies in the Persian vases tremble. She tries to make Ellsworth see how art connects to life, but Ellsworth, ultimately, prefers to stand and look at the stars.

The plot of "The Blues I'm Playing" echoes Hughes's falling out with his white patron, Charlotte Mason, in 1930. Mason, like Mrs. Ellsworth, supported several artists. Hughes was sorry about the break, but he realized that their views of the roles of black artists were too incompatible to resolve. He believed that Mason's views were too restrictive. Oceola, like Hughes, is genuinely sorry when the end comes.

Mrs. Ellsworth is firmly entrenched in white society. Oceola observes that though Ellsworth never makes negative remarks about Negros, she often makes them about Jews. Jones makes neither racist nor anti-Semitic remarks. Their views of art also differ. Oceola, unlike Mrs. Ellsworth, sees art not as sublime but as integral to humanity, though Jones clearly disagrees with some of her fellow artists, who believe that art can break down color lines. Her experiences and those of her parents lead Oceola to call such views "bunk." Ellsworth's views differ both from Oceola's and from those of the other artists. Though Mrs. Ellsworth is not totally an unsympathetic character, she clearly represents the dualism of Western culture, the binary opposition between soul and body, heart and mind. In Oceola's final attempt to make Mrs. Ellsworth connect, she plays the blues and tells Dora Ellsworth that the music is both sad and gay, white and black, man and woman. The final blues song is clearly a triumph of Oceola's view of the synthesis of art and life.

THE NEGRO SPEAKS OF RIVERS

First published: 1920
Type of work: Poem

"The Negro Speaks of Rivers" is a succinct and powerful poem that ties black history to the rivers of the world.

"The Negro Speaks of Rivers" is perhaps Langston Hughes's most anthologized poem. Written in the first person, the poem begins, "I've known rivers." The "I" is a collective voice of black people from ancient times (3000 B.C.) to the present. The narrator's voice speaks of bathing in the Euphrates, building a hut near the Congo, raising pyramids by the Nile, and watching the sun set on the Mississippi. The refrain, "My soul has grown deep like the rivers," links the movement and endurance and power of the great rivers to black history.

The repeated "I," beginning seven of the ten lines, focuses the reader on the narrator, the black person who speaks of rivers, and on the effects of the tie between his history and the rivers.

In Hughes's autobiography *The Big Sea*, he says that he wrote the poem on the back of an envelope on a train just outside St. Louis on his way to Mexico to visit his father during the summer of 1920. Hughes says that he was feeling very bad, because he was thinking of his father's strange dislike of his own people. Hughes, who liked his people very much, says his thoughts then turned to history, the Mississippi, and finally the other rivers of the world. Within ten or fifteen minutes, he had written the poem. Hughes concludes that he no doubt changed "a few words the next day, or maybe crossed out a line or two."

"The Negro Speaks of Rivers" was positively reviewed by both black and white critics, and it even appeared in translation in a paper printed in Germany. The poem has been acclaimed for Hughes's passionate acceptance of his race, his combination of lyric and epic, his embracing of heritage, and his reclaiming of black origins.

THE WEARY BLUES

First published: 1923
Type of work: Poem

"The Weary Blues" blends jazz and poetry to expose the soul of the blues singer.

"The Weary Blues" is about a piano player Langston Hughes knew in Harlem. According to critic Edward J. Mullen, Hughes called "The Weary Blues" his "lucky poem" because it placed first in a literary contest sponsored by the National Urban League in 1925. Unlike "The Negro Speaks of Rivers," however, "The Weary Blues" received greatly mixed reviews from both black and white critics. It was called everything from a masterpiece to doggerel.

The poem itself blends jazz, blues, and poetry into powerful lyric poetry. The narrator's voice begins the poem:

> Droning a drowsy syncopated tune,
> Rocking back and forth to a mellow croon,
> I heard a Negro play.

In these lines, the musical quality of the poem is already evident. Several of the poem's repeated lines, such as "He did a lazy sway" and "I got the Weary Blues," then capture the motion and rhythm of the music. Other refrains, such as "O Blues!" and "Sweet Blues," create the crooning of the blues. Hughes also uses onomatopoeia in the thumps of the man's foot on the floor.

Hughes concludes the image by extinguishing the performance, the stars, and the moon, but showing that the blues remain an integral part of the man:

> The stars went out and so did the moon.
> The singer stopped playing and went to bed
> While the Weary Blues echoed through his head.
> He slept like a rock or a man that's dead.

This final image, so different from that in "The Negro Speaks of Rivers," probably accounts for the mixed reviews of the poem.

Critics who like "The Weary Blues" compare Hughes's poem to the poetry of Carl Sandburg. DuBose Heyward, for example, says their poetry shares a "freer, subtler syncopation" than that of Vachel Lindsay. Other critics see elements of ballads and spirituals in "The Weary Blues." Oddly enough, several early critics praise "The Negro Speaks of Rivers" for the same qualities they condemn in "The Weary Blues." In response, late twentieth century critics have suggested that these critical comments were biased by the themes of the poems. While "The Negro Speaks of Rivers" is upbeat and affirming of black heritage, "The Weary Blues" affirms a specific heritage, one distinctly not middle class, not classical.

MULATTO

First published: 1926
Type of work: Poem

"Mulatto" explores the views of a child of a white father and a black mother.

"Mulatto," written by Langston Hughes in the summer of 1926, appeared both in *The Saturday Review of Literature* and in *Fine Clothes for the Jew* (1927), a collection of Hughes's work. Hughes said that the poem is about "white fathers and Negro mothers in the South."

The opening voice in "Mulatto" is that of the son, who says, "I am your son, white man!" The child stands in judgment of the father's use of the mother's body. The white father renounces the mulatto son (lines 5 and 6): "You are my son/ Like hell!" The next twenty lines of "Mulatto" re-create the image of the white man exploiting the Negro woman. The white man asks twice within the sketch, "What's the body of your mother?" He has answered the question rhetorically, that the boy's mother's body is a toy.

After the brutal sketch of the white father, the voice of the white man's white son renounces the mulatto boy: "Naw, you ain't my brother./ Niggers ain't my brother./ Not ever./ Niggers ain't my brother." Racism has pitted father against son and brother against brother. Another voice, probably the father's (though it could be the white son's), tells the mulatto, "Git on back there in the night,/ You ain't white." The final words are spoken by the mulatto boy to the white man. He repeats his opening words. "I am your son, white man!"

The poem is lyrical and contrasts the warmth of the Southern landscape and nights with the searing heat of anger and racism. Though the jazz syncopation in "Mulatto" is not so evident as it is in Hughes's later poems, the musical quality of the poem marks it as distinctly Hughes's.

Hughes's first autobiography, *The Big Sea*, in two especially memorable passages, touches on the idea of a mulatto child. In the first, Hughes is surprised that in Africa he is considered white. In the second, Hughes tells the story of a mulatto boy who greets the ship as it harbors in Africa. The child wants to know if the sailors have anything in English for him to read, and he longs to go to England. The boy's father, Hughes learns, is a white man, then living in England. The boy's mother is a black woman that his father has left behind. The child, accepted by neither blacks nor whites, hungers for the other half of his family and heritage. "Mulatto," written after Hughes's journey to Africa, seems a sort of synthesis in his treatment of the family destroyed by the deformed values of racism.

"Mulatto" is praised by critics for its craftsmanship and the powerful delivery of the theme. Several critics consider it the masterpiece of *Fine Clothes for the Jew.*

THE NEGRO MOTHER

First published: 1931
Type of work: Poem

Black mothers call to their children to take control of their future, to live with freedom and dignity.

"The Negro Mother" is the title poem in the collection of poetry that Langston Hughes wrote to reach the masses of black people. The twenty-page book and the poem were such an instant success that Hughes told his friend Carl Van Vechten that in Birmingham, Alabama, the book "sold like reefers on 131st Street."

The voice in the poem is that of the black mothers through the ages. In the opening line, the narrator addresses her children. In the narrative that follows, "the Negro mother" depicts the capture and hardship of black slaves and speaks of the will to endure that kept them going. The voice of the Negro mother urges the children to transform the future so that they may live in dignity and freedom from white oppression.

The poem, often referred to as a heritage poem, is highly lyrical, employing both a regular rhyme scheme (couplets) and meter. It was Hughes's intention, he says, that the poems be pleasant to recite and easy to remember. "The Negro Mother" and the success of the volume show how keenly in tune Hughes was with his audience.

Summary

Langston Hughes, in addition to his significant role in the Harlem Renaissance of the 1920's and 1930's and the Black Arts movement of the 1960's, left much powerful literature that breaks new ground in combining elements of blues and jazz with prose and poetry.

Throughout Hughes's writing, his integrity and his commitment to clarity are evident. Through his candid depictions of his characters, such as Jesse B. Simple, Roy Williams, Oceola Jones, and Mrs. Dora Ellsworth, Hughes helps readers understand more about everyday people, about artists, about humanity.

Bibliography

Barksdale, Richard K. *Langston Hughes: The Poet and His Critics.* Chicago: American Library Association, 1977.

Berry, Faith. *Langston Hughes: Before and Beyond Harlem.* Westport, Conn.: Lawrence Hill, 1983.

Dickinson, Donald C. *A Bio-bibliography of Langston Hughes.* 2d ed. New York: Archon Books. 1972.

Jemie, Onwuchekwa. *Langston Hughes: An Introduction to the Poetry.* New York: Columbia University Press, 1976.

Miller, R. Baxter. "Langston Hughes." In *Afro-American Writers from the Harlem Renaissance to 1940*, edited by Trudier Harris. Vol. 51 in *Dictionary of Literary Biography.* Detroit: Gale Research, 1987.

Mullen, Edward J., ed. *Critical Essays on Langston Hughes.* Boston: G. K. Hall, 1986.

Rampersad, Arnold. *The Life of Langston Hughes.* New York: Oxford University Press, 1988.

Carol Franks

ZORA NEALE HURSTON

Born: Eatonville, Florida
January 7, 1891
Died: Ft. Pierce, Florida
January 28, 1960

Principal Literary Achievement

Zora Neale Hurston created a body of literature that celebrates and preserves the sound and spirit of black voices as she knew them.

Biography

Zora Neale Hurston was born on January 7, 1891, though she was later to list her birth date as 1901, taking a full decade out of her life. She was born in Eatonville, Florida, the first black incorporated town in the United States; her father, John Hurston, a local minister, also served three terms as mayor of the town and wrote its laws. Her mother, Lucy Ann Potts Hurston, did the most to encourage young Zora's spirit and learning.

It was when Hurston entered high school in 1917, after having spent some time traveling with a Gilbert and Sullivan troupe, that she came up with her revised birthday, to make herself appear still a teenager. In 1918, she entered the Howard Prep School at Howard University to catch up on missed education, and in 1920 she received an associate degree from Howard.

In 1925, Hurston won second prize in a fiction contest for her short story "Spunk," which also landed her a job as a secretary with one of the contest judges, the popular novelist Fanny Hurst. The same year, she entered Barnard College, the women's division of Columbia University, at the urging of Annie Nathan Meyer, also a novelist, and one of the founders of Barnard. There, Hurston was the only black student. At Barnard, she studied anthropology with Franz Boas, one of the most influential anthropologists of his time, and Hurston was graduated in 1927 as a committed social scientist.

Hurston had arrived in New York during the Harlem Renaissance, the biggest literary, musical, and artistic flowering of African-American culture that the country had ever seen, and she immediately became an important part of it. Among her close associates was the poet Langston Hughes, who later recalled that Hurston seemed to know everyone. With Hughes and some others, Hurston was coeditor and frequent contributor to a short-lived journal called *Fire!!*, which was to have a last-

ing influence in its advocacy of black literature developing an authentically black voice, as opposed to following the traditions of English and European writing.

In 1927 and 1928, with the financial support of Mrs. Rufus Osgood Mason, who had also supported Langston Hughes, Hurston made several folktale collecting trips to Florida and New Orleans, collecting material for what would eventually grow into her first book of folktales, *Mules and Men* (1935). In 1930, she collaborated with Langston Hughes on a comic play, *Mule Bone*, which was to sever their friendship for all time when Hurston tried to copyright the play under her own name. The play was never produced in either of the writers' lifetimes.

In 1933, the writing of *Mules and Men* mostly behind her, a short story Hurston wrote that was published in *Story* magazine, called "The Gilded Six-Bits," led to an inquiry by a publisher, Lippincott, as to whether she were also working on a novel. She began writing a novel on July 1, 1933, and by September 6, she was done with it. In May, 1934, her first novel, *Jonah's Gourd Vine*, was published. An autobiographically based novel, it presents a fictionalized version of her parents' marriage, concentrating especially on John Pearson, a character loosely based on her father. The novel was generally well received, but it was also misinterpreted by reviewers who had a hard time believing that a black preacher could be as eloquent as John Pearson.

It was the publication of *Mules and Men* in 1935 that marked the beginning of the debate over the worth and meaning of Hurston's work which was to follow her throughout her life. It was well received, but also widely criticized for ignoring the harsh realities of life in the South that had hit especially hard during the Depression. Also in 1935, she made an attempt to return to school at Columbia to study anthropology, but in fact she rarely attended classes. In 1936, Hurston was awarded a grant by the Guggenheim Foundation to continue her work in folklore. It was while on a trip to Haiti that she wrote her masterpiece, *Their Eyes Were Watching God* (1937). Like her first novel, the material was her own life and her hometown transformed into art.

In 1938, Hurston's second book of folklore, *Tell My Horse*, much less successful than her first, was published. In 1939, she was hired to teach drama at the North Carolina College for Negroes at Durham, and she married Albert Price III, a twenty-three-year-old man. Their marriage was to last less than a year. In November, 1939, *Moses, Man of the Mountain*, widely considered to be her second-best novel, was published. In 1941, Hurston wrote her autobiography, *Dust Tracks on a Road*, which was published in 1942, with her comments on Western imperialism excised. In 1943, she received several awards, including the Ansfield-Wolf Book Award in Race Relations, and appeared on the cover of the *Saturday Review*. It marked the zenith of her fame.

In 1945, a novel on which she had been working called *Mrs. Doctor* was rejected for publication by Lippincott, and financial worries that Hurston had for years been keeping at bay began to catch up with her. In 1948, her novel about white Southern life, *Seraph on the Suwannee*, was published by Scribner's, the only novel of hers that is generally considered to be an artistic failure.

In 1948, she was arrested on a false charge of molesting a ten-year-old boy. Though the charges were dropped in 1949, Hurston never completely recovered from this or from the downturn in her professional success. In 1950, the *Miami Herald* published an article about Hurston working as a maid to support her writing. Though she published a few essays and stories during the last ten years of her life, she spent most of her time working on a never-to-be-published biography of King Herod. After supporting herself through a number of odd jobs for several years, she suffered a stroke in 1959 and moved into the St. Lucie Welfare Home, where she died on January 28, 1960.

In 1973, writer Alice Walker placed a gravestone remembering Hurston in the graveyard in which she had been buried and, two years later, published an essay in *Ms.* magazine called "In Search of Zora Neale Hurston," which launched the revival of Hurston's literary reputation.

Analysis

Zora Neale Hurston's depiction of black life in her writing stands in sharp contrast to the harsher views of black life depicted in works by such novelists as Richard Wright, who attacked her writing as "counter revolutionary." Unlike the work of Wright, who was committed to using his writing to demand social change, Hurston's writing is first and foremost a celebration of being black in America.

Richard Wright was not the only critic during her lifetime, or afterwards, to accuse Hurston of political naïveté; it is a charge that deserves consideration. It is true that the reader of Hurston's work searches in vain for some sensitive portrayal of the true plight of blacks during the Depression, the period during which Hurston wrote most of her best works. Poverty in the Eatonville she portrays is most likely to be the setting for a story or a joke, rather than a cause for concerted political action. Furthermore, it is equally true that Hurston, who grew up in a nourishing black community, remained a defender of some aspects of racial separatism well after the Civil Rights movement had quite correctly identified integration as its goal; she even criticized the Supreme Court's *Brown vs. the Board of Education* ruling, which demanded desegregation of public schools.

Yet if Hurston thought that blacks should be wary of what integration had to offer, it was because she valued so highly what black culture had to offer and feared the possibility of black culture getting lost in an attempt to homogenize society. The title of her most successful work of folklore, *Mules and Men*, might seem to suggest a grim setting of men being treated like beasts of burden. In fact, though, the stories within the book celebrate a bond of cleverness and zest that the people of the South she chronicles share with the folkloric animals about which they tell stories. It is not that Hurston was not a political writer, but that the politics of her writing came from a greater appreciation for the culture and values that black Americans had developed than for the culture from which they were often painfully excluded. Furthermore, as becomes clear in some of her essays, such as "How it Feels to Be Colered Me" (reprinted in a collection of Hurston's essays, *I Love Myself When I Am Laughing . . .* , 1979, edited by Alice Walker), she understood before many that it was only from a perspective of mutual respect that the black and white races would be able to cooperate.

When Hurston's literary reputation began to be revived in the 1970's, it was as much because of an appreciation of her sexual politics by feminist readers as because of her celebrations of black America. Her great novel, *Their Eyes Were Watching God*, is as much as anything else an account of its main character's, Janie Crawford's, sexual awakening and search for equality in a relationship. Furthermore, her autobiography, *Dust Tracks on a Road*, is an often frank (and sometimes guarded) account of a very independently minded woman's walk through life.

It is generally true that Hurston's political vision, which was shaped within an autonomous black community, applies less well to the poor and often racially besieged black communities that existed elsewhere in the South. It is also generally true that the further she got from the realities of Eatonville as the setting for her writing, the less effectively her imagination and craft seemed to serve her. This can be seen especially in *Seraph on the Suwannee*, her one attempt at centering a novel on mainly white characters; it is the most disappointing of her fictions. The exception to this rule may, with some justification, be said to be *Moses, Man of the Mountain* (1939), her version of the escape of the Hebrews from Egypt and the founding of Israel; in fact, however, *Moses* is successful precisely because it rewrites the story of Moses as a black fable about the establishment of an autonomous nation after the end of slavery.

The most valuable lesson that can be taken from Hurston's writing, and her most important recurring theme, is the enormous beauty and power a distinctive voice can have when it has the courage to show itself as its cultural and personal self rather than hiding behind imitations of others.

MULES AND MEN

First published: 1935
Type of work: Folklore

Hurston returns to her native South to collect folklore.

In writing *Mules and Men*, Zora Neale Hurston not only found a way to make a crucial bridge between her anthropological and literary ambitions but also created a lasting treasure of stories that captured the authentic voices of southern black storytellers in the late 1920's. The book is divided into two parts. The first part details her collecting of folklore in Florida, the second part in New Orleans. The order in which the tales are related is ostensibly random, simply the order in which people told them to her, but as her biographer, Robert Hemenway points out, and as inspection of the text reveals, the clusters of the stories are to some extent thematic.

Though there are a few stories about men and women in the first part of the book, most of the earlier stories deal with the days of slavery and with competition between the races in general. In the tales of slavery, the most common character is John, sometimes called Jack, who is often introduced as "Ole Massa's" favorite slave, though he inevitably ends up tricking the slave owner somehow or another. John is a consummate trickster figure who, though he will often engage in hard physical labor, always triumphs through the power of his wits, and occasionally, good luck. Sometimes John's triumphs are smaller than at others—sometimes he merely survives—but at times, when he has been attacked brutally or viciously, his revenge is brutal indeed, as in "Ah'll Beatcher Makin' Money," where he tricks Massa into killing his own grandmother, then into being drowned. John shows his proudest, most dignified, side in the story Hurston calls, "Member Youse a Nigger," in which he works extra hard for a year to arrange a banner crop for his master, on the condition that he be freed at the end of the year. Ole Massa does indeed keep his side of the bargain, but shows his true self when, as John leaves, he keeps calling to him, "'Member John, youse a nigger." John replies to him after every call, but keeps walking until he gets to Canada.

Many of the other stories are talking animal stories, similar to the ones Joel Chandler Harris had collected in his Uncle Remus stories some years earlier. In many of these, the animals are clever stand-ins for black and whites, such as the story "What the Rabbit Learned," in which Brer Rabbit knows enough to keep away from Brer Dog, despite Brer Dog's protestations that dogs have all agreed to be friends with rabbits. Perhaps the most important of these stories is the story "The Talking Mule," in which an old mule called Bill, after years of doing plowing for the man who owns him, one day speaks up and refuses, which so startles the old man that he runs away as fast as he can. The encoded message, preaching resistance to oppression, could not be clearer.

Part 2 of *Mules and Men* has an entirely different feel to it. In part 1, it is clear that Hurston is collecting stories that she is often familiar with already, in an area that, though she occasionally stands out as citified, she basically considers to be home. Part 2, however, takes her to New Orleans, where she sets about collecting the lore of Hoodoo, which she argues is a suppressed religion. Whereas in the first part, Hurston herself is often as important as the stories she is collecting, in the second part, she removes herself more to the background, usually playing the role of student to the people she writes about.

Part 2 is written as series of profiles of individual Hoodoo doctors. Luke Turner, one such doctor, tells Hurston the legend of Marie Leveau, a famous nineteenth century Hoodoo doctor; Anatol Pierre is a Catholic who also claims to have learned from Leveau. Dr. Duke is a root doctor, who uses herbs and roots he gathers from the swamps. Hurston is very careful about detailing the initiation ceremonies that different doctors make her undergo as well as the elaborate rituals they use to get rid of people, to get people back, and even to kill them. With Kitty Brown, the last Hoodoo doctor profiled, Hurston herself participates in a ritual to cause the death of a man who left one of Kitty Brown's clients. When the man begins, several days later, to feel a pain in his chest, he returns to the woman he left, who in turn quickly has the curse canceled. It becomes very plain in these stories that Hurston takes these rituals very seriously indeed.

One of the complaints some reviewers had about *Mules and Men* was its general reluctance to show the economic realities of the southern blacks about which Hurston was writing. To some extent, this seems to have been the result of a deliberate choice by Hurston to emphasize the qualities she most cherished. The South that Hurston records in this volume of folklore is one fiercely alive with humor, irony, and mystery.

THEIR EYES WERE WATCHING GOD

First published: 1937
Type of work: Novel

A black woman's life becomes a personal odyssey in search of personal values.

Janie Crawford, the main character of Hurston's most important novel, *Their Eyes Were Watching God*, is the granddaughter of a slave woman, Nanny, who was raped by her owner, and the daughter of a woman who was raped by her schoolteacher. It is against the heritage of this racial and sexual violence that Janie tries to find a personally fulfilling life. The novel begins with Janie returning to Eatonville after the death of her third husband, Tea Cake Woods. Janie sits with her old friend, Pheoby, to tell her story, and the bulk of the novel, although narrated in the third person, is the story Janie tells.

Her story begins when her grandmother, Nanny, spies Janie enjoying her first romantic kiss. Realizing that Janie, at the age of sixteen, is almost a woman and that Nanny herself will not be around much longer to take care of her, Nanny quickly arranges Janie's marriage with a local farmer so Janie can be protected. Janie, however, finds no happiness in being Mrs. Logan Killicks, so when Joe Starks comes by, Janie happily runs off with and marries him.

Joe has heard about a black town being formed, Eatonville, to which he wants to move and become a "big voice." From the first day he is there, Joe starts organizing the town around his own principles, opening the first store, then a post office, and finally becoming the first mayor. As the wealthiest man in town, he also builds himself the grandest home. Janie's place in all of this, it turns out, is to reign over the town at his side, but without speaking, and to work in the store while he entertains friends out on the porch.

Starks is a deliberately contradictory character. On the one hand, the reader can admire him for his organizational ability. On the other hand, he organizes Eatonville into a model of the white towns in which he has lived, except with himself at the head of it. Janie herself gets lost in the shuffle. Joe relegates Janie to the role of a voiceless servant and deliberately keeps her apart from most of the town—partly out of jealousy, partly out of contempt for the townspeople.

From Janie's perspective, her marriage to Starks becomes an almost twenty-year-long struggle to assert herself. She finally does, in front of the whole store, when, defending herself against insults about her looks, she hits him with a comment about how old he looks. Taking this wound to his pride as a mortal blow, Joe moves out of their bedroom and sleeps downstairs, and in fact he does die shortly thereafter of kidney failure.

The story of Janie's third marriage, to Tea Cake Woods, takes up most of the second half of the novel, and it involves many interesting and deliberate reversals from the first half. Whereas Janie entered her marriage to Joe as the younger and poorer of the two, she is about twelve years older than Tea Cake and considerably richer. Nevertheless, they fall in love and get married, and move further south so that Tea Cake can do the work he likes best, picking crops and gambling.

The story of Janie's marriage to Tea Cake has troubled many critics. After the long process by which Janie eventually was able to fight her way out of one oppressive marriage, she hardly seems to notice that she has fallen into a marriage with another man who is every bit as dominating as Joe Starks. Tea Cake is portrayed as more genuinely respectful and loving of Janie than Joe ever was, and several scenes between Janie and Tea Cake have an evident erotic charge. Yet he too begins to get violent with Janie when he feels jealous.

Thus, the hurricane from which Janie and Tea Cake flee almost becomes an expression of Janie's subconscious rage. Certainly the rabid dog that bites Tea Cake during this storm and which several days later makes the now rabid Tea Cake sound like a reincarnation of Joe Starks seems to be a deliberate plot device to force Janie to make a painful decision to live: She has to shoot him to prevent him from killing her.

When Janie returns home to Eatonville, she is in a sense returning in failure; the only personally rewarding love she has found was one that was too volatile to hold. She feels satisfied at the end that she found such a love affair at least briefly, but, as many feminist critics have pointed out, Janie's story serves as a better illustration of the need for a mutually respectful relationship than it does as an example of such a relationship.

MOSES, MAN OF THE MOUNTAIN

First published: 1939
Type of work: Novel

A retelling of the saga of Moses, making it particularly relevant to the experience of blacks.

Hurston's *Moses, Man of the Mountain* is a novel about greatness, taking as one of its main themes the sacrifices that are required for a people to become great. Yet the novel itself, despite some excellent passages, falls short of that goal. The conceptual problems Hurston had in putting this novel together are summarized in the character of Moses himself. On the one hand, she sees him as a hereditary Egyptian, and thus as an African. On the other hand, within the metaphor with which she begins and which allows the Hebrews to talk like African Americans, the Egyptians represent white plantation owners. Thus, Moses' speech becomes an inconsistent mixture of black dialect and grand biblical rhetoric.

He is, at any rate, a very interesting character. Though there is a story in this novel that Moses is Hebrew, it is not given any credence by Moses himself. This Moses grows up the grandson of a pharaoh and becomes a military leader before he starts to plead for more humane treatment for the Hebrews. When he kills an Egyptian guard for senselessly beating a Hebrew worker, rumors about his birthright start to spread, and he chooses to exile himself to Midian, across the Red Sea.

In Midian, he becomes a student of Jethro, a monotheist priest who teaches him magic for twenty years, and whose daughter, Zipporah, he weds. After learning all he can from Jethro, he travels to Koptos, where he battles and defeats a deathless serpent to consult the Book of Thoth, which teaches him even greater secrets. Afterward, he is ready to return to Egypt to teach the Hebrews Jethro's religion and demand their release from Pharaoh.

As the leader he becomes in Egypt, Moses is a shrewd politician who is careful not to intimidate Pharaoh too quickly with his series of plagues. He needs the stage that his confrontation with Pharaoh provides in order to establish his credibility with the Hebrews. When he finally does win the Hebrews' freedom, his job as lawmaker has barely begun, as has his task of making the freed slaves understand how perilous a thing their newfound freedom is and how carefully it has to be guarded.

Although it is included for a point, the endless quarreling among the freed Hebrews, especially by Miriam and Aaron, the brother and sister who started the rumor that Moses was a Hebrew in the first place, goes beyond showing the human foibles of a "chosen" people and becomes a sustained and relentless performance of pettiness.

At times, the grumbling of the Hebrews against Moses is played for comedy. Indeed, this comedy of showing the historical Hebrews grumbling like the men outside Joe Clarke's store in the Eatonville of Hurston's youth has an important role in making the connection between the emerging culture of black Americans and the Hebrews after leaving slavery. Hurston's point is that the cultural limitations of slavery take time to overcome. Still, the almost complete lack of faith in Moses by anyone other than Joshua seems more the perspective of the beleaguered Moses himself than of the lover of her own people that Hurston was; one suspects that the writer's real motive was to bring out the contradictions that were part of Moses' character as the giver of freedom and law. He reflects on this paradox when he consistently tells the Hebrews that he did not promise to make life easy, he promised to make them a great nation; he also says, "People talk about tenderness and mercy, but they love force." It is force that Moses has to show, as when he returns from

Mount Sinai to find the Hebrews have built a golden Egyptian idol, and he demands that those who are on his side slaughter those who are not.

Eventually, the contradiction between freedom-giver and patriarchal lawmaker is too great to be sustained, and Moses knows that he will not accompany the Hebrews when they cross the river Jordan to found the state of Israel. By this time, the wandering of the Hebrews in the wilderness has cost the lives of almost all the people who originally fled from Egypt, and the generation that founds the state of Israel were born as free men and women. Moses' work is done.

In one respect, Moses can be read as an idealized version of Hurston's own father, the dynamic preacher John Hurston, who as mayor of Eatonville wrote many of the laws of that town and who was featured in her first novel, *Jonah's Gourd Vine*, as John Pearson. Moses, unlike Hurston's father, who was a noted philanderer, is a man with enough strength of character not to take advantage of such a position. The book is a study of the value such powerful, patriarchal lawmakers can have during a time of transition, but Hurston fully understands the limits of the role, and, in her study of Moses as a person, the heavy burden it places on a person who accepts such a role.

DUST TRACKS ON A ROAD

First published: 1942
Type of work: Autobiography

Hurston recalls her childhood in Eatonville and her success as a writer, and she speculates on great questions.

Though Zora Neale Hurston's autobiography, *Dust Tracks on a Road*, was a success with the general public when it was first published, it has in many respects hurt her reputation in the long run because of its seeming inconsistencies. In part, the inconsistencies in the book's tone come from Hurston's own uncertainty as to who her audience was. At times she seems to be addressing a predominantly black audience, as also seems to be the case in her best fiction. At other times, she seems to want to address a white audience, and the writing becomes stiffer, less lively, and less forthcoming.

The first half of the book, at least, shows Hurston's writing at its best. She begins with descriptions of Eatonville and of her parents before introducing the story of her own birth in a chapter entitled, logically enough, "I Get Born." Beginning with the line, "This is all hearsay," the chapter tells the story of Hurston's birth being midwifed by a local farmer who happened to stop by while Hurston's mother had sent one of her older children out to fetch the local midwife. It may not be entirely true, but that only makes it an appropriate birth for a woman who grew up to record the town's folktales, called "lies" by the tellers.

The chapters that follow chart her growth from young girlhood to young womanhood, and they are written with a zest for recalling herself and the people she knew. In one characteristic passage, recalling the richness of her inner life, she recalls her roughness with toys: "Dolls caught the devil around me. They got into fights and leaked sawdust before New Year's . . . I wanted action."

One of the early lessons she learns in the all-black Eatonville, and which she very much wants to communicate to her readers, is the importance of never seeing her blackness as an encumbrance or excuse. This is a position which has been both applauded and criticized. On the one hand, her admirers point out the courage it took to adopt such a perspective in a society in which black children were often taught early not to forget their place; her detractors, meanwhile, have pointed out the extent to which this point of view led Hurston to underestimate the effect that the harsh political realities of her time had on shaping the lives of her fellow blacks.

One of the most traumatic experiences Hurston describes in her autobiography is the death of her mother, who was the dominant influence on her. This passage, which is written in the figurative language of folklore that sees death as a sentient being stalking the living, tells of Hurston's mother telling the young Zora not to let her father take away her pillow or cover the mirror and clock, as is the village custom with the dying. Zora alone is not able to stand against the custom, however, and she watches her mother die uneasy, feeling that perhaps her mother is berating her for her failure.

Several years after her mother's death, Zora leaves Eatonville with a traveling Gilbert and Sullivan company, and with, as she says, "A map of Dixie on my tongue." Her account of her subsequent schooling up north is as interesting for what it does not say as for what it says. "I have no lurid tales of race discrimination at Barnard," Zora says, and omits mentioning an episode Robert Hemenway reveals in his biography of her in which Annie Nathan Meyer, who had arranged for Hurston's scholarship, forbade Hurston to go to a dance, believing that it would be improper. Such willingness to avoid seeing race prejudice may be partly a capitulation to an assumed white audience for her book, but it is certainly partly an extension of her own feelings about her race.

The outbreak of World War II while Hurston was writing her autobiography caused her to spend an uncharacteristically long time revising the manuscript. For example, at the urging of her editor, she excised comments that were very critical of Western imperialism in Asia. In general, the second half of the book seems to run out of energy. Most of these chapters are topic-oriented essays following Hurston's thoughts, and the writing in some of them gets notably awkward. For example, her chapter on religion lacks the power of the fictional sermons in *Jonah's Gourd Vine* and takes refuge behind an uncharacteristically general rhetorical style which leads her to say such things as "what need of denominations and creeds to deny myself the comfort of all my fellow men?"—which may be a noble thought, but the saying lacks Hurston's personal rhetorical power.

Among the treats of the later part of the book, though, is the chapter entitled "Love," which tells of her on-and-off love affair with a younger man, whom she identifies as A. W. P. Though he seems to bear no resemblance to the character, he apparently served as Zora's model for Janie Crawford's third husband, Tea Cake, in *Their Eyes Were Watching God*. Hurston says that the novel was written in an attempt to "embalm" the tenderness she still felt for A. W. P. after an (unsuccessful) attempt to break up with him.

Hurston's autobiography was motivated as much by the wish to avoid saying too much as it was by a desire to tell her story. Hemenway points out in his biography of Hurston that she was ambivalent about the idea of writing an autobiography, and this ambivalence shows. Nevertheless, much of the book beautifully recounts a spirited black girl's explorations of life and her growth into young womanhood.

Summary

The gravestone that Alice Walker placed on Zora Neale Hurston's grave identifies her as a "Novelist, Folklorist, Anthropologist," and "A Genius of the South." This is an excellent summary of her career. The three occupations combined to form the basis for Hurston's genius. She did not need her training as an anthropologist to convince her that the life of southern blacks was worth recording, but she did use this training to help her record it. The spirit she captured in her writing belonged as much to Eatonville as it did to Hurston herself, and it is a vibrant and lasting spirit.

Bibliography

Gates, Henry Louis, Jr. *The Signifying Monkey: A Theory of Afro-American Literary Criticism*. New York: Oxford University Press, 1988.

Hemenway, Robert E. *Zora Neale Hurston: A Literary Biography*. Urbana: University of Illinois Press, 1977.

Johnson, Barbara. *A World of Difference*. Baltimore: The Johns Hopkins University Press, 1987.

Jordan, Jennifer. "Feminist Fantasies: Zora Neale Hurston's *Their Eyes Were Watching God*." *Tulsa Studies in Women's Literature* 7 (Spring, 1988): 105-117.

Reich, Alice. "Pheoby's Hungry Listening." *Women's Studies* 13 (1986): 163-169.

Washington, Mary Helen. *Invented Lives: Narratives of Black Women, 1860-1960*. Garden City, N.Y.: Doubleday, 1987.

Willis, Susan. *Specifying*. Madison: University of Wisconsin Press, 1987.

Thomas Cassidy

JOHN IRVING

Born: Exeter, New Hampshire
March 2, 1942

Principal Literary Achievement

Bright, imaginative stories of individuality and courage in the face of mediocrity, John Irving's best-selling novels embrace large philosophical ideas within bizarre characterizations and unique plot situations.

Biography

Born into a happy New England family, John Winslow (his mother's maiden name) Irving enjoyed the benefits of his father's position as teacher of Russian history and treasurer of Phillips Exeter Academy. He attended that prestigious school himself, which under various disguises serves as a setting for many of his novels, including *The World According to Garp* (1978) and *A Prayer for Owen Meany* (1989). After several false starts in college, including a year at the University of Vienna, he received his B.A. degree in 1965 from the University of New Hampshire. Following graduate work in the writing program at the University of Iowa, he became an assistant professor at Mount Holyoke College in Massachusetts.

His first novel, *Setting Free the Bears,* was published in 1969 and received more critical attention than most first novels. It is a picaresque novel and a *Bildungsroman.* Irving made use of his Austrian experiences in this novel, and he introduced many of the themes and motifs that were to reappear in his canon, such as caged bears, motorcycles, and bizarre deaths. He continued to write, relying on academic salaries from small New England colleges, writer residencies, and grants from large institutions. Although his next novels, *The Water-Method Man* (1972) and *The 158-Pound Marriage* (1974), sold only about six thousand copies each, he had gained a reputation as an academic writer and was supported by the Rockefeller Foundation in 1972 and a National Endowment for the Arts fellowship in 1974-1975, followed by a Guggenheim Foundation grant in 1976-1977, during which he wrote *The World According to Garp* (1978). He switched publishers, leaving Random House just before completing *Garp.* With the success of this novel, he freed himself from teaching and from needing grants. The book was made into a film in 1982. Two more novels, *The Hotel New Hampshire* (1981) and *The Cider House Rules* (1985) followed, with some success, attributable in large part to massive publicity campaigns by his publisher, Dutton. He switched publishers once again, however, and his novel

A Prayer for Owen Meany (published by Morrow) once again brought him the critical praise he had found with *The World According to Garp.*

The target of criticism for his popularity, he has also written several essays describing and defending his position on writing with "sentimentality," by which he means being in touch with human emotions, and avoiding the postmodern self-consciousness of other contemporary novelists such as John Barth, Thomas Pynchon, and William Gass.

Analysis

John Irving has combined academic status and seriousness with a popular appeal that has made him an immensely successful American novelist. His *The World According to Garp* won several awards, and some 3 million copies of the paperback version were printed. Ironically, that same popular success is the primary criticism that his detractors seem to be able to level at him. Irving does not experiment with the novel form in the postmodern sense of William Gass, John Barth, and others; rather, he creates his content with an eye to its uniqueness. An "academic" writer who has succeeded in pleasing a general public as well, Irving is often accused of retreating from the true "serious" novel form and succumbing to the temptations of financial security and popularity. Admittedly using earlier popular novelists such as Thomas Hardy, Charles Dickens, and Laurence Sterne as his models, Irving maintains that academic experimentation for its own sake has no value. While he makes use of accepted narrative elements to tell his story, the events he describes rival the strangeness of life itself, according to Irving.

Several settings and situations serve Irving over and over in his novels. One is the boys' school setting, like Exeter, but with all the changes and revisions that a novelist would like reality to assume in the fictive form. Another is Vienna—the entire novel *Setting Free the Bears,* but also some of *The World According to Garp* and large parts of *The Hotel New Hampshire,* take place in Vienna. It stands for Old World decadence; if the Nazis are not invading, then terrorists living upstairs in the hotel are planning a bombing of the opera house. Finally, the family unit is a setting for Irving. The family is always a little bizarre, very close, and friendly, a source of warmth for the family members. The father is a strong figure, the mother creative, the siblings close to one another. When, as in the case of Owen Meany, another figure is introduced into the family, his acceptance is total and complete.

Less easy to define and describe is Irving's predilection for the violent. Every novel contains bizarre descriptions or stories of rape, murder, mutilation, torture, or unusual sexual practice, including incest. Since virtually every novel deals with the maturation of the narrator, much loss of innocence, often in odd circumstances, occurs. Garp, for example, is conceived on a hospital bed; his mother is a nurse, and his father is a dying soldier. The union is a "benign rape" of the father by the mother. *The Hotel New Hampshire,* too, focuses on a rape—the rape of the protagonist's sister in high school and her subsequent overcoming of the trauma. Despite the violence, Irving manages to insert a poetic justice into each story, as though in the absence of a god of divine justice or a fair world, the fiction writer has it in his or her power to adjust the events and their consequences to bring a sense of rightness to the story.

Because of Irving's own interest in the sport and recreation of wrestling, many incidents in his novels deal with wrestling coaches and team sports; Irving manages to incorporate elements of his own personal life into his novels without actually writing his autobiography. The reader senses that Irving is thinly disguised in the narrative voice, and that sense gives the novels a depth of understanding. Irving also is fascinated with bears, not only in his first novel, but, for example, in *The Hotel New Hampshire*, where the parents' story of a bear begins the narrative.

Irving moves his novels through time; events occur as early as the late nineteenth century (when reaching back for a story's "prehistory") or as recently as the Reagan administration. His novels often begin in an idyllic boyhood time shortly after World War II (Irving was born in 1942), and the narrative character is often a young boy when the novel begins but a mature young man by the end of the novel. In this sense they are all *Bildungsromanen*, novels of passage from boyhood to manhood, but they are more than that. The father figure is often a dreamer, one whose dreams are never very far away. The family, often large and democratic in style, grows with the father's dreams, usually with the narrator being the most astute observer of the whole situation (one critic has noted the importance of the narrator's being the "third child" of the family). Occasionally the mother disappears from the picture, sometimes by death (as in *A Prayer for Owen Meany* and *The Hotel New Hampshire*), but in *The World According to Garp*, she is there until her murder toward the end of the novel. Ambivalent about his own childhood (his stepfather reared him), Irving seems obsessed with the ideal family in every setting—as he is with incest, usually graphically described and discussed, which becomes a metaphor for the kind of family love beyond which it is impossible to go.

In a way, Irving's repetition of certain motifs is his own novelistic experiment. Rather than avoiding repetition, Irving uses it to build a system of signs for the reader of the entire canon; critics actually look for the motifs and complain when one or another is missing from the most recent novel. Irving is accumulating a considerable body of work, all of it interwoven by these motifs. It can be said that his life work is all one novel, told in various disguises. Irving has one task: to fix the world's injustices by telling of them in his own "repaired" version. He never denies that the bizarre, the accidental, and the "unfortunate" occur, but he maintains that every event serves a purpose in the larger, more positive construction called life. Nothing is an accident; everything that happens is supposed to happen. As Garp says, "Remember . . . everything."

Underneath the quirky invention, the autobiographical convolutions, and the variety of sex and violence is a message of life and hope. Yes, Irving says through the character of Garp, everyone dies, but the main idea is to live—to have an adventure. If the frightening "Under Toad" (a child's misunderstanding of "undertow") lurks for everyone, it can be ignored through giving life and by loving.

SETTING FREE THE BEARS

First published: 1969
Type of work: Novel

A Vienna fantasy turns into a destructive adventure when the narrator sets free some zoo animals, fulfilling the wishes of his dead co-conspirator.

Set in Austria in 1967, Irving's first novel introduced the bizarre style and outrageous imagination that was to become Irving's trademark. The pair of young heroes, Hannes and Siggy, undetached from any kind of worldly commitment, travel by motorcycle through the European countryside, fantasizing, planning, complaining about all manner of authoritarianism, and generally enjoying the life of the free man. One of their imaginary schemes is to free all the animals in the local Vienna zoo as a statement against the encroaching Fascist mentality of Europe, which had been the cause of World War II and was still in evidence after the war. Siggy dies, however, in a strange encounter with a swarm of bees. As a tribute to Siggy, his friend Hannes brings the plan to fruition, using Siggy's elaborate notes about the schedule of guards, the layout, and other details of the zoo.

The novel divides into three parts. The first section describes the meeting of the two protagonists, their picaresque adventures through Europe on motorcycles, and Siggy's bizarre, tragicomic death from bee-stings. The second section is Siggy's diary, a prehistory in that it describes Nazi Germany before his birth. Here the grotesque elements of oppression are highlighted—bizarre, ironic deaths and meaningless slaughter. In the third section, Hannes frees the animals, only to witness their own destruction, a contradiction to the philosophical idea that freedom is necessarily good. The obvious parallel between social oppression and captivity of animals in the zoo is carefully foreshadowed in an incident in part 1, in which Siggy and Hannes free some goats only to have them be destroyed by their freedom. A third character has a love affair with Hannes, but she leaves him after the zoo incident.

The central theme of the book is the question of captivity—whether a human being is captured by the everyday obligations and responsibilities of love, country, family, and the like, or whether one can choose to free oneself and submit to the implicit destruction of that freedom. In this sense, Irving is an existentialist, trying, in the absence of provable larger plans, to establish right action by means of examining cause and effect—the consequence of his actions. Like Heimito von Doderer, the German novelist, Irving tries to discover whether every man is a murderer because of the chained effects of his actions and because people put themselves in self-destructive but redeeming situations. In this respect, "saints" enter Irving's narrators' lives, saints being defined as persons who give their lives to some larger idea than their own ego. Owen Meany (in *A Prayer for Owen Meany*) is an obvious example; Siggy is another, less obvious, example.

Underneath the "coming of age" or *Bildungsroman* style of the novel is a larger philosophical theme. Irving tells his story in a way that enforces the notion of freedom for all individuals, a freedom to find one's own private place. As a first novel, *Setting Free the Bears* is a daring and imaginative work, introducing the predominant themes that were to pervade Irving's subsequent work.

THE WORLD ACCORDING TO GARP

First published: 1978
Type of work: Novel

The fictive biography of a writer in extremis, watching the world around him act out its destiny.

From the opening passages of this novel, the reader knows that an unusual story is about to be told. The prehistory of Garp is a wildly unorthodox conception: His mother, a nurse, physically cuts a soldier making a pass at her in a motion picture theater, then conceives Garp from another, almost comatose, dying soldier. Her life story later becomes her autobiography, *A Sexual Suspect*, "said to bridge the usual gap between literary merit and popularity," and it is in competition with Garp's novel, which is purely literary and not successful. Like Irving himself, the two writers fight with the apparent contradiction in the two approaches. As Garp struggles with his own writing, his life takes on all the aspects of cause and effect that he is trying to express in his work: His marriage almost fails, one child dies in a bizarre automobile accident in the family driveway, and both Garp and his mother are assassinated by ultra-sexist radicals (one male, one female).

As a youth, Garp attends the Steering School, another of the New England private schools that are favorite sites for Irving. One family, the Holms, consisting of Ernie and Helen, a wrestling coach and his daughter, are the nontraditional family that Irving incorporates into virtually all his novels. Garp's first writing environment is Vienna; his mother accompanies him there and she plans to write a little something herself. The writer as subject fills *The World According to Garp* with a second layer of meaning; the novel clearly represents an attempt on Irving's part to reconcile the elements of seriousness and popularity in his own work. Bizarre deaths continue, and accidents show that the plans of the characters must take accident and contingency into account. Irving establishes the notion of improbable events compiling life's experiences.

While Garp is constructing his first book, *The Pension Grillparzer*, he experiences the life of Vienna, in particular through his relations with several prostitutes. One, Charlotte, is a kind of mother substitute for Garp; she dies in a hospital where the nurses think Garp is her son. Meanwhile, his mother Jenny is managing to write a thousand-page autobiography, one which attains great popular success, much to Garp's chagrin. Garp sees a family of circus performers who own a trained bear, once again touching on Irving's preoccupation with caged and captive animals. It is as though all *The World According to Garp* is a reassembly of the symbols from Irving's own life, gathered together for an inventory; "life as a doomed effort at reclassification" is what one critic calls his chapter on *The World According to Garp.*

One of the reasons for this novel's success is its recapitulation of Irving's earlier motifs and their reconstruction around a hero who is, in fact, also a changer of facts to fit a poetic justice of his own. While it is clear that Garp and Irving are two different writers (a point that Irving has made many times in interviews by pointing out that his childhood was happy and his life uneventful), they both engage in the same writer's habits: procrastination, long planning without actual literary output, travel to broaden and enlighten, envy of but disdain for popular writers whose prolific output makes their own "writer's block" even more painful, and, the ultimate novelist's power, the ability to see in bizarre events a greater justice at work.

To live without forgiveness, without understanding, is wrong, according to Garp. He can forgive his wife's sexual infidelity (as she forgives his), even though it is partly responsible for the death of their youngest child. In the final analysis, *The World According to Garp* is a large idea with many digressions, all brought together in the novel's theme: Apparently disconnected events do, in fact, link up into a life, and forgiveness is essential to healing.

THE HOTEL NEW HAMPSHIRE

First published: 1981
Type of work: Novel

A father who is a dreamer seeks happiness for his family by running a series of hotels on two continents.

It is a miracle of novel writing that, once a financially successful and comprehensive novel has been published, the novelist can come up with yet another. The critics are always ready to pounce, and the drain of ideas from the previous novel is bound to tell on the imagination of the next. Irving wrote *The Hotel New Hampshire* in a remarkably short time, given the notoriety of his previous hit and claims on his time from filmmakers and interviewers. Large in scope and covering two continents, it does not stint in imagination, but it does make use of the groundwork of the others. Here, the father does not die in conception but is the hero of the book. The mother dies in a plane crash, as does the youngest child (who has the symbolic name of Egg), and the entire novel moves in a different circle from *The World According to Garp.* Eventually there is incest between a brother and sister (John and Franny), which is inaugurated in a sense by the previous gang rape of Franny, a violent event that John is helpless to prevent. There is also a sense of revenge, of justice done in the fictive world, or rather in the imagination of the author, that sets this book apart from Irving's previous success.

The novel begins with a long remembrance, in which the father of the family, Win Berry, recalls how he met his wife and fathered five children. The couple met at a seaside resort, where among their adventures they meet a Viennese bear trainer named Freud, who has taught the bear to ride on a motorcycle. The father purchases the bear, and Freud returns to Vienna, just before World War II. The resort, called Arbuthnot-by-the-Sea, is idyllic in the father's imagination, but when the family returns to it many years later, it has become run-down and ruined. The father's dream must then be realized, and he turns a former school into the first Hotel New Hampshire. His scheme is financially unfeasible, but he tries it anyway, and the child narrator (whose name, John, and year of birth, 1942, make the connection with Irving more than gratuitous) grows up experiencing the variety of life that temporarily inhabits the place.

The entire novel takes place in a succession of hotels, first at the resort on the seaside, then in the converted schoolhouse in the small town where the Berry family live, then in Vienna, at the invitation of a former guest, the Viennese Sigmund Freud (the bear trainer, not the famous psychiatrist). Win Berry, a dreamer, is always enchanted by the possibilities of the hotels—they are to him an extension of the warmth and love of his immediate family. Freud's trained bear is accidentally shot and is emotionally replaced by Sorrow, a black Labrador retriever who, even in death, is a symbol of the family's ability to revive and survive.

The first Hotel New Hampshire, in an abandoned schoolhouse, is in fact a school for the growth and maturity of the family. The midgets who come as guests, grown-ups in childlike bodies, are the counterparts of the Berry children, growing into their own adulthood in time to partake of the combination of love and violence awaiting them in Vienna. It is in the first Hotel New Hampshire that the family encounters its first series of problems: Franny's rape, the discovery that Lilly has dwarfism, and eldest brother Frank's admission of homosexuality. These problems cannot truly be called tragedies: In Irving's rendition, the family's acceptance of these events, without the destructive rancor and self-incrimination that usually taints such occurrences, renders them harmless, and the family remains intact and happy. Only during the transition from one hotel to another can true tragedy intervene. It is during this transition that the mother and Egg, the youngest child, die in a plane crash.

The second Hotel New Hampshire is in Vienna. Another bear enters the picture: a woman disguised in a bear suit, a strange lesbian character who first seduces Franny, then converts her to a feminist perspective. The prostitutes who live on one floor, and the terrorists on another, are a microcosm of the forces of the world—sex and violence—housed and even protected in the Hotel New Hampshire. Both groups believe "in the commercial possibilities of the ideal," the subject of more than one analysis of this novel. The climax of the novel, which takes place in a New York hotel, allows Franny, the sister, to get revenge (although her relationship to her teenaged rapist is more complex than that) and frees her finally from the inability to act that has haunted her since the rape. Another sister, Lilly, becomes a novelist; her first story, *Trying to Grow*, tells the family history from her perspective and is a success. In this respect she represents an aspect of Irving's own writing career, much as Garp's mother did in a previous novel.

Although John is the narrator for all the events of this story, his older sister, Franny, is the hero. The eventual punishment of Franny's rapist (with the improbable name of Chipper Dove) is an example of the overly romantic nature of Irving when dealing with his version of poetic justice. The incestuous affection between brother John and sister Franny is consummated near the end of the novel, but in a way that frees them both from any subsequent anxiety about their attraction.

The father is more important in this novel than in others from Irving's pen; he is a "dreamer" who is directly compared to Jay Gatsby, F. Scott Fitzgerald's creation, with his "white dinner jacket." Despite the recurring elements (such as Vienna and bears), Irving refers to this novel as a fairy tale. "You enter it . . . and while you're in it, its rules apply, yours don't."

For Irving, all the hotels are hostels, refuges against the madness outside the family unit, whether represented by political insanity or personal madness. Yet even inside the hotel there is madness—not only the obvious, such as that of the terrorists, but also the madness of John's desire for his sister, Franny; the inability of Franny to forget the rape; and the father's dreams that will always fail. The narrator can only watch as one hotel after the other rises and falls, always with a "bear" in the picture, another sign of violent life lived without guile. The mother's death, along with the suicide of a young prostitute, prompts John to remember and use over and over the admonition, which becomes a family motto, "Keep passing the open windows." It is the last line of the novel, and one of the first lines Irving wrote when beginning it. Irving told one interviewer that he knew how the novel would end, and he only had to fill in the rest.

THE CIDER HOUSE RULES

First published: 1985
Type of work: Novel

A doctor in an orphanage practices safe abortion while rearing a protégé who eventually rejects his philosophy.

Told in an omniscient style, *The Cider House Rules* is a Dickensian novel about the disenfranchised; it is unusual for Irving in that he does not make use of his "props"—Vienna, bears, and motorcycles. It is also an examination of the family from an entirely different perspective—an orphanage—and the abortion discussions in the book are another example of the violence inherent in the world as Irving sees it. It is a novel with a frankly social point of view, a "polemic," as some critics claim, yet Irving's actual stand on the issue of abortion is not clear at the end of the book. Dr. Larch, assigned to an orphanage in the small town of St. Cloud's, tries to prevent the pain and dangers of illegal abortions by performing them himself to "save the mothers." Many of the abortions are the result of incest, of girls being raped by their fathers or brothers. Dr. Larch is both obstetrician and abortionist; his protégé, Homer Wells, eventually takes a different view of abortion, and the novel's dynamics emerge from the contradiction.

The graphic descriptions of abortions and birth, together with fetuses and physical after-effects of the two processes, make this book a difficult one to read without some guidance. It is not so much a polemic in favor of a certain procedure as it is a frank, if fictive, discussion of the subtle consequences of both sides of the controversy—a graphic description of the less than ideal life of the orphan and the ruin of the mothers (especially those suffering from incest), compared with the very real deaths of the fetuses. By contrasting Dr. Larch with Homer and showing both as sympathetic characters, Irving manages to create a dynamic about the controversy. Especially impelling is the series of scenes in which Dr. Larch chooses to offer antiseptic, safe abortions as a defense against the abortions obtained in the abortion dens that cause more suffering than they alleviate.

One of the orphans, Homer, starts to learn the doctor's trade. Homer's gradual education about the ways of orphanages and about birth and death leads to a kind of apprenticeship with Dr. Larch, one which eventually will result in a false doctorate for Homer so that he can succeed Dr. Larch, who dies accidentally while inhaling ether—a habit he formed when trying to relieve his own gonorrhea.

Homer was born and reared in the orphanage and, through a series of "aborted" adoptions, has grown to be a part of the orphanage—to be "of some use." The story moves toward and away from a reconciliation of the basic premise—saving mothers or saving babies—and Homer himself is an example of a "saved" baby. It is a difficult and complex argument that brings Irving toward this fictional reconciliation and which gives this novel the sense of a "polemic" in a way that no other of his novels achieves.

At the center of Homer's argument against abortion is the idea that everything should be wanted, that a child not wanted is a contradiction in terms. Into maturity, he finds a couple to live with in a sunny part of Maine, conceives a child called Angel, and eventually returns to St. Cloud's under the fictitious name of Dr. Stone to continue the work of Dr. Larch. The sunny seaside where Homer goes with a young couple is the antithesis of the St. Cloud's atmosphere in which he was reared, and the "cloud" of his belonging to the orphanage is temporarily raised. When he and his lover, Candy, go back to the orphanage to have the baby Angel, he has returned in yet another capacity to the place of his own birth. He subconsciously wonders if he is in fact "wanted" on this earth, a perennial fear of all orphans, especially those abandoned intentionally by their parents.

Clearly discussing the problem of the morality of abortion, Irving is at the same time examining kinds of freedom. The orphans, while not exactly prisoners or animals in a zoo, are locked into their situation (the fact of their orphanhood). Homer has even made a "home" of his parentlessness after several parents have tried to make him their child (the last couple who try to adopt him are drowned in a log jam, another bizarre death).

In the act of writing a false history of the orphanage, Dr. Larch is in a sense the fictive novelist once again, this time writing to preserve and defend his point of view. He actually invents a fictional character, a doctor (given the name Stone) with a pro-life point of view, and elaborately underwrites his credentials, in order for Homer to be able to return to the orphanage and assume the fictive persona.

The character of Melony (misnamed from "Melody" at birth), young Homer's first lover, is another example of the strong, domineering, searching female in Irving's novels. She spends much of the novel's time searching for Homer, to remind him of his broken promise never to leave her. He first meets Melony when he begins reading Charlotte Brontë's *Jane Eyre* (1847) to the girls' side of the orphanage—Melony is the oldest and most sexually developed of the girls. The theme of incest in Irving's novels is more than a prurient aberration; it represents the combination of the two major love drives, that of the opposite sex and that of the family. By combining the two, Irving is saying that true love must somehow combine the two, not separate them.

This novel is much more linear than Irving's previous novels and is told by an omniscient narrator. Although the reader follows Homer in his growth into experience, he is definitely not the narrator as a child. The novelist does not define himself inside a character who is a writer; this is the world of doctors and orphanages. When the scene of the novel moves away from the orphanage, the reader is slightly uncomfortable, just as Homer is in the sunny seaside world that is the antithesis of St. Cloud's. One knows that he will return eventually to take Dr. Larch's place and sees this temporary adoption (although he is now an adult) as a sidetrack for Homer, who "belongs to the orphanage."

The central and often-repeated phrase, "to be of some use," is in fact the statement of purpose for all novelists of Irving's predilections. This "polemic" has a use if it enlightens the reader about the complexity of the problems of abortion versus orphanage, unwed motherhood, and incestuous unions and if it shows that the mother needs to be "saved" as well as the child. While it is true that the child who is "stopped" (in Dr. Larch's euphemism) leaves behind its fetus for Homer to discover, it is also true that the damage to the mothers of those children is less visible, except in the offices of the illegal abortionists, who extract for payment a promise to prostitute for them in the future. This cycle of depravity and uncleanness must be stopped, in Dr. Larch's view, and his way, the "Lord's Way," is to make the process hygienic and guilt-free, at least to the best of his ability.

That Irving writes an equally strong character, Homer, to offer counter-arguments shows that Irving himself sees the issue as immensely complex. He has focused on one single bizarre and unexplainable aspect of real life and shown how the novelist can "fix" it or can at least describe it in a way that the reader can decide which view is right. The reader is first introduced to Dr. Larch's point of view in some convincing scenes, first showing the terror of the illegal abortion room, then showing the positive results of his intervention. Later, as Homer grows up, the novelist shows the other side of the argument in equally convincing scenes, such as the discovery of the aborted fetus. Irving himself thereby takes the novelist's view, which is to describe and to locate the centers of each argument within the rhetoric of fiction.

A PRAYER FOR OWEN MEANY

First published: 1989
Type of work: Novel

The "hagiography" of Owen Meany, a tiny saint with a large voice, who is the essence of everything larger than life.

"'INTO PARADISE MAY THE ANGELS LEAD YOU,'" quotes Owen Meany over the grave of the narrator's mother. Tiny Owen Meany is an alter-ego for the novel's narrator, John Wheelwright. From the vantage point of the late 1980's, Wheelwright, a schoolteacher in Toronto, Canada, remembers the 1960's, when he and Owen were growing up in the small town of Gravesend, New Hampshire.

The story begins with an odd death of the sort that frequently occurs in Irving's novels: Owen accidentally kills John's mother by hitting a baseball which strikes her in the head. John, who takes his surname, Wheelwright, from his mother's family because his father is unknown, spends a good part of the novel wondering who his father is; at the moment of her death, he realizes his mother was waving to his father in the stands.

Owen, who never reaches normal adult stature, comes from an indrawn family, the local quarry owners. His relationship with John is like that between soul and body, separate but united; he eventually becomes the love interest of John's sister. At one point Owen plays the Christ child in a Christmas pageant. Indeed, Owen is Christlike in several respects; all of his lines appear in capital letters, reminiscent of red-letter Bibles that highlight the words of Jesus. Owen's words, in capital letters, are much more than conversational responses or innocuous chatter. By putting them in capitals, Irving gives them an importance that cannot be denied by even the casual reader. Everything Owen says seems practical, even wise, by comparison with those around him. His voice is large, both in print and in the rooms of the narrator's home. John's grandmother often remarks about the strange little boy with the big voice, a voice she and John hear long after Owen is gone. Owen is God's instrument; he has dreamed of his death: "AND NOW A DREAM HAS SHOWN ME HOW I'M GOING TO DIE. I'M GOING TO BE A HERO! I TRUST THAT GOD WILL HELP ME, BECAUSE WHAT I'M SUPPOSED TO DO LOOKS VERY HARD."

Owen and John practice a strange game of basketball, in which Owen is lifted up to the basket by John. This odd practice, apparently so trivial and removed from the important parts of life, will eventually save the life of some small children threatened by a terrorist's bomb. Irving is saying that the most trivial incident has a meaning and a purpose in a larger scheme.

In the climactic moment of the narrative, Owen saves the lives of some children by putting a bomb out of reach, imitating the basketball motions that he and John had practiced for so long. He dies in the subsequent explosion, but his life has been justified. The hours of practice with John have paid off in an unusual way, and the "sin" of killing John's mother with a baseball has finally been expiated.

The Irving ideology requires that the reader make a leap of faith from the improbable to the fictionally possible, here again establishing the novelist's power to make a world that is "righter" than the real world. If Irving has any single point to make, it is that fiction is not merely a form of autobiography; the world he creates is far from his own. If the real world were fairer or more just, he would not have to write fiction to fix it.

At the center of the novel is Owen's idea that there is no such thing as an accident—the "accident" of the baseball, for example, had its importance somewhere. In the final scene, all the seemingly arbitrary events come together. Just as the events of everyday life come together to have a meaning, so the novelist can supply effects to causes and tie together into a comfortable ideological package the incidents in the novel. Irving has mentioned in interviews that one of the major difficulties in writing a novel is hiding the seams, blending the diverse ideas from which the novel was generated into a coherent whole. Many critics see *A Prayer for Owen Meany* as the culmination of Irving's efforts to create such a seamless vision.

Summary

In order to write about the real world, Irving has tried to meet the extraordinary in combat and beat it at its own game. Throughout his sometimes echoing, recurring, and reflective novelistic worlds, a rightness prevails, guided by the hand and eye of the novelist, whose real job is "freeing the bears" of natural human impulses. There is no such thing as seediness or sin in Irving's novels—all smallness is strengthened by the largeness of life's positive value, and all sin is washed away by uplifting human emotions.

Bibliography

Atlas, James. "John Irving's World." *The New York Times Book Review*, September 13, 1981, p. 36.

Haller, Scot. "John Irving's Bizarre World." *Saturday Review* 8 (September, 1981): 30-32.

Harter, Carol C., and James R. Thompson. *John Irving*. Boston: Twayne, 1986.

Miller, Gabriel. *John Irving*. New York: Frederick Ungar, 1982.

Nelson, William. "Unlikely Heroes: The Central Figures in *The World According to Garp, Even Cowgirls Get the Blues*, and *A Confederacy of Dunces*." In *The Hero in Transition*, edited by Ray B. Brown. Bowling Green, Ohio: Bowling Green University Popular Press, 1983.

Thomas J. Taylor

WASHINGTON IRVING

Born: New York, New York
April 3, 1783
Died: Sunnyside, New York
November 28, 1859

Principal Literary Achievement

Recognized as the United States' first important writer, Irving is renowned for his influential prose style, native humor, and the creation of many memorable characters.

Biography

Washington Irving was born in New York City on April 3, 1783. He was the youngest of eleven children born to William and Sarah Irving. Washington was named after the first president of the United States and was once briefly presented to the founding father. William Irving was a stern figure who had come to America to seek his fortune and did achieve some financial success. Sarah and the numerous brothers and sisters indulged and pampered Washington. The family noted that the youngest child was a charming, sensitive, adventurous, imaginative individual who was a keen observer of life around him—traits that would stand him in good stead as a writer.

Irving was an indifferent student at school and often daydreamed. He showed great interest in English, literature, and fine arts but was bored with science, math, and the classical languages. His favorite writers were Joseph Addison, Oliver Goldsmith, Samuel Johnson, Miguel de Cervantes, Henry Fielding, and François Rabelais. Unlike his older brothers, Irving did not attend nearby Columbia College. In 1801, he began studying law privately. The following year, in 1802, his brother Peter established the *Morning Chronicle*, a partisan Manhattan newspaper. Irving began writing articles for him signed under the pseudonym "Jonathan Oldstyle," a practice he would continue during his literary career. The nineteen-year-old fledgling writer took the name from the rustic hero Jonathan in Royall Tyler's *The Contrast* (1787). Irving commented on many topics in a humorous vein, particularly on the theater.

Irving and his relatives published the *Salmagundi* papers from 1807-1808, a mixture of sensible and silly comments "to instruct the young, reform the old, correct the town, and castigate the age." The sensational success of "old Sal" made Irving realize that a living could be made as a writer. On December 6, 1809, under the name of "Diedrich Knickerbocker," Irving published the humorous book *A History*

of New York, from the Beginning of the World to the End of the Dutch Dynasty, a two-volume effort that made Irving famous in New York City. The book was written after a prolonged bout of melancholy brought on by the death of his fiancée, Matilda Hoffman, a tragedy that propelled him into permanent bachelorhood because "her image was continually before me, and I dreamt of her incessantly."

For the next decade, Irving half-heartedly plunged into his family's import business, briefly became editor of *Analectic Magazine*, and served as a colonel in the New York Militia in the War of 1812. Three years later, he went as a business representative for his family's company to England and remained for seventeen years. His mother's death and the failure of the business, for which he was partly responsible, triggered his second severe depression. The creative period which followed resulted in *The Sketch Book of Geoffrey Crayon, Gent.*, published in 1819-1820 in America and England. Written under the alias of Geoffrey Crayon, *The Sketch Book* is Irving's most important work. It spread his fame worldwide and earned for him literary immortality. Within four years he wrote *Bracebridge Hall* (1822), still under the pseudonym Crayon, and *Tales of a Traveller* (1824), both humorous works. Irving thought the latter book to be his best work, so the hostile reception by the American critics greatly disturbed the sensitive writer. In time he turned away from humorous pieces and began exploring the history genre.

Irving's career took a diplomatic turn in the 1820's, and he served at the U.S. legation in Madrid (1826); in 1829, he was appointed secretary of the legation in London. During that period, he wrote a number of historical works: *The Life and Voyages of Christopher Columbus* (1828), the first work under his own name; *A Chronicle of the Conquest of Granada* (1829); *Voyages and Discoveries of the Companions of Christopher Columbus* (1831); and *The Alhambra* (1832), perhaps his best unified work.

In 1832, Irving returned once again to the United States and his beloved New York. He was determined to remain in America "as long as I live," a promise broken only once by an appointment as ambassador to Spain from 1842 to 1846. Irving was widely hailed on his return home. He was lionized by dignitaries, awarded honorary doctorates by Columbia and Harvard colleges, and given many testimonial dinners. He bought property and considerably enlarged a house in Sunnyside on the banks of the Hudson River near Sleepy Hollow, establishing it as a retreat. Later it became his beloved home, where the curious and the famous sought him out.

Irving could not remain still for long and was soon bitten by the travel bug. He took off to see the American West, particularly to explore the Indian Territory. His travels resulted in three books: *A Tour on the Prairies* (1835), again by Crayon; *Astoria* (1836); and *The Rocky Mountains*, also known as *The Adventures of Captain Bonneville* (1837). For the next decade or so Irving wrote only one work, the *Biography of the Late Margaret Miller Davidson* (1841), a young woman poet who died at sixteen. Between 1848 and 1851, publisher George P. Putnam issued a fifteen-volume collection of the "Author's Revised Edition" series of Irving's work, beginning with *A History of New York* and closing with *The Alhambra*. It was a publishing first for America, proving profitable for both author and publisher, and it introduced a better sense of financial security to the writing profession. His last works were biographical affairs resulting in studies on the lives of Oliver Goldsmith (1849), Mahomet (1849), Mahomet's successors (1850), and George Washington (1855-1859), the latter a five-volume work. A few months after completing it, Irving died on November 28, 1859.

Analysis

Although best known today as an American humorist, Washington Irving's literary career also encompassed historical works and biographies. He was a prolific writer who took great delight in describing whatever interested his curious intellect. The author was a superb and influential prose stylist who influenced other writers, and he became America's first successful man of letters.

Irving's work can be categorized by the changes in his temperament, which also followed a chronological pattern. Beginning in 1802, this first period was marked by a certain recklessness of attitude. Irving assumed the persona of "Jonathan Oldstyle," and he reflected his own and the nation's positive exuberance following the overthrow of British tyranny. Serving out his literary apprenticeship, Irving's merry and vulgar Oldstyle looked at the citizens of New York City and found something to say about their culture, society, and politics. By the time Irving penned his burlesque *A History of New York* in the second period, he had settled down and developed into a stylish and confident amateur. The work is one of the great comic masterpieces of American literature, and "Diedrich Knickerbocker" was an original, almost mythical character. "Father Knickerbocker," in his recognizable tricorn hat, is still New York's official symbol. In the third and most creative phase, a mature Irving found his greatest literary expression in *The Sketch Book*, followed by two other pieces.

Critical reaction to Irving's humorous material forced the insecure author to become interested first in history and later in biography. The resultant histories of Spain and the American West are marred by an unscientific approach and are filled with romantic overtones. The biographies on Goldsmith, Mahomet, and Washington that appeared when the author was in his sixties are tired efforts and are marred by sentimentality. Irving's contributions to history and biography in the last period of life have not stood up well over time and are rarely read.

Irving penned most of his best work under a pseudonym, beginning with the Oldstyle pieces. He did so initially while he searched for an authentic voice, a practice that would take a lifetime. Irving always remained unsure of himself as a writer and undertook elaborate steps to disguise his own identity. Once a publisher provoked Irving's fury by appending the author's real name under the pseudonym to a published work (*A Chronicle of the Conquest of Granada* by "Fray Antonio Agapida").

Irving suffered from paralyzing bouts of melancholy during his life, usually following the death of a loved one. The depressed state would then be followed by a creative burst of energy that pushed aside the gloom. Yet his work characteristically contained a certain morbidity and fascination with cemeteries and death that seemed inappropriate in his lighter work. Even in his delightful *The Sketch Book*, there are some lachrymose pieces— "The Broken Heart," "The Widow and Her Son," and "Rural Funerals"—that underscore a subconscious preoccupation with death. Irving's literary career was not a smooth one. Throughout his life, he endured fallow periods when he wrote absolutely nothing. The dry spell could range anywhere from five to ten years, after which he would become productive again. Overall, his six decades of interrupted writing activity produced a voluminous amount of literature.

Irving's influence on American society during and after his lifetime was great. A complete set of his works in a private library was once considered the hallmark of an educated individual. Numerous writers, including nineteenth century American writers Herman Melville, Nathaniel Hawthorne, and Edgar Allan Poe, owe Irving a great literary debt, and his reputation, although dimmed by time, remains secure as America's first important writer. He is especially revered for his stories of native American humor, which found its best expression in *The Sketch Book*, particularly in the tales of "Rip Van Winkle" and "The Legend of Sleepy Hollow."

THE SKETCH BOOK OF GEOFFREY CRAYON, GENT.

First published: 1819-1820
Type of work: Short stories and essays

This disparate collection of short pieces reflects the author's catholic tastes and includes two classic tales of American literature.

Irving's *The Sketch Book of Geoffrey Crayon, Gent.* was first published in 1819 and 1820 in America in seven paperbound installments and then in two volumes in England. It became an immediate best-seller in both countries and started a line of other "sketch books" as imitative writers sought to capitalize on its success. *The Sketch Book* remains Irving's most important, influential, and popular work.

Irving became an overnight literary sensation and the first American writer to be lionized in England and Europe. The author, living in England at the time of publication, took the unusual step of publishing his work on both sides of the Atlantic because he feared that a pirated edition of his work would make its way to Britain. It was a well-founded fear, because there was no international copyright law to protect literary property, and pirating of popular material was a common practice. Irving's stratagem, therefore, was a clever move and protected his material from unscrupulous publishers. It also established a practice that other writers would emulate.

Irving's use of the character "Geoffrey Crayon" was a masterstroke. He fashioned an admirable figure by which to bring together his diverse collection of short pieces. Common themes run throughout *The Sketch Book* that tie the various stories together. The most prominent includes imprisonment, shipwreck, sterility, financial loss, and the function of the storyteller. The book brims with Jeffersonian idealism. Crayon is quick to point out America's vitality and growing importance even in his English pieces. In one essay, "English Writers on America," he condemns their temerity and suggests that England is a pygmy when compared to the United States. In the fifth part of *The Sketch Book*, Irving wrote a quintet on impressions of Christmas that is sometimes printed and lavishly illustrated separately as *Old Christmas.*

The Sketch Book is actually a literary potpourri designed to appeal to a variety of tastes, both American and English. It is made up of some thirty pieces. Each one marks a deliberate shift in tone and mood. About half of them are based on specific observations of life in England. There are also six literary essays, four traveling reminiscences, three short stories, and two pieces on the American Indian; three pieces defy easy classification. The work focuses on England, since only four contain specifically American content; however, two of those four— "Rip Van Winkle" and "The Legend of Sleepy Hollow"—have become legendary.

RIP VAN WINKLE

First published: 1819
Type of work: Short story

A henpecked village loafer wanders into the Catskill Mountains, sleeps twenty years at a single stretch, and returns to find that his familiar world has changed.

"Rip Van Winkle" is an American masterpiece of the short story. It is based on local history but is rooted in European myth and legend; it is the first American tale. Irving reportedly wrote it one night in England, in June, 1818, after having spent the whole day talking with relatives about the happy times spent in Sleepy Hollow. The author drew on his memories and experiences of the Hudson River Valley and blended them with Old World contributions.

"Rip Van Winkle" is such a well-known tale that almost every child in the United States has read it or heard it narrated at one time or another. Rip is a simple-minded soul who lives in a village by the Catskill Mountains. Beloved by the village, Rip is an easy-going, henpecked husband whose one cross to bear is a shrewish wife who nags him day and night. One day he wanders into the mountains to go hunting, meets and drinks with English explorer Henry Hudson's legendary crew, and falls into a deep sleep. He awakens twenty years later and returns to his village to discover that everything has changed. The disturbing news of the dislocation is offset by the discovery that his wife is dead. In time, Rip's daughter, son, and several villagers identify him, and he is accepted by the others.

One of Irving's major points is the tumultuous change occurring over the twenty years that the story encompasses. Rip's little Dutch village had remained the same for generations and symbolized rural peace and prosperity. On his return, everything has drastically changed. The village has grown much larger, new houses replace old ones, and a Yankee hotel occupies the place where the old Dutch inn once stood. The people are different, too. Gone are the phlegmatic burghers, replaced by active, concerned citizens. Rip returns as an alien to a place that once considered him important and discovers that life has passed on without his presence.

Irving makes clear that change is inevitable and that one pays a huge price by trying to evade it. Yet he also makes it clear in "Rip Van Winkle" that certain fundamental values may be lost when people prefer change to stability and are willing to sacrifice everything for material prosperity. Rip's return shows him to be completely disoriented by the march of time. Irving takes pity on his comical creation, however, and does not punish him. Instead, Rip is allowed back into the new society and tolerated for his eccentricities, almost as if he were a curiosity. Rip has slept through vital political, social, and economic changes, including the Revolutionary War, and he returns ignorant but essentially harmless. Irving's suggestion, then, is that Rip is a perfect image of America—immature, careless, and above all, innocent—and that may be why he has become a universal figure.

The recurring theme of financial failure evident in two pieces preceding "Rip" is also found here, as is the concept of sterility. Rip awakens twenty years later and discovers that his gun and his faithful dog are gone. He notes the changes in the village and sees another Rip Van Winkle character there, has a sudden loss of identity when he returns, and realizes that there has occurred the birth of a new nation, with the replacement of King George by George Washington. Irving emphasizes the comic rather than the tragic, because Rip turns all the above into a positive affirmation of himself. He acquires a new identity and has a wondrous tale to tell of irresponsibility which counterpoints the stress of puritan ethics.

The tale of "Rip Van Winkle" has found expression in other artistic mediums. Five stage plays have been made of the story, beginning in 1829. There have been three operas, several children's shows, and a television film by Francis Ford Coppola in 1985. Perhaps the most famous adaptation was made by noted nineteenth century American actor Joseph Jefferson III, who played the role of Rip for forty-five years in a very popular and much-beloved interpretation. Jefferson's vehicle proved to be one of America's most successful plays of the period. In the theater, it far surpassed in popularity Irving's other masterpiece—"The Legend of Sleepy Hollow."

THE LEGEND OF SLEEPY HOLLOW

First published: 1820
Type of work: Short story

A lanky, calculating schoolteacher is bested in romantic rivalry and driven away by a "demon" who preys on his deep-seated fear of the supernatural.

"The Legend of Sleepy Hollow," represents Irving's other comic masterpiece, a ghostly tale about "things that go bump in the night." The specter in question here is the mysterious Headless Horseman, said to be a Hessian trooper who lost his head in a nearby battle. Each night he roams the countryside in search of it. The unlikely hero in this tale is Ichabod Crane, an itinerant schoolmaster, whose name suits him perfectly.

> He was tall, but exceedingly lank, with narrow shoulders, long arms and legs, hands that dangled a mile out of his sleeves, feet that might have served for shovels, and his whole frame most loosely hung together.

Irving opens his tale with a marvelous and evocative description of the lush, charming Hudson Valley region of Sleepy Hollow near Tarry Town, the delightful and dreamy atmosphere pervading the place, and the tale of the Hessian trooper's ghost that supposedly roams near the churchyard. He then introduces the reader to Ichabod, a poor Connecticut Yankee who is very interested in marrying the wealthy, lovely, and flirtatious Katrina Van Tassel, daughter of the richest man in the area. Ichabod's plan is to ingratiate himself into her life, winning her hand in marriage. He arranges to teach her psalmody and is therefore permitted to visit Katrina on a regular basis at her family's prosperous farm. His interest in Katrina, however, is less than honorable. Ichabod wants to acquire her hereditary wealth and sell it off. His chief rival is a brawny local named Brom Bones, who loves Katrina for herself. Both men despise each other (Irving adroitly contrasts Yankee opportunism with Dutch diligence). Ichabod attends a party given by Katrina's father one night and later, on his way home, meets the terrifying Headless Horseman (Brom Bones in disguise), who drives the superstitious victim out of Sleepy Hollow forever.

Unlike "Rip Van Winkle," which appears among the first pieces in *The Sketch Book*, Irving placed "The Legend of Sleepy Hollow" last and followed it in a brief piece summarizing his final thoughts on the book. It too is set in the Hudson Valley, but Irving's point in this tale is markedly different. In "Rip Van Winkle" the old order gives way to the new, but the reverse is true here. The hypocritical Yankee Ichabod is defeated by the stalwart Dutch Brom, who represents the old order. The contrast between both men could not be more startling. Ichabod is a skinny, shrewd, calculating, sterile (and comic) individual, devoid of human affections, who relies on wit in his attempt to defeat his erstwhile rival. He is also a very gullible individual who believes in the supernatural, thus providing his opponent with the weapon that will destroy him. Brom, on the other hand, is a swaggering, athletic type inclined to mischievous pranks, but he does have deep romantic feelings for the beauteous Katrina. Brom is desperate to win her love, but he realizes that he cannot physically challenge his rival to a fight; hence, he devises a stratagem to prey on the schoolmaster's fear and drive him away from Sleepy Hollow.

Although "The Legend of Sleepy Hollow" is as familiar a tale as "Rip Van Winkle" to generations of schoolchildren, it has not had much success on the stage because of the difficulty of staging the thrilling chase scene at the end between Ichabod and the Headless Horseman. It has twice, however, been turned into a motion picture. The first was made in 1922, when the great cowboy humorist Will Rogers starred in a silent screen version retitled "The Headless Horseman," and the second in 1949, when Walt Disney created a full-length animated feature with Bing Crosby as narrator. It was also made into a television film in 1980.

"The Legend of Sleepy Hollow" is an endearing and charming tale full of good humor, yet it has serious social implications. It questions whether change and progress are better than stability and order. The old virtues of the settlers are more important than those of the destroyers. Irving sides with Katrina, who has rejected Ichabod's advances, and Brom Bones, who defeats his rival by playing on the hero's irrational fears. Irving implies that the practical man always will defeat the dreamer. With the creation of "Rip Van Winkle" and "The Legend of Sleepy Hollow," even if Irving had written nothing else, he would be elevated to literary greatness, because he fashioned two great American myths that perfectly symbolized American ideals and aspirations.

Summary

Washington Irving's monument near his beloved Sunnyside states that he was an "Essayist, Poet, Historian, Diplomat, Soldier." He was all those and much more. During his life, Irving wrote fables, legends, chronicles, tales, sketches, criticisms, plays, biographies, and histories in his impeccable prose style. His literary output was prodigious and fills many volumes. Future writers will forever be indebted to him. Irving achieved a large, adoring public and was widely admired at home and abroad; above all, he will forever be immortalized for his masterpieces "Rip Van Winkle" and "The Legend of Sleepy Hollow."

Bibliography

Bowden, Mary Weatherspoon. *Washington Irving*. Boston: Twayne, 1981.

Hedges, William L. *Washington Irving: An American Study, 1802-1832*. Westport, Conn.: Greenwood Press, 1965.

Langfeld, William R., and H. L. Kleinfield, eds. *Bibliography of Washington Irving*. Port Washington, N.Y.: Kennikat Press, 1968.

Leary, Lewis. *Washington Irving*. Minneapolis: University of Minnesota Press, 1963.

Myers, Andrew B., ed. *A Century of Commentary on the Works of Washington Irving*. Tarrytown, N.Y.: Sleepy Hollow Restorations, 1976.

____________. *Washington Irving: A Tribute.* Tarrytown, N.Y.: Sleepy Hollow Restorations, 1972.

Roth, Martin. *Comedy and America: The Lost World of Washington Irving*. Port Washington, N.Y.: Kennikat Press, 1976.

Williams, Stanley T. *The Life of Washington Irving*. 2 vols. New York: Octagon Books, 1971.

Terry Theodore

HENRY JAMES

Born: New York, New York
April 15, 1843

Died: London, England
February 28, 1916

Principal Literary Achievement

Celebrated in the final years of his life as "the Master," James was perhaps the greatest chronicler of the mores of the Anglo-American ruling classes in the age of imperialism.

Biography

Henry James, Jr., was born in New York City on April 15, 1843, the son of Henry James, Sr., the Swedenborgian philosopher, and Mary Robertson Walsh. The younger of two sons (his brother was the philosopher and psychologist William James), he also had a younger sister, Alice. As is clear from the second volume of his autobiography, *Notes of a Son and Brother* (1914), and from letters, Henry, Jr., often struggled in the shadow of his successful elder brother and strove all his life to carve out an independent career to rival William's.

Although a New Yorker by birth, James grew up principally in Cambridge, Massachusetts, with several important trips to Europe punctuating his youth and early manhood. Educated for the most part privately, the two James brothers pursued distinctive trajectories. William was to become a professor at Harvard University, marry, and rear a family, while Henry remained a bachelor all of his life and plied his trade as a writer almost exclusively abroad.

Having traveled in Europe several times between 1869 and 1875, James removed himself there permanently in October, 1875, rarely returning to the United States during the next forty years. Like many of the characters in his novels and tales, James was an émigré. His earliest works mined what he himself termed "the international theme," chronicling the lives of Americans encountering the exhilarating but often dangerous atmosphere of European culture and society.

Never so well off that he could simply write whenever and whatever he pleased, James nevertheless earned enough from his fiction, essays, and travel writings to sustain a comfortable upper-middle-class existence, traveling to the continent frequently while maintaining his principal residence in London and later at Lamb House in Sussex. His fiction of the 1870's, while it is still read and appreciated—in particular

The American (1877) and *Daisy Miller* (1878)—scarcely would qualify him as a major writer. With the publication of *The Portrait of a Lady*, however, which began serial publication in *Macmillan* magazine in October, 1880, it was clear that he had entered a new period, what F. O. Matthiessen would call his "major phase."

Throughout the 1880's and 1890's, James wrote steadily, even prolifically, producing many of the novellas and short stories on which his reputation in those genres now securely rests. Somewhat inexplicable, however, is the fact that this period saw the publication of none of what would now be considered his most important novels. In the mid-1890's he made a disastrous foray into the theater. The fiasco of *Guy Domville*, which opened at St. James's Theatre on January 5, 1895, to a hostile audience and an even more hostile critical reception, ended James's hopes that he might be released from financial necessity by becoming a popular dramatist. Stung by the experience, he retreated into a series of novels and tales of psychologically wounded children, emerging only after the turn of the century to explore once again the intricacies of adult mental life.

It is idle to speculate what James might have written had his dramas not failed so miserably. What is certain is that between 1900 and 1909, the mature writings on which his later reputation would be based fairly flooded from his pen—or, to be more precise, from his mouth, since he had by that time hired a stenographer, to whom he dictated his prose. Three enormous novels, *The Wings of the Dove* (1902), *The Ambassadors* (1903), and *The Golden Bowl* (1904), appeared, along with the classic tales "The Beast in the Jungle" (1903) and "The Jolly Corner" (1909). James also returned to the United States for a year's visit in 1904, his first since 1883. Out of his travels—partly a lecture tour—he wrote one of his finest, if least appreciated, pieces of cultural criticism, *The American Scene* (1907).

The crowning achievement of this, James's last fertile period, was the monumental "New York edition" of his novels and tales, over which he labored from 1907 to 1909. James undertook the enormous task of selecting and, in many cases, closely rewriting his earlier fiction, arranging it in a sensible order (not purely chronological) and, most important of all, providing a series of magisterial prefaces to the various volumes. Although they are (at best) ambiguous guides to the stories they introduce, these prefaces remain a landmark in the theory of fiction, as Richard Blackmur shrewdly discerned when he collected them into a single volume under the title *The Art of the Novel: Critical Prefaces by Henry James* (1934).

Commercially, the New York edition was not successful; it was the crowning disappointment for a man who had borne more than his share over the years. It is probably fair to say that James's reputation during his lifetime, while it remained high among a select audience of high-culture consumers, never reached the level it would during the years following World War I, when his works became one of the staples of college and university literature courses in the English-speaking world. Awarded the Order of Merit on New Year's Day, 1916—he had become a British subject in July, 1915—James would outlive the honor by less than two months. He died on February 28, 1916, from the lingering effects of a stroke suffered the previous December.

Analysis

The distinctive focus of James's early fiction is undoubtedly what James himself dubbed "the international theme." From *Roderick Hudson* (1875) and *The American* to *Daisy Miller, The Portrait of a Lady,* and "The Aspern Papers" (1888), James wrote about Americans in Europe. One might invoke the "innocents abroad" of the Mark Twain title to characterize James's overarching sense of how his countrymen, generally wealthy and in search of a cultural breadth and depth unavailable in the Gilded Age United States, came to grief when they encountered the older, more settled, socially entrenched European culture.

The classic examples are *Daisy Miller* and *The American*. In the former, the ingenue heroine dies when she foolishly ignores warnings not to venture out in the Roman evening when the danger of contracting fever is greatest. Her life and death allegorize the classic Jamesian sense that Americans are vulnerable when they go to Europe, that they are simply naïve in the ways of the world and thus easily fall prey to the wiles of the more cunning and worldly Europeans. *The American* makes the same point less dramatically, depicting the tragic involvement of Christopher Newman, a disillusioned robber baron who has come to Paris to escape the ruthless competition of American business, with an old French family whose daughter he loves and wishes to marry. Newman thinks that his money (which the family desires) and native good sense will be proof against the family's determined resistance to accepting him as a son-in-law. Too late he realizes that the rules of society are completely different in Europe, that discriminations and nuances that have matured over generations count for more than personal determination and a hefty bank balance.

James would never abandon the international theme entirely; it would in fact be central to his late masterpieces, *The Ambassadors, The Wings of the Dove,* and *The Golden Bowl*. From *The Portrait of a Lady* onward, however, the capacity of Americans to deal on equal terms with Europeans, to hold their own in the strategic game of manipulating social power, demonstrably improves. It may be that this raising of Americans' stock, as it were, reflected James's own growing confidence in himself, both socially and artistically. What seems more likely, however, is that James lived through a period when the balance of economic—hence social—forces had begun to shift dramatically in favor of the United States, particularly in relation to Britain and France, the two countries he knew best. Americans had been going abroad in growing numbers since before the Civil War; James's own family was a prime example. With the definitive triumph of Northern industrial capital over the Southern plantocracy, however, the stage was set for a massive expansion of the American economy, with the building of the railroads, heavy investment in coal and iron production, and the opening of the Western prairies for capitalist agriculture. By the 1880's, and increasingly in the decades preceding World War I, American economic power was challenging Britain for global supremacy; often the Americans were getting the best of it. This, one may surmise, is the relevant background to the demonstrably more powerful American characters who inhabit James's mature fiction.

Much has been written about James's prose style, especially about its growing complexity—even obscurity—in the last twenty years of his life. Close attention to the texts, however, reveals that while the periodicity of his sentences did grow as he matured, it is less their syntactic oddity—James's sentences characteristically parse perfectly well—than their figurative richness that makes James's prose bewildering.

The difficulty of James's later writings is related to another feature that, while it was always observable in his fiction, assumes greater prominence in the texts of his final period. These narratives are often controlled by central symbols announced in the title: for example, the biblical image of the Holy Spirit in *The Wings of the Dove*, or the famous *objet d'art* in *The Golden Bowl*. The symbolic power of these central figures ramifies through the texts in subtle and occasionally explicit ways, but it is never obvious how one is to resolve their meaning. James was notoriously resistant to stating his thematic purposes openly, as the prefaces to the New York edition and his notebooks testify, and this tendency to circumlocution, obliqueness, and downright reticence became more and more the norm in his writing from the late 1890's onward. It has often been remarked that the archetypal Jamesian tale is "The Figure in the Carpet" (1896), a maddeningly elusive story about the fruitless search for the key or secret to a fictional writer's corpus. Unlike Irish writer James Joyce, whose fondness for more or less rigorous allegorical systems led him to construct codes by which to decipher the large-scale structures underlying his narratives, James neither professed nor (apparently) ever seriously entertained the notion that his texts could be interpreted by reference to a fixed code or system of controlled meanings.

Indeed, it is often all but impossible to state directly what James's texts are finally about. To say that *The Ambassadors* or *The Wings of the Dove* is about renunciation, or that "The Altar of the Dead" (1895) is about mourning, is not so much wrong as it is banal. At this level, one might say that thematic accounts of James inevitably fail. The subject matters of his texts are invariably less interesting than the intricate moves and countermoves plotted and enacted by the characters set down in the situations James has concocted for them. Similarly, as James's prose becomes more and more figuratively dense and textured, the weight of analysis must fall on the rhetorical structure of his sentences. Although reading the later James is probably an acquired taste, patience and close attention to the figural dimensions of his language will repay the effort.

DAISY MILLER

First published: 1878
Type of work: Novella

On a trip abroad, a guileless American ingenue dies from a fever contracted when, against all advice, she goes out in the disease-ridden air of Roman evenings.

"Daisy Miller" was James's first commercial success; it made him immediately famous as the chronicler of "the international theme" and remains, after "The Turn of the Screw" (1898), probably his most widely known work. A characteristic example of James's early fiction, which is indebted to the allegorical tradition of Nathaniel Hawthorne, the novella establishes a recurrent theme that would be reworked with increasing complexity as James's career developed.

On an excursion to Vevey, Switzerland, to visit an aunt, Frederick Winterbourne, an expatriate American resident for a number of years in Geneva, encounters the Miller family, wealthy Americans touring Europe. While the businessman father has remained home in Schenectady, Mrs. Miller, her son Randolph, and her daughter Daisy are sampling the pleasures of European tourist attractions. Winterbourne is immediately attracted to the young, beautiful, and flirtatious Daisy, who innocently ignores all the social conventions governing the conduct of young women in Europe, scandalizing Winterbourne's aunt, Mrs. Costello, but charming and intriguing Winterbourne himself. Daisy extorts from him a promise to visit her in Rome in the coming winter, and the tale turns to their relations there.

In the intervening months, Daisy has taken up with a handsome Italian named Giovanelli, with whom she has rendezvouses in the evenings—against the advice of both her mother and the resident American hostess, Mrs. Walker. They warn her about the insalubrious Roman air, but it is clear that, for Mrs. Walker at least, the impropriety of meeting handsome men, unaccompanied, is the more pressing danger. On one evening, Winterbourne accompanies Daisy, much to his consternation, for he is, it seems evident, both attracted and unable to comprehend her. He remarks:

> It was impossible to regard her as a perfectly well-conducted young lady; she was wanting in a certain indispensable delicacy. It would therefore simplify matters greatly to be able to treat her as the object of one of those sentiments which are called by romancers "lawless passion." . . . But Daisy, on this occasion, continued to present herself as an inscrutable combination of audacity and innocence.

As Winterbourne attempts vainly to warn Daisy that she is becoming the talk of the American colony, the young, headstrong woman continues to ignore him and all the proprieties. The climax of the story occurs when Daisy again ventures out into the Roman night—this time even her Italian admirer Giovanelli counsels against it—and encounters the furious Winterbourne in the Colosseum. With Giovanelli's consent, he insists they return home, but the rescue comes too late. Daisy contracts the "Roman fever" (malaria, one presumes) and dies shortly thereafter. Belatedly, Winterbourne realizes that he had done Daisy an injustice by believing the worst of her, and he assuages his guilt by returning to Geneva, where he is, depending upon which reports one believes, either engaged in study or involved with "a very clever foreign lady."

The allegory and the moral situation in "Daisy Miller," are simple enough. What remains ambiguous, as it does so often in James, is the ending. What is one to make of the contradictory reports of Winterbourne's life in Geneva? How is one to interpret his expressed intention to return to the United States in the wake of Daisy's death, and then his not doing so? The interpretive dilemma at the end, with all its moral and psychological ramifications, appropriately forecasts the characteristic difficulties involving plot and character in virtually all James's future fiction.

THE PORTRAIT OF A LADY

First published: 1880-1881
Type of work: Novel

A young American heiress traveling in Europe is duped into marrying a cultured but passionless American expatriate, discovers her mistake, and is confronted by the dilemma of what to make of the marriage.

The Portrait of a Lady is James's first unarguably major work. Technically his third novel (though the early *Watch and Ward*, published in 1871, is by general agreement unworthy of mention), it represents a quantum leap in sophistication and moral complexity over *Roderick Hudson* and *The American*. Thematically continuous with "Daisy Miller" in that it treats the perils of an innocent American heiress abroad, the novel probes the psychology of its heroine, Isabel Archer, to infinitely greater depths than does the earlier novella.

The reader first encounters Isabel Archer at the English country house of the Touchetts, relations by marriage. Her aunt, Lydia Touchett, has brought her from the United States after the death of Isabel's father. Pursued by the feckless British aristocrat, Lord Warburton, and the crude American, Caspar Goodwood, Isabel is also especially admired by her invalid cousin, Ralph Touchett, who gives her an enormous bequest from his father's estate.

While visiting her aunt in Italy, Isabel meets Madame Merle, an elegant, cultured woman who maintains a respectable life by imposing on the hospitality of her wealthy acquaintances. Madame Merle introduces Isabel to Gilbert Osmond, an American expatriate living in quiet retirement in a Roman villa with his daughter Pansy. Disarmed by Osmond's cultivation and taken with Pansy, Isabel accepts Osmond's offer of marriage, only to discover that he has effectively imprisoned her and, to her immense dismay, that he was formerly Madame Merle's lover and Pansy is their illegitimate offspring. Isabel realizes that any attempt to sunder their bond will lead to Pansy's suffering; since Isabel genuinely cares for Pansy, she is caught on the horns of a classic Jamesian moral dilemma.

Summoned to England to see her dying cousin Ralph, Isabel encounters both Lord Warburton, who offers to marry her (she declines), and the egregious Caspar Goodwood, who in a rare scene of explicit passion in James, forcefully embraces Isabel:

> His kiss was like white lightning, a flash that spread, and spread again, and stayed; and it was extraordinarily as if, while she took it, she felt each thing in his hard manhood that had least pleased her, each aggressive fact of his face, his figure, his presence, justified of its intense identity and made one with this act of possession. So had she heard of those wrecked and under water following a train of images before they sink. But when darkness returned she was free. She never looked about her; she only darted from the spot . . . She had not known where to turn; but she knew now. There was a very straight path.

As in much of James's writing, while the meaning of this ending (the finale actually comes some lines later, when the reader learns that Isabel has returned to Rome) seems clear enough, what will become of Isabel when she rejoins Osmond is far from certain. In a gesture that will become the very signature of James's mature fiction, she renounces her freedom and assumes the moral burden of defending Pansy from Osmond's revenge. Yet whether she will remain, as she had been prior to the discovery of Osmond's and Madame Merle's machinations, a submissive and suffering spouse is more difficult to determine. If James's later heroines are any guide here, it may be surmised that Isabel will now be more than a match for her unscrupulous and soulless husband.

Along with *The American*, *The Portrait of a Lady* was one of the texts James revised most heavily for publication in the New York edition of his novels and tales. In general, these revisions did not alter the basic elements of the plot, but they tended, in line with James's later conception of his work, to render more ambiguous its ultimate outcome.

WHAT MAISIE KNEW

First published: 1897
Type of work: Novel

Shuttled off by her divorced parents to various caretakers and minders, young Maisie Farange discovers truths about human selfishness while contriving to secure a stable home for herself.

When Mr. and Mrs. Beale Farange are divorced, they receive joint custody of their young daughter Maisie. At first, both jealously guard their privileges, using Maisie as a weapon to wreak revenge on each other. Then, as they themselves become involved with new lovers, Maisie is increasingly forgotten, left to fend for herself with little more guidance and affection that what is to be had from her ridiculous governess, Mrs. Wix.

As it happens, Ida Farange's new husband, Sir Claude, has some scruples and is genuinely fond of Maisie. It is he who takes over her care—indeed, her entertainment—for the most part, while her selfish and heedless parents all but abandon her. Sir Claude and Ida eventually go their separate ways, however, and he takes up with

Beale's new wife, Miss Overmore. This puts the highly scrupulous Mrs. Wix in a compromising position, which she applies equally to the hapless Maisie, who would, it seems, be quite content to go on living with Sir Claude and his new mistress.

At this point, the extent of Maisie's extraordinarily canny grasp of her situation and of the intricate amorous games being played all around her becomes clear. She quite brazenly bargains with various adults to secure her own care, preferably with Sir Claude. He takes her to France with Mrs. Wix, only to be pursued there by Ida, or Mrs. Beale, as she is most frequently called. In a climactic confrontation, Sir Claude dispatches Maisie and Mrs. Wix back to England, promising never to abandon Maisie, although he seems to have returned to Ida, who, presumably, has no desire to have her gay life interrupted by the duties of caring for a young child.

The novel takes a pathetic subject and treats it with extraordinary tact and splendid comedy. James claimed in the preface to this text in the New York edition that the entire interest of the tale lay in its being told as if from the point of view—though not in the language—of the child. This consciously imposed constraint makes for occasionally difficult going, since while Maisie's consciousness demonstrably matures in the course of the novel, it is not always immediately clear what she beholds, since her knowledge of adult relations is for quite some time rather inexact. Still, *What Maisie Knew* remains among James's minor masterpieces, perhaps the first of the mature texts that someone new to the Jamesian manner should attempt.

THE TURN OF THE SCREW

First published: 1898
Type of work: Novella

In an English country house, a high-strung governess discovers that her charges are in the power of ghosts who have corrupted them.

Ghost stories would appear at first not to be James's natural genre, but like all of his mature fiction, "The Turn of the Screw" exhibits important complications. In the first place, the tale is framed by a nameless narrator's relating how one evening a man identified only as Douglas read a manuscript—which is the story one is about to read—to an audience eager to hear a ghost story. From the outset, then, the story is placed at several removes from the reader. Questions about Douglas, the narrator, and the authorship of the manuscript all remain maddeningly unresolved. It is also futile to attempt to resolve the question of whether the ghosts in the story are real.

The tale itself is simple enough in outline. The nameless governess has been hired by her similarly nameless employer to look after his orphaned nephew and niece, Miles and Flora. Sent down to the employer's country house for this purpose, the governess encounters the ghosts of Peter Quint, her employer's dead former valet, and Miss Jessel, her predecessor as the children's governess. From the housekeeper, Mrs. Grose, the governess learns that Quint and Miss Jessel were intimate, and that they may have corrupted the children. In a series of bizarre incidents, the governess becomes convinced that the ghosts have indeed possessed the children, and she resolves to protect her charges from further harm by keeping them there at Bly—Miles was to have returned to school, having been expelled earlier for possibly immoral conduct—under her watchful eye. Her vigilance fails, however, as Flora is discovered wandering near the lake one night where Mrs. Grose sees the ghost of Miss Jessel. Directing Mrs. Grose to take Flora to her uncle, the governess confronts Miles alone and tries to liberate him from the ghosts by extracting a confession of his past sins. At the climactic moment, Quint's specter appears at a window, in response to which the governess shields Miles, who confesses his crimes and then dies in the governess' arms.

There the story ends, and one can see why it has elicited the large volume of commentary that it has. The reader cannot know whether the ghosts are real or are a product of the governess' hysteria. One does not know if Miles is guilty, as he admits, or is prodded into a false confession by the governess' incessant inquisition; the reader is not told why Miles dies. It is most unlikely that this series of questions will ever be definitively answered—which is, one imagines, precisely what James intended.

THE AMBASSADORS

First published: 1903
Type of work: Novel

A middle-aged American comes to Paris to rescue a young friend from the clutches of a European woman but discovers that the conventional morals he has been sent to protect must be sacrificed to more cosmopolitan values.

The Ambassadors, the first written but second published of James's final trilogy, resurrects his early preoccupation with the effect of Europe on Americans. James's handling of the theme here, however, is infinitely richer and more nuanced than in his earlier fiction. Above all, the ambiguous relationship between aesthetic sensibility and conventional moral values is rendered with consummate skill.

Lambert Strether, a middle-aged bachelor from Woolett, Massachusetts, has been sent to Paris to bring home the son of the woman whom he is planning to marry. Strether, who has not been abroad for many years, discovers that Chad Newsome is amorously involved with a French woman, though Strether mistakenly believes at first that his love interest is the young Jeanne. Charmed by the manner in which Chad has matured during his time in Paris, Strether delays to the point that the Newsomes themselves (absent the mother) appear on the scene to take matters in hand. Strether is in a difficult position, since his material well-being depends significantly on Mrs. Newsome's good will.

While on a solitary excursion into the French countryside, Strether fortuitously encounters Chad in a romantic interlude with his lover, who turns out to be the middle-aged Marie de Vionnet, Jeanne's mother. Shocked, but finally persuaded that the principles by which he has lived have deprived him of a fulfilling life, Strether decides to return to the United States without disclosing the secret of Chad's illicit liaison. In the final scene, Strether, having renounced his obligation to the Newsomes, is approached by Maria Gostrey, a woman who has been pursuing him discreetly ever since his arrival in Europe. Strether declines her invitation to remain in Europe with him, thus reasserting his basic dignity and moral sense and depriving himself of pleasure he might otherwise have enjoyed. That Strether has in some sense matured does not mean that all of his ethical values have been nullified.

Declared by James himself to be his most structurally perfect work, *The Ambassadors* does exhibit an uncharacteristic economy and tightness in plotting. The shortest of the final three novels, it is also on the face of it the least substantial, taking as its theme the moral dilemma of a somewhat priggish man confronting the fact of adultery. Unlike *The Wings of the Dove* and *The Golden Bowl*, where the sexual relations of major characters constitute a direct betrayal of the heroine, in *The Ambassadors*, Strether is merely disillusioned by Chad's having concealed the truth about his affair with Madame de Vionnet. Readers must decide, as many have, that the problem of a middle-aged man being initiated into a broader, more aesthetic universe is of intrinsic interest in order for this novel to be valued. It is an open question whether the notion of aesthetic education, on which the novel turns, can bear the weight James attributes to it.

THE GOLDEN BOWL

First published: 1904
Type of work: Novel

A young American heiress marries an impoverished Italian prince, only to discover that an old friend, who has become her widowed father's wife, has been carrying on an illicit affair with the heiress' husband.

The last of James's completed novels, *The Golden Bowl* is arguably his crowning achievement, gathering together many of the major thematic concerns that dominated his entire career and weaving them into a rich tapestry of intrigue and psychological warfare. As nearly always in James, marriage and money are basic ingredients, but here these provide only the barest givens. The real force of the story derives from the subtle maneuverings, first of Charlotte Stamp and later of Maggie Verver (with some considerable assistance from her father, Adam), to secure the love of Maggie's husband, Prince Amerigo.

On the eve of Maggie's and the prince's marriage, Charlotte Stamp, an old friend of Maggie, arrives in London to attend the ceremony. Unknown to Maggie, Charlotte was once the prince's lover, and she enlists his help in choosing an appropriate wedding gift—the gilded crystal bowl of the title. After the wedding, Charlotte remains, at Maggie's urging, to act as companion to Maggie's father, the millionaire Adam, whom Maggie feels she has abandoned. Adam ultimately asks Charlotte to marry him, and in the course of the two couples' life together, she resurrects her affair with the prince. By chance, Maggie discovers that Charlotte and the prince had purchased the bowl together, surmising the truth about their past and the painful reality of their present relations.

Maggie is thus confronted with a dilemma: Either she must continue to tolerate her husband's adultery or she must contrive to send Charlotte away, with the result that she will be deprived of her father. Opting for the latter, Maggie persuades her father to return with Charlotte to America and undertakes the daunting task of constructing a secure relationship with her husband. While the fate of Maggie and the prince remains in the balance at the end, the real losers are surely Adam and Charlotte, the former because he is now forever separated from his daughter, the latter because she is exiled from the only amorous ties to which she can aspire—it being reasonably clear that Adam is impotent.

While the plot of *The Golden Bowl* is in a way simple, and the premise uncomplicated, the rich, textured performance of the novel transforms the materials into a powerful portrait of the complex psychology of adultery and power. Maggie's ostensible maturity in accepting the fact of her husband's adultery is matched by the ruthless cunning she evinces in removing her rival from the field—this all without ever openly declaring her knowledge or her intentions. It is by no means clear at the end that Maggie and the prince's relations can be so readily resolved, although the prince's dependence on Maggie's fortune will surely constrain his behavior, as it motivated him to marry her in the first place. Beneath this plot of love and intrigue lies a fable about the growing hegemony of American wealth in the world market, for it is that which has brought Maggie and the prince together and sustains their marriage. If the impotent Adam Verver is one side of James's image of the American *haute bourgeoisie*, the resourceful and single-minded Maggie is surely the other. Bereft of her innocence in much the same way as Isabel Archer, Maggie Verver contrives a more forceful plan of action that, if it does not absolutely ensure her supremacy over her husband, gives her a much more powerful hand to play.

THE ASPERN PAPERS

First published: 1888
Type of work: Short story

Having learned that some letters of poet Jeffrey Aspern are in the possession of the poet's former mistress in Venice, an American editor attempts to purloin them from her.

A minor masterpiece, "The Aspern Papers" is perhaps not so familiar to non-aficionados of James as "The Beast in the Jungle" or "The Turn of the Screw." Combining intrigue, seduction, and James's great gift for psychological subtlety, this tale deserves to be ranked among James's greatest short fictions.

A nameless editor who has devoted his life to publishing all the bits and scraps he can gather of the fictional American poet Jeffrey Aspern learns that Aspern's former lover, Juliana Bordereau, who resides in Venice, has kept Aspern's love letters to her. Realizing that procuring the letters will be no easy task, the editor schemes to obtain them by first renting rooms in the palazzo occupied by Juliana and her spinster niece Tita, then attempting to charm both the women. As the tale unfolds, it becomes clear that the conniving editor, whom Juliana will call a "publishing scoundrel," is himself being manipulated. He believes that by wooing Tita he will gain access to the letters, and indeed one night does steal into Juliana's quarters, only to be caught in the act by Juliana herself.

He leaves Venice in shame, returning to discover that Juliana has died and the papers are in Tita's hands. She has been ordered to burn them rather than let anyone else see them, but offers that Juliana's edict would not apply to a family member. Repulsed by the prospect of marrying the plain and somewhat dull Tita, the editor flees, only to return in the evening and request an interview with Tita the next day. As she enters the room, he beholds her transformed (by his imagination) and realizes that he is indeed willing to "pay the price," as he puts it. He has come too late, however, Tita has already destroyed the papers. In a fine touch of cruelty, worthy of the dead Juliana herself, Tita observes that she burned them one at a time and that consequently "It took a long time—there were so many."

Doubtless this story resonates with James's own fears as a writer of having his bones picked over after death, but the tale's power derives less from this personal anxiety, which many writers have experienced, than from its taut plot with its delineation of cunning and calculation. The unscrupulous editor is finally no match for the wily Juliana, nor even for the suddenly crafty Tita—or has Tita's guile been there all along? Has she been a willing accomplice to Juliana's machinations? The tale leaves this as a tantalizing possibility. Like Aspern's letters, which are never actually produced, the contents of Tita's consciousness remain an insoluble mystery to the end.

Summary

Henry James's fiction, especially his later works, is complex—psychologically, stylistically, and morally. T. S. Eliot once observed that James "had a mind so fine no idea could ever violate it." While literally untrue—James's problem was precisely that he had too many ideas and that all of them qualified and altered each other ceaselessly—Eliot's judgment does suggest something important about James's writing. "Fineness," in the sense of precision, is just what James's fiction seeks most relentlessly. Reading his work should be proof against any tendency to reach hasty conclusions about human motivation, about human action, and indeed about knowledge itself.

Bibliography

Anesko, Michael. *"Friction with the Market": Henry James and the Profession of Authorship.* New York: Oxford University Press, 1986.

Bell, Ian F. A., ed. *Henry James: Fiction as History.* Totowa, N.J.: Barnes & Noble Books, 1985.

Edel, Leon. *The Life of Henry James.* 5 vols. Philadelphia: J. B. Lippincott, 1953-1972.

Gale, Robert L. *Plots and Characters in the Fiction of Henry James.* New York: Shoe String Press, 1965.

James, Henry. *The Art of the Novel: Critical Prefaces by Henry James.* Edited by R. P. Blackmur. New York: Charles Scribner's Sons, 1934.

Matthiessen, F. O. *Henry James: The Major Phase.* New York: Oxford University Press, 1944.

Rowe, John Carlos. *The Theoretical Dimensions of Henry James.* Madison: University of Wisconsin Press, 1984.

Wicke, Jennifer. *Advertising Fiction: Literature, Advertisement, and Social Reading.* New York: Columbia University Press, 1988.

Michael Sprinker

ROBINSON JEFFERS

Born: Pittsburgh, Pennsylvania
January 10, 1887

Died: Carmel, California
January 20, 1962

Principal Literary Achievement

Unique in his achievements in narrative, lyric, and dramatic poetry, Jeffers centered his work on the characters and landscapes of the California coast, capturing their stark grandeur.

Biography

John Robinson Jeffers was the first son of William Hamilton Jeffers, professor of Old Testament literature at Western (Presbyterian) Theological Seminary, and Annie Robinson Tuttle, a gifted amateur musician. On both sides, Jeffers was descended from generations of strict Calvinists. For seven years an only child, he was treated as a prodigy by his father, who introduced the boy to reading Greek at five, after working on English and French. His early education included extended travel to England and the Continent. This home tutoring continued throughout most of his early life, while he attended various private schools near Pittsburgh and in Europe. At fifteen he entered college in Pennsylvania, transferring to Occidental College in California when his parents moved there a year later. In 1905, he began graduate studies in literature at the University of Southern California.

There he met Una Call Kuster, a fellow student who was already married to a Los Angeles attorney. Jeffers, with little worldly experience, was overwhelmed by her combination of beauty, polish, and sophistication. The couple fell in love, and Una considered divorce, at that time still a radical, socially unacceptable act. The two were separated forcibly: Una went to live with relatives, in the East and then in Europe, and Jeffers embarked on tour with his parents. He broke with them, however, declaring independence at the age of nineteen, and enrolled briefly in the science curriculum of the University of Zurich. From there he returned to USC, entering medical school and completing the three-year program, although he did not take his degree.

This was an eight-year span of acute emotional turmoil and social experimentation in his life, and it was the only time he pursued the bohemian life-style of young intellectuals. He lodged anywhere from his professors' homes to beachfront cottages

to laborers' boarding houses, and he did things as diverse as winning the heavyweight college wrestling championship and spending a summer bumming on the beach. Two elements, however, survived this upheaval. One was his dedication to poetry; from age fifteen he had vowed to become the American equivalent of English poet and painter Dante Gabriel Rossetti, the leader of the nineteenth century Pre-Raphaelite movement. Though the kind of poetry he aspired to write would change, the intensity of his dedication never wavered. The second was his love for Una.

After leaving medicine, Jeffers moved to Seattle, where he spent a year studying forestry. In 1912, he returned to Los Angeles; a small bequest allowed him to publish *Flagons and Apples* (1912), a collection of largely derivative, competent lyrics in traditional forms. The next year he was back in Washington, where Una finally acquired her divorce; they were married on August 2, 1913. This was the turning point in Jeffers' life, for Una proved exactly the person to stiffen his will.

Not that they lived without trouble—in the first year of their marriage, first Jeffers' father died; then the couple's newborn daughter survived only one day; and World War I, the cataclysmic event of their generation, broke out in Europe. They needed a solitary retreat to recover their balance, which they chanced upon in the then-remote Carmel, on the Monterey peninsula. They rented a cottage in the pines. As their stay extended to several years, they came to identify, spiritually and emotionally, with the rugged coast. Eventually Jeffers purchased several acres, on which he began constructing, from native stone and mostly by his own effort, the house-and-tower complex he named "Tor House." There he and Una reared and educated their twin sons, Donnan and Garth, born in 1916.

That year also saw the publication of his second volume, *Californians*, which, while accomplished, falls short of distinction; he had not yet found his voice and his form. That would take him several years, and exactly how he did so remains a mystery. It was influenced by the experience of building Tor House, and also by the war, in which Jeffers, after some delay, volunteered to serve; he was still awaiting a commission when hostilities ceased. The two events together caused a spiritual awakening in the thirty-one-year-old poet akin to religious conversion. That awakening brought him a new voice, new forms, and new themes, all centered on the country and people of the Carmel coast.

The new voice declared itself in a variety of novel nonrhyming narrative measures, most of them flexible five- and ten-stress lines largely unprecedented in English. The closest analogues are some ancient Greek and Hebrew narrative measures. Subsequently they have been adapted effectively in translations; when Jeffers introduced them in 1924 they were unique, however, opening up an entirely new dimension for English poetry.

Jeffers published the work *Tamar and Other Poems* (1924) privately, after eight years of routine rejections. The reception was so enthusiastic that an expanded volume—*Roan Stallion, Tamar, and Other Poems* (1925)—was published the next year. This was a poetic best-seller, establishing Jeffers as one of the few poets of his time to become (and remain) commercially successful. Like the visions of many other innovative writers of the mid-1920's—Sherwood Anderson, Ernest Hemingway, Sinclair Lewis, William Faulkner, and F. Scott Fitzgerald—Jeffers' was bleak, bitter, and harsh, a pungent antidote to the easy optimism of the era's boosterism and boom times. It ripped off the mask of complacency with which the industrial United States covered its injustices.

Thereafter, volume followed volume almost annually. *The Women at Point Sur* (1927) did not enjoy the critical acclaim and popular sales of *Roan Stallion, Tamar, and Other Poems,* but the poem—a depiction of a minister who loses faith, develops a natural religion of abandon, and finally is destroyed by the unconstrained animalism he preaches—is in many ways his most ambitious and complex achievement. *Cawdor and Other Poems* (1928) and *Dear Judas and Other Poems* (1929) recaptured much of his audience, though the liberties he took in "Dear Judas" offended the orthodox. "The Faithful Shepherdess" and *Descent to the Dead: Poems Written in Ireland and Great Britain* (1931) are among his most memorable works. *Thurso's Landing and Other Poems* (1932) and *Give Your Heart to the Hawks and Other Poems* (1933) secured his hold on the public.

Thereafter, his success with narrative poems declined, especially when he voiced what were taken to be anti-American sentiments during World War II. In retrospect, however, these seem consistent with his earlier vision, which was never pro-American, and they certainly call for re-examination in the light of postwar history. His final successes were in different venues. His 1946 translation of Euripides' *Medea* (431 B.C.) was a theatrical hit in 1947, and the dramatic versions of *The Tower Beyond Tragedy* (1951) the *The Cretan Woman* (1954) were both well received. Una died in 1950, and Jeffers' final volume to be published in his lifetime, *Hungerfield and Other Poems* (1954), is a collection of lyric memorials to her and their life together. He died on January 20, 1962.

Analysis

Since first gaining public attention in 1925 with *Roan Stallion, Tamar, and Other Poems,* Robinson Jeffers has been remarkable primarily for his metrical innovations; for graphic, even sordid, plots set in scenes of spectacular beauty; and for themes that eventually resulted in the philosophical attitude he called "Inhumanism." In all three respects Jeffers stands alone; however, as time passes, he appears increasingly to have anticipated later developments with uncanny foresight.

The metrical innovations—and the purposes to which he put them—are most immediately evident. Narrative poetry in the 1920's held a larger share of popular culture than it would later; still taught as a literary staple in the schools, it appealed to a wide audience. In 1920, nineteenth century American poet Henry Wadsworth Longfellow was easily the most popular poet in the country, as the English poet Alfred, Lord Tennyson had been twenty years before; Stephen Vincent Benét would have several best-sellers in the two decades following. All of them wrote in traditional rhymed or unrhymed regular four- or five-stress patterns that had been familiar for centuries. Jeffers himself used these in his early narratives. For *Tamar,* however, an updated version of a myth variously recounted by the Greek poet Hesiod in *Theogony* (c. 800 B.C.) and by the authors of the biblical Book of Samuel, Jeffers believed that he needed English verses with the rhythmic suppleness of the Greek and Aramaic originals.

Few examples were immediately available in the English poetic repertory. True, there was the precedent of Old English verse, which Jeffers had studied and which Ezra Pound had raised to the status of cult object. Transcribed as nearly verbatim as possible into modern English, it produces a line with four or five stresses and a variable number of sequences of unstressed syllables. Literal translation of some Greek and Hebrew measures creates a similar effect. Measures such as those had been used in English poetry before, notably by Christopher Smart and William Blake, but without great success.

Jeffers had the genius to make his adaptation seem so natural that subsequent poets would routinely use the terms "four- and five-stress lines." Basically, he doubled the five-stress line, thereby creating a ten-stress form unlike anything heard before; yet it sounded as inevitable as nature. It is more sinuous and patterned than the finest, most contoured prose, less precious and confined than any regular meter. It is relatively easy to read, yet it embeds itself effortlessly in the mind. It made Jeffers the most read narrative poet of the twentieth century.

Jeffers' second distinction is his choice of plots and settings. The building of Tor House caused him to feel that he had come to the "inevitable place" and that it was his vocation to capture its spirit. His scientific training in geology and biology had taught him that in the scales of cosmic time and space, humankind had hardly nudged the beam. The full course of human history cast a shadow as trivial as that of a single man on the face of Big Sur. Furthermore, he knew that as products of evolution, human beings were closer to the animals than to the angels. Their behavior was only fitfully rational; otherwise, primitive instincts dragged them, hopelessly trailing platitudes and rationalizations. His viewpoint was close to one expressed by Irish satirist Jonathan Swift, who in *Gulliver's Travels* (1726) declared humankind "the most pernicious race of little odious vermin that nature ever suffered to crawl upon the surface of the earth."

If his Calvinistic upbringing had indoctrinated him in the conviction of universal human depravity, his study of the writings of Charles Darwin and Sigmund Freud reinforced those views. Yet it gave him a different perspective. Humans were not responsible for their depravity: They were merely irredeemably animal. In fact, they made themselves worse by pretending to be more. Denying those impulses forced them to repress their animal instincts, which did confer a superficial propriety. Repression, however, far from eradicating instincts, merely held them at bay for a time. When they finally found an outlet, they exploded with accumulated pressure. Because these explosions of passion were unintentional, humans were not responsible for them and therefore could not be considered evil. They were, rather, as innocent as animals—which also meant they could not be considered good, either. Instead, they should be viewed indifferently, as part of the process of life.

These views gave Jeffers a predilection for plots of intense sensuality, irregular passion, and brutish violence, whether he was retelling ancient myths or creating more realistic, more contemporary narratives. This first appears in *Tamar*, which details multiple incidents of incest—brother-sister, father-daughter (implicit), second generation brother-sister—as well as lesbianism, seduction, a séance of sorts, murder, arson, and self-immolation, all presented almost as everyday events. *Roan Stallion*, Jeffers' most widely circulated work, includes a fantasized act of bestiality between stallion and woman, wife rape, and retaliation in which the woman uses the stallion to kill her husband before the eyes of their child. *The Tower Beyond Tragedy* (1925) complicates Aeschylus' *Oresteia* by making explicit the sexual relationship between Agamemnon and Cassandra, by suggesting that all the sexual relationships are mechanical when not forced, by emphasizing the callousness of the execution of Cassandra, and by expanding the multiple incestuous links among the characters. *The Women at Point Sur* (1927) includes father-daughter incest in a kaleidoscope of permissive sexual debauchery and violence that struck most readers as excessive, even by Jeffers' standards.

This focus on the unrepressed savage or animalistic behavior of humankind is consistent throughout his life's work. In "Dear Judas" and "The Loving Shepherdess" (1929), he does find something to admire in humanity. Yet even here, what he admired—zest for life and self-realization in the character of Jesus, and, in "The Loving Shepherdess," Clare Walker's clear-eyed acceptance of suffering and her determination to guarantee the best part of life for her doomed baby—did not strike everyone else as positive. His explicit repudiation of divinity, to say nothing of virtue, in Jesus appeared aggressively blasphemous. The term most often used by critics to describe Jeffers' attitude is "tragic"; nearly as common is the adjective "unrelieved."

Jeffers himself called his orientation "Inhumanism"; although he did not specifically define it until near the end of his career, it underlies all of his poetry. Inhumanism characterized the viewpoint that humans needed to acquire, in Jeffers' view, in order to escape the limits and errors of human-centered thought and action. He considered all previous philosophies defective because they regularly assumed that existence pivoted on man. The ancient Greek commonplace held that man was—or should be—the measure of all things. Moreover, that attitude underlies all systems of thought which use human reason as the means of analysis. Jeffers believed that this imparted a human bias to assessments to the universe and man's role in it.

To correct this, Jeffers proposed a view which moved man from being the center to being part of the complex whole. This was not novel with him; it was consistent with contemporary perspectives of biology, geology, and cosmology, having been expressly formulated by Charles Darwin in *On the Origin of Species* (1859). Although some aspects of Darwinian thought had been accepted, his displacement of man (and God) from central roles in the continuing evolution of the cosmos had not. That concept, however, allowed Jeffers a stark objectivity in his treatment of characters and plots.

TAMAR

First published: 1924
Type of work: Poem

At an isolated Carmel farm, a girl, Tamar, becomes involved with her brother, learns of her father's own incest, and commits suicide by conflagration.

In capsule, the action of *Tamar* seems so contrived and decadent as to defy plausibility. Yet it is actually an expansion of a generation myth told briefly by Hesiod and retold in a paragraph at the end of Herman Melville's *Pierre: Or, the Ambiguities* (1852). Another version, with Tamar as the main character, appears in chapters 13 and 14 of the Second Book of Samuel. In contrast, Jeffers' development of the material is leisurely and expansive. Furthermore, it is presented in such compelling rhythms, such detail, and such a matter-of-fact way that the question of plausibility hardly arises during reading. The poem is sixty-two or seventy-two pages long (varying with edition) so that the story's development is ample.

The narrative begins with a prelude in which Lee Cauldwell, Tamar's brother, falls with his horse from a cliff during a drunken dare. Near death, he is nursed back to health by Tamar. The two grow closer after this. The house in which he lies recovering broods forebodingly, however; a midnight storm stirs the uneasy souls of their father David and their aunts Stella Moreland, a ghost-seer, and Jinny Cauldwell, who is mentally disabled. By the following spring, Lee has recovered, and he finds himself increasingly drawn to his sister—to the point that he drives off a suitor. He stops going to local parties, giving up his former carousing. His father warns him that he will not have time for socializing once he is drafted for the war.

That April, they stop one hot afternoon to bathe in a stream. Overcome with passions for which she cannot even find words, Tamar tries to drown herself. As her brother rescues her, they find themselves instinctively making love. Afterward he despairs, but she accepts responsibility and declares her love for him.

Shortly afterward, Tamar interviews her Aunt Stella when Stella is in a trance; she learns that her father had been incestuous with his sister Helen, now dead. Feeling that her own relationship with Lee is foredoomed, she continues it in despair, until she discovers that she is pregnant. After a vision in which she surveys all the various peoples who have lived along the coast, she rides to the Andrews farm, where she seduces Will so that she will have someone whom she can blame for her pregnancy.

This sets the stage for the longest, most detailed section of the poem. The mid-August heat frazzles Tamar; she begs Aunt Stella to summon the dead. That evening, they proceed to a nearby fjord, where Stella once more enters the trance state. Several voices speak through her, but primarily a spokesman for the Indian people who once held rites in that place. He commands Tamar to dance naked as the pregnant Indians did, to placate the spirits. Her dance turns into a frank, sensual invitation to the spirits to couple with her. Finally spent, she is allowed to speak to Helen, her father's sister-lover, through Stella. The two harangue each other. Suddenly the séance is interrupted by an alarm bell from the cliff-house above. The voice announces that Tamar's attempt to burn the house has failed.

Tamar loses her child and requires bed rest for recovery. Her father denounces her and Lee for their sin, demanding retribution, and she has a vision of impending war. Mysterious events haunt the house. Lee tells Tamar that their father was going to kill him but relented when Lee offered to join the Army and not return until Tamar is married and David is dead. Tamar believes that Lee has betrayed her for the easy French women available overseas. The old man returns to denounce Tamar; she defies him, accusing him of hypocrisy and extorting from him a confession of lust for her and a condemnation of Helen. Meanwhile, Stella is able to induce a clairvoyant state in Jinny; she sees Tamar ablaze while Helen laughs and the old man has a rope around his neck.

Lee returns to find the two women—with Helen speaking through Stella—trying to get into the locked room. Tamar opens it for Lee; he finds Tamar in command and his father, broken, on his knees. Tamar taunts Lee, saying that not he but another lover had fathered the child, and Helen and Tamar continue wrangling. Tamar sets the signal for Will Andrews, to bring her three lovers together under one roof.

Lee enters to bid farewell. Tamar entices him to carry her to her bedroom, where she goads him until he strikes her with a riding whip. Soon Will arrives; Lee has been waiting for him. While he goes to bring David, Tamar tells Will that the two have beaten her, causing her to lose their baby. Will insists on taking her with him. Lee resists, and Will hits him. When the women intervene, Lee knifes Will. Jinny seizes the chance to thrust a piece of paper into the lamp, setting herself and the room on fire. Lee struggles to escape, first with Tamar and then alone, but the dying Will hampers him, and Tamar will not let him go. All die in the fire.

The poem has justly been praised for its elemental, mythic quality. It has the compelling quality of myth, an inner intensity that defies logic and plausibility because it possesses its own internal truth. Jeffers captured the essence of the way irrational human impulses operate.

ROAN STALLION

First published: 1925
Type of work: Poem

After establishing a rapport with their prize stallion, a California peasant woman flees to it for protection from her abusive husband; the horse kills the man.

"Roan Stallion" is the best-known and most often reprinted of Jeffers' narrative poems; it is also the most compact and most concentrated. Unlike the majority of the others, it is simple in plot construction, makes little use of the abnormal, and is concrete in detail. It consists of three episodes, each connected directly to the one following.

The first introduces California, a twenty-one-year-old quarter-Indian, quarter-Spaniard, half-Scot woman, whose husband, Johnny, has just won a prize stallion by gambling. Preoccupied by the game and his habitual drinking, he has neglected to get anything for their daughter, Christine, for Christmas. To make up for it she will have to go to Monterey on Christmas Eve. She tries to leave early, but he demands that she sleep with him before leaving. His insistence and lack of compassion make her late. As a result, she cannot return before nightfall, and she must ford a rain-swollen river. Twice the mare balks, the second time nearly overturning the wagon, apparently startled by the apparition of the infant Jesus. Finally California abandons the wagon and swims the mare across, careful not to damage her daughter's presents.

In her memories of the apparition, she persistently mixes the image of the stallion with the image of God. That spring, after spending a day breeding, Johnny leaves to spend the weekend drinking. Restless, California goes out after nightfall to ease herself with a moonlit ride into the hills, only to find that Johnny has taken the mare. Fantasizing a sexual union with the stallion, she decides to take it instead. The climb is ecstatic. On the peak, she feels herself rapt in union with the power that is God and the spirit of the horse, and she dreams of the unions of powers, animal and human, that have generated existence. They walk back down the hill.

Johnny returns the next evening, half-drunk, orders that the child be put to bed, and demands that California drink with him, after which he threatens her. The contrast between the real power she has known and his puny swaggering disgusts her, and she escapes outdoors. He calls the dog to track her, planning to run her down like an animal. She retreats to the corral, where the dog begins feinting with the stallion; Johnny climbs the fence, pursuing her.

Meanwhile, Christine awakes, becomes aware of the commotion, and wanders down to the corral. Seeing the stallion strike down the pursuing figure, she runs back to the house to fetch the rifle. She returns to find her mother watching the dog protect the crawling Johnny from the frenzied horse. Taking the rifle, California deliberately shoots the dog, then rests the rifle, saying that the moonlight had darkened the sights. While the child begs her to shoot, the stallion stamps the man into the mire. With infinite reluctance she raises the rifle and dutifully kills the man-killer, feeling that she has killed God.

Like most of his early poems, "Roan Stallion" incorporates mythic material, this time primarily concerning Egyptian and Near Eastern projections of beast-gods and of beast-god couplings. More notable is the use Jeffers makes of his material. He shows that humans such as California, sensitive to all aspects of their psycho-spiritual heritage, can respond instinctively to affinities higher than transient human ties. This is his first formulation of the doctrine he would later call Inhumanism. As he phrases it here,

Humanity is the mould to break away from, the crust to break through, the
coal to break into fire,
The atom to be split.
Tragedy that breaks man's face and a white fire flies
out of it; vision that fools him
Out of his limits, desire that fools him out of his limits, unnatural crime,
inhuman science,
Slit eyes in the mask; wild loves that leap over the walls of nature, the wild
fence-vaulter science,

. . . .

The heart of the atom with electrons: what is humanity in this cosmos? For
him, the last
Least taint of a trace in the dregs of the solution; for itself, the mould to
break away from, the coal
To break into fire, the atom to be split.

THE LOVING SHEPHERDESS

First published: 1929
Type of work: Poem

A shepherdess, abandoned by the lover who has killed her father and shunted the blame onto her, wanders the cliffs with her bedraggled flock until her death.

Suggested by a character created by Scottish writer Sir Walter Scott and transposed to the California coast, "The Loving Shepherdess" is the most straightforward and simplest in texture of Jeffers' narrative poems. It lacks both the mythic overtones and the thematic commentary of the others. Structurally, it simply traces the course of Clare Walker's last, doomed journey, during which she refuses to avert the suffering derived from her previous actions.

The poem opens with a ragged Clare leading her flock, reduced from fifty to ten, past a one-room schoolhouse at recess. The children jeer at her and threaten her, reminding her that she had killed her father and then been abandoned by her lover. One boy alone protects her, warning her to avoid the cattle ranches, where the dogs would be set on her sheep. Clare wanders on, obviously distressed in mind and body, but devoted to her sheep. Near Fogler's ranch his dogs attack; he comes out to drive them off. Recognizing her, he wants to offer her shelter, but knows that his wife will object. Hastily he packs some food, gathers a pair of old shoes, and kisses her, shame-faced, as she leaves.

They wander northward. Clare has moments of pastoral bliss, but all pleasures are overshadowed. Near Point Sur, forgetting for the moment that she is in cattle country, she is warned off the pastures by a young cowboy, Will Brighton. He shows her an abandoned house, telling her that she can shelter there. To thank him, she sleeps with him. While their attention is diverted, two of the sheep fall into an old, half-collapsed well. They are able to save one, badly lamed, but the second dies.

The next day she climbs Sur Hill, then spends the night there; in the morning, she seeks help from a passing horseman. He is Onorio Vasquez, an itinerant visionary who figures in several of Jeffers' poems. She tells him that her purpose in life is to care for her sheep until she dies, which will happen in five months. Thinking she is referring to something learned in a vision, he tries to reassure her, but she says that her trouble is physical. They are interrupted by a hawk attacking a heron; her sympathetic distress is physical. Vasquez observes that her love for animals is universal. After they get the sheep to water, he points her toward a nearby cabin.

Finding no pasture there she presses on, reaching a farmhouse where an old hand offers them the use of the barn, mentioning that the owner is dying and will not notice. During the night he comes twice to visit, complaining that, though old, he is cursed with young feelings. She offers herself to him, explaining that since her trouble she finds herself filled with love for all, willing to please anyone in her short remaining time. She finds no food, though the sheep have hay.

Now in the rainy season, she continues north, hungry and deteriorating, as is her flock, two of which are suffering from bad feed. Onorio once again appears, bringing food and fire. Sheltering for the night under a bridge, Clare tells the story of her affair with Charlie Maurice, who had actually killed her father; she had lied to cover for him, because she was pregnant. At that time she contracted influenza and miscarried. The attending doctor told her that it was a blessing in disguise: A deformed pelvis would have caused the death of both baby and mother. Somehow, out of this suffering, she has learned that "all our pain comes from restraint of love."

Later, a shipwreck occurred offshore near her farm. She did what she could to help the survivors, but in their hunger they began to slaughter her sheep, so she led them away. She found no forage for them and no food for herself, however, and she was starving when rescued and nursed to health by a vagrant. Eventually he asked for sex. Despite the danger, she consented, out of gratitude and love. By midsummer she was pregnant again.

Onorio offers to procure an abortion, but Clare cannot bear to cause the death of anything. Moreover, she believes that the period of intrauterine development is the most serene, blessed time of life; how can she deprive her baby of that? Onorio has a vision of cosmic order, in which the incidents of one individual life dwindle to the infinitesimal, yet the revealed order is compellingly beautiful. When Clare awakes, she tells that she has seen the same vision in a dream. They are so caught up in the vision that they forget about the sheep, which drift off. Suddenly Clare realizes they are gone. When they find the animals, two have been attacked by a lion, and one is dead. Onorio offers to put her up at his father's farm, but Clare has to follow her destiny. Onorio plans to stay with her, but a vision of Christ going up to Calvary deflects him.

Clare continues wandering, getting help periodically but becoming increasingly fearful and distraught. She watches a salmon struggling upstream to spawn and die, and she sees this course as parallel to her own. She becomes increasingly disordered as her flock dwindles away. She is last seen at a hobo camp. Finally her pains claim her; as she retreats, she calls the names of her now nonexistent sheep. Jeffers in this poem realized the objective incarnation of the idea of Inhumanism.

DESCENT TO THE DEAD

First published: 1931
Type of work: Poetry

In a series of sixteen poetic meditations on scenes in Ireland and England, mostly archaic, Jeffers contrasts past with present and Old World with New.

Descent to the Dead, occasioned by a visit Jeffers and Una paid to Ireland, the land of their ancestors, and England in 1929, is the major sequence of short poems composed by the poet. Most of them commemorate monuments of ancient cultures—cairns, cromlechs, graves, and standing stones—attempting to re-create the human consciousness that entered into their construction. Jeffers is most concerned with drawing connections between disparate moments of time, both to bridge the immense gulf between them and to mark man's beautiful insignificance in the context of cosmic time. It is another means of disclosing Inhumanism.

Because Jeffers had chosen the Carmel coast—the final West—as his inevitable place and had accepted as his vocation the revelation of man's essential triviality in that context, he had symbolically turned his back on the culture of his own country—thus his need to forge new poetic forms. By that same measure, he had rejected even more the culture of the Old World. This is the "dead" to which he descends, dead in two ways: It represents a rejected or transcended culture, and it is the culture of his ancestors, dead in a real sense. His object is both to reveal its irrelevance and to record its paradoxical beauty.

The poems focus on monuments of internment—"Shane O'Neill's Cairn," "Ossian's Grave," "In the Hill at Newgrange," "Iona: The Graves of the Kings," "Shakespeare's Grave"—and of religious ritual—"The Broadstone," "The Giant's Ring"—because these are what the days and works of the dead have come to. The contrast between lofty aspirations and the cold reality of those graves (literally memorials to nothing, for nothing is left in them) is telling. Jeffers sees the end of man in this, and he accepts it; it is enough, for there is a great beauty and fitness in these places.

The primitive character of the places reinforces the theme; it brings to mind the brutishness of the lives so crudely remembered. Shane O'Neill was a name of power four centuries ago, controlling life and death for many; now he has shrunk to an empty grave surmounted by senseless blocks, and he is considered a petty king of an insignificant and primitive people. Moreover, this condition afflicts even the truly notable: lip-service is paid to Homer and Shakespeare, but twenty-six hundred years after his death only a few can read what the former composed, and the same will become true of the latter.

Jeffers believed that only from such a perspective could man accurately assess the role of humankind. For although man may be insignificant and his self-importance a bloated lie, seen against the background of cosmic immensity his few moments of insight and self-realization can also appear heartbreakingly beautiful.

Summary

Robinson Jeffers is unparalleled among twentieth century poets in the range of his achievements, his technical innovations, and the cast of his vision. He alone reached master status in lyric, narrative, and dramatic poetry, and he created a unique voice and idiom in each genre. Much of this eminence derived from his radical approach to the writing of poetry in English: He wrote as if poetry in his time stemmed from the same impulses that produced poetry in ancient Greece and Israel. To communicate his vision, he invented flexible five- and ten-stress lines rare in English before him; he projected a Darwinian vision of man as only one life form in a complex ecosystem.

Bibliography

Bennett, Melba. *The Stone Mason of Tor House.* Los Angeles: Ward Ritchie, 1966.

Boyers, Robert. "A Sovereign Voice: The Poetry of Robinson Jeffers." In *Modern American Poetry: Essays in Criticism*, edited by Jerome Mazzaro. New York: David McKay, 1970.

Brophy, Robert J. *Robinson Jeffers: Myth, Ritual, and Symbol in His Narrative Poems.* Cleveland: Case Western University Press, 1973.

Carpenter, Frederic I. *Robinson Jeffers.* New York: Twayne, 1962.

Nolte, William H. *Rock and Hawk: Robinson Jeffers and the Romantic Agony.* Athens: University of Georgia Press, 1978.

Zaller, Robert. *The Cliffs of Solitude: A Reading of Robinson Jeffers.* Cambridge, England: Cambridge University Press, 1983.

James L. Livingston

SARAH ORNE JEWETT

Born: South Berwick, Maine
September 3, 1849
Died: South Berwick, Maine
June 24, 1909

Principal Literary Achievement

Jewett's stories about women and girls show a feminine side of nineteenth century American life; they usually tell of ordinary people in rural areas.

Biography

Theodora Sarah Orne Jewett was born in South Berwick, Maine, on September 3, 1849, the middle of three daughters of Caroline Frances Perry Jewett and Dr. Theodore Herman Jewett. Her family was wealthy, thanks to an inheritance and to her father's successful medical practice. She remained financially independent throughout her life and, therefore, felt little pressure to marry or to work for an income.

Jewett's childhood experiences growing up in southern Maine became the main source of her stories. South Berwick, in her time, was an abandoned seaport, with memories of grand days when ships from the Maine coast sailed around the world, bringing back the riches of Europe and the Orient. As a child, she spent hours listening to her grandfather and his friends spinning yarns of trade and adventure as world merchants. People such as these, who remembered and mourned a better, lost time became the characters of her best-remembered stories. Because she was often unwell as a child, her father took her on his country rounds, where she could benefit from the bracing air and where she met the rural people and learned about the landscape that became central in her fiction.

When she was graduated from Berwick Academy in 1866, she was well educated. Her parents had encouraged her to read the classics and more recent works—John Milton, Laurence Sterne, Henry Fielding, Jane Austen, and Alfred, Lord Tennyson among them—but she seems to have been especially impressed by Harriet Beecher Stowe's *The Pearl of Orr's Island* (1862), which showed her what could be made of her own locale.

She had begun writing poetry and fiction in her childhood, and within a year after being graduated, Jewett was submitting stories to magazines under various pseudonyms. Her first published story was "Jenny Garrow's Lovers" (1868), a melodramatic tragedy of two brothers in love with the same woman. In 1868, she im-

pressed William Dean Howells, who eventually became the powerful editor of *The Atlantic Monthly.* When he accepted her story "Mr. Bruce" (1868), her career was off to a good start. Though her early stories were generally aimed at teaching good behavior to young girls and so are not of great interest to modern readers, they were widely published. Jewett's confidence in her writing grew along with her willingness to experiment. She became interested in essay/sketches of Maine life, some of which she gathered into her first book, *Deephaven* (1877).

After the death of her father in 1878, Jewett became friends with James T. Fields, publisher of *The Atlantic Monthly,* and his wife, Annie. This friendship brought Jewett into Boston literary circles. James Fields died in 1881, and Jewett and Annie Fields began to live together. They remained close friends throughout Jewett's life, traveling often together in the United States and Europe. Jewett divided her time between her childhood home in South Berwick, where she wrote, fished, rode, skated, and walked, and the two residences of Annie Fields, where she conversed with many of the literary eminences of her day. Their circle of friends included Harriet Beecher Stowe, Oliver Wendell Holmes, John Greenleaf Whittier, and Mary E. Wilkins Freeman. In Europe, she met and visited with many of the great writers, including Henry James, Christina Rossetti, and Tennyson.

In this atmosphere, her writing flourished. Her short stories continued to appear in popular magazines, and she regularly published book collections. Her second and third longer books, *A Country Doctor* (1884) and *A Marsh Island* (1885), were reasonably successful attempts at traditional novels. *A Country Doctor* tells the story of Nan Prince, who follows the path that Jewett dreamed of, becoming a physician like Dr. Jewett. Dr. Leslie, Nan's supporter, is much like Jewett's father.

A White Heron and Other Stories (1886) marked Jewett's entrance onto the stage of world literature. The title story and several others from this collection have continued to be anthologized and have helped, along with the others that American novelist Willa Cather collected in her edition of *The Country of the Pointed Firs and Other Stories* (1925), to sustain Jewett's reputation. In the early twentieth century, the discovery of Herman Melville and Emily Dickinson, the tendency of the novel to overshadow short fiction, and many other factors in literary studies tended to obscure Jewett's achievement, so that nearly all of her work went out of print and could only be found on the shelves of larger libraries. By the end of the century, new factors in literary studies, notably feminist criticism, helped to bring more of her works back into print and contributed to her rediscovery.

In the last fifteen years of her writing career, Jewett produced a memorable body of fiction, beginning with *A White Heron and Other Stories, A Native of Winby and Other Tales* (1893), *The Life of Nancy* (1895), *The Country of the Pointed Firs* (1896)—her masterpiece— and *The Queen's Twin and Other Stories* (1899).

In 1903, on her fifty-third birthday, Jewett was seriously injured in a carriage accident. Unable to write fiction in her last years, she nevertheless continued her correspondence and formed the friendship with Cather that was so important to that writer's career. She died in her home in South Berwick on June 24, 1909.

Analysis

Few writers have so successfully described Jewett's achievement and characteristics as Cather does in her preface to *The Country of the Pointed Firs and Other Stories.* Cather says that Jewett "once laughingly told me that her head was full of dear old houses and dear old women, and that when an old house and an old woman came together in her brain with a click, she knew that a story was under way."

Jewett's best fiction deals mainly with women, especially older women, in the villages and towns and on the farms of Maine. Her themes generally concern the beauty and dignity of these characters, who live in the shadow of a more prosperous and culturally richer past and who often have suffered great loss themselves—husbands and sons to the sea, comparative wealth and independence, and friendship to accident, time, or human weakness. She shows how these people succeed or fail at transcending their circumstances. Many of her stories deal with the relations of the individual to the larger community. Sometimes, an individual must withdraw from an oppressive community in order to create or strengthen the independent self, as in "A White Heron" (1886). Sometimes, the individual who has experienced unhealthy separation must be gathered into a vital community in order to find happiness, as in "Miss Tempy's Watchers" (1888). Human happiness in Jewett's works always involves finding a balance between the need to be a self and the need to belong intimately to a community. Perhaps her best representation of this ideal of balance is Mrs. Blackett in *The Country of the Pointed Firs.*

Cather praises Jewett for possessing "the kind of beauty we feel when a beautiful song is sung by a beautiful voice that is exactly suited to the song." Jewett has not been widely recognized for her style, but it is a very important aspect of her writing. Cather points out that Jewett's subjects are not often "exciting" in the usual sense: She "wrote of people who grew out of the soil and the life of the country near her heart, not about exceptional individuals at war with their environment." For example, "A Native of Winby" (1893) concerns not the heroic actions of Joseph Laneway but rather his evening's visit with a dear friend of his youth. This choice of subject creates two major problems of style: how to make the stories interesting and how to avoid sentimentality.

The development of Jewett's writing career is in part an illustration of how to find the right tone. Jewett learns to vary her tone within a fairly narrow range, rising quietly to heights such as the vision of the heron in "A White Heron" and the moments of self-transcending sympathy in "Miss Tempy's Watchers," without creating a false melodrama of pastoral/urban opposition in the former or Gothic mystery in the latter. This command of style is crucial to the success of stories such as "Martha's Lady" (1899), in which a servant woman builds her self over a lifetime out of a brief summer visit from a lovely and loving lady, remembering her chiefly by means of a few relics of their short time together.

Cather implies that Jewett's strength of style arises from a personal gift that was central to her becoming a great writer. The great writer, says Cather, has the gift of sympathy: "That alone can make his work fine. He fades away into the land and people of his heart." It was this sort of sympathy that inspired Jewett to write about the vanishing culture of the Maine coast and that earned for her the label as one of the most accomplished writers of the regional school of the end of the nineteenth century. While Jewett did not consider herself a member of a school of writers, she did share with a number of her contemporaries, notably Mark Twain, the wish to preserve in art a beautiful and valuable aspect of American culture that seemed destined to disappear in the new industrial age.

Cather also notes Jewett's humor: "She had with her own stories and her own characters a very charming relation; spirited, gay, tactful, noble in its essence and a little arch in its expression." Though always subtle and quiet in tone, some of Jewett's stories are among the funniest in nineteenth century American literature. "The Flight of Betsey Lane" (1893) provokes laughter as Betsey's aging almshouse friends toil out to the pond to see if she might have drowned herself, when in fact she has used a small legacy to visit the Philadelphia exposition. "The Guests of Mrs. Timms" (1895) exploits irony and humor reminiscent of Jane Austen as two women go to the city to visit a woman who invited them insincerely. "Miss Debby's Neighbors" (1884) is almost a tall tale in the vein of Twain, telling of spiteful brothers moving their houses until one house gets caught on the railroad tracks.

All Jewett's most memorable themes and all the best qualities of her writing appear in her generally recognized masterpiece, *The Country of the Pointed Firs*, the unusual novel that Cather equates with Nathaniel Hawthorne's *The Scarlet Letter* (1850) and Mark Twain's *The Adventures of Huckleberry Finn* (1884).

A WHITE HERON

First published: 1886
Type of work: Short story

Young Sylvia resists the temptation to tell a charming hunter where to find the nest of a beautiful bird.

"A White Heron" is Jewett's best-known short story and the only one to have an entire critical book written about it, Louis Renza's *"A White Heron" and the Question of Minor Literature* (1984). Though Jewett wrote many other stories at this level, this one has been most often anthologized and it connects thematically with works that have much greater reputations, such as Melville's *Moby-Dick* (1851), Henry Thoreau's *Walden* (1854), and William Faulkner's "The Bear" (1942).

Sylvia, a shy nine-year-old, is bringing home the milk cow when she meets a young ornithologist who is hunting birds for his collection of specimens. He goes with her to her grandmother's house. Mrs. Tilley has rescued Sylvia from a crowded home in the city, where she was languishing. The farm has proven a good environment for her. The handsome hunter, however, awakens Sylvia's interest in a larger social life. He is friendly and sociable. He offers money and other rewards for information about where he can find the white heron he has seen. He spends a day with Sylvia looking for the heron's nest, during which Sylvia comes to find him increasingly attractive, even though she is repelled by his killing birds. She knows where the nest probably is, but she hesitates to tell him.

On the second morning of the hunter's stay, Sylvia climbs a nearby landmark pine at dawn to see the heron rise from its nest. She seems to have decided to help the ornithologist; however, at this point Jewett uses some special narrative devices to subvert Sylvia's apparent intentions. Shifts in verb tense and point of view create an intimate unity between the narrator, the reader, and Sylvia herself. One effect of this unity is probably to help the reader share Sylvia's enriching mystical union with nature that leads her finally to decide not to tell what she has found. Sylvia is not yet ready to surrender a life "heart to heart with nature" for the "great wave of human interest" represented by the hunter. Before she can return to the more various social life she has temporarily left behind to live on the farm with her grandmother, she must come surely to possess herself. For her, this can happen best in the comparative isolation of country life.

Though it is easy to read this tale as extolling a life close to nature over a richer social life in the city, Jewett's story seems more complex. Jewett herself lived alternately in the quiet, rural village of South Berwick and in the cosmopolitan social and literary life of Boston, and she often traveled to other cities (and several times to Europe). The story deals with several of Jewett's major themes, one of which is the necessity at some times and for some people of withdrawing from social life into a simpler set of relations where the self can be fostered or renewed. The story does not imply that Sylvia will find a lifetime of happiness only on her grandmother's farm—though indeed she may—any more than Thoreau's discoveries at Walden Pond require that he live all the rest of his life there.

The ornithologist is attractive as well as a little dangerous; the wave of human interest he represents is, for most of Jewett's characters, necessary to happiness. Sylvia simply is not yet ready to enter into the great stream of social life, and to do so too soon would threaten her ability to create and maintain a strong self. Were she to help the young man now, she would come to love and serve him "as a dog loves." Such a love does not suggest the most rewarding kind of love between strong equals.

MISS TEMPY'S WATCHERS

First published: 1888
Type of work: Short story

Sarah Ann Binson comforts Mrs. Crowe as they keep watch in Temperence Dent's house on the night before her funeral.

"Miss Tempy's Watchers" is one of a number of Jewett's subtle and moving tales of the lives of older women who must deal with loss and hardship. Just before they drift off into a short sleep, as Sarah Ann Binson and Mrs. Crowe watch together in Tempy's house, Mrs. Crowe reflects that Tempy always made the best of everything. For example, she made excellent quince preserves by taking care of a thorny old tree with such attention and good cheer that she seemed to "kind of expect" it into blooming. Sarah replies, "She was just the same with folks." This is a story about blooming—about how, with the deceased Tempy's help, Sarah begins to replace her, and so helps Mrs. Crowe to begin to bloom into a more generous person.

Tempy's spirit hovers over a scene she has created by asking her two friends to watch together in her house. The women reflect repeatedly upon how they seem to feel her living presence as they converse through the night, and the narrator adds touches that contribute to the reader believing that Tempy is spiritually present even apart from her friends' memories and talk. Left alone together for the long night, the women find themselves confiding private thoughts and fears.

Mrs. Crowe, especially, has much to confess. Tempy's death has made her feel more than ever the pain of her stinginess. Because she is rich and socially powerful, Mrs. Crowe's small contributions to the community earn her praise and gratitude out of proportion to her true generosity, and she knows this. Though she is not fully aware of the degree to which Sarah follows Tempy in giving all she possibly can for the happiness and well-being of children and the more needy, she does know what Tempy has done. This knowledge humbles her "to the dust," and she has resolved to make Tempy's example her own. Confiding this commitment to Sarah will help Mrs. Crowe to carry it out; moreover Sarah knows who is in need, since she is not insulated by wealth from suffering in the community.

When Sarah and Mrs. Crowe go upstairs to check on Tempy, Mrs. Crowe is reminded of her fear of death, about which she cannot speak directly. Sarah sees this and speaks directly to her fear, quoting Tempy first and then the minister. This discussion moves into a discussion of aging as the women eat a snack. Before they drift into sleep, Sarah reflects as Mrs. Crowe and she did at the beginning of their more intimate conversation, that she cannot imagine getting on without Tempy. She wishes that folks could come back once after they die, to explain where they have gone.

In fact, Tempy has returned to them, but not in the way Sarah imagines. Tempy has used her death to create the situation in which she can "expect" these women's friendship into blooming. By bringing them together so successfully, she has left a duplicate of herself in the world: a woman with the knowledge of how to be generous and another with the means to be generous, wedded in what promises to be a productive friendship. Tempy has gone into their hearts to live.

"Miss Tempy's Watchers" embodies the opposing theme to "A White Heron." Here, a woman who has been unhealthily alienated from her community is gathered in, drawn to the center by acts of communal and personal love. Mrs. Crowe's latter years promise a greater happiness than she yet has known.

A NATIVE OF WINBY

First published: 1893
Type of work: Short story

The successful businessman, soldier, and politician Joseph Laneway quietly visits his birthplace at Winby.

While not one of Jewett's best-known stories, "A Native of Winby" is typical of her better work. Jewett carefully presents four scenes of return, showing different kinds of welcome Senator Joseph K. Laneway receives when, after about fifty years, he visits Winby, the New England town where he was born and where he lived for thirteen years before his family went west. Laneway has been an enormously successful businessman, a Civil War general, and a leading United States senator from an influential western state. He is at first surprised and a little pleased to find that no one recognizes him in Winby. His anonymity allows him to make three quiet pilgrimages before the public can lionize him.

First he visits the country school he attended as a child. The story opens from the point of view of the young teacher, Marilla Hender, struggling to get her students to work on a warm May afternoon and inspiring them with reminders of their distinguished schoolmate, Senator Laneway. She and the students do not recognize him in the elderly visitor who asks to observe them for awhile. After he has enjoyed evoking his childhood memories, he identifies himself and gives them a short speech admonishing them to be brave and good.

As he walks on his second pilgrimage, he reflects that the first was not entirely satisfactory, even though it had its moments—noticing that his speech really inspired a few students and seeing the amusing caricature of himself in one student's arithmetic book. He walks to his old home, where he is disappointed to find a ruin. A remnant of the rose bush his mother missed in the West evokes memories that make him linger at the spot, but finally he is humbled and made aware of his mortality and his comparative unimportance in the great scheme of things.

Disappointed and depressed, he is forced at the end of the day to seek shelter at the home of his closest school friend, Marilla's grandmother, Abby, where he finds what he has been looking for. She knows him at first sight, seeing through all he has done and become to the boy he was when she knew him last and that he still is in his deepest self. As they talk through the evening, Jewett shows how each has been of at least equal value to the world. Each has shown courage and strength, has striven for the good and kept faith with their youthful hopes, and has lived a satisfying and productive life despite hardship, loss, and pain.

Joe and Abby's visit becomes a communion of the sort that Jewett consistently presents as the ideal in human relationships. As a result, when Marilla, excited by the public welcome he receives on his departure, returns from accompanying him to the Winby train station, the reader sees as clearly as Abby does that this acclaim, while deserved, is not really what Joe wanted in Winby. What he wanted was to go with Abby down to the cellar to draw some of her cider that tastes like the month of October and to share it, their memories, and a cheerful laugh.

THE COUNTRY OF THE POINTED FIRS

First published: 1896
Type of work: Novella

Hoping for quiet isolation, a writer flees for the summer to a rural, coastal village, but she finds there a vital community that distracts and renews her.

Readers wishing to experience *The Country of the Pointed Firs*, Jewett's generally acknowledged masterpiece, as she originally published it, should seek out an edition such as that of Mary Ellen Chase (published by Norton in 1968 and 1981), which reprints the first edition. Willa Cather's 1925 edition interpolates three later stories that use the same characters and setting: "A Dunnet Shepherdess" (1899), "The Queen's Twin" (1899), and "William's Wedding" (1910, unfinished at Jewett's death). These three stories, as well as a fourth Dunnet Landing story, "The Foreigner" (1902), are among Jewett's best, but when shuffled into the novella, they considerably complicate the question of its unity. Despite Cather's rather puzzling reorganization of the novella, however, her assessment of its worth is often quoted with approval: she said that *The Country of the Pointed Firs* stands with *The Scarlet Letter* and *The Adventures of Huckleberry Finn* as a nineteenth century book most likely to remain a classic.

Cather's statement usually seems odd to modern readers, because they have all heard of Hawthorne's and Twain's classics but have rarely heard either of Jewett or of this short novel. Recent critics have asserted, with some justice, that Jewett's work has not been given a fair chance. Powerful early twentieth century male literary critics and historians too easily dismissed her work as of minor importance to modern literature and history. Her fiction was characterized as essentially nostalgic, local, and antiquarian in its appeal. More recent critics, stimulated by feminist reevaluations, have come to see this novella and Jewett's other fiction as being about the dignity and rich variety of the life and culture created and sustained by women even when the masculine interests of trade and adventure diminished in nineteenth century Maine. Marjorie Pryse points out, in her 1981 introduction to *The Country of the Pointed Firs*, that while male characters tend to become lost and alienated in the economic decline of New England, the female characters and the men who learn from them carry on life as full and happy as ever.

The overall structure of *The Country of the Pointed Firs* is simple, but within that structure, Jewett creates a variety of complex connecting images and oppositions that make the work a rich text for study and discussion. The story opens with an unnamed woman narrator explaining the attractions of Dunnet's Landing. She loved it at first sight and dreamed of it as a place of retirement, where she could escape the bustle and distractions of city life in order to complete a piece of writing. She finds, however, that she has moved to another center. She has engaged a room in the home of Almira Todd, the sixty-seven-year-old village herbalist and center of communion.

Communion is a key idea in the book, for Mrs. Todd is a purveyor not of gossip, but of visiting, the kind of news and talk that connects the entire community in a deep, sustaining fellowship. The narrator is often mystified at how well people seem to know one another, when their surface lives seem so placid and uncommunicative. Some people, in fact, seem to be in almost mystical communication. Mrs. Todd, for example, simply knows when she begins one of her infrequent visits to her aged mother, Mrs. Blackett, that she should take an onion, because her mother's are probably gone.

One way of viewing the overall structure of the novella is as the progress of the narrator's ability to understand how these people communicate and, thereby, to join in that communication. The narrator has the necessary talents for this task of learning: quick observation, tact, the desire to cultivate friendship, and the golden gift of sympathy she finds in Mrs. Blackett: a perfect forgetting of the self. From this point of view, the book can be seen as a series of visits that gradually add to the narrator's understanding of the community and ability to commune with these people. As her intimacy increases, so does her appreciation, until at the end of her summer, she feels herself so at home that leaving is painful.

The narrator and Mrs. Todd quickly become so intimate that the narrator is unable to write in Mrs. Todd's home and, therefore, rents the schoolhouse as a summer office. There she is visited by Captain Littlepage, a man alienated in time and place by the loss of his profession as a sailor. Though a small, dried-up grasshopper of a man, he comes to vivid life when he tells his fantastic tale of a "waiting place" near the North Pole, where the dead go to wait until they can enter the next world.

Her next major visit is to Mrs. Todd's mother and brother out on Green Island. There her friendship with Mrs. Todd deepens when she meets and becomes intimate with her relatives. Mrs. Blackett is presented as the center of the village, even though she lives on its far periphery and rarely comes to the mainland. As the oldest member of the Bowden family, which is the largest family in the area, she is seen by all as its matriarch. The narrator sees Mrs. Blackett as the perfectly developed social person, with a self so strong and secure that she is completely free to give herself to her family and community. All have felt and believe in her love for them, and a constant if intermittent stream of affectionate communication flows like the tides between her and all who recognize her for what she is. The chapters that complete this revelation and show the narrator reaching her fullest understanding of and intimacy with the community are the centerpieces of the book. The main remaining incidents are a visit by Mrs. Fosdick to Almira, the Bowden family reunion, and the narrator's visit with Captain Tilley.

Mrs. Fosdick is a "professional visitor." She is highly desirable company as a sort of traveling newspaper. Instead of reporting the political and general news, however, she helps examine family and communal events and helps to keep them clearly within the context of the community's history. Her main story is of "Poor Joanna," a woman who became angry with God when her betrothed jilted her. Having committed "the unpardonable sin," she thinks herself no longer fit to live among folks and so isolates herself on Shell-Heap Island. This portrait of a person who cut herself off from a community as rich and sustaining as Dunnet's Landing is a continuing cause of wonder for all three women and has been one of the outstanding historical events in the community, though it would hardly interest the newspapers.

The story of Joanna, like the Bowden reunion and the narrator's solo visit with Captain Tilley, illustrates the degree to which the narrator has entered into the life of the community. She is welcomed without reserve into Mrs. Fosdick's conversation. She sees in Joanna an image of herself as she was at the beginning of the summer—very distant from what she has become. At the Bowden reunion, she is made an honorary Bowden, and she almost feels as if she really is a member of the family. With remarkable tact and sensitivity, she succeeds in drawing out Captain Tilley.

Tilley has sought her out in the way Littlepage did earlier in the summer. When Tilley opens himself to her, she is more successful at relating to him than she was with Littlepage. Tilley's story is about how, after his wife's death, he has come to identify with her and so to understand her and love her even more than he did in life. This communion has sustained him in his loneliness. Tilley's multifaceted story brings an appropriate end to the narrator's brief stay, for it reminds her of what she learned on Green Island and shows how she may continue to commune with Dunnet's Landing after she leaves.

Seeking a hermitage, the narrator of *The Country of the Pointed Firs* finds a home, a true retreat. She never reveals whether she completed the writing she intended at Dunnet Landing, but this book is proof that she finds a subject there that is, perhaps, of greater importance.

Summary

Sarah Orne Jewett's fiction has become increasingly admired as literary scholars give more attention to the functions of women in American culture. Her stories are mainly about women and girls creating themselves in relation to nature and others and about the intimate communion with others that is one of the central values of social life. They thoughtfully show a feminine side of nineteenth century American culture. Jewett's best fictions are beautiful, moving, and often humorous tales of quiet, ordinary people in rural areas who create rich and full lives, often out of slender resources.

Bibliography

Cary, Richard. *Appreciation of Sarah Orne Jewett: Twenty-nine Interpretive Essays.* Waterville, Maine: Colby College Press, 1973.

____________. *Sarah Orne Jewett*. New York: Twayne, 1962.
Donovan, Josephine. *Sarah Orne Jewett*. New York: Frederick Ungar, 1980.
Frost, John E. *Sarah Orne Jewett*. Kittery Point, Maine: Gundalow Club, 1960.
Matthiessen, Frances O. *Sarah Orne Jewett*. Boston: Houghton Mifflin, 1929.
Nagel, Gwen. *Critical Essays on Sarah Orne Jewett*. Boston: G. K. Hall, 1984.
Nagel, Gwen, and James Nagel. *Sarah Orne Jewett: A Reference Guide.* Boston: G. K. Hall, 1978.
Sherman, Sarah Way. *Sarah Orne Jewett: An American Persephone.* Hanover, N.H.: University Press of New England, 1989.

Terry Heller

GARRISON KEILLOR

Born: Anoka, Minnesota
August 7, 1942

Principal Literary Achievement

Keillor's humorous comments on American life, especially in his tales of the fictional Lake Wobegon, Minnesota, have prompted comparisons with Mark Twain.

Biography

Gary Edward Keillor was born August 7, 1942, in Anoka, Minnesota, the son of John Philip and Grace Ruth Denham Keillor. His father was a railway mail clerk and carpenter. Keillor attended the University of Minnesota at Minneapolis, where he worked as a staff announcer for the campus station, KUOM Radio, from 1963 to 1968. This job began a long career in radio, during which he took the more formal Garrison Keillor as his professional name. He married Mary C. Guntzel on September 11, 1965, and one son, Jason, was born of their union. He received a B.A. from the University of Minnesota in 1966 and briefly sought a writing job in New York. He had hoped to join the staff of *The New Yorker*, a magazine he had admired since boyhood. He was not at that time successful, so he continued in broadcasting. In 1971, he began working as an announcer and producer with Minnesota Public Radio in St. Paul. In 1974, he launched the highly successful weekly program, *A Prairie Home Companion*, for which he served as host and principal writer. He was divorced in May, 1976.

A Prairie Home Companion, inspired by the *Grand Ole Opry* radio program, was broadcast live before a theater audience on Saturday nights. The program ran for more than a decade. It was carried by more than two hundred American Public Radio stations and was televised during its final season on the air. It was a variety show made up of an eclectic musical component, comic sketches (written or cowritten by Keillor), and the host's weekly monologue about the goings-on in his fictional hometown of Lake Wobegon, Minnesota. Keillor's leisurely monologues drew heavily upon his small-town upbringing, although he has always insisted that Lake Wobegon is a romantic creation, not a caricature of his actual hometown. Keillor grew up in a Fundamentalist sect called the Plymouth Brethren, whose strictures made other Fundamentalist denominations appear rather "loose." The monologues often treated the American practice of Christianity humorously, but also gently and

affectionately. *A Prairie Home Companion* was interspersed with commercials for fictitious businesses and products: Ralph's Pretty Good Grocery, Bertha's Kitty Boutique, the Chatterbox Cafe, Bob's Bank, the Sidetrack Tap, Scottie's Cough Syrup for Dogs, and—most popular of all—Powdermilk Biscuits.

Although never perhaps reaching the mass audience available to commercial radio, the show was a phenomenal popular success for public broadcasting. It was also a critical success, receiving the George Foster Peabody Broadcasting Award in 1980 and the Edward R. Murrow Award from the Corporation for Public Broadcasting in 1985. On December 29, 1985, Keillor married Ulla Skaerved, a social worker and a native of Denmark. Together they have four children. During the run of *A Prairie Home Companion*, Keillor, who had contributed to *The New Yorker* and other magazines for several years, published two books: *Happy to Be Here* (1982), followed by an expanded edition in 1983, and *Lake Wobegon Days* (1985). The success of these—especially the latter, which was a huge best-seller—helped to broaden his listening audience. The growing popularity of the show eventually prompted a special on public television, which was followed by a regular spot on the schedule of the Disney Channel.

In 1987, Keillor announced that he was ending the show so that he could move with his wife and family to her native country. There, having freed himself from the weekly grind of producing and performing, he would devote himself to his writing. *A Prairie Home Companion* had been based in and around St. Paul, Minnesota, during its entire tenure on the air, and the last regularly scheduled show was broadcast from that city on June 13, 1987. Keillor subsequently brought out two more books: *Leaving Home* (1987) and *We Are Still Married* (1989). He did move to Copenhagen but lived there for only a few months before returning to the United States. He and his family took up residence in New York City, where he became formally associated with *The New Yorker*. He also returned to radio, which he admitted to missing more than he had anticipated. He performed at the National Convention of the Democratic Party at Atlanta, Georgia, in 1988. He also began a series of annual "farewell performances" of *A Prairie Home Companion*. The first was broadcast and telecast from New York City in 1988, the second from Dallas, Texas, in 1989. In the autumn of 1989, he launched a new show on public radio; it originated in New York City and had a different title and cast as well as an altered format. In 1990, he toured with a two-man show, featuring himself and guitarist Chet Atkins, a frequent guest on the old *A Prairie Home Companion*.

Analysis

With the publication of his second book, *Lake Wobegon Days*, Garrison Keillor was crowned the new Mark Twain. He has consistently disavowed the epithet, insisting that he has no such grand illusions about his work. He has turned the comparison aside with a jest by remarking that the Eastern literary establishment considers any humorist from west of Eighth Avenue the new Mark Twain. Still, the comparison is understandable. Keillor, like Twain, is the product of a small town in middle America. Twain's best work features the mighty Mississippi River, which he had known intimately from boyhood, and for thirteen years Keillor's popular broadcasts emanated from St. Paul, Minnesota, on the banks of the Mississippi. For *The Adventures of Tom Sawyer* (1876) and *The Adventures of Huckleberry Finn* (1884), Twain created the idyllic river town of St. Petersburg, and Keillor portrays life in the mythical hamlet of Lake Wobegon. Like Twain, Keillor is at his best in the short story or sketch, and his long works, like Twain's, are actually a stringing together of such shorter pieces. Both men eventually moved to the East after making their reputations in the West. Some of these parallels are superficial, others less so. It can be said, at least, that Keillor follows in the tradition of Mark Twain and Will Rogers—writers also widely known as performers.

Twain attempted several times to give up his lecture tours but was forced to resume them because of the press of financial need. In 1987, Keillor gave up the radio program which had made him famous with the stated intention of devoting himself exclusively to writing. Although the decision took his fans by surprise, it probably should not have. On his show, he repeatedly referred to himself as a writer, suggesting pretty clearly that his performance on stage was a subsidiary, not his primary, activity; however, he is a brilliant monologuist with a rich speaking voice and impeccable comic timing. His old-fashioned, leisurely style of storytelling, which does not rely upon gags and never rushes in order to elicit laughter, is unique in contemporary show business. His regular listeners were understandably unwilling to see him give up something he did so remarkably well. After a few months, he announced that he would resume occasional performances of *A Prairie Home Companion*. Keillor, who also has a pleasant singing voice, had regularly sung with his musical guests. He declared that this singing was what he had missed most during his brief absence from radio.

Keillor's humor has a characteristically gentle tone, but it ranges from good-natured farce to satire that is not always so gentle. He was selling whimsical pieces to *The New Yorker* and *The Atlantic Monthly* as early as 1970. His usual method was to take some American practice bordering upon absurdity and embellish it into hilarity. His spoofs seemed to have no particular political orientation, no ax to grind. The satire was Horatian, gently chiding and essentially free of animus. Stories and sketches from this early period, 1970-1982, were collected in his first book, *Happy to Be Here*. His period of great popularity, both as a writer and a performer, was inaugurated by an article he did on the Grand Ole Opry in the spring of 1974. This piece, which appeared in *The New Yorker*, was the biggest sale he had made up to that time, but, more important, it started him thinking about the possibility of doing a radio show modeled after the original *Grand Ole Opry*. Keillor believed that over the years that program had strayed from its original simplicity and lack of pretension. He would attempt to recapture these qualities in a live broadcast done before a theater audience and directed toward whatever group of people would stay home on Saturday evenings to listen to the radio. The result was *A Prairie Home Companion*.

The show had an anachronistic quality about it from the beginning. It featured old bluegrass and gospel numbers. The central segment of the show came to be Keillor's long monologue on the week's happenings in his imaginary hometown, Lake Wobegon, Minnesota. For many listeners, *A Prairie Home Companion* was a repository of traditional Midwestern—and, by extension, American—virtues. Such adjectives as old-fashioned, wholesome, clean, and decent were frequently applied to Keillor's humor. *Lake Wobegon Days* was, among other things, a history of the hamlet from its founding to the present day. The book was greeted with overwhelming approval by both the reading public and the critics. In *Leaving Home,* Keillor rewrote and collected thirty-six Lake Wobegon monologues from the show. *We Are Still Married* is composed of stories, sketches, letters, and light verse. Although the Keillor persona of the first three books still dominates the text, it is fair to say these pieces are more urban, more personal, more political, and more caustic than the earlier work.

To return to the comparison which Keillor resists, it may be that he is attempting to do what Mark Twain also attempted (without much success). Twain eventually became somewhat embarrassed by his frontier persona and wished instead to be remembered as the author of *Personal Recollections of Joan of Arc* (1896). Keillor's appealing humor and literary craftsmanship certainly predate his creation of Lake Wobegon, but many of his readers have come to love the residents of that little town and are reluctant to give them up.

HAPPY TO BE HERE

First published: 1982
Type of work: Short stories

The fads, fashions, and everyday absurdities of contemporary American life are treated in roughly thirty short comic pieces.

Happy to Be Here is subtitled *Stories and Comic Pieces.* The original version contains twenty-nine selections and is divided into five parts (an expanded edition appeared the next year). Most of the selections can be classified as short stories, although some are parodies of other genres or brief comic sketches. Most are humorous, although a few are mood pieces that scarcely rely upon humor at all. The book's title story, which originally appeared in *The New Yorker* under the title "Found Paradise," is a monologue by a writer who has left the city for the dubious paradise of a Minnesota farm. It is an example of the polarity found in so much of Keillor's work: the narrator's being tugged at simultaneously by the charm—and often the absurdity as well—of rural and small-town life on the one hand and the glamor of the city on the other.

The reader meets quite a gallery of characters: The title character in "Jack Schmidt, Arts Administrator" is a private eye who has turned to grantsmanship on behalf of such clients as the Minnesota Anti-Dance Ensemble (they do not believe in performance). Don of "Don: The True Story of a Young Person" is the leader of Trash, a punk-rock band; Trash becomes famous—or notorious—for eating live chickens during the act. Slim of "The Slim Graves Show" presides over a country and western radio program that evolves into a singing soap opera, with the listening audience voting for its favorite member of the love triangle. In "Friendly Neighbor," Walter "Dad" Benson is the star of a curious radio show on which the fictional Benson family listens to another show, piped in from an adjoining studio. The show within the show is a dramatization of the family life of the Muellers, equally fictional. Mr. Mueller's indiscretion at Christmastime, 1958, shocks the Midwestern audience by setting such a poor example for Christian listeners, especially during the holy season. Dad strongly states his disapproval of Mr. Mueller's decision to spend Christmas at his girlfriend's house rather than with his wife and children. Dad's audience is not placated, however, having decided that the Bensons probably should not have been listening to *The Muellers* to begin with; on New Year's Day, 1959, the parent show, *Friendly Neighbor*, leaves the air. Keillor's many years as a broadcaster in the Midwest are apparent throughout *Happy to Be Here*.

Keillor's interest in baseball, evident in all of his books, is reflected in several pieces from *Happy to Be Here*. "Around the Horne" is a parody of a sports column, the subject of which is a losing baseball team, the Flyers. Bill Horne is sick, and his substitute columnist is a psychologist, much under the influence of *I'm OK, You're OK*, a popular self-help work published in 1969. Ed Farr managed the team from a Fourth of July doubleheader until the end of the season, giving the players intense one-to-one and group therapy all along the way. He explains that the problems of the pitching staff resulted from their having suffered "pitcher's block." Similar problems in hitting and fielding resulted from the fans sending a clear message that the Flyers were not OK. Farr looks to the coming season with high hopes for his charges' personal growth and increased self-esteem. "Attitude" outlines the proper approach to playing slow-pitch softball. One should chatter continuously, spit frequently, pull up tufts of grass, and become involved with dirt. These mannerisms represent real ball and will compensate for any amount of inept play. "The New Baseball" argues that the existential response to modern life is altering the traditions of the game. The emphasis upon performance, the use of umpires, the keeping of the score—all will ultimately disappear. The static conventions of three strikes and three outs will wither away as players become more concerned with experiencing at-batness than with getting hits. The final salutary development will be the abandonment of the arbitrary distinction between player and spectator. "How Are the Legs, Sam?" examines the baseball career of the narrator, who played one game in 1965, one game in 1966, and has been inactive from 1967 to 1970.

The final section of the book—containing the pieces "The Drunkard's Sunday," "Happy to Be Here," and "Drowning 1954"—is more melancholy or wistful than humorous in tone. The collection represents the sort of work Keillor has been doing as a free-lance contributor to *The New Yorker* for more than a decade; most of the pieces in the book, in fact, appeared originally in that magazine.

LAKE WOBEGON DAYS

First published: 1985
Type of work: Novel

The novel is a portrait of the fictitious Minnesota town—its history and its current inhabitants.

The narrator is Garrison Keillor, but, like the Dante of *La divina commedia* (c. 1320; *The Divine Comedy*, 1802), he must be understood to be a fictional character created by the author, not the author himself. The narrative is actually many small narratives skillfully connected by means of association. The history of Lake Wobegon, Minnesota, population 942, is interwoven with present-day events, the narrator's childhood and adolescence, and his musings on the significance of being a Wobegonian. The two qualities that have defined Lake Wobegon life down through the years are happenstance and patience.

There are two contenders for the title of first European to arrive at what is now Lake Wobegon. In 1836, an Italian, Count Carlo Pallavicini, searching for the headwaters of the Mississippi, took one look around and decided he was not there. The previous year, a French priest, Father Pierre Plaisir, had visited what the *voyageurs* came to call Lac Malheur, but, since he mentions nonexistent mountains in his memoir, he may well have been farther to the west. Next, in the early 1850's, came a party of Unitarian missionaries from Boston, led by Prudence Alcott, who intended to convert the Indians to Christianity by means of interpretive dance. The New Englanders gave the name New Albion to the village they settled. One of Miss Alcott's companions, a poet named Henry Francis Watt, composed the first account of Lake Wobegon to reach the East, a poem of 648 lines entitled "Phileopolis: A Western Rhapsody—Thoughts Composed a Short Distance Above Lake Wobegon." Watt, armed with the spurious degrees of Ph.D., Litt. D., and D.D. (all conferred upon him by a coffee broker and land speculator named Bayfield), established New Albion College. The college eventually boasted an enrollment of thirty-six but, after a bear ate one of the scholars, only one student remained for the following spring term (it was later determined that his mind was unhinged, and he was removed to the state asylum). New Albion College was forced to close its doors.

A group of Norwegians arrived on May 15, 1867. Having been fishermen in the old country, they had emigrated deep into the Dakota Territory under the mistaken notion that they would find a huge lake with bountiful fishing. On the weary return trip, they stopped and settled in Lake Wobegon. Then came the German immigrants, who were headed elsewhere but had misread their map. They chose to stay in Lake Wobegon rather than admit they had made a mistake. The Norwegians, who are Lutheran, and the Germans, who are Catholic, have become the dominant ethnic groups in Lake Wobegon. In 1880, the Norwegians finally gained control of the city council and officially changed the name of the town from New Albion to Lake Wobegon. They liked the sound of the word. Wobegon, or "Wa-be-gan-tan-han" in the Ojibway tongue, can be translated as "the place where we waited all day in the rain" or, more simply, as "patience."

Lake Wobegon is located in the appropriately named Mist County. Unfortunately, because of a series of surveying errors, the town has never appeared on any map. When the legislature discovered that the lines drawn by four teams of surveyors had overlapped badly in the middle of the state, they simply reproportioned the state by eliminating the overlap. The result of this action was to remove all of Mist County from the map. The State Map Amendment of 1933 was an attempt to rectify the situation, but it was attached to a bill requiring the teaching of evolution in all secondary schools and it failed. Wobegonians are sanguine about their official anonymity, just as they are about all of life's vicissitudes. They have learned that things seldom work out. A case in point is the town's one genuine athletic hero, Wally ("Old Hard Hands") Bunsen. Wally was a great ball player who had spent a part of the 1933 season with the Chicago Cubs, batting an impressive .348. As his nickname suggests, however, he had learned to play without a glove. A glove threw him off his game, and he begged to be allowed to play without one. The Cubs were adamant: No true major leaguer played without a glove. Wally came home. He died a tragic death in 1936 when he fouled an inside fast ball off his head while playing for the local team.

Keillor fleshes out his portrait of Lake Wobegon with descriptions of such local institutions as the Living Flag, the Sons of Knute lodge, the statue of the Unknown Norwegian, and the Viking runestone (which proves conclusively that Viking explorers visited Lake Wobegon in 1381). He lards the text with footnotes to fictitious sources: reference works, correspondence, even a book of etiquette. The reader is introduced to dozens of well-characterized residents of contemporary Lake Wobegon. Critics greeted the novel almost unanimously as a comic tour de force.

LEAVING HOME

First published: 1987
Type of work: Short stories

Keillor reworked a number of his radio monologues, each about the week's happenings in Lake Wobegon, into a collection of short stories.

The subtitle of *Leaving Home* forthrightly announces the nature of the volume: *A Collection of Lake Wobegon Stories.* Keillor had already performed each of the thirty-six stories as a monologue on *A Prairie Home Companion*. He announces at the beginning of the book that the stories have been altered somewhat from their original form.

The book's title may be ambiguous. Some of the characters in the stories do leave home; others would like to, or dream of doing so. Still, the reader is tempted to apply the title to the author as much as to his characters. Keillor chooses to begin his book with the text of a song he sometimes sang on *A Prairie Home Companion*—the lament of an absent Wobegonian who longs to see the old hometown one more time. This is followed by an introduction, "A Letter from Copenhagen," dated July 3, 1987. He muses therein about leaving behind one's homeland and all that is familiar but also reminds the reader that he has left his radio show after thirteen years. Lake Wobegon came to life each week within the twenty-minute monologue which was the centerpiece of the show. Was *Leaving Home* the author's last, long good-bye to Lake Wobegon? Two years later, his next book would contain only sixty-six pages of Lake Wobegon material out of a total of 330, and his new radio shows would feature no Lake Wobegon segment.

In the stories themselves, however, there are plenty of characters who are leaving home. In "Darlene Makes a Move," after thirteen years, Darlene is leaving her job as waitress at the Chatterbox Cafe on January 1. She is going to Minneapolis to settle matters with Arlen, the husband with whom she has not lived for many years. Then she will seek adventure. And in "A Glass of Wendy," Father Emil, who has been pastor at Our Lady of Perpetual Responsibility for over forty years, is retiring the day after Easter. In "Dale," Dale Uecker leaves a blossoming relationship with Carla Krebsbach behind to go off to the Navy (after he finally finds the key to his car). In "David and Agnes, a Romance," Val Tollefson reads his father's love letters to the woman with whom he ran away in 1946. Perhaps the most amusing of all the stories is "Truckstop." Myrtle Krebsbach has decided, based upon the question-and-answer column in the newspaper, that she has cancer. She is required to go to Minneapolis for her examination, since the local physician, Dr. DeHaven, and all the doctors in nearby Saint Cloud have pronounced her cancer free. She is driven by her husband, Florian, whose eyesight is poor and who has put only 47,000 miles on his 1966 Chevrolet. While Myrtle is using the ladies' room at the truckstop, Florian absentmindedly drives off without her, then gets off the interstate highway and gets lost.

Each of the stories begins with the sentence, "It has been a quiet week in Lake Wobegon," which was always the opening sentence of Keillor's monologue on *A Prairie Home Companion*. In the final story, "Goodbye to the Lake," the narrator, who is going to Copenhagen, takes a panoramic look at Lake Wobegon and her inhabitants on a rainy Wednesday in June. He announces that this will be his last view of them for a while. The writing in *Leaving Home* does not rise to the level of that in *Lake Wobegon Days*. The stories were originally written for oral delivery and do not require the stylistic dexterity found in so much of the earlier book. The stories are well constructed, however, and frequently employ Keillor's familiar blend of comedy and pathos.

WE ARE STILL MARRIED

First published: 1989
Type of work: Short stories

A comic potpourri of short stories, sketches, letters, and poems.

Although Keillor has always been at his best in the short narrative, the flawless anecdote, *We Are Still Married* conveys much more of the pastiche effect than do his first three books. The political satire is harsher, more focused, and more partisan. A number of the pieces, while extremely entertaining, seemed mainly to be apologias for the author's recent decisions regarding his personal and professional life. "Reagan," written just prior to the presidential election of 1988, is in places pure political commentary. "A Liberal Reaches for Her Whip" is more in the vein of earlier Keillor whimsy, but it too includes a direct attack upon Ronald Reagan, George Bush, and the political atmosphere they have fostered in the United States. "Patmos," the account of a trip to Greece, is sprinkled with comment on the fateful nature of the 1988 American presidential election, which is occurring at the same time. Previously, Keillor's narrator persona generally responded with bemused tolerance for the foibles of his fellow man, including his political foibles. Keillor's political commentary is exceedingly mild by comparison to the Juvenalian assaults launched daily by the Washington-based columnists; still, it is a relatively new—and, to some readers, troubling—aspect of his work.

Other pieces—"Who Do You Think You Are?" "Regrets," and "My Life in Prison"—hint at the strained relationships and acrimony which must have accompanied his termination of *A Prairie Home Companion* while it was at its peak in popularity and his subsequent move from St. Paul to Manhattan by way of Copenhagen. The reader recalls the segment in *Lake Wobegon Days* wherein Johnny Tollefson, prospective freshman at St. Cloud State College, is longing to change places with Tony Flambeau of the Flambeau Family mystery series. The Flambeaus have a spacious apartment overlooking Central Park. Emil Flambeau is a Nobel laureate microbiologist, Eileen Flambeau is a former screen star, and teenaged Tony Flambeau drinks wine (Pouilly-Fuissé) with his parents and calls them by their first names. If Johnny Tollefson had actually succeeded in making it to Manhattan, he would surely have left some ruffled feathers behind him in Lake Wobegon.

We Are Still Married is composed of five sections. Section 1, "Pieces," includes thirteen short works, highlighted by the brilliant parodies "The Current Crisis in Remorse," "The Young Lutheran's Guide to the Orchestra," "A Little Help," and "Lifestyle." Section 2, "The Lake," is a five-part miscellany featuring familiar characters from Lake Wobegon. Section 3, "Letters," begins with a how-to essay on letter writing, which is followed by thirty-one letters of various sorts. "House Poems," the fourth section, contains eleven pieces of entertaining light verse. "Stories," the final section, is composed of eleven stories, the last of which also furnishes the title of the book.

Familiar motifs reappear—for example, sports and what they say about American attitudes. "Three New Twins Join Club in Spring" is a humorous response to the Minnesota Twins' victory in the 1987 World Series, and "Home Team" is a bittersweet rumination on the same subject. "The Babe" recalls the day a sick and aging Babe Ruth came barnstorming through Lake Wobegon. "What Did We Do Wrong?" is a short story about Annie Szemanski, the first woman to play in the big leagues. "Basketball" recounts Keillor's making three of four shots while taping a piece promoting the NCAA tournament for CBS, and "Puck Drop" describes his role in the season-opening ceremonies of the Minnesota North Stars.

The contents of *We Are Still Married* range from seventeen unsigned essays, observations, and reflections appearing much earlier in *The New Yorker* to selections which appeared in periodicals only shortly before their inclusion in the book. The narrator left Lake Wobegon in the last story in *Leaving Home*, and *We Are Still Married* seems to signal further movement away from that mythical community.

Summary

The titles of Garrison Keillor's four books and the order of their publication serve as a summary statement of his career. In *Happy to Be Here*, a major comedic talent appears on the literary scene. *Lake Wobegon Days* showcases his powers of invention and his impressive prose style in a sustained narrative; *Leaving Home* announces that the author's Lake Wobegon period is coming to an end. In *We Are Still Married*, Keillor's center of consciousness is no longer located in the Midwest. It can now be found in New York City. Perhaps the title is both a plea and a pledge to the readers who loved Lake Wobegon so much.

Bibliography

Black, David. "Live from Wobegon." *Rolling Stone* 348 (July 23, 1981): 8, 13.

Blount, Roy, Jr. "Garrison Keillor." *The New York Times Book Review*, February 28, 1982, pp. 12, 18.

Geng, Veronica. "Idylls of Minnesota." *The New York Times Book Review*, August 25, 1985, pp. 1, 15.

Hughes, Glyn. "Grace and Fate." *New Statesman* 111 (March 7, 1986): 26-27.

Mano, D. Keith. "Here at *The New Yorker*." *National Review* 33 (December 11, 1981): 1492.

Paterson, Katherine. "Tales from the Town That Time Forgot." *Book/World* 15 (September 1, 1985): 1-2.

Thorpe, Doug. "Garrison Keillor's 'Prairie Home Companion': Gospel of the Airwaves." *The Christian Century* 99 (July 21-28, 1982): 793-796.

Patrick Adcock

WILLIAM KENNEDY

Born: Albany, New York
January 16, 1928

Principal Literary Achievement

Writing about his hometown of Albany, New York, Kennedy has made important contributions to contemporary American literature by revitalizing fictional regionalism.

Biography

William Joseph Kennedy, Jr., was born in Albany, New York, on January 16, 1928, to William Joseph and Mary Elizabeth McDonald Kennedy. Kennedy grew up as an only child in a working-class family whose Irish ancestors had come to Albany five generations earlier. Kennedy's mother worked for many years as an accountant, while his father moved from job to job as a barber, foundry worker, pie salesman, and deputy sheriff.

The older Kennedy was a regular in the saloons, political clubs, and pool halls of Albany's North End, and, like many other young Irish Catholics, he became a petty player in the city's great political machine run by boss Daniel P. O'Connell. As a child, Kennedy often accompanied his father, who served as a ward heeler, making rounds to the gaming rooms and meeting halls where bribery, payoffs, and crooked dealings were the custom.

On his own time, Kennedy visited the pool halls and bowling alleys and followed with great interest the careers of all the day's legendary baseball players and hustlers. At the same time, in keeping with his Irish Catholic upbringing, the young Kennedy served as an altar boy and attended Christian Brothers Academy in Albany. After high school, Kennedy enrolled in Siena College, a Franciscan school in Loudonville, New York, where he originally planned to study chemical engineering. A failing grade in geometry, however, made him decide to switch his major to English. In preparation for a career in journalism, he served as editor of the college newspaper; he received his bachelor's degree in 1949.

After college, Kennedy accepted a position as sportswriter with the *Post-Star* in Glen Falls, New York. He continued his journalism career as a sports editor and columnist for the United States Army newspapers and rose to the rank of sergeant before completing his military service in 1952. He then returned to his native Albany to join the *Albany Times-Union* as a reporter covering city hall.

Growing tired of his job and of Albany itself, Kennedy accepted a job in Puerto Rico and in 1956 became the assistant managing editor for a new English-language newspaper called the *Puerto Rico World Journal*. The newspaper went out of business only a few months after his arrival, and Kennedy moved to Florida, where he briefly worked for the *Miami Herald*. Returning to Puerto Rico in 1957, he served as Puerto Rican correspondent for Knight newspapers and Time-Life publications and married Ana Daisy Dana Segarra, a dancer, singer, and actress from Puerto Rico. In 1959, Kennedy helped found the *San Juan Star* and served as its managing editor until 1961.

It was during his time in Puerto Rico that Kennedy became interested in writing fiction and began studying under Pulitzer Prize-winning novelist Saul Bellow at the University of Puerto Rico. In 1961, Kennedy was suddenly called back to Albany to care for his sick father. During his father's illness, Kennedy worked as a full-time fiction writer until 1963, when he took a part-time job with the *Albany Times-Union* writing local color stories and film reviews. His in-depth reporting focused on Albany's history, ethnic groups, politicians, and vagabonds. In 1965, Kennedy received a Pulitzer Prize nomination for a controversial series he wrote about the city's slums. A strike at the *Albany Times-Union* inspired Kennedy's first published novel, *The Ink Truck* (1969), and many of the drifters and derelicts he encountered as a reporter became models for the characters in his later novels. In 1970, Kennedy left the newspaper and served briefly as book editor for *Look* magazine. He then took a position as a part-time lecturer at State University of New York, Albany, where he was made a tenured professor of English in 1982.

After eight drafts, Kennedy's second novel, *Legs*, was published in 1975, and *Billy Phelan's Greatest Game* followed in 1978. Both novels, set in Albany, tell the legendary stories of some of the city's most notorious characters, including gangster Jack "Legs" Diamond and political strongman Boss O'Connell. Both novels failed to achieve wide critical attention (neither was reviewed by *The New York Times*). It was the publication of *Ironweed* in 1983 that brought Kennedy fame. Viking and twelve other publishing houses had initially rejected *Ironweed* because Kennedy's previous novels were such commercial failures. A supporting letter from Saul Bellow, however, persuaded Viking to reconsider and not only publish *Ironweed* but also reissue *Legs* and *Billy Phelan's Greatest Game. Ironweed* received wide critical acclaim, winning both the National Book Critics Circle Award (1983-1984) and the Pulitzer Prize (1984).

In 1983, Kennedy was awarded the prestigious MacArthur Foundation Award, a fellowship for "exceptionally talented individuals," which brought him $264,000 over three years, tax free. With some of the proceeds from his fellowship, Kennedy established the Writers Institute at Albany in 1984 and began his term as its director. He also won the New York State Governor's Award and was honored in his hometown by a four-day "William Kennedy's Albany" celebration, featuring a party in the park, historical exhibits, tours on the town, and a talk by Kennedy himself.

In 1983, Kennedy published *O Albany! An Urban Tapestry*, a collection of essays on the town's history and folklore, and in the same year worked with Francis Ford Coppola on a script for the film *The Cotton Club* (1984). *Quinn's Book*, the fourth novel in what has become known as Kennedy's "Albany cycle," was published in 1988. In addition to his six published books, Kennedy is the author of numerous monographs and brochures for New York's educational institutions, libraries, and museums.

Kennedy and his wife live in a nineteenth century farmhouse in Averhill Park, a suburb of Albany, and Kennedy has an office in a former rooming house in downtown Albany where Jack "Legs" Diamond was murdered. The Kennedys have three children. Their daughter Katherine works as Kennedy's secretary, transferring her father's typewritten, hand-edited manuscripts to the word processor.

Analysis

In his early attempts at writing fiction, Kennedy turned to exotic locales and set his stories in Puerto Rico, where he worked briefly as a newspaper reporter and editor; however, like William Faulkner, James Joyce, and other notable writers before him, Kennedy soon realized that his most valuable fictional subject was his own hometown—Albany, New York. Kennedy points to his time in Puerto Rico as an important stage in his development as a writer. Being away from home gave him the distance he needed to fictionalize the New York town he had come to know so well.

With the guidance of novelist Saul Bellow, who taught at the University of Puerto Rico, Kennedy began writing about what he knew best, the people and places of Albany, New York. Uninterested in sanitizing his city's past or present, he relinquished traditional civic pride and directed his attention to Albany's most infamous citizens. Kennedy's cast of characters includes the legendary gangsters, politicians, and everyday drifters who inhabit Albany's Irish Catholic North End. During his days as a reporter for Albany's *Times-Union*, Kennedy had come to know these people, their history, and their ways of talking and living.

Kennedy's earlier works, particularly *Legs* and *Billy Phelan's Greatest Game*, reflect his training as a newspaperman and are told in a fast-paced journalistic style. These first two novels of Kennedy's Albany cycle are action-packed exposés of the city's seamy underworld run by cunning gangsters and a corrupt political machine. Both novels are told with an episodic quality that naturally creates a level of suspense appropriate to such sensational subject matter. While recounting the escapades of some of Albany's more infamous citizens, *Legs* and *Billy Phelan's Greatest Game* both present a similar psychological theme in their exploration of the ambiguous appeal of underworld life. Similar in many respects, the narrators of the two books are both peculiarly envious of the exciting, though often illegal, adventures of those whose stories they tell. With frank honesty and ironic humor, Kennedy adeptly explores this odd American fascination with immorality.

In *Ironweed*, Kennedy largely abandons his journalist style and adopts a more lyrical, poetic approach. Still focusing on the psychological implications of immorality, Kennedy turns his investigation inward and explores the soul of a man haunted by his own sins and indiscretions. Unlike Jack "Legs" Diamond and Billy Phelan, Francis Phelan of *Ironweed* is no one's hero. He is a bum on the run who must live with the guilt of knowing that he has let almost everyone in his life down, most of all himself. Taking an almost surrealistic approach, Kennedy literally resurrects the dead to talk to Francis and haunt him into confronting his disturbingly violent past. With the external action kept to a minimum, *Ironweed* is a powerful saga that draws its strength from one man's internal struggle to find forgiveness from himself and from others.

Though it marks a noticeable stylistic break from the previous works, *Quinn's Book*, like *Ironweed*, also shows a man struggling to come to terms with himself. A coming-of-age story set in nineteenth century Albany, *Quinn's Book* traces young Daniel Quinn's development into an artist and a lover. Kennedy uses authentic historical idiom and typical nineteenth century rhetoric to create characters of Dickensian proportion. Still using Albany's colorful history as a backdrop, Kennedy employs a much more elaborate and grand style to bring nineteenth century Albany to life.

Without question, the most prevailing and distinguishing feature of Kennedy's work is its strong sense of time and place. Throughout the years, Albany has suffered the fate of existing in the shadow of its more cosmopolitan neighbor, New York City. By comparison, Albany gained a reputation as a singularly unromantic, provincial city. Kennedy embraces this unlikely setting, peoples it with old, sick, poor, and degenerate characters, and out of it all manages to spin magical tales, full of feeling and importance.

Kennedy's fiction focuses on the down-and-out—people in extreme situations, pushed to their limits, with their souls laid bare. The setting itself—Albany, in all its sordid splendor—acts as a character, a visible force shaping the lives of those who call the city home. In all of his novels, Kennedy treats his characters and their home with reverence and respect, never satirizing, sentimentalizing, or apologizing for their shortcomings.

In his raucous New York town, Kennedy creates a microcosm and paints a vivid picture of all that was wicked and corrupt and splendid in America's not-so-distant past. Writing with an undeniable knowledge of the people, the idioms, and the history of his hometown, Kennedy creates an Albany alive with mythic possibilities and lavishes enthusiastic attention on those generally neglected by others. Kennedy's work hails Albany as a durable town held up by a cast of resilient characters whose main concern, and talent, is survival. With a witty, ironic style, Kennedy blends nostalgia with serious history to create believable fiction. As Saul Bellow commented, upon the publication of *Ironweed*: "These Albany novels will be memorable, a distinguished group of books."

LEGS

First published: 1975
Type of work: Novel

A devoted friend and lawyer recounts the escapades of his boss, legendary gangster Jack "Legs" Diamond.

In *Legs*, Kennedy creates a fictional biography recounting the last year and a half of the life of Albany's most notorious gangster. Jack "Legs" Diamond—a real-life bootlegger, murderer, drug dealer, and rascal—lived above the law, carrying out his business in upstate New York during Prohibition in the 1920's and early 1930's. Kennedy's fictional account of this legendary figure was five years in the making, the result of painstaking historical research and eight drafts.

Legs is, however, more than a catalog of one gangster's exploits. It is a psychological and sociological look at America's fascination with gangsters, murderers, and bad men of all types. Jack, like many gangsters of his era, was a celebrity, a national obsession. The newspapers were filled with details of his every move. He received fan mail, and cheers fill the courtroom when he was acquitted of one particularly brutal assault.

Legs is narrated by Marcus Gorman, Jack's employee, friend, and admirer. The two first meet in the Catskills in 1925 when Marcus impresses Jack with his eloquent praise of Al Jolson, one of Jack's own favorite musicians. Later, Jack sends Marcus, an ambitious young lawyer, six quarts of Scotch in exchange for a pistol permit from Albany County. Attracted to the excitement and intrigue that surrounds this Irish-American gangster-bootlegger, Marcus signs on as Jack's personal lawyer in 1930. While acknowledging the violence and crime, Marcus nevertheless idolizes his boss and recounts their days together with heartfelt admiration and devotion. Marcus declares that Jack was, above all, a man of integrity and deserves at least some credit for being an honest thief.

Working out of his headquarters in the Catskills, Jack made his money running liquor across the border from Canada during the days of Prohibition. His operation was huge and elaborate, with flocks of carrier pigeons used as messengers to avoid telephone wiretaps. Jack came to upstate New York after leaving New York City, where he had shot a customer at his nightclub—once in the stomach, once in the forehead, twice in the temple, and twice in the groin—then hit the man's brother over the head with the spent revolver. Marcus tells the details of several other of Jack's gruesome deeds. Once upstate, Jack tried to hang a local farmer, then did away with a competing rum-runner by dismembering him and burning his body in a still. Wherever Jack went, he left a trail of crime. He killed and tortured, dealt in liquor and heroin, and betrayed his associates. He bought judges, politicians, and policemen, and to many he seemed unstoppable. His body was filled with bullets and crossed with scars that his mistresses traced with their fingers. He was a ladies' man who frequented whorehouses while his devoted wife, Alice, remained true to him to the end.

In 1931, Jack's empire began to fall. Franklin Delano Roosevelt, then governor of New York, brought a fourteen-count indictment against him. The new federal crowd seemed unbuyable, and in a raid on his headquarters in the Catskills, ten million dollars in warehouse stock alone was seized. Later that year, he was gunned down in a rooming house wearing only his underwear.

Kennedy writes with wit and energy as he brings to light the moral ambiguity of success. With vivid language, Marcus' powerful narrative evokes a strong sense of time and place and tells an engrossing story of violence, sex, love, and comedy. In Marcus' mind, Jack never really died. He, in many ways, personifies the American Dream. He embodies the rags-to-riches story, rising to the top by shooting his way to fame. More important, as Marcus sees it, Jack "Legs" Diamond is a prototype for modern urban gangsters and lives on as one of the founding fathers of criminality, whose legacy is sure to be felt for years to come. As Marcus says in his tribute to one of Albany's most memorable bullies, "Why he was a pioneer, the founder of the first truly modern gang, the dauphin of the town for years."

BILLY PHELAN'S GREATEST GAME

First published: 1978
Type of work: Novel

An Albany newspaper columnist recounts the story of Billy Phelan, a small-time hustler who finds himself in the middle of a kidnapping and extortion plot.

Like *Legs, Billy Phelan's Greatest Game* tells a story of Albany's seamier side, based on an actual incident from the city's history. In this second novel of what is often called the "Albany cycle," Kennedy fashions his work of fiction around the real-life 1933 kidnapping of John O'Connell, Jr., the nephew of Mayor Dan O'Connell and the heir apparent to Albany's omnipotent Democratic machine. In Kennedy's novel, the year is moved forward to 1938, the O'Connells become the McCalls, and John Jr. is known as Charlie Boy. Caught in the middle, torn between lending his services to the kidnappers or to the politicians, is Billy Phelan. Billy is a thirty-one-year-old pool hustler, bowling ace, poker player, and bookie, who feels right at home in the tough streets of this Depression-era town.

Along with its other similarities to *Legs, Billy Phelan's Greatest Game* shares a similar narrative structure. Billy's story is told by Martin Daugherty, a world-weary columnist from Albany's *Times-Union* (the newspaper Kennedy worked for before becoming a full-time fiction writer). Like Marcus Gorman in *Legs,* Daugherty acts as foil to the protagonist. Daugherty is a fifty-year-old husband and father, a man burdened with responsibility. With sympathy and understanding, he tells the story of

Billy Phelan, a tough street-smart young man of hardy Irish stock, and like *Legs*'s Martin Gorman, he looks on the shady adventures of his subject with a certain degree of envy. As a reporter, Daugherty has seen too much of the world, and with the eye of a cynic, he looks with disgust at the political corruption that has become a way of life in his town.

The action of the story centers on the bizarre kidnapping of the political boss's nephew. Billy, who is a small cog in the McCall machine, gets pulled in as reluctant go-between. He is pushed to turn informer and must decide whether to uphold his underworld image or comply with the demands of his political patrons by informing on the kidnappers.

Typical of Kennedy's style, *Billy Phelan's Greatest Game* is narrated in vivid, fast-paced cinematic prose that mirrors the swift, suspenseful action of the rough and sweaty city his characters call home. The shabby but ever resourceful underworld figures move at night, hiding in the shadows, occasionally illuminated by the glow of neon signs. They inhabit the rough world of the Irish working class where being a survivor is all that counts.

Like *Legs*, *Billy Phelan's Greatest Game* enjoyed a respectable number of favorable reviews but failed to achieve wide critical recognition or commercial success. Prominent critic Doris Grumbach commented in a 1978 article for the *Saturday Review*:

> [Kennedy's] pitch is perfect. . . . The cast of *Billy Phelan* is, quite simply, a wonder—a magical bunch of thugs, lovers, and game players. No one writing in America today . . . has Kennedy's rich and fertile gift of gab; his pure verbal energy; his love of people, and their kith and kin.

IRONWEED

First published: 1983
Type of work: Novel

Francis Phelan, haunted by ghosts from his past, returns home after twenty-two years of life on the run.

With the publication of *Ironweed* in 1983, Kennedy suddenly found himself at the forefront of contemporary American fiction. This third novel of Kennedy's Albany cycle received wide critical acclaim, winning both the National Book Critics Circle Award (1983-1984) and the Pulitzer Prize (1984). Ironically, *Ironweed* was initially rejected by thirteen publishing houses. Because of the commercial failings of *Legs* and *Billy Phelan's Greatest Game*, the editors at Viking were reluctant to undertake the publication of another Kennedy novel. A scolding letter from novelist Saul Bellow, however, Kennedy's first fiction writing teacher, changed their minds and gave Viking the idea of reissuing Kennedy's two previous novels and marketing the trilogy as what Bellow called the "Albany cycle." In his letter, Bellow reprimanded the editors at Viking, saying, "That the author of *Billy Phelan* should have a manuscript kicking around looking for a publisher is disgraceful."

In *Ironweed*, Kennedy continues his story of the fictional Phelan family and focuses his narrative on Billy's father, Francis. Among other ties to the previous Albany novels is the brief appearance of Marcus Gorman, the narrator of *Legs*; he serves as Francis' lawyer in *Ironweed*. In Kennedy's Albany cycle, the cast of characters usually overlaps slightly from one book to another. While the reappearances and intertwining plots are interesting to note, each novel in the Albany cycle is self-contained and ultimately stands on its own, independent of its predecessors.

In both *Legs* and *Billy Phelan's Greatest Game*, the narrators themselves develop into main characters and supply important secondary plots. *Ironweed*, however, is told from a third-person instead of a first-person point of view, and the character of narrator is thus eliminated. *Ironweed* is the story of one man's physical and emotional struggle for survival and redemption. All the narrative energy and insight is focused on this one main character, Francis Phelan.

A man haunted by his past, Francis has been wandering from flophouse to flophouse after walking out on his family twenty-two years ago. The novel spans two days and two nights, Halloween and All Saints' Day in 1938. Francis has returned to his hometown of Albany, New York, lured by the city's election and a crooked politician's offer of five dollars per vote. Eager to make some easy money, Francis has voted twenty-one times. Caught in the act, he is now spending his Halloween digging graves in a local cemetery to pay his legal expenses.

A former major-league third baseman, Francis had abandoned his wife and two children after the tragic death of his thirteen-day-old son. Francis accidentally dropped the infant while changing his diapers and now bears the grim responsibility of his own son's death. His newborn son was not the only person to die at Francis' hands. In a trolley-workers' strike, he killed a scab with a blow from a well-tossed rock; over the years, Francis has been witness to more than two dozen other deaths.

The opening scene of *Ironweed* finds Francis in an Albany graveyard, face-to-face with the ghosts of these and other victims of his past violence and neglect. In this fictional world where the line between fantasy and reality is obscured, the dead are very much alive, watching with great interest those they left behind. As Francis rides into the cemetery, his mother fidgets in her grave while his father, amused by his wife's nervousness, smokes a pipe and reflects on how much his son has changed. With an elegiac tone and at times surrealistic style, Kennedy is able to make these strange grumblings from the dead seem natural, even believable.

Francis lives on the streets and inhabits a dirty world of depressed and diseased winos. He moves from flophouses to missions to hobo jungles with a frail woman named Helen, his companion in homelessness. Shifting from past to present, reality to illusion, Kennedy vividly creates this haunted world of the bums where Francis seeks refuge from his disturbing past.

In one of the book's most moving scenes, the fifty-eight-year-old Francis returns home to his family with a turkey under his arm for dinner. Reunited with his faithful wife, Francis is shocked to learn that she has never blamed him for their son's death, never even told anyone that it was Francis who dropped the baby. In a departure from the fast-paced journalistic style of his previous novels, Kennedy uses poetic prose, compassionate yet unsentimental, to show a man coming to terms with his own sense of guilt.

A passage from The Audubon Society's *Field Guide to North American Wildflowers* serves as an epigraph for the book and explains that ironweed is a common flowering weed with a particularly tough stem. Indeed, Francis is resilient like the ironweed of the title. He is a survivor, an unromantic antihero caught in a seemingly never-ending quest for forgiveness from both the dead and the living.

QUINN'S BOOK

First published: 1988
Type of work: Novel

Daniel Quinn comes of age as a writer and as a lover in nineteenth century Albany.

Many critics have argued that *Quinn's Book* should not be considered a part of Kennedy's Albany cycle. In both style and setting, *Quinn's Book* stands apart from Kennedy's previous works. Though set in Albany, *Quinn's Book* shows New York's capital city as it was in the nineteenth century and marks a break from Kennedy's previous preoccupation with twentieth century Albany. The style of writing also looks back to an earlier time, often imitating the melodramatic, convoluted rhetoric typical of nineteenth century prose.

Quinn's Book is a fictional autobiography narrated by Daniel Quinn, who at the start of the book is a fourteen-year-old skiffman on the Hudson River. The book opens on a cataclysmic day in Albany in 1849. A boat crossing the Hudson capsizes after being struck by an ice floe. The legendary actress-courtesan Magdalena Colon, better known as La Ultima, is one of the ill-fated passengers thrown overboard to her death. Her body is heroically pulled from the icy waters by young Daniel's boss, John the Brawn. Daniel, on a rescue mission of his own, assists La Ultima's bewitching twelve-year-old niece Maud Fallon to safety. Meanwhile, a nearby bridge collapses and more than a hundred onlookers plunge into the frozen Hudson. Calamities continue as the rush of ice causes a tidal wave that in turn starts a fire raging through the city. Amid the chaos, young Daniel, Maud, and John seek refuge and rush La Ultima's body to the grand mansion of one of Albany's oldest Dutch families. Here, in a frenzy of necrophilia, John resuscitates La Ultima through rigorous intercourse as Daniel and Maud look on with great fascination.

With this apocalyptic start, the novel is set in motion. Daniel reminisces, with great energy, about this important life-changing day, the day he met and fell in love with the beautiful Maud. The rest of the novel tells of Daniel's fifteen-year artistic and romantic quest as he struggles to become a writer and to forge a union with the elusive and, at times, infuriating Maud. This fictional coming-of-age story takes place against a busy historical backdrop. As a journalist, Daniel is particularly aware of events going on around him, and much of his narrative is devoted to first-hand accounts of these historic moments. The Civil War rages on while the Underground Railroad leads escaped slaves to freedom; closer to home, unrest grows among local iron-foundry workers, and the New York draft riots break out in 1864. True to the detail and language of the period, all of these events, complete with races at Saratoga and spectacular theatrical productions, take place alongside Daniel's own raucous odyssey. History and fiction are interwoven with authentic rhetorical gusto using a rich variety of nineteenth century literary styles, ranging from bombastic melodrama to comic sportswriting. With originality and humor, this picaresque novel blends fact and fiction to create a panoramic view of Albany's colorful history.

Summary

Speaking about his hometown of Oxford, Mississippi, William Faulkner once said, "I discovered that my own little postage stamp of native soil was worth writing about and that I would never live long enough to exhaust it." William Kennedy seems to have discovered a similar truth about his own "little postage stamp of native soil," Albany, New York. With its strong sense of time and place, Kennedy's fiction has given regionalism a new validity.

For the most part, Kennedy's stories are dark tales tempered with ironic wit and played out against a background of stark realism. He writes of the lower regions of humanity and shows how these often desperate people manage in their own small ways to transcend their limitations and survive from one day to the next.

Bibliography

Clarke, Peter P. "Classical Myth in William Kennedy's *Ironweed*." *Critique: Studies in Modern Fiction* 27 (Spring, 1986): 167-176.

Hunt, George W. "William Kennedy's Albany Trilogy." *America* 150 (May 19, 1984): 373-375.

Koenig, Rhoda. "Search and Destroy." *New York Magazine* 20 (May 23, 1988): pp. 93-94.

Mitgang, Herbert. "Reading and Writing: Inexhaustible Albany." *The New York Times Book Review*, November 13, 1983, p. 35.

Prescott, Peter S. "Having the Time of His Life." *Newsweek* 103 (February 6, 1984): 78-79.

Quinn, Peter A. "Incandescent Albany." *Commonweal* 115 (May 20, 1988): 308-309.

Winch, Terence. "The Albany Novels." *The American Book Review* 7 (May/June, 1985): 19.

Molly Brown

JACK KEROUAC

Born: Lowell, Massachusetts
March 12, 1922

Died: St. Petersburg, Florida
October 21, 1969

Principal Literary Achievement

Combining expressive poetic language with a fine ear for the patterns of American speech, Kerouac captured the romantic appeal of the archetypal American quest for adventure and renewal.

Biography

John Louis Lebris de Kerouac was the younger son of Leo Alcide Kerouac (a job printer) and Gabrielle Ange Levesque Kerouac, immigrants from Quebec who grew up in New England milltowns. He attended a parochial school in accordance with his family's Catholic background and complemented his education with frequent trips to the Lowell Public Library. At the age of five, he lost his brother Gerard to rheumatic fever, an event which haunted his dreams and became a focal point for the family saga he wrote in later years. Both an enthusiastic student and a fine athlete, he played football and starred in track for the Lowell High School team. His mother's tales of his Gallic and Celtic heritage intrigued him, as did the stories of his father's drinking companions, and although he had spoken French for his first six years, he was proficient enough in English to qualify for admission to Columbia University in 1940.

He had an athletic scholarship and played football until he broke his leg during his freshman year, which led to his dropping out of school temporarily. He shipped aboard a freighter to Greenland in 1942 but was drawn back to Columbia by the excitement of life in New York—its jazz clubs, emerging underground bohemian culture, and interesting mix of companions, eventually including the poet Allen Ginsberg, who was also enrolled at Columbia, and the somewhat bizarre genius William Burroughs. When the coach kept him on the bench in a game in 1942, Kerouac left school again and, in 1943, joined the U.S. Navy. He was discharged on psychiatric grounds after six months, and after rejoining his family in the borough of Queens, he shipped out again to Liverpool to gather experience for a writing career based on "what I'd seen with my own eyes." From 1944 to 1947, Kerouac moved among the people he called "the subterraneans," acting instinctively and impulsively. He mar-

ried and separated from Edie Parker in 1944, and met Neal Cassady, his spiritual "road brother" and the model for Dean Moriarty in *On the Road* (1957), in 1946, the same year his father died.

His father's death drew him closer to his mother, and after spending nearly two years traveling, he moved back in with her, beginning a pattern which was to continue until his death. He completed *The Town and the City* in 1949; after an initial rejection, the book was published in 1950. In the same year, Kerouac briefly married Joan Haverty—who gave birth to his daughter in 1951 after they had separated—and began to write the manuscript which became *On the Road*. Robert Giroux made some editorial suggestions to which Kerouac responded, but the finished book was not published for another six years; neither were the other manuscripts on which Kerouac worked during the 1950's. At the same time that he was writing, he followed a pattern of visiting friends in various parts of the United States and working on various odd jobs, including brakeman on the Southern Pacific in 1952 and fire watcher in the Cascade Mountains in 1956, as well as jobs in restaurants and aboard ship. In 1955 he was present at the landmark reading at the Six Gallery in San Francisco where Ginsberg presented "Howl," Kerouac assisting by chanting "Go" at the end of each line, and spent time with Gary Snyder, the poet and naturalist who became the narrator's climbing guru in *The Dharma Bums* (1958) as Japhy Ryder.

When *On the Road* was published by Viking Press in 1957, Kerouac found himself suddenly a celebrity and a center of controversy as traditional literary commentators assailed the book. Kerouac did not enjoy his prominence and did not approve of the steady stream of would-be road followers and beatniks who flocked to him for advice and inspiration. He did appreciate the opportunity to get his work into print, however, and published *The Subterraneans* and *The Dharma Bums* in 1958, and *Doctor Sax*, *Maggie Cassidy*, and the book of poems *Mexico City Blues* in 1959. Various personal problems, including a paternity suit, a general physical decline, and the psychic damage wrought by too much alcohol and other drugs pulled Kerouac off the road and into a kind of seclusion with his mother. His sister's death in 1964 bound him even closer to her, and although he traveled occasionally, he was primarily a sedentary person. His marriage to Stella Stampas in 1966 and his return to Lowell in that year completed a cycle out into the world and back to his origins; in his hometown he spent his last days working on *Vanity of Duluoz* (1968), the final chapter of a family saga almost Faulknerian in dimension. In 1968 Neal Cassady died in Mexico, and in October, 1969, Kerouac was "gone in October" (as his friend John Clellon Holmes put it), dying of a hemorrhage in his mother's house in St. Petersburg, Florida.

Analysis

The power of Jack Kerouac's writing comes from two distinct sources. The one that has been recognized by most commentators was Kerouac's extremely incisive, essentially instinctive ability to register the first crest of a wave of cultural change that was about to break over the entire American continent. The other, less accepted, source is the solid background in literature which Kerouac brought to his earliest work. The story of how Kerouac typed, at about a hundred words a minute, the entire manuscript of *On the Road* onto a huge roll of paper in twenty days is well known, but during the time that the book remained in manuscript form, Kerouac revised it with care and diligence, even becoming close friends with the editor Robert Giroux. He recalled that long before he began work on *The Town and the City,* his first book (which covered his early life in Lowell, Massachusetts), at the "age of 11 I wrote whole little novels in nickel notebooks . . . The first 'serious' writing took place after I read about Jack London at the age of 17. . . . At 18 I read Hemingway and Saroyan. . . . Then I read Tom Wolfe. . . . Then I read Joyce. . . . Then came Dostoevsky. Finally I entered a romantic phase with Rimbaud and Blake. . . . At the age of 24 I was groomed for the Western idealistic concept of letters from reading Goethe's *Dichtung und Wahrheit*."

The leap of genius that Kerouac made was to join his substantial, primarily self-directed education with a sense of several stylistic experiences that were taking place in the mid-1940's, including the nascent open measures and long lines of Allen Ginsberg's poetry, the postmodern, stream-of-conscious narrations of William Burroughs, the "marvelous free narrative letters" of Neal Cassady, which bolted and surged in digressive bursts of energy like Cassady's conversation, and elements from popular culture and street speech including the rhythms of jazz, folk blues, gutter argot, and the arcane vocabulary of the underground drug culture. Then, as he developed a style which became a kind of model for his generation and the next, Kerouac placed his technique in the service of a dual vision: Its first component was a history of a family—New England French-Canadian in the middle of the twentieth century; its second was a traditional quest for wisdom and a profound knowledge of the true self in defiance of the conventional values offered by a worn-out, hollow, complacent social order.

The Duluoz Legend, "Kerouac's great sprawling vision," as Ken Kesey calls it, presents the background of the Kerouac family in terms of the author's development into the artist who wrote *On the Road* and *The Dharma Bums*, the books which are most typically expressive of his search for a mystic enlightenment. The "Duluoz" books include *Maggie Cassidy,* perhaps his tenderest rendering of a youthful romance; *Desolation Angels* (1965), which covers the years just before *On the Road* was published, when Kerouac was living in Tangiers and Mexico as well on both coasts of the United States; *Vanity of Duluoz*, his last book, which Allen Ginsberg called "Jack's best retrospective of America's Golden Disillusionment"; *Doctor Sax*, which ranges over his earliest childhood memories; and *Visions of Gerard* (1963), which mixes memory, family legend, and iconography about Kerouac's angelic younger brother, who was loved by everyone in Lowell.

In these books, the often raw details and coarse behavior of the characters—an assortment of Americans of primarily working class origins and experiences—is underpinned by what Kesey calls "a continual current of gentleness . . . illuminating and glorifying all the dim little scenes of our daily mundanities." Now that the initial furor over the supposedly wild antics of the Beat generation has subsided, and the style and attitude which Kerouac almost invented has been pulled into the mainstream of American life by such varied avatars of adventure as James Dean, Bob Dylan, Marlon Brando, and Bruce Springsteen, the rather traditional literary elements of graceful prose, psychological penetration, sense of place, and solidity of structure which were always a part of Kerouac's best writing may be seen as the foundation upon which the more innovative, flashy aspects of his work were placed.

ON THE ROAD

First published: 1957
Type of work: Novel

With Dean Moriarty, a "western kinsman of the sun," narrator Sal Paradise travels across the American landscape in search of love, adventure, and enlightenment.

Because *On the Road* was published near the end of the 1950's, when the conformism of the Eisenhower era was at its most numbing, the book has generally been regarded as a forecast of the counterculture explosion of the next decade. While it certainly contributed to the developing sensibility of the generation which came of age in the 1960's, the book actually belongs to an earlier era in American life. Critics have pointed out how much Kerouac's sense of America is derived from the Transcendentalists of the previous century—men such as Ralph Waldo Emerson, Henry David Thoreau, and Nathaniel Hawthorne, who shaped and shared the literary heritage of New England, Kerouac's home ground—and how Kerouac appropriated nineteenth century American poet Walt Whitman's signature image of the open road as a symbol and source of possibility and self-discovery.

In addition to those distinguished ancestors, however, Kerouac's work is closely related to two contemporaries and to another powerful artist from the nineteenth century. Sal Paradise, the narrative consciousness of *On the Road*, shares a number of significant attributes with Holden Caulfield, the somewhat younger but equally sensitive and artistic consciousness of J. D. Salinger's *The Catcher in the Rye*, published in 1951. That was the year that Kerouac composed the original draft of *On the Road*, which is set in the late 1940's, the same era as *The Catcher in the Rye.* Holden is at the pivotal point between adolescence and adulthood, while Paradise is a college student in his early twenties, with a wife from whom he has separated as the book begins, but both young men are examples of injured innocence. Their lives in the present are made uneasy by the falseness they see around them, their sense of future rendered vacant and cloudy by their inability to see how they can use their artistic inclinations in any productive fashion. Both men are essentially idealists with a vision of America that has been formed from their extensive reading and a romantic optimism that protects them from cynicism or despair in their discouragement. Neither character can depend on a parental home for refuge, and both are strongly influenced by flawed "hero" figures. Holden is almost made inert by repression, however, while Paradise uneasily but instinctively resists the limits proposed by the forces of authority. Each has a special place which offers sustenance and retreat, but in the major divergence between the books, Holden's "place" is a small quarter of the Northeast, whereas Paradise attempts to encompass the entire nation as his ground for restoration. This is the aspect of *On the Road* that bears comparison to two other American masterworks.

The American landscape through which Paradise moves is very similar to the land that John Steinbeck described in *The Grapes of Wrath* (1939) ten years earlier. It has remained relatively unchanged by the intervening decade in which the United States concentrated on the war, and in the rhythms of his evocative observations of geography, his use of place names, his delight with the wonderful eccentricity of the American character as expressed in local dialect and regional styles, Kerouac has produced a paen to the same awe-inspiring, endlessly intriguing reaches of space, terrain, and unique settlement that Steinbeck extolled. Like Whitman, the master who created the genre, Steinbeck and Kerouac both use a kind of folk voice to convey the emotional surge at the core of their characters' passion for an almost mythic America. Paradise is almost dazed with ecstatic delirium as he sees

> for the first time in my life . . . my beloved Mississippi River, dry in the summer haze, low water, with its big rank smell that smells like the raw body of America itself because it washes it up. Rock Island—railroad tracks, shacks, small downtown section; and over the bridge to Davenport, same kind of town, all smelling of sawdust in the warm midwest sun.

Passages such as this one occur throughout the book as Paradise is rescued from sadness at his friends' messed-up lives and dejection over the seeming impossibility of establishing a harmonious relationship by a kind of god-spirit in the land itself. This kind of response is a part of the veneration that forms the basis for environmental consciousness as well, and it helps to explain why Kerouac and Gary Snyder, a pioneer of ecological awareness, got along well in spite of their differences in temperament.

The journeys that Paradise makes across the United States are not only an aspect of Whitman's call to the open road but are also an echo of other American voyages of exploration, particularly the trip made down the heartland river by Mark Twain's famous wanderers, Huck Finn and the black man called Jim. Paradise's adventures, "too fantastic not to tell," are like Huck's escape from civilization (the regularity, predictability, and conformity of conventional expectations) into the vast space of wilderness, where a young man could feel, as Paradise says, "like an arrow that could shoot out all the way." Like many traditional voyagers, Paradise is guided and tempted onward by a "youth tremendously excited with life," the semi-mythic Dean Moriarty (based on Kerouac's friend Neal Cassady). Moriarty is both angel and demon, touched by extraordinary gifts of perception, physical agility, linguistic facility, and charm, but tainted by the obverse of these qualities, hyper-sensitivity and narcissism, selfishness and egocentricity, incipient madness and the need for new sensations. Like Jim in *The Adventures of Huckleberry Finn* (1884), Moriarty represents the impulse beneath the veneer of civilization to live as a natural man; he is the "other" who is feared by proper people but who also fascinates them.

While many reviewers qualified their praise for Kerouac's powers of language when the book originally appeared with criticism of what they regarded as its lack of structure, the separate parts have a cohesion based on the evolution of Paradise's friendship with Moriarty. In part 1, Moriarty is introduced but remains on the fringes of Paradise's thoughts as the narrator crosses the country going west for the first time; in part 2, Moriarty comes into focus as a great energy source, an intellectual and social dynamo. In part 3, Moriarty and Paradise move closer, so that their friendship becomes so intense that their fears and desires become temporarily intermingled in a merging of the self; part 4 records the development of Paradise's perception of how potentially destructive and attractive Moriarty is. Throughout the narrative, the road that Paradise follows becomes more and more divergent from the fabled Route 66 that he initially decided to follow straight across the country, and in part 5, the journey is toward the even more mysterious landscape south into Mexico at the "end of the road." In this last section, Paradise and Moriarty part in an open-ended conclusion that reaches toward the future. In a paragraph-long Joycean reverie, Paradise restates the amorphous goal of his quest for knowledge in terms of the unanswerable questions of existence. Anticipating the postmodern emphasis on process, Paradise realizes that the goal of the journey was the journey itself. The "end of the road" is always out of reach on the horizon, the deep mysteries of the cosmos forever unsolved. Summarizing his burning need to know and his realization that there will always be another mystery, Paradise repeats, almost like a mantra, "I think of Dean Moriarty, I even think of Old Dean Moriarty the father we never found, I think of Dean Moriarty," the name of his friend crystallizing the infinite wonders of life.

THE DHARMA BUMS

First published: 1958
Type of work: Novel

A wandering writer and Zen initiate from the Atlantic seaboard learns the practice of the wild from a poet/ecologist in the West.

As much as Jack Kerouac admired Neal Cassady, the "greater driver" (in Allen Ginsberg's description) living in a "pious frenzy," he knew that Cassady's high-intensity existence carried the potential for destruction and despair for himself and his friends. While not dismissing Cassady's danger-ridden enthusiasms or condemning his impulsiveness, Kerouac had begun to wonder if a life "on the road" in a perpetual search for ecstasy was the only route to be followed. His interest in Buddhism, combined with his previous background in Christianity, suggested that a kind of serenity beyond sensation was possible. In *The Dharma Bums*, he examined an alternative approach to his previous quest for enlightenment. Concentrating on a man who seemed to have a vital, productive, and deeply satisfying manner of living, and who was also an active artist, a master climber, a political radical, a loyal friend, and a powerful thinker, Kerouac created a comic (but serious) balance to the tragic (but often hilarious) vision of *On the Road* in his portrait of the poet Gary Snyder in *The Dharma Bums.*

Snyder had just begun to publish his poetry in 1955 when Kerouac met him in San Francisco days before the famous reading at the Six Gallery. Kerouac was impressed by Snyder's good sense, and he was as rapturous about the natural world in Snyder's company as he had been about anything he had previously experienced. They shared an enthusiasm for literature, language, Eastern philosophy, and many basic social values, and although their essential natures differed tremendously, the points of correspondence plus the respect they had for each other led to a solid friendship. Kerouac's admiration for Snyder contributed to the somewhat idealized depiction of Snyder as Japhy Ryder in what is probably Kerouac's most accessible novel, the one in which he reached the furthest into the world before his long retreat back into his past in his later years.

Just as Moriarty was Sal Paradise's guide to life on the road, Ryder is Ray Smith's guide to life in the wild. As a lifelong expert in "the practice of the wild," Snyder knew the old ways of the native Americans who lived for eons in the Sierra and Marin county mountains, and Kerouac's description of his home, his work, his mountaineering technique, and his temperament show a man who can combine the exuberance of a child with the gravity of a philosopher. When Ryder literally runs down a mountain after their first climb "in huge twenty-foot leaps, running, leaping, landing with a great drive of his booted heels, bouncing five feet or so, running, then taking another long crazy yelling yodelaying sail down the sides of the world," he incarnates the same abandon and exuberance that Moriarty displayed, but with a self-possession and precision of purpose that is the essence of the "dharma bum." This amalgam of East and West, a "Zen lunatic" or wise angel/being, seemed an alternative possibility for Kerouac, who had rejected the corporate concept of America in the early 1950's and was now beginning to reject the counterculture clichés that many of his acquaintances had blindly grasped in its place. In his two climbs with Ryder that form the dramatic highlights of the book, as well as representing some of the finest writing about the American landscape, Kerouac showed how accurate an observer he was. His commitment to this kind of life was brief, however, and his enthusiasm, while genuine, was very transitory.

The sixty-day sojourn as a fire watcher on Desolation Peak in the Cascades which concludes the book is Kerouac's testament and tribute to what Snyder calls "the power vision in solitude." Ryder has departed for an apprenticeship in a Zen monastery in Japan, and without his constant stimulus, Kerouac cannot sustain the consciousness that this life requires. Yet as the whole book proves, for a short time before he was engulfed by his demons, Kerouac felt a relief from pain and sadness in the company of a poet/seer whose own inner life has ratified the promise Kerouac detected in its early stages.

Summary

The body of Kerouac's work will remain the province of those who can appreciate the mastery of style, depth of learning, boldness of vision, and knowledge of time and place that it exhibits. *On the Road* and possibly *The Dharma Bums*, however, have earned a permanent place in American popular culture as well. *On the Road* provided a model for the exuberant literary expression and cultural stances of succeeding generations of rebels, mystics, and artists. The book's revelations of crucial facets of the American psyche now seem more enduring and incisive than other, more highly praised, works by contemporaries; Kerouac's writing can be seen as part of an American tradition dating from Whitman and Thoreau in the nineteenth century.

Bibliography

Donaldson, Scott, ed. *On the Road: Text and Criticism*. New York: Viking/Penguin, 1979.

Gifford, Barry, and Lawrence Lee. *Jack's Book: An Oral Biography of Jack Kerouac*. New York: St. Martin's Press, 1978.

Hunt, Tim. *Kerouac's Crooked Road: Development of a Fiction*. Hamden, Conn.: Shoe String Press, 1981.

McNally, Dennis. *Desolate Angel: Jack Kerouac, the Beat Generation, and America*. New York: Random House, 1979.

Nicosia, Gerald. *Memory Babe: A Critical Biography of Jack Kerouac*. New York: Grove Press, 1983.

Tytell, John. *Naked Angels: The Lives and Literature of the Beat Generation*. New York: Grove Press, 1986.

Leon Lewis

KEN KESEY

Born: La Junta, Colorado
September 17, 1935

Principal Literary Achievement

Kesey's two novels contrast the maverick frontier spirit of independence, individualism, and toughness with the repressive, dehumanizing authoritarianism of institutions that value control, cooperation, and conformity.

Biography

Ken Kesey was born September 17, 1935, in La Junta, Colorado, the son of Fred A. Kesey and Geneva Smith Kesey, dairy farmers. His grandmother taught him a love of down-home yarns and biblical stories, while his strong-willed father communicated his love of the outdoors and of physical competition. Kesey's Springfield, Oregon, high school class voted him most likely to succeed. Kesey played football as a freshman at the University of Oregon in Eugene before receiving a scholarship as the outstanding college wrestler in the Northwest. He majored in speech and communications, acted in a number of campus theater productions, and spent summers in Hollywood trying out for parts in films. On May 10, 1956, he married his high school sweetheart, Faye Haxby, by whom he has had three children (a fourth child was born to Carolyn Adams).

After graduation with a B.A. in 1957, he received a Woodrow Wilson fellowship to Stanford University, where he was exposed to a radical perspective that led to a bohemian existence, leadership in the psychedelic counterculture movement, and trouble with the law. Kesey predated Timothy Leary in using LSD and experimenting with other hallucinogenics. A 1959 Saxton Trust Fund fellowship motivated him to write about his Stanford and North Beach experiences. The same year, Kesey volunteered for drug experiments at the Veterans Administration Hospital in Menlo Park. Later he became a night attendant in the VA psychiatric ward, an experience that inspired *One Flew over the Cuckoo's Nest* (1962). Kesey's creative writing professor at Stanford, Malcolm Cowley, encouraged him and critiqued that book. In June, 1961, Kesey moved back to Oregon to research *Sometimes a Great Notion* (1964). With money earned from his first published novel, he bought La Honda, which became the base of operations of the Merry Pranksters, whose 1964 cross-country ride in a psychedelic 1939 International Harvester school bus and the "happenings" associated with it inspired hippies worldwide. In 1965, Kesey hosted an

extended party for the Hell's Angels at La Honda.

Early in 1966, having been arrested twice for possession of marijuana, Kesey fled to Mexico to avoid a harsh sentence, but he finally turned himself in in San Francisco about six months later. He spent five months in the San Mateo County jail and then the San Mateo County Sheriff's Honor Camp. Afterward, he settled on a farm in Pleasant Hill, Oregon, where he turned away the Merry Pranksters and devoted himself to his family, his farm, and, to only a minor degree, his writing; since his announced shift from literature to life, he has not completed another novel. Instead he has published *Spit in the Ocean* magazine and a series of sketches, essays, travelogues, and film scripts, most of them autobiographical. These include *Kesey's Garage Sale* (1973), *Demon Box* (1986), and contributions to the *Whole Earth Catalog* (particularly in 1971). His descriptions of farming and farm animals are particularly notable. Kesey covered the Beijing Marathon in China and probed the secrets of the pyramids in Egypt. He is devoted to his farm and farm activities. In 1988 he was given the Western Literature Association annual award for Distinguished Achievement in Writing.

Analysis

Ken Kesey's critical reputation rests on his two novels, *One Flew over the Cuckoo's Nest* and *Sometimes a Great Notion*, both of which value physical and moral strength, personal courage, self-reliance, independence, self-sufficiency, privacy, and nature as opposed to fear, passivity, timidity, dependence, group effort, committees, unions, and mechanization.

Although Kesey has said that no writer is better than his first book, perhaps no writer is better than a book which comes at a perfect time. *One Flew over the Cuckoo's Nest* certainly came at a time in American history when its messages could be uncritically admired by a hugely varied audience. The explosion of the counterculture in the 1960's, an explosion that Kesey helped detonate through the Merry Pranksters and Tom Wolfe's descriptions of them in *The Electric Kool-Aid Acid Test* (1968), was a reaction to the staid propriety of the previous decade. Young readers especially were ready to be told that the "Combine," a sinister force as ill-defined as the notorious "Establishment," was a life-denying malevolence opposed to all the good things in life, such as youthfulness, freedom, smoking, free access to the World Series, prostitutes, and gambling, and all the other indulgences inmate Randle Patrick McMurphy brings to the ward. The message, that the carnal and sensuous are good, that self-indulgence can be a virtue, that too much is not enough, may have been a bit horrific in 1962, but five years later, young people were moving on San Francisco, and on Kesey's Oregon farm, by the thousands. The timing of *One Flew over the Cuckoo's Nest* could not have been better—as partial cause of a phenomenon it became one of the artistic totems of the period, along with Joseph Heller's *Catch-22* (1961) and Richard Fariña's *Been Down So Long It Looks Like Up to Me* (1966). Pauline Kael, in her December 1, 1975, review of the film version of *One Flew over the Cuckoo's Nest* in *The New Yorker*, noted that the novel "preceded the university turmoil, Vietnam, drugs, the counterculture," yet it "contained the prophetic essence of that whole period."

Kesey's "radical" message was all the more acceptable for being encapsulated in very traditional and even conservative American symbols. McMurphy is clearly a Westerner, a free spirit at home in any cowboy bar. His league with Chief Bromden creates an unlikely alliance with an Indian against the civilizing influence of Big Nurse as schoolmarm. McMurphy is also a Christ figure, a stock character learning to sacrifice himself for others. On the darker side, the attractive figure of McMurphy is also opposed to both blacks and women, calling on easy prejudices against both groups. In the novel, women, in the main, represent the oppressive forces of Sunday school, the educational system, and the Combine, and they value conformity and socialization, with blacks their tools for oppression. The anti-feminist subtexts of the novel have been thoroughly explained by James F. Knapp, who also points out the ironic fact that one of McMurphy's main weapons against the Combine and Big Nurse is another "Combine" or organization, the community he builds among the patients.

Another traditional element in both Kesey's novels is the role of nature, particularly in the American Northwest. Kesey associates nature with beauty, freedom, and raw power; it revives and challenges man. In *One Flew over the Cuckoo's Nest*, Chief Bromden's childhood memories of his Indian home include the beauty of the Oregon gorge, the splendor and power of the waterfall, and the flight of the wild geese. The inmates' fishing trip proves therapeutic because of the invigorating fresh air, the salt spray, and the challenge of the fish that fight and struggle against man's encroachments. McMurphy, a natural man, untamed by civilization, wears on his shorts a symbol of that natural power and challenge, the white whale. It is the power of the waterfall that challenges greedy men to harness and tame it, however, just as it is the power of the whale that leads men to hunt it to near extinction. Man, to be free, must accept nature's challenge, rely on himself, and discover his own inner strength, as does Broom when he lifts a seemingly impossible weight, smashes through the prison bars, escapes the mental asylum, and takes off across the open field toward the distant mountains of his youth.

In *Sometimes a Great Notion*, the untamed frontiers beckon man farther westward, testing the limits of his endurance and will. The main character therein, Hank Stamper, is made all the stronger and the more independent when an Oregon river, the Wakanda, floods his home, kills his loved ones, and thwarts his purposes. His deep inner strength comes from meeting its challenges as a logger—wrenching trees from the forest and using the current to further his will as it transports his goods to market. Nature has taught him a fierce individualism, self-reliance, and a wild sort of freedom, but it has also brought him an almost transcendental awareness of the spiritual power of sunset and forests, the mystic union of man and nature.

Set in opposition to nature is social man—the group, the organization, the corporation, and the union, with their focus on conformity, submission, and uniformity. These have no place for the wildcat logger, the cowboy, or the maverick; they doom the Paul Bunyans, the Lone Rangers, and even the Santa Clauses. The opposition to nature and the natural man is summed up in the "Combine," a giant corporation, like a giant farm machine that collects, orders, and processes all in its path. Its ultimate effect is dehumanization—like the inmates in Bromden's nightmares who are being repaired at night in a surrealistic and mechanistic hell, where humans are robotized, infused with transistor parts that make their smiles mechanical and their movements stiff.

Kesey's imagery pits nature against machine, the warm vitality and uniqueness of whales and geese, rivers and forests, against the cold metallic harshness of the mechanical and robotic. The opposition is a classic one in American literature, the machine against the garden, the mechanical against the organic.

The movement in both works is from fragmentation to wholeness, from weakness to strength and "grit," from an "unnatural" female dominance to a more "natural" male dominance, with woman's role as nurturer. Males who are pampered and controlled by females grow up less than men, with no true sense of themselves and their power; those more strongly affected by a male society prove tough and independent and strong because of the challenges they face and overcome on a daily basis.

The point of view in both novels is experimental. In *One Flew over the Cuckoo's Nest* it is the confused musings of Chief Bromden, a confirmed schizophrenic, institutionalized for life. As such it reflects the changing nature of Chief Bromden's self-confidence and the concomitant shifts in his perception. Bromden tells the reader that the events he describes are the truth, even if they did not happen. He records his memories of a lost way of life, the mental fog that shuts out the real world from a mind confused by electroshock and drugs, the progression of time as it slows down for bad experiences and speeds up for pleasant ones, the comments and dialogue overheard in the ward and in the staff meetings in the past and in the novelistic present. Supposedly deaf and dumb, he observes all with impunity. As Bromden's sense of self changes, his style and the quality of his observations subtly shift until, at the end, the speaker is a whole man, sane and ready for action, a man who has come to terms with his nightmares and who has finally met the challenge of his life.

Sometimes a Great Notion, on the other hand, constantly and rapidly shifts perspective and point of view to examine the same situation from different angles and perspectives, thereby providing a rounded multiplicity that lends depth and strength to character and act. What one sees and hears on the surface is supplemented by what is going on in the minds of the Wakanda characters, including Hank's dog Molly and the ghost of old Jonas, and by a third-person omniscient authorial voice. Only the typography provides partial clues to a confusing shift of voices. There are idyllic pastoral descriptions, local conversations in regional dialect, spoken words and hidden thoughts, yearnings, fears, and surmises. The effect is the exploration of relationships, attitudes, and motives from so many different angles that one realizes that surface revelations in no way capture the depth and hidden currents of events.

ONE FLEW OVER THE CUCKOO'S NEST

First published: 1962
Type of work: Novel

Randle Patrick McMurphy finds his release from a mental institution dependent on conformity to hospital regulations but chooses to sacrifice himself to inspire rebellion.

The title, *One Flew over the Cuckoo's Nest*, which echoes a children's song ("One flew east, one flew west, one flew over the cuckoo's nest"), puns cleverly on a variety of themes covered in the book: the sadness of the "cuckoos" confined in the insane asylum, the freedom enjoyed by the geese far above the nest, and the sterility of the nest itself. Kesey's novel can be read at many levels. It is a tall tale about a conflict of wills and a social tract attacking the medieval and inhumane treatment of mental patients and calling for reform. On a broader level, it is a microcosm, with the insane asylum a representative small world reflecting a macrocosmic conflict between the individual and society, freedom and restraint, nature and technology. Ex-marine McMurphy had experienced the horrors of brainwashing in a Red Chinese prison camp only to be exposed to the same process on home grounds. His battle with Big Nurse and, by extension, the Combine, is against all systems which try to narrow and limit human nature. Big Nurse is precise, efficient, and machine-like (the values of pragmatic technology), while McMurphy is associated with wild geese and other elements of nature.

The story is in the tradition of a tall tale, a Western shoot-up, or a cartoon or comic book story, with its characters larger than life and with exaggerated black/white, evil/good relationships. A tough, swaggering convict, Irishman, and logger, Randle McMurphy has himself transferred from jail to a mental asylum because of his wild behavior. He thinks it will be an easy time, with the extra attraction of a chance to con a few inmates out of spending money. He challenges the authority of Big Nurse, the ward superintendent, whose fake smile and feigned concern turns men against one another, preys on their fears, and weakens their nerve. To counter her techniques, McMurphy provides a model of rebellion; he uses laughter, comic exaggeration, and absurdist acts to build up their sense of manhood and teach self-reliance. He defies Big Nurse openly, breaks her rules with impunity, and wins the admiration of the men, who slowly begin to join in his acts of defiance.

The knowledge that most of the inmates are volunteers, whereas he is committed until released by Big Nurse, at first cows McMurphy, but when Big Nurse once more begins to undercut the men, the con man gives way to the hero. With iron in his boots, McMurphy "blows up big as a house" (a Chief Bromden metaphor for power) and smashes his fist through the glass barrier of Big Nurse's station to retrieve his confiscated cigarettes. The inmates respond positively to this defiance and ultimately work up the courage to vote for a fishing trip that Big Nurse has done her best to thwart, a trip that gives them a taste of normality and power. McMurphy smuggles the two prostitutes who accompany them on the trip into the ward for a nighttime party that ends tragically when Big Nurse discovers their game, isolates the weakest inmate, Billy Bibbit, and drives him to suicide. McMurphy responds by ripping Big Nurse's blouse to expose her large breasts and to undercut her power. In doing so he dooms himself but gives his fellow inmates hope and self-assurance. Big Nurse "crucifies" this Christ figure with electroshock treatments and then a lobotomy that leaves McMurphy a vegetable. As a result, the volunteer inmates leave the asylum to face the real world. In the last scene, Chief Bromden smothers the husk that was McMurphy, lifts the control panel that McMurphy had been unable to move, hurls it through the barred window, and escapes across the fields. His final words, "I been away a long time," indicate the distance he has come from the reader's first view of him and the power of McMurphy's restorative sacrifice.

SOMETIMES A GREAT NOTION

First published: 1964
Type of work: Novel

Hank Stamper, longtime community rebel and hero, opposes a union strike and, even when undercut by his own flesh and blood, ultimately, through sheer will-power, lives up to his reputation.

Sometimes a Great Notion is ambitious but marred. Its title derives from a line in the song "Good Night, Irene": "Sometimes I get a great notion to jump in the river an' drown." The novel chronicles man's relationship with the river—with its beauty and resources, but also with its unpredictability and cruelty as its rising waters sweep away land, homes, and people.

At the beginning of the novel, a critical contract to supply the sawmill of a national logging corporation with cut timber has almost expired, but a union strike keeps the local community from completing the quota and delivering the timber. The Stampers (their motto is "NEVER GIVE AN INCH") defy the union and go ahead with the work. Because of their shortage of manpower, they send for Leland "Lee" Stanford Stamper, Henry Stamper's younger son and Hank Stamper's half-brother. Lee, a graduate student at Yale University, who has never forgiven his aggressive older brother, backwoodsman Hank, for his sexual liaison with Lee's mother and for her suicide, returns home to get revenge. A central part of the novel is the competition and conflict between the two brothers. While Hank pushes himself to fill his logging quota and to retain his values and integrity while withstanding community pressure to conform to the union rules on strikes, he must also try to come to terms with Lee and to teach his brother self-worth and the family heritage.

Lee's resounding self-warning, "WATCH OUT," makes him suspect even the most innocent of acts. Lee shirks work, claims a cold and fever, and gradually wins the affection of Hank's beloved wife, Viv, with his poetry and his need for mothering. He taunts Hank with his seduction of her. Lee's timing is particularly nasty: Cousin Joe Ben, pinned under a fallen log, has just drowned in the rising river. Henry, his arm torn off, lies on his deathbed, and Hank is nearly battered to death by union thugs. Hank swims the raging river to try to stop his brother's betrayal, but he arrives too late, succumbs to sickness and defeat, gives up his plan to meet the contract, and submits to taunts and "generosity." The town is depressed and terrified by their loss of a defiant rebel of heroic stature. Only when the sly and selfish Lee returns to tempt Viv to leave with him and then goads Hank into a fight in front of her does Hank regain his old force and self-integrity. He beats up his brother, ties his father's severed arm where all the townsmen can see it, its middle finger extended in a symbol of defiance, and, aided by his suddenly transformed brother, begins the river trek to market. Viv leaves without a word. Kesey's basic argument is that a community needs its heroes and its rebels and that each is stronger because of the existence of the other—the community providing the hero with a challenge, the hero providing the community a model to strive to emulate.

Summary

Ken Kesey transforms the local and the particular into the universal, so that the insane asylum of *One Flew over the Cuckoo's Nest* and the logging town of *Sometimes a Great Notion* become microcosms of the conflicts and trends of American society. His fiction demonstrates the importance of individualism and rebellion to social health, contrasting those traits with repression and dehumanizing institutions.

Bibliography

Beidler, Peter G., and John W. Hunt, eds. "Perspectives on a Cuckoo's Nest: A Symposium on Ken Kesey." *Lex et Scientia* 13, nos. 1-2 (January-March, 1977). Special Kesey issues.

Boardman, Michael M. "One Flew over the Cuckoo's Nest: Rhetoric and Vision." *Journal of Narrative Technique* 9 (1979): 173-183.

Carnes, Bruce. *Ken Kesey.* Boise, Idaho: Boise State College Press, 1974.

Handy, William J. "Chief Bromden: Kesey's Existentialist Hero." *North Dakota Quarterly* 48, no. 4 (1980): 72-82.

Leeds, Barry. *Ken Kesey.* New York: Frederick Ungar, 1981

Northwest Review 16, nos. 1-2 (1977). Special Kesey issue.

Porter, M. Gilbert. *The Art of Grit: Kesey's Fiction*. Columbia: University of Missouri Press, 1982.

Tanner, Stephen L. *Ken Kesey.* Boston: Twayne, 1983.

Andrew Macdonald
Gina Macdonald

STEPHEN KING

Born: Portland, Maine
September 21, 1947

Principal Literary Achievement

Generally acknowledged as the finest writer of horror novels in modern times, King has greatly increased both the popularity of the horror novel and its critical appreciation as a serious art form.

Biography

Stephen Edward King was born on September 21, 1947, in Portland, Maine. He was the second son of a middle-aged couple, Donald and Nellie King. In 1949, Donald King disappeared and was never seen or heard from again by his family. Stephen and his elder brother David were brought up in straitened circumstances by their mother, who was forced to rely upon the charity of relatives. The family spent several years in Fort Wayne, Indiana, and Stratford, Connecticut, before settling down, in 1958, in Durham, Maine, where Nellie cared for her aging parents.

Stephen King was a rather sickly child, and illness once kept him out of school for an entire year. To entertain himself, he began writing at about the age of seven, first copying stories from children's books and later creating his own fantasy tales. By age twelve, he was cranking out science fiction stories on an old Underwood typewriter his mother had given him; he even sought, unsuccessfully, to have them published. In 1959, in a box of his father's old books stored in an attic, he discovered collections from *Weird Tales*, a fantasy and horror magazine of the 1940's, as well as a volume of stories by the famous horror writer H. P. Lovecraft. Horror tales soon became an obsession, and he eventually came upon those of Richard Matheson, another prominent writer of the genre. King has frequently acknowledged Matheson's great influence on his own writing.

As a high school student, King made copies of his stories on an old printing press his brother had acquired and sold them at school. Though these first efforts at professionalism were quickly aborted by the school principal, King had become certain of his ultimate commercial success. To his friends, he seemed a relatively normal teenager, but he was already fired with a vision of his own identity as a writer.

After graduation in 1966, he entered the University of Maine at Orono, majoring in English. As a freshman, he wrote his first professionally published short story, "The Glass Floor," which appeared in a collection entitled *Startling Mystery Stories*,

edited by Robert Lowndes. He also completed his first novel, a psychological thriller called *Getting It On*. By his junior year, he had completed another novel, a long story of a high school race riot, and several more short stories. Though he completed several creative writing courses, they seemed only to stifle him, and he finally asked the instructor of a poetry seminar he was taking, Burton Hatlen, to read one of his novels. Hatlen's enthusiastic response bolstered King's self-esteem and reinforced his ambition to become a professional writer.

Throughout his college career, King published many stories in college literary magazines, as well as writing a weekly opinion column in the school newspaper, but he had to support himself by working part time in the university library. While there, he met another less-than-affluent student, Tabitha Jane Spruce. After a somewhat halting courtship, they were eventually married in January, 1971, seven months after King was graduated with teaching certification in English. Tabitha King, like her husband, eventually became a successful novelist.

Unable to find a teaching position immediately, King worked as a day laborer in an industrial laundry, while his wife was a waitress. Writing at night, he sold several stories to men's magazines such as *Cavalier*, and refined his novel *Getting It On*, which he submitted to Doubleday, a large New York publisher. Though Doubleday did not publish the book, King did manage to find a teaching job at Hampden Academy, near Hermon, Maine, in the fall of 1971.

His teaching duties and financial worries prevented King from being very creative, and, bereft of new ideas, he expanded an old short story he had written, called "Carrie," into his first horror novel. He did not think much of it, however, and only reluctantly sent the manuscript off to Doubleday. He was much surprised when, in the spring of 1973, he received a check from the publisher for $2,500 as an advance against royalties on the hardcover publication of *Carrie* (1974). Several months later, the paperback rights were sold for a sum large enough to allow King to leave teaching and become a full-time writer.

Carrie appeared in bookstores in the spring of 1974 and was modestly successful. King soon finished and published another novel, *'Salem's Lot* (1975), which was nominated for a World Fantasy Award; several more of his short stories also appeared. It was not until the following year, however, that his career really took off. That spring, a motion picture version of *Carrie*, directed by Brian de Palma, was released, and its spectacular success suddenly made Stephen King the most popular horror writer in the country. He has retained this position, and it has been consistently reinforced through a string of best-selling novels and short stories as well as several successful screenplays.

Today, Stephen King splits his time between a summer home on Kezar Lake in rural Maine and a large Victorian house in Bangor. He continues to turn out new works, mostly horror novels and short stories, but also fantasies (such as *The Dark Tower* series) and more mainstream tales (such as those in the collection *Different Seasons*, published in 1982), with almost assembly-line regularity. He has also written several novels and stories under a pseudonym, Richard Bachman. He occasionally teaches courses as a guest lecturer at his alma mater, the University of Maine at Orono, and he is frequently called upon to help in the production of films of his works. To his small circle of close friends, however, he remains a somewhat withdrawn individual, obsessed with the nonstop creations of his fertile imagination.

Analysis

Stephen King occupies an unusual position among modern American writers. He is, first, a phenomenally successful commercial writer: His novels and short stories, in both hardcover and paperback editions, have sold many millions of copies; each new work he writes is virtually assured of best-seller status; films, teleplays, and other "spinoffs" from his stories have made his name nearly an ironclad guarantee of profitability. At the same time, he can also lay a valid claim to being a "serious" writer who treats universal themes with great originality. The vehicle he uses is often—but by no means always—the horror novel, and the question he most often addresses is that of the nature of evil. Though this theme has been central to many of the greatest works of literature, today's secularized modern society has generally rejected traditional beliefs in absolute good and evil. King's works do not suggest any specific moral or religious doctrines, but he does seem to be asserting that evil is real, absolute, and inherent in nature.

In several of his works, evil is portrayed as a supernatural force which takes over some object or human being. In the novel *The Shining* (1977), for example, a demoniac power has occupied the old Overlook Hotel, and it gradually possesses Jack Torrance, the hotel's caretaker, and drives him insane. In *The Stand* (1978), Satan takes on the human form of Randall Flagg, one of the few survivors of a biological holocaust, in an attempt to conquer what remains of the world. An automobile is evil's habitat in *Christine* (1983), and the vehicle's new teenaged owner is transformed by the car into a murderer.

Though King's heroes and heroines are frequently victims of this supernatural power, often they fall into the clutches of evil through some weakness or temptation. Thus, in *Pet Sematary* (1983), Louis Creed allows both his curiosity and remorse at the death of his cat to draw him into a haunted Indian burial ground. A corpse buried there, it is said, will return to life. He buries his cat, and it does indeed return, but as a foul, murderous parody of its former self. Even after seeing the results, Creed again succumbs to temptation when his wife dies. In *Carrie*, a young girl is obviously a victim of two kinds of evil: her mother's religious fanaticism and the cruelty of her teenage peer group. Pushed beyond any acceptable limits of humiliation, however, she uses her telekinetic power to destroy everything and everyone around her—thus, in a sense, immersing herself in evil for revenge. Jack Torrance, the hero of *The Shining*, falls prey to the forces of the Overlook Hotel at least partly through guilt and weakness—he is a recovering alcoholic whose uncontrollable temper has often led him into trouble.

Occasionally, King has created terror without invoking supernatural forces. The monster of *Misery* (1987) is entirely human—an insane fan who holds her favorite writer captive and forces him, through torture, to write a novel especially for her. In *The Running Man* (1982), written by King under the pseudonym Richard Bachman, a corporate future society provides a setting of repression, deception, and brutality. The hero, Ben Richards, must himself descend to violence and murder to escape and expose the villainous rulers.

In all these situations, however, King seems to be asking the same fundamental questions that have troubled the human psyche since the days of the great Greek playwrights: Are humans the victims or the masters of their fates? Can evil possess people against their will, or is there something deep inside each individual that connives at its ultimate victory?

Yet evil does not always win. In *Rita Hayworth and the Shawshank Redemption*, one of four novellas in *Different Seasons*, a confessed murderer confined in Shawshank Prison is redeemed through his growing friendship with another inmate who is really innocent, and the two of them escape. All the nastiest monsters ever conceived are rolled into one in the massive *It* (1986), more than a thousand pages long, but this ultimate horror is ultimately defeated, not once, but twice, by the same group of six people—first as children, then as adults. Most often, however, even when King allows his monsters, demons, aliens, or greedy politicians to get their comeuppance, a question is always left in the reader's mind: Is evil really defeated? The reader almost always suspects that the answer is negative.

While Stephen King's approach to the question of evil is the most profound element of his writing, his novels and short stories succeed primarily because of his craftsmanship in creating fascinating, extremely believable characters and settings. He is especially adept at portraying the unique perceptions of children. The ability of King's youthful protagonists to believe and experience what adults usually ignore or deny renders them more open and aware of evil and, occasionally, equips them to fight it in ways their elders cannot comprehend. His adult characters generally are relatively ordinary people placed in extraordinary circumstances. They react in ways that are sometimes heroic, sometimes cowardly, but they are always believable because of King's talent for accurately depicting tiny descriptive details. The reader can almost always readily identify with King's people, and this makes it nearly impossible to put a King book down.

CARRIE

First published: 1974
Type of work: Novel

A telekinetic teenager wreaks vengeance on her fanatic mother and the classmates who have humiliated her.

Stephen King's first published novel, *Carrie*, is also one of his most unusual efforts in its style. Only about half the story is written in traditional narrative form; the remainder uses what is called the "epistolary" style, meaning that the action is carried forward through the use of fictional letters, newspaper pieces, academic journal articles, and selections from books written by witnesses to the events long after their occurrence.

The novel's main character is Carrie White, a high school senior trapped between two equally horrible kinds of existence. At home, Carrie is smothered by a mother who is a fanatical religious fundamentalist and has cut the girl off from all normal social life. To Margaret White, all women are, like Eve, egregiously sinful. Carrie is God's punishment for her own sin of once allowing her now-dead husband to touch her. The daughter has spent her whole home life praying, asking forgiveness for her sins, or being locked up in a closet as punishment for unholy thoughts.

The other half of Carrie's life is perhaps even worse: At school, she is a social pariah. Her quiet religious demeanor, modest clothing, clumsiness, and dull appearance have made her the perpetual target of teasing, crude practical jokes, and all the meanness that children can inflict upon one another. The novel begins, in fact, with an incident which illustrates Carrie's terrible predicament. While showering after gym class, Carrie experiences her first menstruation. She has no idea what is happening, since her mother, believing that periods are the evidence of sin, has never mentioned them. Quite logically, Carrie believes she is bleeding to death. Her classmates, however, unaware of Carrie's ignorance, begin contemptuously laughing, chanting "PER-iod!" and throwing tampons at her. Carrie's screams bring in her gym teacher, who begins to understand the situation and helps Carrie to recover and go home.

With the onset of her womanhood, Carrie for the first time becomes fully conscious that she possesses a tremendous telekinetic power ("telekinesis" is the purported ability to move or affect physical objects using only the power of the mind). In the locker room, in agony, Carrie had unconsciously blown out light bulbs and knocked things over. Now, in her long-pent-up resentment toward both her classmates and her mother, she will begin to take control of the power and learn to use it for an ultimate, terrible, vengeance.

The leader of the "in" group of girls at school is Chris Hargensen, the epitome of the spoiled brat. Typically, she had led the hazing of Carrie in the shower. When the gym teacher punishes all the girls, Chris refuses to accept the punishment; the principal then bans her from attendance at the senior prom. Seeing Carrie as her nemesis, Chris determines that she will get revenge. She is given her opportunity when Sue Snell, another of the "in" group, experiences so much guilt after the shower incident that, as a kind of atonement, she persuades her boyfriend to ask Carrie to the prom. When Chris learns this, she helps to ensure that Carrie and her date are elected queen and king so that they will be onstage for the ultimate humiliation that Chris and her thug boyfriend have planned: They arrange for large buckets of pig's blood to drop on Carrie and her date just as they are being crowned.

After being drenched, Carrie's shame and anger explode, and she unleashes her tremendous power to burn down the school and destroy much of the surrounding town. She also confronts her mother, whom she had defied to attend the prom. In a religious frenzy, Margaret White stabs her daughter, wounding her fatally, but Carrie strikes back with her mind, killing her mother. She then finds Chris and her boyfriend and kills them, too, before dying herself in the arms of Sue Snell.

Carrie is an excellent example of Stephen King's talent for characterization. Though by the end of the novel, Carrie has become an insane engine of destruction, the reader cannot help but sympathize with a young girl whose spirit barely escapes annihilation by forces which have sought constantly to humiliate her and make her conform. Chris and her boyfriend are portrayed as so believably evil that Carrie's retribution, trapping them in a mangled and burning car, seems appropriate.

Like most of King's novels, *Carrie* examines the nature and power of evil, which is represented by Carrie's two tormentors, her mother's religious mania and teenage society's demands that everyone conform to preconceived notions of beauty and success. As he was later to make more explicit in *The Stand*, King sees evil as an inevitable part of both nature and civilization. Carrie herself is a victim, and her telekinetic power is a curse which begins to manifest itself without her bidding. Her eventual use of it for wantonly destructive ends is simply a defensive reflex against the humiliation she has suffered. Thus, though *Carrie* seems on the surface to be simply a novel about a terrible supernatural power, it is also a social commentary on the consequences of religious fanaticism and the intolerance of adolescent peer groups.

'SALEM'S LOT

First published: 1975
Type of work: Novel

A novelist returns to the small town of his youth, only to discover that it is being taken over by vampires.

Stephen King's second published novel and first best-seller was *'Salem's Lot*. It is a variation on the famous vampire novel of Bram Stoker, *Dracula* (1897), but is set in the modern world and, like most of King's novels, in a remote area of rural Maine. The main character is Ben Mears, an author who has recently lost his wife in a motorcycle accident. Unable to conquer his grief after many months, he returns, after an absence of twenty-five years, to the town of Jerusalem's Lot, known by most of its inhabitants as " 'salem's Lot."

As a child, Ben had spent four years in 'salem's Lot, which he remembers fondly with the idyllic images that most Americans have of life in a small town. He hopes to rekindle pleasant memories, regain a sense of home, and find some peace of mind. Entering the village, however, he is startled by his sight of the Marsten House, a great mansion built on a hill overlooking the town. Ben is filled with foreboding, and the reader knows that the Marsten House is going to be a central factor in the events to come. King describes the mansion as if it is alive, almost conscious, and full of evil. It had been built many decades before by a mobster named Hubie Marsten, who shotgunned his wife to death and then hanged himself. When he was nine, Ben had visited the abandoned building on a dare and had seen an apparition—Marsten's spectral corpse swinging from a roof beam. Now, he feels almost as if the house has been waiting for his return.

Despite his memories and fears, Ben settles comfortably into 'salem's Lot. He soon meets a young woman, Susan Norton, and a budding romance begins. A cast of interesting characters who live in 'salem's Lot appears, and the reader is lulled into believing that this is simply a nice little town like a hundred others. Yet something is wrong; there is an undercurrent of dissatisfaction, a sense that nothing and no one are going anywhere in 'salem's Lot, a kind of "deadness." These feelings seem to be prophetic, for two young boys, Danny and Ralphie Glick, become the first victims of the vampire Barlow, who has occupied Marsten House and is served by his oily assistant Richard Straker. Converted by Barlow into undead zombies, the Glicks begin attacking others, including young Mark Petrie, a former playmate. Though Petrie drives the Glicks away with a cross-shaped toy tombstone, Barlow's flock of vampires begins to grow as spouses, friends, and relatives spread the plague.

On an impulse, Susan Norton goes to Marsten House, where she meets Mark, who has figured out that the house is the source of the evil. Susan and Mark discover Barlow and attempt to kill him, but they are captured by Straker. Mark escapes to tell Ben what has happened, and Ben teams up with Mark and two friends, Dr. Jim Cody and the alcoholic priest Father Callahan, to raid Marsten House. There they find Straker, hanged and drained of blood by Susan, who is now a vampire. Ben is forced to kill her; Barlow, however, is nowhere to be seen.

The following evening, Barlow attacks and kills Mark's parents and confronts Father Callahan. The priest brandishes a cross at Barlow, but it fails to drive the vampire away because Father Callahan had long before lost his faith in its power. Callahan leaves the town in shame, but Ben, Mark, and other friends yet untouched by the vampire go throughout the town driving stakes through the hearts of every vampire they can find. Though Dr. Cody is killed by Barlow, Mark and Ben succeed, in a violently bloody scene, in killing the chief vampire.

This is not the end, though, for Mark and Ben cannot be sure that all the vampires have been eliminated. They flee across the country, winding up in Mexico, where they hope they will be able to rebuild their lives. Ben, however, keeps up on events in Maine by getting old copies of a Portland newspaper. When he reads a report of strange goings-on in the area of 'salem's Lot, he decides he must once more return to finish the job of destroying the vampires. He and Mark burn the town, yet the reader is left with the uneasy feeling that the vampires may yet come again.

'Salem's Lot is a relatively straightforward horror story which succeeds primarily because it is well-crafted and very frightening. King's carefully wrought descriptions of physical details, as well as his fascinating, often humorous, outsider's view of small-town characters, bring the village to life and render the horrors of its creep-

ing vampirism all the more gripping and terrible in their irony. Especially poignant is the agonizing necessity Ben faces of having to destroy Susan, who had begun to repair the damage caused by his wife's death. In the end, Ben's fury at Barlow as the chief vampire is compounded by the fact that Barlow has stolen his love and second chance at happiness. As with any good scary story, at its conclusion King leaves the reader in doubt about whether evil has really been vanquished.

'Salem's Lot is also one of the grimmest of King's novels. Though most of King's works involve horrific violence, copious quantities of blood, and human weakness in the face of almost overwhelming evil, *'Salem's Lot* is one of the few that do not offer the reader some kind of catharsis through the redemption or victory of the hero. In interviews, King attributed the novel's dark tone to the background of what he felt were frightening political events occurring at the time he was writing. His own fears about the future of the country are supposedly reflected in *'Salem's Lot*. The degree to which a writer's psychological moods are related to his writing is debatable, but the effectiveness of *'Salem's Lot* as an outstanding horror novel is not.

THE SHINING

First published: 1977
Type of work: Novel

The caretaker of a haunted hotel is driven insane by its demons and tries to murder his family.

As *'Salem's Lot* is dominated by the brooding presence of Marsten House, *The Shining* is similarly largely occupied with the evil possessing the Overlook Hotel, an elegant old resort on a remote Colorado mountain. Built early in the twentieth century, the Overlook has passed from owner to owner, unprofitable and unlucky for all of them. It has frequently been the scene of murders, suicides, and other unspeakable crimes. Within the hotel lives a demoniac spirit that has corrupted nearly everyone who has spent time there.

When the hotel prepares to close down for the winter, as it does every year, Jack Torrance is hired to maintain the building and grounds through the off season. Jack is a writer and former English teacher trying to recover from alcoholism. He has also inherited a volcanic temper from his father. Though he loves his son Danny deeply, Jack once broke Danny's arm in a fit of anger. He lost his last job when he beat a rebellious student, and he has frequently abused his fragile wife Wendy, who has borne her own cross of a hateful mother. Through a friend's help, however, Jack has gotten a last chance to knit his life and family back together by working for the Overlook Hotel as the winter caretaker.

Upon the family's arrival at the hotel, Danny senses that something is terribly wrong; He is haunted by visions of "REDRUM" ("murder" backwards) and a monster trying to kill him. As they tour the hotel, the Torrances meet Dick Hallorann, the black cook, who has "the shine"—psychic perception. Dick recognizes that Danny, too, has this ability, and to a much greater degree than himself. Before he leaves for his winter home in Florida, Dick warns Danny to stay away from room 217. He also tells Danny to call him telepathically if he gets into serious trouble.

After everyone else leaves, the Torrances begin to settle into a routine, and Jack repairs the hotel roof and tends the Overlook's dangerously unreliable boiler. The evil spirit, however, has decided it wants Danny, and it begins to work through his father. Soon, the snows isolate the hotel from the outside world. In the boiler room, Jack discovers an old scrapbook filled with items about the hotel's scandalous past, and he becomes obsessed with the history of the hotel. He soon begins to exhibit his old temper and all the characteristics of a drunk, even though he has not had a drop.

In the meantime, Danny, drawn by nightmares and visions, has begun to explore the hotel, led by an imaginary friend Tony, who is actually an older version of Danny himself. The boy cannot resist going into room 217, where he is nearly strangled by the ghost of an old woman who had committed suicide there. In the manager's office, over a CB radio, Jack hears the voice of his long-dead, drunken, and abusive father telling him to kill Wendy and Danny. Terrified, Jack smashes the set, cutting the snowed-in hotel's last link to the outside. The hotel's demon now takes nearly complete possession of Jack, and, when Wendy insists that they leave by the hotel's snowmobile, Jack sabotages it. Drawn by ghostly revels to the Overlook's bar, Jack gets drunk on imaginary booze, and the specter of Delbert Grady, a former caretaker who had murdered his family and then killed himself, urges Jack toward similar actions.

Wendy and Danny are now thoroughly frightened by Jack's strange behavior, and with his mind Danny calls out for help to Dick Hallorann, who eventually arrives by snowmobile. Jack attacks both Wendy and Hallorann and corners Danny. The son now knows that it is not his father, but an evil spirit occupying Jack's body, and he refuses to bend to its will. The real Jack surfaces long enough to express his love for Danny and to tell him to run away. As Danny, Wendy, and Dick Hallorann escape, the hotel boiler, which the possessed Jack has neglected to watch, blows up, consuming both Jack and the hotel. The spirit, however, is not destroyed, but only dispersed.

The Shining is one of King's most thematically potent novels. On the surface, the demoniac possessor of the Overlook Hotel seems to be a force independent of the human beings it uses and consumes. Yet, as the scrapbook Jack finds makes clear, many of the people who have been associated with the hotel's destructive power were already evil long before they had any contact with the Overlook. Those the hotel has destroyed also seem always to have had some kind of weakness which the spirit could manipulate. Jack, too, has been "marked" by inheriting his father's alcoholism and abusive temper. Thus, King appears to be suggesting that evil cannot operate without some sort of cooperation from, or at least weakness in, its human tools.

Another interesting element in *The Shining* is Danny's psychic power. King has frequently employed children as the conduits for supernatural powers, both for good and for evil. The openness of children and their willingness to believe—what is often called their "innocence"—make them especially appropriate for this role. Though Danny is a precocious child, he is nevertheless only five years old, and his telepathy and precognition are limited and distorted by his youthful inability to read the messages he receives clearly. In the end, it is the stubbornness of Danny's love for his father as much as his psychic powers that allows him to cheat the grasp of the demon. While love may not be able to conquer all (death, for example) it may ultimately provide the only redemption from the power of evil.

THE STAND

First published: 1978 (unexpurgated edition, 1990)
Type of work: Novel

Most of the world's population is destroyed in a biological holocaust, and good and evil fight for possession of the souls of the survivors.

The Stand almost defies classification. While it is certainly a horror story in the sense that frightening events and supernatural powers are depicted, it also qualifies clearly as science fiction or epic fantasy and even as a political allegory. This last aspect is immediately apparent in the events which open the novel: Nearly all the world's population (99.4 percent) is killed in only three weeks after a superflu virus escapes from a U.S. Army biological warfare installation. The world as all have known it is destroyed.

A few people inexplicably survive to pick up the pieces. Stu Redman, a laconic Texan, is taken to a disease laboratory in Maine, where the few remaining government scientists hope to discover what has given him immunity. Realizing that the government plans to use him as a guinea pig, Redman flees the laboratory and soon meets Glen Bateman, formerly a New Hampshire sociology professor. Other survivors throughout the country also appear: Nick Andros, a deaf-and-dumb genius, is wandering around rural Oklahoma, where he meets the retarded but amiable Tom Cullen. Larry Underwood, a rock singer on his way to New York, finds the city devastated. Soon, they and other characters begin having disjointed, prophetic dreams of a "dark man," Randall Flagg, the personification of evil, and of Abigail Freemantle, a black woman more than a hundred years old who serves as God's instrument and prophet. Each character is drawn toward one of the two: Some find Abigail in her old cabin in a Nebraska cornfield; others follow Flagg in what appears to be the beginnings of a reborn American society in Las Vegas.

Flagg gathers to himself a large number of average citizen types, who are deceived by his cunning into believing that they are salvaging civilization. He has also claimed many of the dregs of surviving humanity, such as Donald Elbert, a mad pyromaniac, and Lloyd Henreid, a mass murderer. Together, they help Flagg assemble a massive arsenal of destruction. As his technological power grows, Flagg begins to display supernatural powers: He can transform himself into animals and control minds.

With little more than Abigail's goodness and visions to guide and inspire them, Redman, Bateman, Underwood, and Ralph Brentner (a good-hearted farmer) undertake a long and torturous journey on foot to Las Vegas, where they plan to battle Flagg face to face. Redman breaks his leg in the desert and must be left behind, but the other three are eventually picked up by police cars under Flagg's authority. In a tense encounter with Bateman, Flagg forces Henreid to shoot and kill the sociologist; despite his superiority in numbers and weapons, Flagg has begun to fear the power of goodness. He stages a melodramatic public trial, accusing Underwood and Brentner, held captive in steel cages, of trying to sabotage his new society. The crowd of ordinary people, beginning to be aware of Flagg's deception and evil, starts to protest, but Flagg silences them with a display of supernatural malevolence, burning a protester down with a fireball.

Suddenly, Elbert, who had been sent by Flagg to find an atomic bomb, returns with it in tow on a cart. The bomb's radioactivity has sickened him and driven him insane, but he has persisted in his mission. Flagg becomes nearly hysterical with fear, for the fireball he had launched has grown in the sky and assumed the shape of a great blue-fire hand—the hand of God—headed for the bomb. Flagg disappears and in his place for only a moment is a half-seen vision of a horrible being, perhaps Satan. The hand of God reaches out and ignites the bomb, destroying all.

Back in the community started by Abigail and her followers, called the Free Zone, Redman, who was rescued and has recovered, is disturbed by the way in which all the flaws of pre-superflu America seem to be reappearing: creeping red tape, bureaucracy, and even authoritarianism. He senses that the victory over Flagg's forces may not, after all, be complete. In the final scene, Redman and a few others decide to leave the Free Zone and head for Maine, where, perhaps, they can live without the evils which seem inevitably to arise from civilized society.

The Stand is an extremely complex work. King has intricately interwoven his fears about the political direction in which he believed the United States was moving with a more universal story of the clash between good and evil. Yet the question recurs: How are good and evil to be defined? Many, perhaps most, of Flagg's followers are average people simply seeking to re-create the life they had known before the superflu destroyed almost everything. They are used, manipulated, and deceived by Flagg for his own purposes, yet King seems to be saying that they are somehow responsible, too—that evil is inherent in the order and rules necessary for any society's continued existence. Even the Free Zone is not immune.

For the first time in King's novels, *The Stand* takes an explicitly theological position: While Satan is never specifically named or portrayed, it is clear that God is the force behind Abigail and that faith in God is what sustains and gives power to her followers. Clearly, then, God is the source of goodness, but what, exactly, does that mean? Stu Redman, Larry Underwood, and the others who work for the Free Zone are certainly not saints, and their faith is often weak, yet they remain the representatives of what King sees as good. The critical point appears to be that they also have faith and trust in one another, and humanity in general, and they simply wish to avoid harming anyone. While this may be a simple message, King shows that translating it into action is supremely difficult.

MISERY

First published: 1987
Type of work: Novel

A novelist is held captive and tortured by an insane fan.

Misery is the darkest of Stephen King's novels. Not only is it frightening, it is also depressing. Part of the explanation lies in the fact that, unlike most of King's works, it contains nothing of the supernatural but is a story of psychological terror. The villain in *Misery* is all too human and all too believable. She is Annie Wilkes, a very hefty and very insane former nurse who had murdered scores of patients but always managed, cleverly, to escape being caught. Finally, though, she came under sufficient suspicion to be tried for killing several infants. The prosecution failed to get a conviction, but Annie found it prudent to retire to a farm in the remote mountains of Colorado.

Into her life comes Paul Sheldon, a writer of historical romances. In a blinding snowstorm, his car has careened off the road, and his legs are crushed in the ensuing crash. Annie finds him, pulls him out, and takes him home. She goes through his wallet, only to discover that she has rescued her favorite writer. She is Sheldon's "number one fan" and has read all of his books. Unfortunately, Sheldon had tired of the main character of these romances, Misery Chastain, and, at the end of the latest one, *Misery's Child*, he contrived her death. Annie is outraged at Misery's death, and she now insists that Sheldon write a new book and bring Misery back. To be sure he does so, she keeps him locked in a back room, supplying him with a wheelchair, paper, a typewriter, and a pain-killing drug to which he becomes addicted.

A frightening battle of wits ensues as Sheldon desperately seeks a way of escape while working on the new novel, *Misery's Return*. Each time he tries to leave or to fool her in some way, he is foiled by Annie's paranoiac cleverness. Each time, too, she punishes him horribly. At first, in the power of this immense, crazy woman, he is angered and tries to resist, but, as she terrorizes him, his will begins to break down. Finally, when she slices off one of his feet and a thumb, his spirit is nearly crushed.

In the meantime, under such immense pressure, he has been writing the greatest novel of his career. His missing car is finally discovered, and a state patrolman visits to question Annie. Sheldon throws an ashtray out the window and begins shouting, but Annie attacks and disables the trooper; she then runs over his head with her riding lawnmower. Despite carefully concealing the evidence, she realizes that the police will return and suspect her—after all, she has a history of scandal. She indicates to Sheldon that *Misery's Return* must be finished very soon. Sheldon infers, correctly, that she plans to murder him and commit suicide as soon as she reads it.

Though by this time he has often hoped simply to die, Sheldon now conceives a plan for revenge: As soon as he finishes the novel, he will burn it in front of her. He manages to find a can of lighter fluid and hide it. When the completion is announced, he soaks the manuscript in lighter fluid and ignites it before her. She explodes in rage and agony and tries to grab the burning pages, catching fire herself. Sheldon throws the typewriter, an ancient and very heavy office model, at her, and she collapses. In a dramatic struggle with the writer, Annie finally expires.

Sheldon is rescued by the police, who have returned to investigate the disappearance of the state trooper. He, in turn, rescues much of *Misery's Return*, and it is immediately a best-seller. Despite this success and much physical recovery, however, Sheldon cannot seem to shake almost constant terrifying nightmares and a sense that he somehow lost his manhood during the terrible humiliations of his captivity. He is drinking heavily and believes that he will never write again. Then, as he limps down a New York street, he sees a little boy leading what at first appears to be a cat, but on closer examination is obviously a skunk. Struck by this image, he returns to his apartment, and an idea begins to coalesce. He begins, once more, to write.

The growing terror and suspense of *Misery* make it one of Stephen King's most effective page-turners, but it is also an interesting discussion of insanity, the vicissitudes of the novelist's creative process, and the way in which personality and dignity can break down under tremendous stress and threats. Annie is frightening, but also fascinating in her manic depression and paranoia, and she exhibits a bewildering variety of moods, amounting almost to multiple personalities. In his initial responses to her, Sheldon mistakenly assumes that he can outsmart her, but he is constantly amazed and beaten by her craftiness. Throughout *Misery*, King also gives the reader an inside look at some of the pains and pressures a novelist endures by sharing portions of the novel-within-a-novel Sheldon is writing and discussing, through Sheldon, many of the techniques of the novelist's craft.

The most depressing aspect of *Misery* is the graphically illustrated disintegration of Sheldon's will and personality under Annie's awful terrorism. His nightmares of captivity merge with the terrible pain of his injuries as he becomes both addicted to and shamefully aware of his dependence on the drugs she brings him. He cajoles, flatters, lies, and totally humbles himself to gain her good will, only to learn later that she has seen through him. He grimly watches himself become accustomed to, then almost comfortable with, his confinement. In the moments before she mutilates his body, he begs incoherently, screaming for mercy, promising her anything she wants if only she will stop, but she is inexorable, and his pleas turn into howls of pain. In King's depiction of Sheldon's deterioration and the almost symbiotic relationship that develops between himself and Annie, the reader begins to share Sheldon's desperate belief that he will never escape and that even if he does survive he will always be haunted by his humiliation. In the end, Sheldon can only release his pent-up shame in tears as he begins to write again. Though for him, as well as for the reader, this is a kind of catharsis, the reader is nevertheless left depressed and is relieved only that *Misery* has finally ended.

Summary

Perhaps more than any other modern novelist, Stephen King has demonstrated that it is possible to combine phenomenal commercial success with serious artistic purpose and achievement. He shares with other great authors the talent to produce works which can be read and enjoyed on more than one level. His frightening plots, believable characters, and rich descriptive details make his works outstanding as pure entertainment, while his perceptive analyses of the many natures of evil contain profound ideas worthy of serious consideration.

Bibliography

Beahm, George, ed. *The Stephen King Companion*. Kansas City, Mo.: Andrews and McMeel, 1989.

Blue, Tyson. *The Unseen King*. Mercer Island, Wash.: Starmont House, 1989.

Collings, Michael R. *The Annotated Guide to Stephen King*. Mercer Island, Wash.: Starmont House, 1986.

____________. *The Many Facets of Stephen King*. Mercer Island, Wash.: Starmont House, 1985.

____________. *Stephen King as Richard Bachman*. Mercer Island, Wash.: Starmont House, 1985.

Collings, Michael R., and David Engebretson. *The Shorter Works of Stephen King*. Mercer Island, Wash.: Starmont House, 1985.

Magistrale, Tony. *Landscape of Fear: Stephen King's American Gothic*. Bowling Green, Ohio: Bowling Green State University Press, 1988.

Reino, Joseph. *Stephen King: The First Decade, "Carrie" to "Pet Sematary"*. Boston: Twayne, 1988.

Underwood, Tim, and Chuck Miller, eds. *Kingdom of Fear: The World of Stephen King*. New York: New American Library, 1986.

Winter, Douglas E. *Stephen King: The Art of Darkness*. New York: New American Library, 1984.

Thomas C. Schunk

MAXINE HONG KINGSTON

Born: Stockton, California
October 27, 1940

Principal Literary Achievement

Kingston has impressed critics with her unique linguistic style, part memoir and part myth, and her sensitivity in revealing cultural conflicts experienced by people of Asian heritage living in the United States.

Biography

Maxine Hong Kingston, an American writer born of stern immigrant parents, writes simultaneously from her past Chinese heritage and from her present American experiences. Such a conflicting blend is not always easy reading, but it is always vivid and lively.

Her father, Tom Hong, was a scholar and village teacher in China before emigrating to the United States. In New York City, he opened a laundry business with three other Chinese men that became very successful. Meanwhile, his wife, Ying Lan Hong, completed medical school in Canton and established a practice there. Impatient at her husband's absence and recovering from the loss of their two young children, she gave up her career and joined him in America in 1939. Kingston was conceived in New York and born in Stockton, California, where her parents moved after her father's partners cheated him out of his share of the laundry. Her paternal grandfather had visited California three times from China and established the family's claim to U.S. citizenship. Kingston's father, meanwhile, began to manage a gambling house in Stockton's Chinatown, which the police eventually shut down, but he took the name for Maxine Hong, his first American daughter, from a blonde American woman who was a frequent and lucky gambler at his casino. Attending American school and Chinese school simultaneously, Kingston became aware of cultural conflicts early in life.

She received an A.B. from the University of California, Berkeley, in 1962, the same year that she married Earl Kingston, an actor. She earned a teaching certificate in 1965 and taught English and mathematics for the next two years in Hayward, California. In 1967, she and her husband moved with their son, Joseph, to Hawaii. She has taught in secondary schools and colleges in and around Honolulu.

She and her family eventually moved to Oakland, California. Her son became a musician, and Kingston gave up teaching to become a full-time writer. She visited China for the first time after the publication of her second book, *China Men* (1980). She said she felt that she wanted to write about Chinese myth, which had affected her life so strongly, before visiting China itself and acquiring a new set of memories. Having begun writing as a child, her love of words and her memories of her mother "talking stories" to her certainly influenced her career. She only took one creative writing course in college, which she says was mainly a reading course, though she has taught creative writing.

Kingston has her own unique style of poetic eloquence and brash vitality, combining personal biography and cultural mythology. She does acknowledge stylistic influence from several writers she admires. From Virginia Woolf she learned an unconventional use of time, alternating wide expanses of time with detailed little moments. She believes that she has carried forward the tradition of American literature that William Carlos Williams had expressed in *In the American Grain*, published in 1925. Nathaniel Hawthorne's puritanism and his sense of a woman's place she believes is reflected in "No Name Woman" in *The Woman Warrior: Memoirs of a Girlhood Among Ghosts* (1976). Finally, she uses Gertrude Stein's notion of creating authentic speech as a new style fabricated from sentences and syntax, rather than, as Mark Twain did, from making a representative dialect out of spelling variations and apostrophes.

Kingston has been given the National Book Critics Circle Award in nonfiction twice, for *The Woman Warrior* and *China Men*. *The Woman Warrior* was also named one of the top ten nonfiction works of the decade by *Time* magazine in 1979. She was a National Education Association writing fellow in 1980, the same year that she was named a Living Treasure of Hawaii.

Analysis

Maxine Hong Kingston writes biography and autobiography in a very non-traditional way. She does not strictly adhere to chronology for her organizational structure (except in the case of *Tripmaster Monkey: His Fake Book*, 1989, which is largely fiction). She "creates" events in the lives of the real people in cases where she is not privy to what actually happened; she may even create several contradictory variations to explain any one given event. She is not above tampering with ancient Chinese myth, legend, and history as well, feeling that doing so gives her writing a larger and more important truth. The entire question about what is fact and what is fiction in her writing is an open one; it is an issue that she says is, finally, unimportant. She believes that she had less freedom in her first two books because, being largely stories about her relatives and her own childhood, their raw material was preordained. In *Tripmaster Monkey*, however, the book that she calls her first "novel," she enjoyed the freedom to write whatever she chose. Like Wittman Ah Sing, the book's hero, she was also a Chinese American in San Francisco during the 1960's, so the reader can conjecture that she perhaps had as lively a social life as he did.

Both Kingston and her critics are in agreement about the major themes of her writing: female identity, familial identity, and ethnic identity. All these themes function importantly in her three books and reflect Kingston's own struggle to find her particular place in the world. As an American woman born of Chinese parents, Kingston keenly feels allegiances and sensibilities that pull her in two often conflicting directions. Her works make clear the pain that she and her parents have endured because of their ethnicity, and they also reveal the concomitant humor and richness that result when two heritages come face to face.

The title *The Woman Warrior* indicates that Kingston's conception of female identity is a strong, even aggressive, one. The women whose lives she explores—from mythical hero to mother to self—are all strong characters who operate under the idea that they have control of their lives. They all have a vision of themselves that they have worked hard to attain.

The realization of that vision is more difficult than might be supposed, because Chinese culture traditionally devalues women. The birth of a daughter is thought of as only a "small happiness" in comparison to the birth of a son. Kingston's first two books are full of examples that illustrate this idea—male children being given presents or taken on trips while female children are expected to stay quietly and uncomplainingly at home, for example. Adolescent girls are sold into slavery at Chinese markets in *The Woman Warrior,* a practice Kingston has found even more baffling than the use of black slaves by white plantation owners in early U.S. history. The elevation of woman as warrior is established in a mythical Chinese figure, but it is represented as well by Kingston's mother, Brave Orchid, who became a medical doctor and who, in fact, was in a position to purchase and employ as assisting nurse her own adolescent female slave. Brave Orchid gives up her successful position in society, however, to join her husband in the United States. Brave Orchid holds the family together in *China Men* when her husband becomes unemployed and mentally distracted, and she is always resourceful and wise. She is also domineering, her self-control becoming parental control in her desire to have too strong a hand in shaping her daughter's life. Not surprisingly, Kingston rebels by cultivating American traits that her mother cannot understand.

Though the main character in *Tripmaster Monkey* is male, the book's female characters are very strong. Nanci Lee resists being seduced by Wittman's poetry. Taña de Weese, the Caucasian beauty Wittman marries on a lark to avoid the draft, makes two things very clear to him: She will remain with him only as long as she is attracted to him, and she will not act the role of the wife, shouldering the bulk of the domestic duties. In fact, she would prefer it if he would do that. Popo, Wittman's grandmother, abandoned at the side of a mountain road by his parents, may be the strongest female character in the book. Despite her age, she has independently carved a present existence that is enviable, and she is happy to share her good fortune with Wittman, the only relative who seemed genuinely to care for her. Finally, it is always the female characters who "talk-story" in Kingston's writing. They know all the old tales and superstitions, they keep alive ancient values with oral tradition, and they are more than ready to give advice based on their personal experience. They are creators and nurturers and emerge as characters more fleshed out than the angry, silent male relatives Kingston depicts.

Familial identity is a second meaningful issue for Kingston; she believes that being a strong individual must be carefully balanced with being a meaningful part of a collective community. There is no question of spousal fidelity. Men who wish more than one partner take an additional wife or wives, and women are unequivocally faithful to a single husband. The one episode in *The Woman Warrior* of a married woman who bears a child by a lover is so embarrassing to Kingston's mother that she never tells Kingston the woman's name, despite the fact that the woman is Kingston's aunt.

One expectation underlying *The Woman Warrior* is that the daughter will tacitly adopt her mother's values and priorities:

> To make my waking life American-normal, I turn on the lights before anything untoward makes an appearance. I push the deformed into my dreams, which are in Chinese, the language of impossible stories. Before we can leave our parents, they stuff our heads like the suitcases which they jam-pack with homemade underwear.

Kingston is full of questions she wants to ask her mother about the conditions surrounding her aunt's adulterous affair, and she has hundreds of frustrations that she is burning to vent but is unable to do so, suppressed by her mother's control.

Her father, as he is represented in *China Men*, is even less approachable; he is not forthcoming about his own background. His secret "father places" are off limits to other people. Even his appearance is so elusive that the children once mistake another man for him. Yet the family unit is sacred. Elderly relatives are unquestioningly taken in by adult children. Kingston's military brother is expected to hunt up distant relatives in Hong Kong when the Navy takes him there. The family unit is more structured in China than in contemporary California, though the first place Wittman goes after his impromptu marriage is the home of his parents.

Ethnic identity, however, which brings with it the fact of racial prejudice, is the most forceful issue that Kingston explores. Much puzzlement and pain comes with having an ingrained cultural heritage from one country and living in quite a different country, and it is apparent that Kingston has not resolved the issue for herself even by the end of her third book.

Already in *The Woman Warrior*, Kingston identifies "the enemy" as "business-suited . . . modern American executive[s]," the meaning of "racist" overlapping with that of "tyrant." The well-meaning but insensitive Hawaiian grade school teacher who could not understand the Chinese children's discomfort in singing "land where our fathers died" might have been unconsciously racist. Overtly and brutally racist, though, were the white bosses in *China Men* who made life miserable for one laborer grandfather on a Hawaiian plantation and another grandfather on a railroad crew in the Sierra Nevada. It is probably not a coincidence that Kingston stakes her bitter, brief essay, "The Laws," exactly at the midpoint of *China Men*, for it is a shocking chronology of 110 years of U.S. legislation against the Chinese people. Its detached, historical tone has a strong emotional impact on the reader.

Racism is only an undercurrent in *Tripmaster Monkey* until Wittman's closing thirty-page monologue, in which he angrily relates the discrimination he has felt as a Chinese living in the United States. He feels insulted by the newspaper reviews of his play that praise it for its Chinese aspects, because he wants to be accepted as an American playwright. He is resentful of the American ideal of beauty that has led some of his Asian friends to have plastic surgery to remove the upper fold of their eyelids, resulting in what Wittman derisively called "the jalapeño look." He is appalled by the roles, either minor or undesirable, in which Asian actors are always cast. He wants to "unbrainwash" Americans from their racist attitudes and pleads for them to accept him as an equal:

> Once and for all: I am not oriental. An oriental is antipodal. I am a human being standing right here on land which I belong to and which belongs to me.

Working through her own conflicts of identity has led Kingston to realize that her writing is, finally, much more American than Chinese. One reviewer of *Tripmaster Monkey* called that book the "novel of the sixties." Kingston believes that her writing is a way of claiming the English language for herself; in claiming the language, she has also claimed America.

THE WOMAN WARRIOR

First published: 1976
Type of work: Autobiography

A Chinese-American woman strives to resolve the conflict between her past heritage and her present environment by exploring her relationship with her mother.

The title *The Woman Warrior: Memoirs of a Girlhood Among Ghosts* is descriptive of both the violence and strength, the death and endurance, that have been a part of Kingston's life and that she seeks to resolve by examining her relationship with her mother. The five sections of the book are five vignettes, separate memories culled from Kingston's past, that depict terror at being an emotional outsider and that give the reader her own life as well as a collective biography of suppressed ethnic and sexual minorities. Kingston's personal identity is central to the second and fifth sections, in both cases connected with a legendary warrior woman, and the remaining three sections are devoted to stories of her female ancestors. Although chronologically organized, the book is plotless in the conventional sense; each segment can be read and appreciated separately.

The title of the first section, "No Name Woman," is loaded with meaning, for none of the three major female characters—the adolescent girl narrator, her mother who tells her a family secret, or her deceased aunt who is the subject of the story—is named. Such namelessness gives the story permanence and wide relevance; important information is revealed about the entire Chinese people—their behavior and customs—that is more significant than an isolated incident about one individual family. The lack of identity also brings with it a sense of alienation and anonymity which is mysterious and slightly sinister.

The story the mother tells her daughter is a confidential tale of family shame. It focuses on the girl's aunt, who became pregnant years after her husband had departed to America to seek his fortune, then drowned herself and her baby in the family well. The daughter spends considerable time mulling over the bare details her mother gives her, but she cannot ask her mother what she really wants to know—was the woman raped, was she profligate, or was she genuinely in love?

At once more metaphorical and more personal is the second section of the book, "White Tigers." Here the concept of "warrior" suggested by the book's title is developed. Along with continuing a feminist theme begun in section 1, real bitterness and rage at the traditional Chinese devaluation of the female gender is revealed. As with "No Name Woman," a Chinese mother is "talking stories" to the narrator daughter, this time about a mythical Chinese swordswoman heroine, Fa Mu Lan. The line between fantasy and reality is blurred in this bedtime story format, as the narrator daughter imagines herself a child who follows a bird into the mountains and is tutored by an old couple for fifteen years to become a warrior.

The ordeal of her training is arduous both physically and mentally. The old couple teach her "dragon ways," her body becoming so strong and controlled that she can will her pupils to dilate, and her parents use sharp blades to carve out oaths of revenge on her back. Companionship of a beloved husband and an infant son are followed by agonizing loneliness when she must send them away to fight her village's enemies, but she is equal to the challenge. The narrator struggles with what relevance the swordswoman could have to her own present desperate life and how that vision might help her do something important for her people in the light of the racial and sexual discrimination she experiences in the United States and remembers from China.

The book's third section, "Shaman," is both Kingston's personal tribute to her mother and a cultural explication of Chinese myth, medicine, religion, history, and politics. At the To Keung School of Midwifery at Canton, her mother is at the top of her class, but her academic achievements are no less remarkable than her psychological strength. For example, she willingly spends the night in a "haunted" room of the women's dormitory, from which she exorcises a threatening "Sitting Ghost."

As a respected village doctor, she delivers babies and encounters demoniac beings. Then, in her forties, she sacrifices money and power to join her husband in America and help him run a laundry, rear six children, and battle the non-Chinese "ghosts" of a strange world. The chapter ends with an adult Kingston on her annual visit to her parents' home. Now a seasonal worker in a tomato field, her mother has put on weight and seems beaten down by the speed of American society, though she is still the family's strength.

In part 4, "At the Western Palace," Kingston and her siblings play only minor roles in the reunion of her sixty-eight-year-old mother, Brave Orchid, and Moon Orchid, the sister she has not seen for thirty years. Moon Orchid lives for a number of weeks at her sister's home, painstakingly folding towels and shirts at the laundry and meekly acquiescing to Brave Orchid's insistence that they drive to Los Angeles to confront Moon Orchid's rich and successful husband. The encounter, when it happens, is a disaster. Brave Orchid has tracked down the husband at his downtown office, where he is a classy and respected surgeon. He has remarried and makes it clear that he has no place for his Chinese wife in his present life. Moon Orchid becomes a paranoid schizophrenic who dies in a state mental asylum, and Kingston and her sisters vow never to love an unfaithful man.

The book's final section, "A Song for a Barbarian Reed Pipe," is a memoir of Kingston's early school days, when she was more or less mute, intimidated by a society and behavior that she did not understand. While she proudly paints her grade school pictures a solid and uniform black, intrigued by the "possibilities" that she has represented, her teachers see only products of a disturbed mind. She rebels against her parents by purposely excelling in things they do not value. In a long and angry tirade against her parents toward the end of the book, she vents cultural and personal frustrations, bitter about having to leave home in order to find herself. Even as an adult, she struggles with the distinction between what is real and what is not.

CHINA MEN

First published: 1980
Type of work: Autobiography

A Chinese-American woman explores her own identity through the lives of her father and other male relatives.

Originally conceived as a single work, *The Woman Warrior* and *China Men* express two halves of the whole of Kingston's life, examining her heritage and attempting reconciliation with, first, female ancestors and, second, with male ancestors. While Kingston's mother appears garrulous and larger than life, her father is taciturn and does not share his history with her, so his biography and motivations are approached more speculatively, with Kingston at times posing several possible explanations for one event. Though the narrative line in *China Men* is simpler, moving consistently toward the father, the book as a whole seems more complicated reading than *The Woman Warrior*, especially to an audience unfamiliar with Chinese culture and myth.

There are six major sections to the book, following two short introductory pieces, one a personal reflection about elusive fathers and the other a scathing feminist essay protesting ancient Chinese customs which degrade or torture women. Together, the two brief essays set the tone for the entire book: angry, speculative, magical, and powerful. Brief lyrical pieces that may or may not directly involve Kingston's relatives close out each major section. These generally use Chinese myths or history to express themes of deception, suffering, or isolation.

Her own father is the subject of two central sections of the book. In the first major section, "The Father from China," Kingston traces her father's birth and childhood, his success at the excruciating Imperial Examinations, his marriage to a woman who would not kowtow to him, and his unsatisfactory job as a village schoolteacher. The reader is then given a "legal" and an "illegal" version of how her father came to the United States. In the illegal version, he crosses the ocean furtively, nailed inside a crate. The legal version has him detained by immigration officials in San Francisco before settling in New York City and opening a successful laundry. He is joined there by his wife after she finishes medical school, but when his business partners swindle him out of his share of the laundry, the couple moves to California.

In "The Great Grandfather of the Sandalwood Mountains," Kingston "talks story" about her great-grandfather Bak Goong, who was lured to Hawaii with promises of getting rich quick. His optimism, fueled by the aromatic flowers and plentiful fruit, is soon dampened by harsh plantation labor under heartless foremen. The story of Bak Sook Goong is interjected—another great-grandfather laboring in Hawaii, who brings a Hawaiian woman back to China as his third wife.

In "The Grandfather of the Sierra Nevada Mountains," Kingston recounts the hard labor and exploitation of her grandfather Ah Goong while building the Central Pacific Railroad. He is resourceful, strong, and lucky, resilient to hardships created by white "demon" bosses and dangerous working conditions. With other workers, he organizes a strike, which results in only a small wage increase. He is swindled out of half of his gold for a parchment "citizenship" paper and the other half for a surprisingly small bracelet that he brings back to China for his wife, but he never loses his optimism. He is important as the family claim to the United States; he has legally established citizenship for the entire Hong family.

"The Making of More Americans," the fourth chapter of *China Men*, offers both a personal and a cultural transformation of ethnic Chinese into Chinese Americans, first with Kingston's childhood memories of her third and fourth grandfathers, then with the story of another male relative, whose nightmarish visions of his dead mother drive him back to China to appease her memory. Another grandfather living in America, a former riverboat pirate, vacillates between remaining in California and returning to his wife in China. At his death, the family performs an elaborate Chinese funeral ritual that embarrasses Kingston because her sensibilities are now more American than Chinese. Aggressive and talkative Uncle Bun is an unusual relative who is obsessed with the ideas of Communism and wheat germ. He becomes paranoid that his relatives are stealing his money and that the government is trying to force-feed him garbage. In the final episode of the chapter, Kingston's aunt "talks story" about her vacillations between great prosperity and difficult suffering during her marriage to a strange man.

The elusive, haunting, evocative beginning of "The American Father," which reads like legend, mirrors the tone of the short essay that follows. Like Li Sao, wandering through the world asking questions that have no answers, Kingston's father is misunderstood in his adult life. Friends cheat him out of his laundry, police shut down his gambling house, and unemployment plunges him into morose despair. Even his own children turn wild. When he opens a new laundry establishment and plants fruits and flowers in his yard, his equilibrium returns. The book is brought full circle with this chapter, showing the father as the book's most fully realized hero. The final chapter focuses on Kingston's own generation.

"The Brother in Vietnam" traces Kingston's earliest memories of the births of her younger brothers. Descriptions of cruel war cartoons and brutal accounts of wartime torture of prisoners precede the main narrative, a biography of her youngest brother. A prime candidate for the draft, he enlists in the Navy, resolving to follow all rules except a direct order to kill. He teaches remedial reading aboard the *U.S.S. Midway* during the Tet offensive and accepts invitations from his pilot friends to ride along on the bombing missions. Fearing that he is being solicited to serve as an interrogator-torturer, he declines his commanding officer's request to study languages. He survives the Vietnam War without being killed or killing anyone else, but finally his life seems meaningless to him.

China Men spans two continents and several generations and illustrates how Kingston's male relatives, especially her father, laid claim to America. Kingston's love for her father is at war with her anger toward him, and she fills in the gaps of her ignorance of his life with her imagination. She finds, at last, that there is a great distance between them and that she may never fully understand him. The heroic status she accords him through specific detail and poetic fantasy is, at last, indicative of her respect for all China men who immigrated to America.

TRIPMASTER MONKEY

First published: 1989
Type of work: Novel

Wittman Ah Sing, a hippie playwright, searches for synthesis and resolution to his Chinese ethnicity in 1960's America.

Tripmaster Monkey: His Fake Book is Kingston's first novel; she says that it was written after she had exhausted all the stories she knew about China. A densely packed four hundred pages, it is the story of the pranks and high jinks of twenty-three-year-old Chinese-American hippie playwright Wittman Ah Sing, who lives in San Francisco in 1963. The book covers two months, September and October. Wittman is as free-spirited, independent, and garrulous as Walt Whitman, the nineteenth century American poet who is his namesake, yet he is equally as Chinese as Monkey, the mythical trickster-saint who brought Buddhist scripture to China from India. Wittman's picaresque life is part serendipity and part fantastic journey, and his goal is to stage his epic dramatic production based on Chinese novels and folktales. Told in nine chapters of roughly equal length, the novel moves in a seamlessly chronological and fantastical story line, using third person limited omniscient point of view; the reader accompanies Wittman on his adventures and is privy to his thoughts through the commentary of a wise, indulgent, and engagingly intrusive seer-narrator.

When the novel opens, Wittman has been out of college for a while and is puzzling about his future. He contemplates suicide in such a slapdash way that the reader cannot take him seriously as he walks the streets of San Francisco, his observant mind and quick wit attuned to nuances in the behavior of strangers and microscopic features of inanimate objects. Aboard a city bus, he reads aloud passages from Rainer Maria Rilke's *Die Aufzeichnungen des Malte Laurids Brigge* (1910; *The Notebooks of Malte Laurids Brigge*, 1930), regaling (or at least not annoying) fellow passengers. He enjoys a cappuccino with Nanci Lee, a beautiful Asian acquaintance and aspiring actress in whom he is romantically interested. When he brings her to his apartment and reads his poetry to her, however, she neither understands nor appreciates his work and walks out.

After working on a play in progress all night long and sleeping for a few hours, Wittman goes to his job as toy clerk at a department store. He is offensive to customers and inept at assembling a display of bicycles. He attends a management trainee conference at a fancy hotel (under false colors, since he has been demoted) and is an embarrassment to the three other Chinese Americans also present. Back at the job, Wittman maneuvers a toy organ grinder monkey and a Barbie bride doll into an obscene position in full view of shocked customers, which gets him fired.

For something to do, he sees the movie *West Side Story*, but he is put off by the falsity of Hollywood. He boards a bus for Oakland and endures the self-interested chatter of the plain, aggressive Chinese-American girl who sits next to him. His destination is a party at the home of good friends who have recently married. The party is well attended. Wittman eventually is enchanted by Taña de Weese, a Caucasian with long blonde hair and sandals who recites poetry while looking directly into Wittman's eyes.

Wittman and Taña and a few other guests stay up all night and then share a breakfast omelet. Wittman reads aloud a long excerpt from his play, and everyone discusses acting in it. Wittman and Taña visit her apartment, which Wittman finds enchanting, and where they declare their love for each other. The next day they do some sightseeing and encounter a hippie claiming to be an ordained minister, who spontaneously marries them.

The next stop is Sacramento to visit Wittman's parents. His mother is hosting a game of mah-jongg, so Wittman is able to introduce Taña to family relatives and friends. He searches the house for his grandmother, and his mother is elusive about her whereabouts. His father, playing poker at a friend's house, also will not give

Wittman a straight answer, except to say that they had taken her to Reno and she had not returned with them. Taña and Wittman drive to Reno but fail to find the grandmother. Instead, they enjoy dinner at an expensive restaurant that is partially marred by racist jokes they overhear at an adjacent table.

The next morning Taña goes to work, and Wittman goes through the seemingly interminable application process for unemployment compensation. Later, meandering through the lights of Chinatown, he unexpectedly meets his grandmother. Her abandonment by Wittman's parents in the Sierra Nevada has worked to her advantage; she was picked up by a wealthy Chinese man who married her. She presses money into Wittman's grateful hands before they depart.

Wittman uses a pay telephone to contact friends and relatives—everyone he knows in the area—to assemble an acting company and an audience for his play, which is to open on Halloween night. The play turns out to be a complex and fast-paced blend of slapstick and magic, wit and rage, with the actors playing eccentrics, freaks, and mythical heroes. The cast and growing audience love it, and critics rave. So frenzied are the events that the audience finds it impossible to take it all in at once. Police are called because of the pandemonium. It becomes a climactic free-for-all, with everyone fighting everyone else, and it culminates in an explosion of fireworks. A book that has begun with reference to suicide ends in a roaringly good time.

After things settle down, Wittman takes center stage and "talks story" about the formative influences in his life and the larger dilemma of all Chinese living in the United States. As his name echoes Walt Whitman's, so this is his equivalent of Whitman's "Song of Myself." His extended monologue is touching, bitter, and humorous as he describes his personal experiences of racial prejudice. His narrative reveals the agony, pain, and bafflement of trying to synthesize past Chinese heritage with present American culture, yet his invectives and fevered eloquence end in optimistic determination for the future.

Summary

The timeless debate about whether a person is more a product of heredity or environment is given full illustration in Kingston's writings. She does not wish to rid herself of either influence but to reconcile the differences implied by her mixed identity and to chart her own course in her own way. Playing out a real-life struggle in one's professional writing is not unusual for a writer, though the style and format in her unconventional autobiography, biography, and fiction are extraordinary. Ultimately, she emerges as strong and visionary as Fa Mu Lan, as lucky and clever as the Monkey, and as American as she could ever have dreamed.

Bibliography

Juhasz, Suzanne. "Maxine Hong Kingston: Narrative Technique and Female Identity." In *Contemporary American Women Writers*, edited by Catherine Rainwater

and William J. Scheick. Lexington: University Press of Kentucky, 1985.
Pfaff, Timothy. "Talk with Mrs. Kingston." *The New York Times Book Review*, June 15, 1980, 1, 17-25.
Rabinowitz, Paula. "Eccentric Memories: A Conversation with Maxine Hong Kingston." *Michigan Quarterly Review* 26 (Winter, 1987): 177-187.
Sledge, Linda Ching. "Maxine Kingston's *China Men*: The Family Historian as Epic Poet." *MELUS* 7 (Winter, 1980): 3-22.
Smith, Sedonie. "Maxine Hong Kingston's *Woman Warrior*: Filiality and Woman's Autobiographical Storytelling." In *A Poetics of Women's Autobiography: Marginality and the Fictions of Self-Representation*. Bloomington: Indiana University Press, 1987.

Jill B. Gidmark

JOHN KNOWLES

Born: Fairmont, West Virginia
September 16, 1926

Principal Literary Achievement

Although he has been a prolific professional writer of high stylistic caliber for more than thirty years, Knowles is primarily known and praised for a single work, *A Separate Peace.*

Biography

John Knowles, American novelist, short story writer, and essayist, was born September 16, 1926, in Fairmont, West Virginia, the son of the vice-president of a major coal company. In 1945 he completed his high school education at Phillips Exeter Academy, a private boys' school in Exeter, New Hampshire, and then went to Yale University, where he received a B.A. in English in 1949. While at the university, he served as editor of the *Yale Daily News*, and several of his early stories were published in student magazines. From 1950 to 1952, Knowles was a reporter for the *Hartford Courant* in Connecticut. He then turned to free-lance writing for several years, then served as an associate editor of *Holiday* magazine from 1957 to 1960.

During this ten-year period he was already writing short sketches of what would later be the subject matter of his first novel; he detailed the struggles of adolescent boys striving to discover their mature selves within the restrictive environment of a boarding school. His short story "A Turn With the Sun," written in 1949 when he was twenty-three years old, details the accidental death by drowning of a prep school boy scorned by his classmates. This was followed by "Phineas," written in 1953 and published in May, 1956, by *Cosmopolitan* magazine, an early rendering of what would later be reworked as the first four chapters of *A Separate Peace* (1959). In this short tale, Knowles created the character of Phineas as "the essence of careless peace," a prototype of the free-spirited Finny of the later novel.

Following the immense success of his short novel *A Separate Peace*, Knowles devoted himself full time to writing. He traveled extensively for two years, recording his impressions in a narrative diary which served as a basis for *Double Vision: American Thoughts Abroad* (1964), a nonfiction travelogue sparked with commentary on the foibles of the human condition as observed within the diverse cultures of Europe, Asia, and the Middle East. He served as writer-in-residence at the University of North Carolina in 1963-1964 and at Princeton University in 1968-1969. Dur-

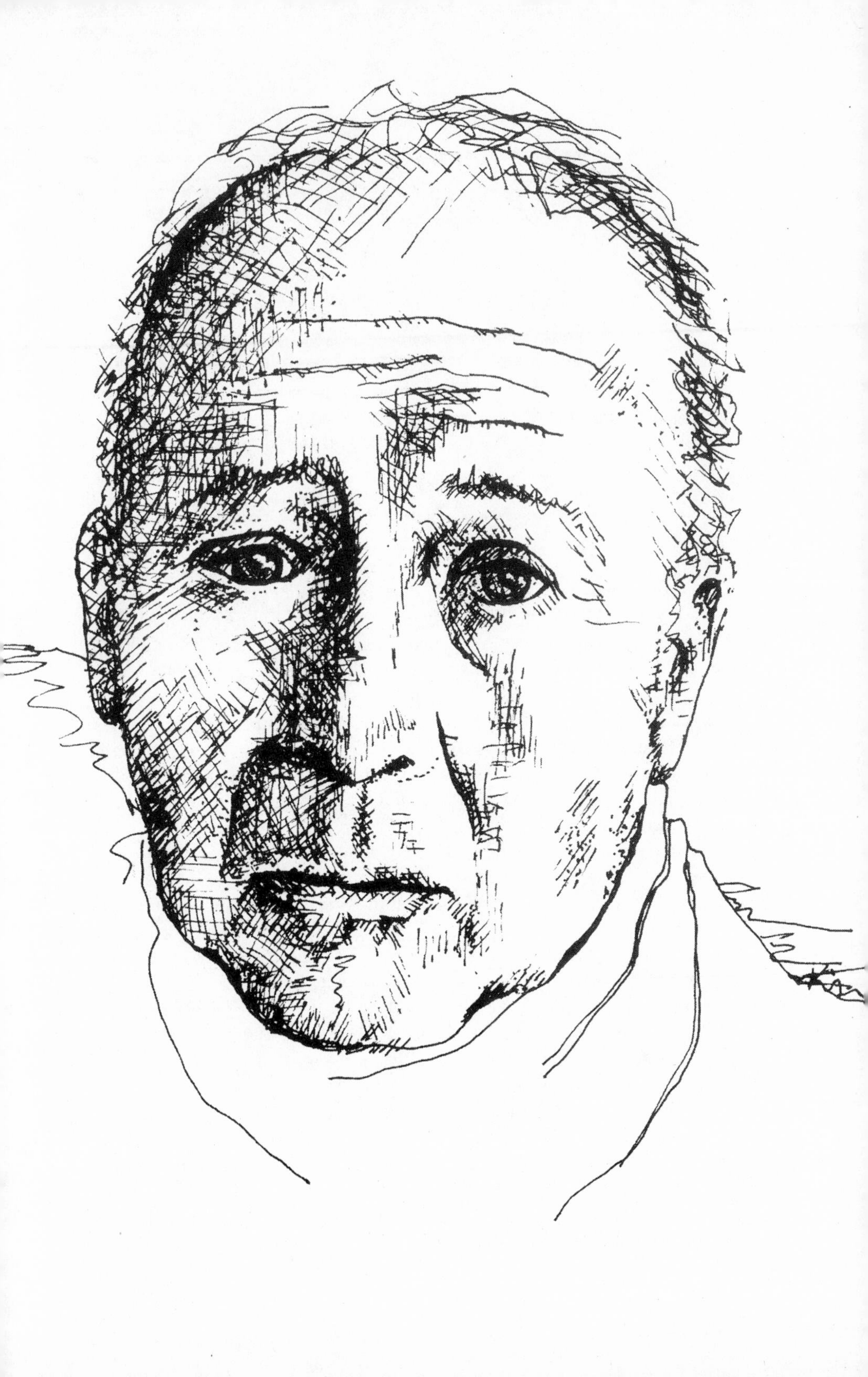

ing the 1960's Knowles published two more novels, *Morning in Antibes* (1962) and *Indian Summer* (1966), as well as a collection of short stories, *Phineas and Other Stories* (1968).

In *The Paragon*, published in 1971, he returned to the depiction of bonding and bickering among young students with the tale of the tenuous and shifting relationship between two Yale University roommates of opposite temperament and life-style—post-adolescent cynical heroes, disillusioned with their parents, their country, and their world. Three years later, Knowles completed *Spreading Fires* (1974), a novel set on the Riviera in the south of France, an area whose decadent atmosphere had intrigued him during his earlier travels. This was followed by *A Vein of Riches* (1978), Knowles's only novel set in his home territory of West Virginia. Here he depicted the struggles of a coal dynasty family faced with the loss of their fortune and power.

Knowles completed two more short novels in the 1980's, *Peace Breaks Out* (1981) and *A Stolen Past* (1983). In *Peace Breaks Out*, he turned once more to the theme of maturation through the achievement of self-acceptance. The action takes place in the same Devon prep school setting as *A Separate Peace*, five years after the events of the earlier novel. The characters are again high school lads whose careless cruelty results in the death of an unpopular classmate, a death whose circumstances might even be construed as murder. The boys must face their subsequent experiences of guilt as part of their growing into manhood.

Analysis

A view occasionally voiced among literary critics is that most writers have but a single message to share, and they simply repeat it in various guises from work to work throughout their writing careers. Such a judgment might be made concerning the great majority of the novels and short stories of John Knowles. In his extended nonfiction piece *Double Vision: American Thoughts Abroad*, he asserts that "the American character is unintegrated, unresolved, a careful Protestant with a savage stirring in his insides." Knowles views life in American, Western culture as having "an orderly, rather dull and sober surface, but with something berserk stirring in its depths." It is this duality of character, this coexistence of the moderate, the gentle, and proper with the treacherous urge to destroy what cannot be controlled, that Knowles repeatedly presents to his readers for their understanding.

Knowles has placed his novels in settings that influenced his own personal world view. He has made repeated use of the emotionally charged environment of boarding institutions such as he attended during his secondary and college years, finding there an ideal milieu for illustrating the effects of cultural duality. In such settings, characteristically ricocheting between the opposing demands of undisciplined and frequently cruel peer expectations and constrictive adult regulations, he found a microcosm of the wider society he wished to illustrate.

A particular talent of Knowles is the evocation of atmosphere through the careful presentation of physical details of a setting and the use of associative imagery. He stages his plot action using techniques similar to those of the theatre set designer. The hot, turgid atmosphere of the summer Riviera reflects the emotional state of characters in *Morning in Antibes*; the ever deepening grayness of the West Virginia coal town of *A Vein of Riches* mirrors the grim descent to poverty of the wealthy mine owner's family. In *A Separate Peace*, Knowles employs meticulously developed details of landscape, such as a single great tree and two rivers, as symbolic devices around which he weaves his plot.

Knowles's skillful use of imagery and his grace of phrase and metaphor are generally acknowledged by critics as his greatest strength. While praising him as a fine craftsman of language, these same critics are equally agreed that his shortcoming as a novelist is a lack of convincing character development. His protagonists, with the notable exception of Phineas of *A Separate Peace*, are seen as mediocre creations—as passive, ruminating characters, more acted upon than acting, unable to arouse reader empathy. There may be several sources for such a judgment.

Perhaps, having created the marvel of Phineas in his first novel, Knowles reached a level of characterization that he has not been able to achieve again, and all of his characters therefore seem pale in Phineas' shadow. To have achieved that height even once in a literary career is far beyond the capacity of many writers. It may also be that critics view as underdevelopment the very qualities of character which Knowles has striven to achieve. The men and women of Knowles's works are not exceptional beings of peerless courage and unassailable virtue. They are persons meagerly shaped by the meagerness of their environment; as sharers in the imperfect human condition, they search for the truth of themselves amid the savagery and greed of humankind masked by twentieth century hypocrisy. Their victories are small, the victories of ordinary people facing ordinary difficulties. Perhaps it is that very ordinariness which acts as a barrier to reader empathy; it is not comfortable to see one's own experience as merely ordinary.

A few analysts of Knowles's work label his novels, especially the later ones, as trite, disjointed, and derivative, stating that he reworks elements from his own and other writers' works. What is viewed by some as derivative, however, is seen by others as placing Knowles significantly within the mainstream of key American literary traditions: the young hero's search for the true center within the self, the self-testing of an imposed view of life, the fall from moral innocence through the tragic experience of evil in one's self and in trusted friends. John Crabbe, author of a critical review of *A Separate Peace*, calls Knowles's works "a treatment of American innocence in the tradition of Hemingway, Fitzgerald and Salinger." To his list might be added Herman Melville, Mark Twain, Henry James, and many others.

Morning in Antibes clearly echoes the sense of rootlessness and the alienation from one's homeland which is found in many of Ernest Hemingway's works and particularly in *The Sun Also Rises* (1926). The young iconoclastic hero of Knowles's *The Paragon* bears close resemblance in word and action to the gullible, love-blinded Jay Gatsby of F. Scott Fitzgerald's *The Great Gatsby* (1925); Phineas, too, is akin to Gatsby in directing his actions by substanceless dreams and paying the same price of life itself. Though much has been suggested concerning the similarities between Gene in *A Separate Peace* and Holden Caulfield in J. D. Salinger's *The Catcher in the Rye* (1951), Gene realizes the root of evil within and reconciles himself with that knowledge, whereas Holden views evil only as a threat from without and seeks refuge from it in a temporary mental breakdown.

Knowles does come alarmingly close to reprising his own material in *Peace Breaks Out*, a rather weak rewriting of his highly successful *A Separate Peace.* He repeats the setting, character types, plotting, and resolution from the earlier work, and none of these elements is improved in the reworking. Indeed, one reviewer saw *Peace Breaks Out* as a stain on an otherwise unblemished career and wondered how Knowles could have allowed the novel to be published. In assessing Knowles's writings, however, it is finally less important to consider whether such resemblances are to be censured as being too derivative than it is to approach them as the attempt by a writer of cultivated style and craftsmanship to demonstrate once again humankind's enduring efforts to find meaning within the flawed human condition. The overall positive acceptance of Knowles's work by the reading public is an acknowledgment of his success in achieving just such an end.

A SEPARATE PEACE

First published: 1959
Type of work: Novel

In a world at war, a young shoolboy must fight his own inner moral battle and make peace within himself to achieve full maturity.

With its publication in the United States in 1960 (it was first published in England), John Knowles's short novel *A Separate Peace* became an instant success with young readers. Within that year, the book was granted three awards: the first William Faulkner Foundation Award, the Rosenthal Award of the National Institute of Arts and Letters, and the National Association of Independent Schools Award.

The novel has a simple story line presented initially by a first-person narrator, but it quickly modifies to a dual view of events as experienced in a flashback view of incidents which occurred fifteen years before the opening scene, coupled with a mature assessment of those incidents. This combination of narrative voices gives the tale the immediacy of an eyewitness account while providing the author wide-ranging possibilities for omniscient commentary on the larger meaning of events.

The main setting of the novel is the Devon School in the hills of New Hampshire during the summer session of 1942 and the academic year which follows. Action focuses on a small group of boys completing their junior year by taking accelerated summer courses to allow them the extra time they will need as seniors to participate in training activities readying them to join the armed forces at war in Europe and Asia. The war and their proximity to participation in it are sustained factors in the minds of the boys, though they feign a youthful indifference to its threat. Fear is their constant unacknowledged companion, fear of the unknown horrors which lie ahead and fear of their inability to conduct themselves well in battle.

Though they would not likely consider it as such, these boys are already engaged in a battle in the quiet halls of Devon. This is their battle with some of the many fears that teenage youths must face while growing to maturity: fear of not belonging or being displaced in the affections of one's friends; the proud fear of loss of status, of not performing up to other's expectations; even fear of surrendering to irrational hatreds caused by jealousy and to the latent violence that each boy senses within the self and others. Knowles leads the reader through skirmishes of this battle by detailing the experiences of two boys in this group, Gene Forrester and Phineas.

Gene is an intelligent, cautious boy reared by a supportive Southern family. He has enjoyed three academically successful years at Devon and is well respected by his professors and classmates as a scholar and athlete. In contrast to Gene's moderation in all things, Phineas, his Bostonian roommate, known to all as "Finny," is possessed of a uniquely free spirit. Finny, who lives always for the exhilaration of the moment, is a peerless athlete of perfect physical coordination. He views life as a great playing field on which all are engaged in a romping game of friendly competition and everyone is a winner. With these two characters, Knowles presents the dichotomous aspects of the mythic "American male"—half conservative intellectual, half noble savage. A major premise of his novel is the necessity for the reconciliation of these two aspects as one.

Finny's charming manner and facile tongue make it possible for him to escape with ease the usual disciplinary consequences of every wild scheme his unfettered imagination can propose. One such scheme is the Super Suicide Society of the Summer Session. Members of this elite club are initiated by a single perilous jump from the limb of a great tree into the Devon River, which runs through the school grounds. Gene and Finny, however, as the clubs only charter members, must make the leap every night.

As the summer moves toward its close, Gene becomes concerned about his grades and begins to resent Finny's continual demands on his time through this and other impromptu interruptions of his study hours. He begins at first to feel that Finny is deliberately trying to make him fail in his bid for top student of the class while Finny himself will continue to be lauded as the best athlete. Gene lacks self-awareness of the growing anger he feels toward his roommate and of his jealousy of Finny's ability to get by with outrageous behavior. At first he is able to cloak these feelings with the self-lie that Finny is in turn jealous of him. When he at last realizes that this is not so, he sees himself as inferior to Finny even in this, and his anger cannot be contained. At a nightly meeting of the suicide club, in an unreasoned, unplanned act that Gene later blames on "some ignorance inside me, some crazy thing . . . something blind," he bounces the limb, causing Finny to fall awkwardly onto the bank below, splintering the bones of one leg so severely that the doctor predicts he will never play sports again.

At the opening of the fall term, Gene visits Finny at his home in Boston, where he is still recuperating, and there makes an awkward attempt to confess his guilt for the supposed accident. Finny brusquely refuses to accept Gene's admission; he is unable, in his total truthfulness, to believe that his closest friend could betray him. As the term goes forward, Gene sets himself to atone for his action against Finny by staying out of sports. He occasionally even wears some of Finny's clothes in a vain attempt to put on the mind and spirit of the friend he has maimed through unreasoned jealously. It is a period of moral agony and doubt for Gene as he feels the war within his heart increase in intensity parallel to that of the war raging across the world outside the haven of the Devon school.

Gene's confession, blurted out clumsily in Finny's home, is not enough to cleanse his guilt and fear. Reconciliation is vital for both boys; neither can escape the necessity of forgiving and being forgiven. Though they are able to avoid the pain of that action for several months after Finny returns to Devon, in the final week of their last term, the moment of reconciliation comes. A mock investigation is proposed as a jest by a few boys, purporting to uncover the facts of Finny's accident. The truth of Gene's action is finally forced upon Finny, and in dashing from the scene in angry confusion, Finny falls once again, injuring himself fatally. In their few moments together on the morning before his death, Gene and Finny at last find peace: Gene in the humbling self-acceptance of the potential for savagery within everyone, and Finny in an understanding and acceptance of such human frailty possible even within a closest friend.

Much allegorical and symbolic material is woven throughout this short novel, which opens it to multiple interpretation of its rich layers of meaning. It can be viewed, for example, as a tale of Original Sin, with the Devon School as an Eden enclosing the great Tree of Knowledge through which humankind falls from innocence but is redeemed by the suffering of a totally innocent one. It may also be approached as a reworking of the classic tale of the need to accept the potential evil within everyone and thus make peace with one's true self.

Summary

Although strong critical acclaim such as he received for *A Separate Peace* has come to John Knowles only once in his prolific writing career, he is nevertheless generally recognized as a writer of considerable skill, able to create striking verbal images of that interior world in which everyone struggles with fear of failure in resisting seemingly uncontrollable pride and jealousy. His central theme—that the only true path to achieving victory over such a common human fear is through acceptance of the common human need for loving forgiveness of each other's and one's own inner weaknesses—has appeal for the reading public beyond that of his literary skills. It is for his insightful expression of this theme, particularly in his tale of Gene and Phineas, that he is most noted.

Bibliography

Ellis, James. "*A Separate Peace*: The Fall from Innocence." *English Journal* 53 (May, 1964): 313-318.

Foster, Ruel E. "John Knowles." In *Contemporary Novelists*, edited by D. L. Kirkpatrick. 4th ed. New York: St. Martin's Press, 1986.

Halio, Jay L. "John Knowles's Short Novels." *Studies in Short Fiction* 1 (Winter, 1964): 107-112.

McDonald, Jane L. "The Novels of John Knowles." *Arizona Quarterly* 23 (Winter, 1967): 335-342.

Mengeling, Marvin E. "*A Separate Peace*: Meaning and Myth." *English Journal* 58 (December, 1969): 1322-1329.

Weber, Ronald. "Narrative Method in *A Separate Peace*." *Studies in Short Fiction* 3 (Fall, 1965): 63-72.

Witherington, Paul. "*A Separate Peace*: A Study in Structural Ambiguity." *English Journal* 54 (December, 1965): 795-800.

Wolfe, Peter. "The Impact of Knowles's *A Separate Peace*." *University Review* 36 (March, 1970): 189-198.

Gabrielle Rowe

LOUIS L'AMOUR

Born: Jamestown, North Dakota
March 22, 1908

Died: Los Angeles, California
June 10, 1988

Principal Literary Achievement

L'Amour is universally recognized as the United States' most popular writer of traditional Western and frontier fiction. Some 225 million copies of his eighty-seven novels and his twenty-one other books are in print.

Biography

Louis Dearborn LaMoore was born in Jamestown, North Dakota, into a pioneer family of English, Irish, French, and Canadian stock. He was the seventh and youngest child of Louis Charles LaMoore and Emily Dearborn LaMoore. His father was a veterinarian, a farm-implements mechanic, a police chief, a civil and political leader, and a Sunday school teacher. He instructed his sons in Western lore, in animal husbandry, and in boxing and was a living example to them of the virtues of hard work—as was his mother. Her father had been a Civil War veteran and an Indian fighter before his marriage. Emily Dearborn trained to become a teacher but married Louis Charles LaMoore instead, in 1892. She is remembered as quiet, fond of gardening and reading, and a captivating storyteller.

Louis L'Amour (as he called himself from the 1940's) enjoyed a Tom Sawyer-like boyhood combining outdoor freedom and voracious reading. When his parents moved to Oklahoma in 1923, young Louis, feeling that school was interfering with his education (as he often put it later), lit out on his own for what he called his knockabout years. He held a variety of jobs that were indirectly educational and which, as he often said, were grist for his writing mill. He was a cattle skinner, migrant farm worker, professional boxer, circus roustabout, lumberjack, miner, longshoreman, sailor, and friend of bandits in China and Tibet. He celebrated his eighteenth birthday in Shanghai. Much later, he became a book reviewer back in Oklahoma, a lecturer, and a neophyte author of many action stories as well as a little wretched poetry (published in book form in 1939). Entering the U.S. Army in 1942, he served in tank-destroying and transportation units fighting in World War II in France and Germany.

The year 1946 found L'Amour in Los Angeles and determined to write for a living. By that time he had published much short fiction in pulp and slick magazines—

mostly mediocre yarns about sailors and detectives, in addition to cowboys. In 1950 his first novel, *Westward the Tide*, was published in London but went unnoticed. On July 5, 1952, a turning point in his life came when *Collier's* published one of his short stories. Called "The Gift of Cochise" (reprinted in a collection of short stories entitled *War Party*, 1975), it formed the basis for his Western classic *Hondo* (1953).

Success and happiness followed instantly. Beginning in 1953, L'Amour was under contract with Fawcett for a novel a year. A few years later he signed with Bantam Books for two (then three) novels a year. In 1956 he married Katherine Adams, an actress who had appeared in *Gunsmoke* and *Death Valley Days* segments. Twenty-six years his junior, she willingly gave up her career to become his devoted wife, editor, business manager, chauffeur, and the mother of their two children.

Durable L'Amour, who was six feet, one inch tall and weighed 215 pounds, established a grueling schedule for himself. On two electric typewriters, he regularly wrote six hours a day, seven days a week. His production was never fewer than five pages a day and was often twice that. He paced himself with afternoon workouts on a stationary bicycle, with weights, and at a punching bag. The L'Amours soon bought a lavish home in Los Angeles. It was an adobe hacienda set on a quarter of a block off Sunset Boulevard, decorated with paintings, Indian rugs, and hunting trophies, and including a library of at least ten thousand books—mostly on Western history—and other Western memorabilia. The L'Amours later bought a California ranch and two condominiums in Durango, Colorado.

Louis L'Amour's biography from about 1960 on is mainly an account of one popular success after another, considerable travel and repeated scouting trips for research and fun, and numerous adaptations of his novels for films and television programs. Three of the best films are *Heller in Pink Tights*, starring Anthony Quinn and Sophia Loren (1960), based on *Heller with a Gun* (1955); *Shalako*, starring Sean Connery and Brigitte Bardot (1968), based on *Shalako* (1962); and *Catlow* starring Yul Brynner, Richard Crenna, and Leonard Nimoy (1971), based on *Catlow* (1963). The best television adaptations were *The Sacketts* (1979), based on both *The Daybreakers* (1960) and *Sackett* (1961) and *The Shadow Riders* (1982), based on *The Shadow Riders* (1982).

The Daybreakers was L'Amour's eighteenth novel, and in it are introduced the Sackett brothers, William Tell (called "Tell"), Orrin, and Tyrel ("Tye"). Their exploits, and those of their cousins far and wide and ancestors way back, are recounted in seventeen novels. In the preface to his thirteenth volume in the Sackett saga, called *Sackett's Land* (1974), L'Amour reveals his grand design:

> Some time ago, I decided to tell the story of the American frontier through the eyes of three families—fictional families, but with true and factual experiences. The names I chose were Sackett, Chantry, and Talon. . . . Story by story, generation by generation these families are moving westward.

His five Chantry and three Talon novels feature characters from both families who sometimes meet, as well as a few cameo appearances by certain Sacketts. *North to the Rails* (1971) is the first Chantry novel; *Rivers West* (1975), the first Talon.

Although he ambitiously planned almost fifty Sackett, Chantry, and Talon books, L'Amour also published many other Westerns and then, late in life, sidetracked himself with *The Walking Drum* (1984), *Last of the Breed* (1986), and *The Haunted Mesa* (1987). The first is a lengthy swashbuckler cast in twelfth century Europe and the Middle East; the second, a thriller about an Air Force jet pilot caught in a twentieth century Cold War plot; and the third, an effort at time-travel science fiction cast in L'Amour's beloved Southwest. L'Amour had at least twenty novels in the planning stage when, though he was a nonsmoker, he abruptly died of lung cancer in 1988.

L'Amour was given several honorary degrees and was voted many awards, the most prized of which was the National Gold Medal of the U.S. Congress (1982); it was presented to the author on the White House lawn by President Ronald Reagan in 1983. L'Amour left a kind of intellectual autobiography in somewhat careless form, which was published as *Education of a Wandering Man* in 1989.

Analysis

Western fiction may be divided into the formulary narrative, the romantic historical reconstruction, and the historical reconstruction. The typical formulary story is set in the Far West and features a tough, laconic hero, usually with a shadowy past, who is familiar with fists, guns, and horses and is obliged to save something or someone in trouble—for example, a disputed gold mine, rustled livestock, or a woman in distress. *Shane* (1949), by Jack Schaefer, is such a novel. The romantic historical novel treats characters and events in greater depth and includes figures from Western history—Billy the Kid, Buffalo Bill, George Armstrong Custer, or a railroad or banking mogul, for example—either glamorized or vilified. *Little Big Man* (1964) by Thomas Berger is an example. The historical reconstruction is more closely based on history, seeks realistic effects beyond the aim of popular formulary and romantic Western writers, and attempts to elucidate the Western past. *From Where the Sun Now Stands* (1960), by Will Henry, is an example.

L'Amour thought that he could write in all three subgroups, but he could successfully manage only the first two. One of his early formulary Westerns is *Utah Blaine* (1954). Its hero rescues an innocent old rancher from being lynched by villains greedy for his land, inherits the grateful man's holdings when the man adopts him but then is murdered, must fight to preserve his new spread from an assortment of thugs, avoids a murdered neighbor's spoiled daughter, regenerates a would-be ruffian by beating him up and then offering him a job, is aided by a newspaperman, and ultimately saves and marries an endangered neighbor woman. Most elements in the stereotypical Western are here in *Utah Blaine*.

One of L'Amour's best romantic historical reconstructions is *Sitka* (1957), in which the hero grows up with Robert J. Walker (1801-1869, a real-life Pennsylvania lawyer, U.S. senator from Mississippi, and federal financial adviser). The hero also meets Jean Pierre Chouteau (1758-1849, pioneer St. Louis fur trader); becomes a merchant sea captain plying the waters between San Francisco and Alaska; and even falls in love with the niece of Czar Alexander II and fights a duel in St. Petersburg, Russia. *The First Fast Draw* (1959) represents an unsuccessful attempt by L'Amour to write historical reconstruction. It purports to narrate the life of Cullen Montgomery Baker (1835-1869), an infamous gunslinger who gained his reputation when Edmund Jackson Davis, Radical-party governor of Texas from 1870 to 1874, tried to enforce unfair laws with scalawag appointees during early Reconstruction days. Baker's depraved life is well documented by reputable historians. L'Amour, rewriting history quite irresponsibly, tries to turn a guerrilla-style killer into a folk hero.

Beginning with *The Broken Gun* (1966), L'Amour branched into the field of the Western detective novel, which several early short stories (later collected in *The Hills of Homicide*, 1983) had prepared him to do. *The Broken Gun* is L'Amour's first novel cast in the twentieth century; still, its hero, though a survivor of combat in Korea and Vietnam, is really a latter-day cowboy, menaced by Old West-style, land-greedy villains and abetted by telephone messages instead of smoke signals; characters ride jeeps rather than horses. Later L'Amour wrote other Western detective novels which are more representative of his talents because they are less innovative; these include *Borden Chantry* (1977) and *Milo Talon* (1981).

A strain of mysticism runs through many of L'Amour's works. His first novel to tap this vein is *The Californios* (1974), in which the hero is aided by a hundred-year-old surrogate father and his literally non-material Indian friends, who move across time barriers effectively symbolized by desert heat waves. Several other L'Amour characters, usually women and often in the Sackett series, also possess extrasensory powers, being able, for example, to predict dangers yet to come. The thread of mysticism is especially vivid in L'Amour's blockbuster novel *The Lonesome Gods* (1983). In this splendid best-seller, an old Indian once again turns up like magic to help the young hero, who quickly learns to telephathize with horses, to empathize with a victim of deformity, and to sympathize with the immemorial desert gods long abandoned by materialistic men and women.

L'Amour's most daring supernatural work is *The Haunted Mesa*, which also stars his most autobiographical hero. When only a teenager, this man worked on a ranch and then in a circus, was a miner along the Colorado River, traveled and studied in the Orient and the Middle East, read widely back home, and did research into occult phenomena. He accepts the challenge to explain the disappearance of thirteenth century Navajo cliff-dwellers in the four-corner area of Utah, Arizona, New Mexico, and Colorado. The narrative dramatizes jumps through an Indian kiva from the present to the past, but it is only partially successful, because of the aging novelist's fatigue.

L'Amour wrote dozens of other novels, and much else besides. Regardless of the specific subject, his best characters may be counted on to be exemplars of the old-fashioned, now somewhat outmoded American virtues of self-reliance, stoicism, domestic reverence, realistic (but never sentimental) racial tolerance, and belligerent patriotism. In addition, L'Amour is noteworthy for being an early environmentalist opposed to the abuse of natural resources and for advocating the free flow of ideas across traditionally hostile borders. L'Amour's style, though that of a born storyteller, often betrays careless haste, grammatical and syntactical errors, inconsistency in managing details, and frequent violations of narrative point of view. (By his own admission, he never rewrote.) As his sales figures make clear, however, his action-packed plots carry millions of readers along at an uninterruptable, wild-gallop pace.

HONDO

First published: 1953
Type of work: Novel

An Army scout in 1874 Arizona aids a deserted ranch wife and mother, is forced to kill her no-good husband, then saves her from Apaches.

Hondo is as fine a Western novel as L'Amour ever wrote. Since its title is synonymous with that of the 1953 Western film classic starring John Wayne, most readers of the novel probably see "the Duke" in their mind's eye as the hero. In the novel, Hondo Lane is the quintessential good guy of the Old West—tall, taciturn, slow to anger but deadly when challenged, lightning fast with firearms, knives, or fists, instinctively pragmatic with women, children, and animals, and restlessly questing. At the same time, in the depths of his being, he is eager to settle down—though strictly on his own macho terms.

The arid Southwest dominates *Hondo.* Fighting with the Apaches, who call the harsh region home and who resist the encroachment of white "civilization," begins and ends the story. The Apaches regard Hondo as their enemy, since he is a scout and dispatch rider for (real-life) General George Crook. Yet Hondo and Vittoro, the Apache chief, admire each other, as well-matched foes often do in L'Amour. This fact, along with the cruel beauty of the fickle desert and an assortment of soldiers (some brave, others bungling), creates the novel's splendid tensions.

Escaping an Apache ambush, Hondo makes it with his fierce dog Sam to Angie Lowe's run-down ranch, where he accepts her hospitality, doubts her when she loyally fibs that her worthless husband will soon return, does some heavy chores for her, and quickly impresses and likes her six-year-old son Johnny. Hondo must leave, since the Army is evacuating the white settlers in the region for their own good. L'Amour, abruptly changing his narrative point of view, begins to humanize the Indians by presenting good Vittoro and evil Silva, his ambitious Apache subordinate. Both are on the warpath. Vittoro whimsically likes Angie, admires her son's spunk, and annoys Silva (who wants Angie for a squaw) by permitting the little family to continue tending their ranch until the rains come. (Weather and seasonal changes are significant here, as they are elsewhere in L'Amour.) Next, L'Amour skillfully sketches the Army post, complete with a motley gallery of soldiers, crisp military talk, cheap whiskey, a poker game, and handsome but no-good Ed Lowe, Angie's neglectful husband. He is laying plans to follow Hondo into the desert to kill and rob him.

In the last half of *Hondo*, L'Amour complicates his plot with cinematic scene shifts and neatly managed coincidences. The upshot of the next episode is that Hondo saves Lowe from an Apache attack but then kills the depraved fool when he tries to steal Hondo's horse. Hondo is captured himself, tortured, and then allowed to duel Silva. He wins the brilliantly orchestrated knife fight but then spares his vindictive adversary's life. This dramatic generosity sets the stage for a tantalizingly delayed climax, rendered more wrenching by Hondo's moral dilemma: Is it right for him to love a woman, however eager, whose husband, however worthless, he has killed?

THE DAYBREAKERS

First published: 1960
Type of work: Novel

Surviving a Tennessee feud, Tyrel and Orrin Sackett escape to New Mexico, where they protect decent Hispanic Americans from land-grabbing Yankees.

The Daybreakers was the first of the seventeen Sackett novels L'Amour published, and it remains one of the best. In it he allows Tyrel Sackett, age eighteen in 1866 when the story begins, to narrate his own adventures in his own intermittently folksy way. In Tennessee, Tye kills a man who was trying to shoot his unarmed brother Orrin, and the two Sacketts evade the law (typically thick-headed here) by heading west—for Abilene, Kansas, and then Santa Fe (in the New Mexico Territory). Between dangerous cattle drives and much derring-do, the brothers fall in love—Orrin unfortunately, with Laura, the selfish daughter of a Yankee land-swindler named Jonathan Pritts; Tye blessedly, with Drusilla Alvarado, the beautiful granddaughter of an endangered Spanish land-grant holder. L'Amour loves to send his heroes far and wide, even as they long for homes to call their own. So Tye must go through experiences in the Idaho goldfields before becoming a lawman in Mora, a little town northeast of Santa Fe. Orrin is already not only the marshal there, but also a quickly disaffected husband and a budding politician. Tye remains the heroic central character of *The Daybreakers* when, in the last chapters, he helps to rout several gunmen hired by Pritts to destroy the Alvarados, saves his brother Orrin's life, and marries Drusilla.

It is not the plot but the assembly of more than sixty characters that makes this novel a valuable Western fictional document. They run the gamut from admirable to villainous, from heroic to pusillanimous, from beautiful to evil-eyed. Several of the *dramatis personae* are especially memorable. Wily old cattleman Cap Rountree is a father figure, and he will reappear in many later novels. Former Army officer and former lawyer Tom Sunday teaches Tye to read but later turns alcoholic, jealous, and grimly disloyal. Professional gunslingers, hailing from both sides of the border, display colorful degrees of viciousness and courage. Tye's Drusilla and Orrin's Laura are starkly contrasted. Widowed old Ma Sackett follows Tye and Orrin to New Mexico to make a new home; she brings along a couple of younger sons, Bob and Joe, but still misses her oldest son, Tell —up north fighting the Sioux.

Though betraying typical L'Amour haste of composition, *The Daybreakers* is both exciting on its own and allusive and open-ended. This permitted the publication of more adventures of Sacketts young and old. The earliest events occur in *Sackett's Land* (1974), featuring Barnabas Sackett, founder of the Sackett dynasty in seventeenth century England and the Carolinas. His sons include Kin Ring, Yance, and Jubal, who rate prime time in several later novels. In his turn, Tell Sackett, Kin Ring's descendant, is himself the narrator of six novels, one taking him into Western Canada in 1870 (*Lonely on the Mountain*, 1980), another into Mexico about 1878 (*The Lonely Men*, 1969). Tye will also reappear in a few later novels but not as narrator. Bob Sackett's murder is the plot trigger in *Borden Chantry.*

BENDIGO SHAFTER

First published: 1979
Type of work: Novel

A young man helps found a Wyoming town, goes to Oregon to buy cattle for it, discusses the West with journalists in New York, then returns home.

Bendigo Shafter seems destined for classic status. This unusually long L'Amour novel has all the necessary ingredients. Bendigo Shafter, the youthful French-Canadian hero and narrator, is eighteen when the action begins, about 1862. In the next six years or so, he moves, as do many of L'Amour's heroes, from youth to early manhood and matures as a responsible pioneer, a hunter, a trail boss, a peace-making friend of Indians, a town marshal, and an author. Trouble takes various forms: violent weather, unpredictably hostile Indians, dangerous rescue missions, the need to build homes and offices in a wilderness and out of its materials, discovery of gold (which attracts would-be robbers and killers), cattle rustlers, and the near impossibility of making independent Westerners see the virtues of a Plymouth Colony-like governmental structure.

The plot divides itself into three numbered parts. The first two are of almost identical length; the third, typically, is cut short. Part 1 is centered on the new townsite, and Ben narrates many episodes of danger (attacks by renegades, avoidance of religious fanatics), rescue (of missing children, Mormons lost in the snow, rather stupid pioneers, and a wounded Shoshone), and plans for the future—better homes, more reading, a school, saving money to buy cattle. In part 2, Ben has adventures along the famous Oregon Trail—proceeding through desert and snow, assembling cattle, hiring Indians to help him drive his livestock home, fighting off thieves—and returning to be elected town marshal. This part is a veritable anthology of trail yarns. Part 3 lacks focus and seems rushed, but it may sufficiently compensate for this by its variety and suspense. Ben is now patiently in love with Ninon Vauvert, a young girl who has left the little South Pass town to become a traveling actress. The pair meet again in dirty, smoky New York City, but then, after lecturing Horace Greeley (1811-1872, the founder-editor of the New York *Tribune*) on the Far West, Ben suddenly takes a danger-fraught train ride back to Wyoming, refreshes his spirit at the sacred Indian Medicine Wheel in the Big Horn Mountains, and goes home again—to face the open-ended challenge of chaotic politics.

Bendigo Shafter includes an unusual variety of women—a learned widow (marvelously depicted) who inspires Ben with her decency and big library, the stolid, work-worn wife of his older brother (named Cain for no discernible reason), a flirt who fails to seduce Ben and then disappears inexplicably from the story, many reliable old frontier wives, and Ninon. She is only twelve at story's start and hence barely nubile, which is convenient for L'Amour because he always declines to present sexual passion in any detail whatsoever. The most attractive character in the whole novel is arguably Ben's ally Uruwishi, an Umatilla Indian so old that he knew Lewis and Clark back in 1805.

THE WALKING DRUM

First published: 1984
Type of work: Novel

A resourceful hero seeks his missing father—and adventure, learning, and love—from France to the Middle East between 1176 and 1180.

The Walking Drum represents L'Amour's serious effort late in his career to escape being labeled merely a frontier novelist. Cast in medieval Europe and the Middle East, it presents panoramic action far from the nineteenth century trans-Mississippi West.

The incredibly melodramatic plot of *The Walking Drum* defies adequate brief summary. At the outset, narrator and hero Mathurin Kerbouchard learns that his mother has been murdered in Brittany and that his father is now languishing in forced servitude somewhere east of Baghdad (the capital of Iraq, which was then called Mesopotamia) and south of Tehran (the capital of Iran, then called Persia). Young Kerbouchard begins a long journey, in search of revenge and his missing father. He grows talented in ways surely unique in history and even in fiction. He becomes a sailor, a horseman, a fierce warrior, a merchant with caravans ("the walking drum" pounds out their marching pace), an acrobat, juggler, and magician, a fluent linguist (in Arabic, Frankish, Greek, Hindi, Latin, Persian, and Sanskrit), a versatile scholar and scientist (mastering botany, chemistry, explosives, geography, history, literature, medicine, military tactics, music, philosophy, and theology), and a storyteller. He is also a L'Amour-style lover. That is, he has several voluptuous girlfriends (Moorish, Spanish, French, and Middle Eastern) but indulges in no bedroom activity.

The novel falls into unnumbered but obvious thirds, the last of which is the shortest. Each has radically different scenery: Spain and its coastal waters, territory from France to the Black Sea, and exotic regions of the Byzantine and Turkish empires. The action features countless fights, imprisonment and escape, theft and ransom and rescue, wounds and injuries aplenty (and a touch of torture), and, in between, much serene study. This last gives L'Amour an opportunity to parade his wide-ranging (if superficial) erudition, as he has Kerbouchard pause between wild acts to absorb wise lore, esoterica, and no little trivia, partly by sitting at the feet of several real-life European and Arabic savants. L'Amour's death prevented him from writing a promised sequel to this glittering medieval adventure novel.

Summary

Louis L'Amour's fiction has been extremely popular: His novels have far outsold those of all leading competitors in his main field, that of Western fiction. He was above all a storyteller, nothing less than a latter-day, frontier troubadour. He dramatized the value of the solid, old-fashioned American virtues—love of nature, self-reliance, and never-say-die patriotism. His stories present rugged heroes challenged by the elements, overcoming dangers, rescuing the less fortunate, dispensing two-fisted justice, and respecting and guarding conservative family values.

Bibliography

Etulain, Richard W. "Louis L'Amour." In *A Bibliographical Guide to the Study of Western American Literature.* Lincoln: University of Nebraska Press, 1982.

Gale, Robert L. *Louis L'Amour.* Boston: Twayne, 1985.

Hubbell, John G. "Louis L'Amour: Storyteller of the Wild West." *Reader's Digest* 117 (July, 1980): 93-98.

Jackson, Donald Dale. "World's Fastest Literary Gun: Louis L'Amour." *Smithsonian* 10 (May, 1987): 154-156, 158, 160, 164, 166, 170.

L'Amour, Louis. *The Sackett Companion: A Personal Guide to the Sackett Novels.* New York: Bantam Books, 1988.

Marsden, Michael T. "Louis L'Amour." In *Fifty Western Writers: A Bio-Bibliographical Sourcebook*, edited by Fred Erisman and Richard W. Etulain. Westport, Conn.: Greenwood Press, 1982.

Nesbitt, John D. "Change of Purpose in the Novels of Louis L'Amour." *Western American Literature* 13 (Spring, 1978): 65-81.

Robert L. Gale

HARPER LEE

Born: Monroeville, Alabama
April 28, 1926

Principal Literary Achievement

Lee's reputation rests on her novel *To Kill a Mockingbird*, a moving account of a Southern lawyer's battle against prejudice and injustice.

Biography

Nelle Harper Lee was born in Monroeville, Alabama, on April 28, 1926. Her father, Amasa Coleman Lee, was the son of a Confederate veteran and a Florida legislator. A. C. Lee himself was a prominent citizen of Monroeville, a practicing lawyer who served in the Alabama legislature for twelve years. He was also involved in the management of the local newspaper. Harper Lee's mother was Frances Finch Lee, whose family had moved from Virginia to Alabama, where they founded Finchburg.

With her sisters, Alice and Louise, and her brother, Edwin, Harper grew up in the quiet little town of Monroeville. In her childhood, like Jean Louise (Scout) Finch in *To Kill a Mockingbird* (1960), Harper used to go up to the courthouse balcony to watch her father appear in court. Like Scout, Harper and Edwin had a friend from the city, Truman Capote, who spent much of his childhood with elderly relatives in Monroeville and who was later to become a distinguished writer. Harper herself had begun writing by the time she was seven.

After attending the public schools in Monroeville, Lee went to Huntington College in Montgomery, Alabama, for one year, then in 1945 transferred to the University of Alabama, where she remained from 1945 to 1950, except for one year spent as an exchange student at the University of Oxford. At the University of Alabama, Lee continued her writing, contributing to various campus publications. Then she made her decision. She must be a writer. Much to her father's disappointment, Lee left the University of Alabama six months short of a law degree. She moved to New York, where she supported herself by working as an airline reservations clerk for Eastern Airlines and British Overseas Airways. Eventually, she took some of her work to a literary agent. He was particularly interested in one of the short stories, and he suggested that she expand it to a novel.

Quitting her job, Lee began working full time on what was to be *To Kill a Mockingbird*. In 1957, she had a manuscript completed; however, the editors at the publishing committee to which she submitted it asked her to rework it, tightening the

structure. She did, and the book was published in 1960.

To Kill a Mockingbird was a best-seller. It was a Literary Guild Selection, a Book-of-the-Month Club alternate, and a *Reader's Digest* condensed book. The novel also gained critical acclaim; in 1961, it won the Pulitzer Prize. The following year, it was made into a motion picture, which won an Academy Award. At that time, Harper Lee announced that she was working on a second novel. During the next three decades, several essays and articles appeared, but Lee published no more fiction. Lee still lives in her native Monroeville.

Analysis

To Kill a Mockingbird is a novel of childhood, but it is not told by a child. The narrator, Jean Louise (Scout) Finch, is an adult, recalling events that occurred in the mid-1930's, when her older brother Jem Finch was nearing his teens and she was four years younger. This narrative stance has several advantages. By using the first person, Lee gains immediacy and dramatic effect; by placing the events in the past, she can evaluate incidents that have become much clearer over the years.

The novel concerns innocence and experience, and its theme is more complicated than it might appear. Scout, Jem, and their friend from Meridian, Mississippi, Dill Harris, are not naturally cruel; however, they have not yet learned to empathize with others. To them, outsiders have no feelings. Therefore, it is all right to run up to the porch of a recluse, as a game; it is all right to rub a poor boy's nose in the schoolyard dirt; it is all right to make a snowman in the image of a neighbor; and it is all right to make fun of crabby old ladies. Although Atticus Finch, the father of the motherless Scout and Jem, is not particularly concerned with proper clothes for them, he is concerned about teaching them to imagine themselves in the position of others, even of people who are not particularly friendly or appealing. In this sense, then, the children's innocence, which dictates instinctive aversion, must be modified. On the other hand, Atticus hopes that his children will preserve another form of innocence—that they will not learn the prejudices that society is so willing to teach them.

Structurally, then, the novel is organized to show the development, or the moral education, of Atticus' children. In episode after episode, the pattern is repeated. The children (or one child) will assess someone by superficial standards; then, either on their own or, more often, in a conversation with Atticus, the children discover the truth—that the person whom they condemned has hidden sorrows and, often, hidden strengths.

Since the first-person narrator is the adult who, as a child, experienced all of these revelations, Harper Lee could have had her introduce the characters in these episodes with a full description and analysis. Instead, she chooses to let the readers follow the children to their discovery of the truth. This technique not only increases suspense, it also dramatizes the process through which the children themselves are going on their way to understanding.

One of those brief but significant episodes occurs at the end of part 1 of the novel, which is divided into two parts. It begins with the narrator's explaining the antipathy that both she and her brother feel toward Mrs. Henry Lafayette Dubose, an old woman who lives alone and whose chief pleasure seems to be sitting on her front porch and shouting criticisms and insults at passing children, especially at Jem and Scout. They cannot understand why their father behaves in so courtly a manner toward Mrs. Dubose. As far as they are concerned, she deserves their hatred.

Finally, Mrs. Dubose hurls one insult too many at the children, this time one equating their father with the blacks and poor whites for whom she says Atticus works. When the children pass her house again a short time after this diatribe, Jem notices that Mrs. Dubose has retreated from the porch; in a fury, he destroys every one of her camellias.

As soon as he has done it, Jem begins to anticipate his father's rebuke. What he does not expect is the punishment that he receives: Atticus not only makes Jem apologize, he also has him offer amends. What Mrs. Dubose decides that she needs of Jem is to have him read to her every day but Sunday for a month. Atticus finds that penalty appropriate and makes sure that Jem lives up to the contract. Even when Jem reports Mrs. Dubose's continuing insults about Atticus helping the blacks, Atticus will not relent. Finally, the month is up, and Jem thinks that he is free of Mrs. Dubose.

Some time later, however, Mrs. Dubose dies; Atticus then feels free to explain to Jem why, despite her prejudice and her crankiness, he considers Mrs. Dubose one of the bravest people he has ever known. Mrs. Dubose was addicted to morphine; however, when she knew that she was dying, she was determined to break that habit, even though by doing so she would ensure herself an agonizing death. Atticus does not have to explain further to his son; Jem now knows that he will never be free of Mrs. Dubose, will never forget the lesson he has learned.

In brief episodes such as this, Lee chronicles the children's moral development. The fact that generally she has her adult narrator move through events like the child she was when they occurred is one reason that *To Kill a Mockingbird* so effectively dramatizes the journey from innocence to experience, from amorality to morality.

TO KILL A MOCKINGBIRD

First published: 1960
Type of work: Novel

Three children learn about goodness and courage from the small-town Alabama lawyer who defends an innocent black man in court despite community disapproval.

To Kill a Mockingbird has been discussed by many critics simply in terms of racial prejudice; however, it is clear that in both the novel and the film the theme is even more universal than a portrayal of the evil of racial prejudice. That evil is shown as an example of man's intolerance. In all of its forms, man's inhumanity to man is the real antagonist of the enlightened. In the novel, there are many minor instances of prejudice, including the encounter between Jem and Mrs. Dubose, with which part 1 of the book ends. These incidents prepare for the concentration on the two major plot lines in part 2. Neither of the plot lines dominates the novel. Structurally, they are brilliantly interwoven. Thematically, they complement each other.

The first of these plots is introduced in the first few sentences of the novel, when the narrator says that the story to be told really began when Dill Harris got the idea of getting Arthur (Boo) Radley to come out. The setting is the small town of Maycomb, Alabama; the time is the mid-1930's. Boo Radley is the neighbor of the Finches. When he was a teenager, he got into minor trouble, and since that time, he has been imprisoned in his home by his father, who is a religious fanatic. Because no one in the community ever sees Boo, much less gets to know him, everyone has come to fear him. At first, the children share this fear. They dare each other to run up to the house where Boo is incarcerated, as if he were a supernatural monster. Gradually, however, they become aware that Boo is observing them and that he wishes them no harm. Indeed, in his loneliness, he reaches out to the children. He keeps Jem from getting in trouble by returning his torn pants, mended; he leaves the children little presents in a hollow tree; he even gets near enough to put a blanket around Scout when she is standing outside to watch a neighbor's house burn. Once the children begin to share secrets with Boo, they have admitted him to their world. He is no longer a stranger; he is a friend. The children have surmounted the prejudice of their community.

There are many parallels between this plot line and the second plot line, which involves a black man, Tom Robinson. Like Boo, Robinson is imprisoned within his community, but unlike Boo, Robinson has never committed any action that might produce punishment. His only crime is to have been born black in a society that has certain assumptions about blacks—among them, the assumption that black men always desire white women. That assumption is based on another assumption: that whites are always superior to blacks.

Like Boo Radley, Tom Robinson is a kind person, drawn toward those he perceives as helpless. Certainly the white girl Mayella Ewell, is pitiable. The entire community, black and white, looks down upon the Ewell tribe, which is headed by the despicable Bob Ewell, Mayella's father. Bob Ewell is the only character in *To Kill a Mockingbird* who has no virtues. He is mean, abusive, filthy, and shiftless. When he is drunk or simply in a bad mood, he beats his children. Given this family situation, it would be natural for anyone to respond to a plea from one of those children. From time to time, when Tom is passing by the Ewell place, Mayella asks him to help her with some heavy task that her father has assigned her to do, and innocently, Tom does what she asks. Unfortunately, like Boo Radley, Mayella is desperately lonely, and she does the unthinkable: She makes a sexual advance to Tom. Shocked and terrified, he leaves; shocked at her own conduct, she connives with her father to accuse Tom of rape. Thus it is Tom's compassionate attempt to transcend community prejudice, to treat an outcast white girl as a friend, which puts him in peril and which finally, despite the impassioned legal defense by Atticus Finch, costs Tom his life.

There is no question that both Boo Radley and Tom Robinson are acting correctly when they reach out to others. By example, Atticus Finch is attempting to teach this kind of behavior to both his children and his community. Yet Atticus would be the first to admit that there is danger in defying prejudice, in breaking down barriers that have been erected over the years and throughout the generations. Tom's moral action is misinterpreted; to believe him would be to admit that a white girl could desire a black man, and thus to upset the entire social hierarchy. Therefore the community must doom Tom, even though many people secretly do believe him. Boo Radley, too, runs a risk by befriending the children, not only from his tyrannical father but also from the law. When Bob Ewell ambushes Jem and Scout, planning to maim or kill them as a revenge upon Atticus, Boo goes to their defense and in the scuffle kills Bob Ewell. Atticus Finch—the man of honor, no matter what the consequences—believes that he must turn Radley over to the sheriff; however, the sheriff refuses to prosecute Radley and persuades Atticus on this occasion to put justice ahead of the letter of the law and to let Radley go free. If the timid recluse had been sent to prison, he would have died as surely as Tom Robinson dies when he attempts to flee.

If compassion in the midst of prejudice costs Tom Robinson his life and puts Boo Radley in peril, it can nevertheless sometimes win a victory. During Tom's arrest and trial, the community tension mounts, and with it, hostility toward Atticus. Finally, a mob gathers at the jail where Tom is being held; outside the jail, Atticus is on guard. Undoubtedly, he would have been attacked, even killed, if a past kindness had not been remembered. Scout had befriended the child of one of the members of the mob. Innocently unaware of the danger, Scout runs to her father and singles out that other father with inquiries about his son. Shamefacedly, he answers, the anger is dispelled, and Atticus is safe. Although she is a realist, Harper Lee refuses to be a cynic. If there is evil in humanity, there is also good, and sometimes the good is recognized and even defended.

Summary

In *To Kill a Mockingbird*, Harper Lee not only captured the essence of what it was like to grow up in a small Southern town in the 1930's, but she also showed what it was to grow up in such a society with a father who was a man of principle, who would risk his reputation and his life to defend a black man accused of a crime that violated the most sacred taboos of his society.

By making Tom Robinson's story only one of a number of episodes in the novel, all with a similar pattern, Lee broadened the subject of her work and expanded its theme. What Atticus is endeavoring to give to his children and to his community is the power to empathize with others and the courage to defend them against injustice.

Bibliography

Betts, Doris. Introduction to *Southern Women Writers: The New Generation*, edited by Tonette Bond Inge. Tuscaloosa: University of Alabama Press, 1990.

Bruell, Edwin. "Keen Scalpel on Racial Ills." *English Journal* 53 (December, 1964): 658-661.

Cook, Martha. "Old Ways and New Ways." In *The History of Southern Literature*, edited by Louis D. Rubin, Jr., et al. Baton Rouge: Louisiana State University Press, 1985.

Going, William T. *Essays on Alabama Literature.* Tuscaloosa: University of Alabama Press, 1975.

Schuster, Edgar H. "Discovering Theme and Structure in the Novel." *English Journal* 52 (October, 1963): 506-511.

Rosemary M. Canfield Reisman

URSULA K. LE GUIN

Born: Berkeley, California
October 21, 1929

Principal Literary Achievement

Though usually categorized as science fiction or fantasy, Le Guin's writing transcends such arbitrary titles, ranging from subtle feminist works to multimedia fiction.

Biography

Ursula Kroeber Le Guin was born in Berkeley, California, on October 21, 1929. Her parents, Theodora and Alfred Kroeber, were both well-educated people; her mother had a graduate degree in psychology, and her father was a well-known anthropologist. Le Guin and her three older brothers, Karl, Theodore, and Clifford, were reared in a household that placed strong emphasis on reading.

Le Guin's father taught at the University of California, Berkeley, and the family spent the academic year in Berkeley. With the arrival of summer, however, the family would move to their forty-acre estate, called Kishamish, in the Napa Valley. Le Guin spent much time exploring the land around the estate with her brothers, which is perhaps why so many of her novels include tales of journeys by foot. Yet even during the summers, visitors to Kishamish included visiting intelligentsia such as Robert Oppenheimer and various anthropological scholars. Le Guin's exposure to anthropology dates from before the time she could read, as her father often told stories about the local Indians to his children.

Le Guin's reading was not confined to anthropology, however, for she read all genres available to her, ranging from the romantic works of Lord Dunsany to the Taoist writings of the legendary seventh century Chinese figure Lao Tze, while still in her teens. In 1947, she was admitted to Harvard University's Radcliffe College, in Cambridge, Massachusetts; in 1951, she was made a member of Phi Beta Kappa and received a B.A. in French and Italian (with an emphasis on Renaissance literature). That year, she entered a master's program at Columbia University, receiving an M.A. in 1952. Although Le Guin continued with her higher education by starting a doctoral program at Columbia University, she ended it when she married Charles Le Guin, a history professor whom she had met while on a ship to France (she was on her way to a Fulbright year in France). They were married, in Paris, in December of 1953.

The end of Le Guin's doctoral aspirations, however, proved to be the beginning of

her career as a writer. Le Guin's mother had been a late bloomer as a writer, not starting until she was middle-aged (her *Ishi in Two Worlds* was published in 1961, a year after the death of Le Guin's father). Le Guin had begun writing much earlier, producing her first fantasy story at age nine, though when her first science fiction story was rejected by a magazine when she was eleven, she waited ten years before submitting another one. With her marriage, she began writing poetry, later collected in *Wild Angels* (1975), and novels, all of which were rejected by publishers because they did not fit neatly into a commercial genre.

Le Guin's real publishing success came with the publication of what is now called the Hainish trilogy: *Rocannon's World* (1966), *Planet of Exile* (1966), and *City of Illusions* (1967). After that, Le Guin no longer had to fear rejection slips. Her 1968 *A Wizard of Earthsea* won the *Boston Globe*-Horn Book Award, and *The Left Hand of Darkness* (1969) won both the Hugo and Nebula awards the next year. When her 1974 *The Dispossessed: An Ambiguous Utopia* accomplished this feat as well, Le Guin became the first writer to win both awards twice for novels. *A Wizard of Earthsea* became the basis of what was called the Earthsea trilogy: *A Wizard of Earthsea*, *The Tombs of Atuan* (1971), and *The Farthest Shore* (1972). Much of Le Guin's work has been ignored as being juvenile or young-adult literature, including *A Wizard of Earthsea*. The epic fantasies of the Earthsea series recount the adventures of a young boy named Sparrowhawk and the young priestess named Arha whom he rescues. *The Tombs of Atuan* and *The Farthest Shore* follow their lives as they mature and develop their individual powers. In 1990, *Tehanu: The Last Book of Earthsea* was published, formally (or so Le Guin has said) bringing the adventures of Tenar (Arha) and Ged (Sparrowhawk) to an end. *Tehanu* is markedly different from the earlier books in the series, however, in that it is written for adults. Perhaps Le Guin wanted to aim it at the audience who had grown up reading her books and was now older and mature—just as Tenar and Ged are in *Tehanu.*

Occasionally, Le Guin has combined her writing career with teaching. She has taught French as well as writing and has spent time as a writer-in-residence at the University of Washington. In 1976, Le Guin was a visiting fellow in creative writing at the University of Reading, in England. She has also participated as a teacher in writing workshops in places such as Melbourne, Australia, and Oregon, Washington, and Indiana, in the United States. Though probably best known for her contributions to the genres of science fiction and fantasy, Le Guin has also written children's literature, including *Solomon Leviathan's 931st Trip Around the World* (1983) and *Fire and Stone* (1989). Her later work has been excerpted in magazines such as *Harper's Magazine* and *The New Yorker.*

Le Guin's books and stories have won many awards and have come to be accepted as literary achievements beyond the categories of science fiction and fantasy.

Analysis

During her writing career, Ursula K. Le Guin's work has expanded significantly outside the genre of science fiction. From "pro-choice" parables in *Ms.* magazine to advice to fellow authors in her book of essays *Dancing at the Edge of the World: Thoughts on Words, Women, Places* (1989), Le Guin has been prolific and diverse in her output.

Strongly feminist, her writing is sensitive but sensible. Her fiction has become accepted by critics because of their recognition of the breadth and depth of her stories and characters. Le Guin's fascination with anthropology, mythology (especially the Norse myths), and identity has led to several approaches by analysts of her work. Probably the most widely discussed approach is that of Jungian analysis of her writing, while another approach uses a blend of feminism and general psychoanalytic theory.

Le Guin's interests in identity and in the clash between human and nonhuman are some of the broadest themes throughout her works, along with that of the difference made by accidents of gender or the difference made, as in *The Left Hand of Darkness,* by lack of gender. Though Le Guin is not considered a mainstream fiction writer, her fantasy and science fiction now are interpreted from a point that transcends those labels. Beyond mere entertainment and escapism, her works probe the conflicts that all races must face in the future. Equally, human and nonhuman (or different cultures of any race or creed) are forced to deal with the issues and problems created in her plots.

Yet Le Guin does not believe that the basis of writing is conflict or that there is no story without conflict. In her essay "Conflict," included in *Dancing at the Edge of the World*, she wrote that to base one's writing on conflict is "to use an aspect of existence, conflict, to subsume all other aspects, many of which it does not include and does not comprehend."

Le Guin's feminist thinking is very apparent in her work. In the short story "Crosswords" (published in the July 30, 1990, edition of *The New Yorker*), Le Guin's main character, Ailie, describes the easiest way of dealing with most men.

> It was easier to smile. It's like there's a kind of oil that makes their wheels go round, and smiling is part of it, women smiling. They expect it, and when they don't get it they may not know what's missing but they tend to seize up and get mean, like a motor you don't oil.

Interestingly, Le Guin said in a 1990 interview with *Publishers Weekly* that "neither [she] nor . . . literature was ready for a female point of view in the early 1970's." For a long time (until writing *Tehanu,* in fact) Le Guin believed herself unable to write fiction from the viewpoint of a mature woman. The absence of females as main characters had been much criticized by some in the feminist movement. Though probably not written for that reason, *Tehanu* has helped fill this gap in Le Guin's oeuvre.

Le Guin has described her works (such as *The Left Hand of Darkness*) as "thought experiments about the meaning of sexuality and gender." She does not blindly assume that female qualities are innately good and male qualities are naturally bad. Her female characters are not perfect; the problems they face are not solved any more easily because they are applying "female intelligence" to them.

Le Guin's preoccupation with identity and naming—the other major aspect of her work—is often discussed in the context of "artistic autism": separation from the world in order to create. Le Guin has said that she does not make up ideas; rather, images present themselves and she writes about these images. Therefore, her choice of a male over a female protagonist is not an antifeminist statement; it is merely based on the image that appears, an arbitrary happening, not a choice. Le Guin does not view feminism as female versus male, and it is a stance that her works reflect. For example, both *The Left Hand of Darkness* and *Always Coming Home* (1985) incorporate sexual plurality, though of different manifestations. In her collection *Buffalo Gals and Other Animal Presences* (1987), her story "She Unnames Them" combines feminism with identity, as she has Eve unname all the animals in the Garden of Eden and then leave Adam—after returning her own name.

Le Guin's talent is in her reversal of social expectations; she surprises the reader by distorting gender and behavioral categories and fashioning new norms by which her characters behave. The fascination of Le Guin's work lies in this sociological creativity.

THE LEFT HAND OF DARKNESS

First published: 1969
Type of work: Novel

An alien envoy tries to convince the inhabitants of the icy planet Winter that there is life beyond their world.

Genly Ai is an envoy from the Ekumen, an ambassador sent to recruit the planet Winter to join an assemblage of planets in a peaceful intergalactic council. The main advantage the Ekumen have to offer is communication with numerous other worlds throughout the star system, worlds that are light years away.

Winter's inhabitants are different from most humanlike beings in that they do not have two separate genders: Each person is a hermaphrodite. Ai, the envoy, is the one regarded as the freak, a person perpetually in a state of *kemmer*, or "heat." Ai's relationship with Estraven, the prime minister of one of the major powers on the planet, provides him with many uncomfortable moments as he tries to come to terms with dealing with someone who is neither male nor female but both. (One of Le Guin's most startling images comes when Ai is told that the king of Karhide is pregnant.)

Political intrigue and physical hardships, however, teach Ai to accept Estraven as what he is: anther human being. Hearth tales separate the narrative chapters, which are told alternately by Ai and Estraven. The hearth tales serve to illuminate social customs, such as the acceptance of incest but the rejection of an incestuous couple who bear a child.

Language and communication are an important theme in this work. When Ai finally manages to "mindspeak" with Estraven, for example, Estraven "hears" his dead brother's voice. Other themes include those of symbiosis (Ai's dependence on Estraven when they are crossing the ice) and isolation (the miles of nothingness Ai and Estraven must cross to reach Karhide), death and rebirth, and sexuality (*kemmer*) and platonic friendship (Ai's and Estraven's purposely nonsexual relationship).

As one critic has noted, "the goals and concerns of Le Guin's characters are closely related to her own." Ai's acceptance of Estraven as a being beyond sexual labeling speaks for Le Guin's hope that one day society will accept all of its members without heed to their sex or sexual orientation.

THE DISPOSSESSED

First published: 1974
Type of work: Novel

An inhabitant of a world without rules or laws visits its exact opposite—a world composed of prisons and barriers, both mental and physical.

The Dispossessed: An Ambiguous Utopia is another example of Le Guin's fascination with the theme "to voyage is to return." For Shevek, the novel's protagonist, "to go was not enough for him, only half enough; he must come back." On the headstone of Laia Asieo Odo, the woman credited with founding Shevek's civilization, is the epitaph *To be whole is to be part; true voyage is to return.*

Odo was a revolutionary anarchist who broke away from the rigid society on her home planet, Urras, to found a society free of regulations on Urras' moon, Anarres. Shevek is a physicist who breaks with the traditions of his planet to reintroduce social contact with Urras (the two planets have maintained trade ties since Anarres broke away 180 years before).

The contrasts between Urras and Anarres include the status of women (they are mere sexual property on Urras, while respected as equals on Anarres), freedom on Anarres from the germs that plague Urras (with the exception of the common cold, the cure of which Le Guin places beyond any known science), and the disdain for power on Anarres that is a reaction to the greed perceived on Urras.

Shevek goes to Urras in hopes of having his "temporal theory" accepted by the scientific establishment there. This theory promises the capability of simultaneous communication in the form of a device called an ansible. (This devise is used by other characters in several of Le Guin's books, including by Genly Ai in *The Left Hand of Darkness.*) Le Guin uses Shevek and Anarres to reveal the inadequacies left by a society that believes nothing is owned and that no one person is more important than another. Shevek is continually thwarted in his work through bureaucratic obstacles and general indifference to his theory. The Anarrasti do not want contact with other civilizations, all of whom are equated with the Urrasti. Although Shevek finds life on Urras to be equally disturbing, he does not give up on his quest to change society. Ultimately, he returns to Anarres, bringing an Urrasti man with him in the hope of inducing some change in his society.

Le Guin subtitles her book *An Ambiguous Utopia* deliberately; at no time in *The Dispossessed* does she advocate Anarres as a solution to intergalactic societal problems. Instead, she uses the contrasts between the two worlds to highlight the best and worst of each, combining her utopian and science fiction themes to create a dialectic on the eternal struggle between the artistic and the political.

ALWAYS COMING HOME

First published: 1985
Type of work: Novel

Living a future that may not exist, a woman recounts events from her past.

Always Coming Home is a multimedia (it includes tape recordings of songs and poetry) fictional historical work set in Northern California that purports to write the history of several peoples in the distant future. When first working on the book, Le Guin found that she had difficulty in writing about the Napa Valley of her childhood ("Na Valley" in the book). To try and work the block out, she wrote a story about an encounter between an elderly neighbor and a mountain lion called "May's Lion" (included in *Buffalo Gals and Other Animal Presences*). From that story came the inspiration that allowed Le Guin to write *Always Coming Home.*

Le Guin writes in her introduction that these peoples may not exist and that their future might not take place. The people are, however, present in the book, if not in the real world—yet. Le Guin talks about the difficulty of translating this story from the language of the Kesh, comparing the book to Lao Tze's *Tao teh ching*—a book translated into Chinese "at every cycle of Cathay," though it is a book that is not available in the original and was written by someone who may not have existed.

The Kesh have a peaceful, matrilineal society. Their opposites are the aggressive, patrilineal Condors. The history of these peoples are told by Stone Telling (who is also known as North Owl, Ayatyu, and Woman Coming Home, depending on her stage of life), a Kesh woman whose mother was a Kesh but whose father was a Condor.

Le Guin's message is that Western civilization's patrilineal aggressiveness needs to be tamed by taking a more matrilineal approach to social structure. Without peace, there may be no future. Her title, *Always Coming Home*, reflects her Taoist leanings—to go is to return. All Stone Telling's journeys lead to her return home.

Always Coming Home was viewed by the feminist movement as a statement that Le Guin had decided to make women the center of her writing. While *Always Coming Home* and *Tehanu* are true women's books insofar as they portray women honestly, Le Guin is not trying to segregate her writing from men. Her stories are meant for both women and men to read. Society is made up of both females and males; without cooperation, they cannot survive together—and they certainly cannot survive without each other.

TEHANU

First published: 1990
Type of work: Novel

The arrival of a fallen "archmage" on a dragon changes the quiet world of a widow who has powers of her own.

In *Tehanu: The Last Book of Earthsea*, the fourth book of Le Guin's Earthsea series, Tenar (who earlier went by the name Arha) has been widowed and is using her Gontish name, Goha. She is called to assist in the treatment of a badly burned and sexually abused young girl, whom Tenar adopts and names Therru. A visit to the now-dying Ogion elicits the information that there is a powerful and dangerous presence in Therru. The dramatic return of Ged aboard the back of the dragon Kalessin, however, occupies Tenar's mind, as she must nurse him—he has lost the powers of archmagery and has returned to his former name, Sparrowhawk.

Tehanu is, like much of Le Guin's work, a careful compendium of names, spells, and physical transformations. Le Guin has said that power is the central theme to this work—physical, mental, and magical power. In these aspects, *Tehanu* resembles Le Guin's earlier work, especially *Always Coming Home.* Where much of her earlier work, however, is geared toward retaining a younger person's interest, *Tehanu* deals with the darker themes of child molestation and abuse and death on a more adult level. In a way, *Tehanu* is also a coming-of-age novel. Instead of becoming an adult person from a youth, however, Tenar becomes a mature and self-confident being from having been regarded too long as "merely a woman."

Summary

Science fiction and fantasy authors are often maligned as inferior writers. Yet the creativity and judgment that go into inventing new worlds and new races of people cannot be dismissed so easily. Ursula K. Le Guin's work is exemplary of the finest aspect of what fiction of any genre can offer its audience: the belief that all beings must be respected, regardless of their appearance or customs.

Le Guin has an optimistic view of the future: She believes that the human race can change and that people will save themselves from the ultimate destruction prophesied by most science fiction authors.

Bibliography

Bittner, James W. *Approaches to the Fiction of Ursula K. Le Guin*. Ann Arbor: University of Michigan Research Press, 1984.

Bloom, Harold, ed. *Ursula K. Le Guin*. New York: Chelsea House, 1986.

Bucknall, Barbara. *Ursula K. Le Guin*. New York: Frederick Ungar, 1981.

Olander, Joseph, and Martin Harry Greenberg, eds. *Ursula K. Le Guin*. New York: Taplinger, 1979.

Selinger, Bernard. *Le Guin and Identity in Contemporary Fiction*. Ann Arbor: University of Michigan Research Press, 1988.

Spivack, Charlotte. *Ursula K. Le Guin*. Boston: Twayne, 1984.

Jo-Ellen Lipman Boon

SINCLAIR LEWIS

Born: Sauk Centre, Minnesota
February 7, 1885
Died: Rome, Italy
January 10, 1951

Principal Literary Achievement

The first American novelist to win the Noble Prize in Literature, Lewis gave the American public its first literary view of the emerging middle class during the 1920's.

Biography

Harry Sinclair Lewis was born in Sauk Centre, Minnesota, on February 7, 1885, the youngest of three sons of a country doctor, Edwin J. Lewis. One year after the death of Harry's tubercular mother, Emma, in 1891, his father married Isabel Warner, whom Lewis felt was psychically his own mother. Unlike his older brother, Claude, Harry cared nothing for sports, was not popular in school, and received little praise from his father. So, like so many lonely children, he found solace in books, read voraciously, and began writing regularly in diaries which he kept throughout his life.

Fred, the eldest son, dropped out of school and worked as a miller all of his life. Claude, however, was a constant success and an example held up to Harry, so that Claude's decision to become a doctor undoubtedly had some influence on Harry's educational plans. After six months of preparation at Oberlin Academy, Lewis enrolled in Yale University, but there again he was friendless, an outsider. He did gain a place on the editorial staff of the *Yale Literary Magazine*, but by the beginning of his senior year he left New Haven to become a janitor at Halicon Hall, the experiment in communal living established by writer and social reformer Upton Sinclair.

After about a month the restless young man went to New York and tried to live by writing; he soon took off for Panama to work on the canal. Lewis decided to return to Yale, and he was graduated in June, 1908. In 1914, when his first novel, *Our Mr. Wrenn: The Romantic Adventure of a Gentle Man*, was published, he married Grace Livingston Hegger and settled down to a life of commuting to Manhattan for his daily stint at Doran Publishing and writing furiously at home. After *The Saturday Evening Post* had accepted several of his short stories at a thousand dollars each, Lewis felt that he could devote his entire time to writing. It was not until 1920,

however, with the publication of *Main Street: The Story of Carol Kennicott*, that Sinclair Lewis became famous. It is significant that Lewis had planned originally to call the novel "Village Virus"; it was unremitting in its scathing criticism of provincial America and of what H. L. Mencken later called "boobus Americanus," and it evoked what Mark Schorer (in his biography of Lewis) calls "a storm of vilification and applause."

Even though his first son, Wells, had been born in 1917, Lewis insisted that the family keep moving about the country, indicating a restlessness that he would never lose. Actually, what he called his "research" made it necessary that he live like a field sociologist, filling many notebooks with intricate maps, accurate descriptions of houses (complete with furniture placement), and verbatim conversations before writing each novel.

As biographer Schorer explains, the next novel, *Babbitt* (1922), caused even more consternation than *Main Street*, and Lewis was denounced as a "villain and a traitor." Yet all over the United States thousands of people bought the book. Lewis next planned to write a labor novel, but while in Chicago, he met a young medical researcher, Paul de Kruif, and the two men began discussions of a book dealing with corruption in the medical profession. They went together to the Caribbean, an important locale of the proposed novel, and then to England, where Lewis began work on *Arrowsmith* (1925).

Although still sharply critical of certain segments of American society, this novel had an idealistic hero and a wife who was almost saintly, so that *Arrowsmith* was a huge success, both critically and financially. It was no surprise, then, when the Pulitzer Prize was awarded to Lewis; it was something of a shock, however, when he refused it. He declared publicly that the prize was awarded only to novels which showed the "wholesome atmosphere of American life," and in his open letter to the Pulitzer Prize Committee insisted that acceptance would indicate that their approval equaled authority to make final literary judgments. There is some suspicion that Lewis would have accepted the prize for *Main Street* or *Babbitt* and that he was "thumbing his nose" at those who had deprived him of the award earlier.

The next major novel, *Elmer Gantry* (1927), dealt with the most negative aspects of evangelical religion, and in typical fashion Lewis carefully cultivated many members of the clergy in Kansas City before beginning to write. The result is possibly the most savage satire in the Lewis canon, with hardly one admirable character surrounding the villainous protagonist. In addition, Lewis featured sex quite prominently, so that it caused the greatest furor of all of his books. The bans which followed, from Boston to Glasgow, had the effect of making the book an immediate best-seller, but Lewis was widely denounced from many pulpits and was even invited to a lynching party in Virginia. By now, his marriage had begun to disintegrate, attributable particularly to quarrels over his addiction to alcohol.

Lewis went to Europe alone, looking for subject matter for his next novel, following his familiar pattern of wandering almost aimlessly. He stopped in Germany, however, when he met Dorothy Thompson, the best-known newspaperwoman in

Europe. After Lewis was granted a divorce from Grace in 1928, the two were married. Although he continued to write for the rest of his life, the last important novel, *Dodsworth*, appeared in 1929. As the decade ended, newer, shriller voices were being heard, and from this point on, Lewis would be considered somewhat old-fashioned.

Nevertheless, in 1930, he was awarded the Nobel Prize in Literature, and his acceptance speech was a benchmark in the history of American literature. In it, he announced: "Our American professors like their literature clear and cold and pure and very dead."

At age forty-six he was the author of twelve published novels and would write ten more in the final twenty years of his life. In 1937, there was the dissolving of his second marriage, with his second son, Michael, remaining with Dorothy Thompson as Lewis continued his peregrinations throughout the world. For a time he became enamored of the stage, and even tried acting himself during the late 1930's and 1940's.

Unfortunately, his problem with alcoholism grew worse as he continued his lifelong pursuit of what Schorer calls "some vague and undefined glimmer of a happier place, a richer life." There may be some doubt about whether Sinclair Lewis had ever really left Sauk Centre, since he admitted that the heroine of *Main Street*, Carol Kennicott, was really he himself, and it is significant that by the novel's end Carol has returned to Gopher Prairie and her dull but steady husband, Dr. Will.

Lewis died among strangers in an Italian hospital on the outskirts of Rome on a rainy January 10, 1951.

Analysis

The principal themes of Sinclair Lewis' major novels are concern with the effects of small-town life and narrow-minded people on those who do not conform to established patterns, and a castigation of American middle-class materialism. His first two successful novels, *Main Street* and *Babbitt*, clearly illustrate these ideas even by their titles. In the first, his main character, Carol Kennicott, tries to raise the level of life in Gopher Prairie, the small town to which she has come after her marriage. She finally "settles" for the dullness of Main Street which typifies such places.

In *Babbitt*, Lewis creates a protagonist so symbolic of the emptiness inherent in the middle-class pursuit of material things that his name can now be found in the dictionary, defined as "a self-satisfied person who conforms readily to middle-class attitudes and ideals." In *Arrowsmith*, Lewis continues his castigation of small-minded individuals, this time showing how their lack of vision and their emphasis on "the practicality of profit" hamper the work of scientific research and negatively affect those in the medical profession. Finally, in *Elmer Gantry*, he draws his most loathsome character, a man who manipulates unthinking people to advance his career in the ministry. By the novel's end, Elmer Gantry has achieved his materialistic goals, but he is shown to be an empty shell of a man, so evil that he is almost unaware of his own hypocrisy.

Lewis' work relies but little on plot. Lewis acts as a photographer of the locales in which his novels are set, creating them and the characters who inhabit them with exactness. He relied heavily on careful research before writing each book, and his ability to re-create so exactly the places, speech, and manners he writes about has made a number of critics call him a consummate mimic. His work is somewhat regional in the sense that his four most outstanding novels are set in the American Midwest, his own bailiwick.

He is a satirist, somewhat sarcastic in tone even when he is drawing the portrait of a character to be admired by the reader. What his work lacks, however, is sufficient probing below the surface of characters to give the reader a genuine sense of each one's motivations. Like a professional photographer, Lewis carefully sets his camera angles to give a particular slant to each picture, a slant usually planned to call attention to the most negative aspects of both the setting and the people pictured.

The era in which Lewis produced his four best novels is an important factor to consider in evaluating them. *Main Street* appeared just after World War I, when small-town America had passed its original frontier days but had not yet truly begun its emancipation from the set patterns and values so much a part of the earlier rural society.

With *Babbitt*, set two years later, he shows the next stage in American development. In mid-sized cities, the emphasis on "not being a hick" has led to an emphasis on the possession of the most up-to-date models of all material objects as being equal to success. It is notable that this novel does not deal with social criticism of genuine business tycoons or "robber barons," as some earlier muckrakers had, but rather with the almost pitiful strivings of those who are the very antithesis of those earlier individualists. To George Babbitt and the other characters in the novel, the most important factor is conformity—being well-liked, being part of the herd.

One of the usual criteria in literary analysis is the manner in which the writer develops characterization. Do the people in the novel exhibit more than a single side or are they so inhumanly consistent that they become stereotypes? With a few exceptions, it is in this area of his work that Lewis may be faulted. Granted, this is the pitfall of the genre—satire—and Lewis based his characters on models he observed in his society. Nevertheless, taking only the photographer's view of his subjects detracts in some cases from the verisimilitude. As critic Geoffrey Moore put it, "Lewis's method was to choose an institution or a class of people, decide on a point of view, and then flatten his characters into the mould he desired. . . . [t]here is no 'innerness.'" When Lewis does go beyond this tendency toward a journalistic style, however, as he does with Carol Kennicott in *Main Street*, Max Gottlieb and Martin Arrowsmith in *Arrowsmith*, and a few other of his creations, he avoids completely the charge of creating caricatures.

Sinclair Lewis can certainly be seen as a critic of the era in which he wrote his best novels, but he was no reformer; he does not suggest solutions. In the manner of some European novelists, such as Émile Zola, he merely points out through satire what he sees.

MAIN STREET

First published: 1920
Type of work: Novel

A young idealistic bride tries unsuccessfully to alter life in a small Midwestern town circa 1920.

Carol Milford, an attractive, eager librarian, marries Dr. Will Kennicott and comes to Gopher Prairie with every expectation of seeing the town through her husband's eyes. Will, a character based to a great extent on the novelist's father and brother Claude, both country doctors, is proud of Gopher Prairie and does not see clearly the faults which become so apparent to Carol almost at once. Carol Kennicott wants to change everything from the dull buildings that line Main Street to the people who inhabit the houses, people whose interests in life are very narrow indeed. Will's friends assume that Carol will "settle in" and embrace their values, and when she does not do so, they are quite disturbed.

Lewis constantly emphasizes the freedom of the countryside surrounding the town, so that nature even in the midst of stormy winter is preferable to the stultifying atmosphere of Gopher Prairie. Some of Carol's happiest times are spent with her husband, tramping through the area appreciating nature.

She tries various plans to "raise the cultural level" of the town. She gives well-planned parties, instead of the usual dull ones that seem to her to be funereal. She offers to use her skills as a librarian to upgrade The Thanatopsis, a ladies' literary discussion group which specializes in brief summaries of the lives of great literary figures; she organizes a drama club to produce plays of more lasting merit than *The Girl from Kankakee.* She consistently fails.

Furthermore, she finds that even in Gopher Prairie, a village of about four thousand souls, there are strict notions of "social class," prejudice against the Swedish and German immigrants, rigid notions about morals, anti-union feeling, an avid love of gossiping, and, above all, a sense of unremitting dullness.

Carol does find a few friends. There is Guy Pollock, a lawyer who at first seems to share her views of Gopher Prairie. There is her hired girl, Bea Sorenson, a young Swedish farm girl who (by contrasting it with Scandia Crossing, population sixty-seven) looks at Gopher Prairie as a big city. There is the town outcast, Miles Bjornstam, an independent "Red Swede" who marries Bea. There is Erik Valborg, a would-be artist/designer who works as a presser in a local tailor shop, and there is Fern Mullins, a young schoolteacher.

Yet each friendship comes to naught. Guy confesses that "village virus" has infected him even unto death; Miles loses his beloved Bea and their little son, Olaf, to death and leaves his farm to travel west; Erik becomes a small-time film actor; and Fern Mullins is forced to resign and is run out of town on a trumped-up morals charge based entirely on malicious gossip.

The Kennicotts have a son, Hugh, and for a while the child fills Carol's life; however, even after she and Will have had an extended vacation in California, she finds that life in Gopher Prairie is intolerable. In addition to the faults Carol has found from the beginning, the town has succumbed to the new "booster" mentality, which has raised the price of land but has not raised the level of everyday life one iota.

With her husband's reluctant approval, Carol and Hugh go to live in Washington, D.C., where she gets a job in the Bureau of War Risk Insurance. It is a first step toward her independence, but she finds a "thick streak of Main Street" even there. After a year, her husband comes to Washington; they take a short trip south, which Will calls a "second wooing," and five months later, Carol decides to return to Gopher Prairie, pregnant with her daughter and determined to continue "the good fight."

Lewis leaves little doubt about his opinion of Gopher Prairie and its faults, but the reader also sees that although Carol has good intentions from the beginning, she is not really focused on what changes she wants to make. She is somewhat immature, perhaps representing the American woman of the postwar period searching for her role in a radically changed society. It is only after she has lived in Washington and had contact with the Suffragettes that she begins to define herself as an individual. Her speech to Will at the end of the book is quite prophetic. She takes him to look at their sleeping baby daughter and says:

> Do you see that object on the pillow? Do you know what it is? It's a bomb to blow up smugness. If you Tories were wise, you wouldn't arrest anarchists; you'd arrest all these children while they're asleep in their cribs. Think what that baby will see and meddle with before she dies in the year 2000! She may see an industrial union of the whole world, she may see aeroplanes going to Mars.

Dr. Will Kennicott seems sometimes to be a father figure to Carol. He loves her deeply and is more than patient with her peccadillos. He is a good doctor, but he sees no romance in his profession; he has accepted some of the less attractive qualities of Gopher Prairie, such as the notion of social classes, as shown in his disapproval of having Carol take Hugh to visit Bea and Miles to play with their son Olaf. He is somewhat interested in making money to secure their future; he is also completely honest, basically kind, and thoroughly loyal. Most of the other inhabitants of Gopher Prairie are not particularly memorable. They are, for the most part, types, rather than distinctly drawn individuals.

The fact that Lewis has put Jim Blausser, the publicity person hired for the booster campaign, so near the end of the novel is significant. This huckster exaggerates everything from the genuine natural beauty to be found in the surrounding countryside to the new "White Way" which is now to be found on Main Street. He assures the citizens that their town can easily expect to become a city of 200,000 and a manufacturing center very soon. As Carol Kennicott wryly comments, "*There's* where I want to go; to that model town Gopher Prairie." Lewis is foreshadowing the next stage in the development of Main Street as he takes it to the city of Zenith, the locale of his next novel.

BABBITT

First published: 1922
Type of work: Novel

George F. Babbitt, representing the new middle class, depends on material possessions and conformity to validate his existence.

Rebecca West, in her 1922 essay "Babbitt," makes a statement that encapsulates Lewis' attitude toward the world of this novel:

> To write satire. . . . [o]ne must hate the world so much that one's hatred strikes sparks, but one must hate it only because it disappoints one's invincible love of it.

This statement also illustrates strikingly the novelist's disappointment in its protagonist, Babbitt. Here is a man with a dim perception that what he has accepted as the "good life" is not entirely satisfying; yet he lacks the power to do more than dream of the "fairy child" who beckons him to a better way. For Lewis, George F. Babbitt is the "Everyman" of his time.

In the real estate business with his father-in-law, Babbitt has convinced himself that he is indispensable as a facilitator. He does not think himself dishonest when he "puts over a deal" whereby a client receives information about a piece of property before the seller is aware of its increased value. He loves his wife, Myra, and their three children, but it is only in times of crisis that he gives them an honest thought. Supposedly a graduate of the state university, Babbitt is really quite ignorant, and in the "poetry" created by one of his fellow Boosters, Lewis has created a hilarious put-down of popular taste in the arts through the verses of T. Cholmondeley Frink, who also writes "Ads, that Add."

George Babbitt thinks that he has many friends, whereas in reality he has but one, Paul Reisling, and it is with Paul on a few days vacation in the Maine woods that Babbitt finds his only true happiness. It is the closeness of a friend which temporarily frees Babbitt from his boring life in Zenith, but this scene serves also as the author's insistence that nature has a salutory effect on all human beings, even the silliest. Paul's wife, Zilla, is a vindictive shrew who finally frustrates her husband to the point of shooting her in the shoulder. In all sincerity, Babbitt goes to Paul's lawyer in an offer to concoct a story to make the crime seem less deliberate, but his suggestion is refused, and Paul goes to state prison for three years. George misses him sorely.

At this time Myra Babbitt and her youngest child, Tinka, go East to visit relatives, leaving only George, his daughter Verona, and his son, Ted. Busy with their own lives, the young people are unconcerned and do little to assuage George's loneliness. His group at the Athletic Club is no help, and he begins to think of female companionship as a viable option. After Babbitt has been further depressed by a visit to Paul in prison, he makes several timorous attempts at flirting with his neighbor's wife and with a young manicurist. Both these women rebuff him, but an attractive widow, Tanis Judique, accepts his attentions after he has found her "just the right apartment."

He feels guilty about his affair and feels anxious about his activities, which include drinking and partying with "the Bunch," a group of Tanis' friends who consider themselves urbane bohemians. He does not stop being "Old Georgie," however, until his wife requires surgery. Meanwhile, Zenith is torn by a strike which divides the city into factions and finds Babbitt confused. He wants to believe that Seneca Doane and the other liberals supporting the strikers have their rights, but he is afraid that those who characterize them as "dirty socialists" will censure him, and he gives in to his fear.

His former friends, the respectable members of the Athletic Club, have formed a Good Citizens League—with all the characteristics of the Ku Klux Klan, minus the white hoods—and George is urged (even mildly threatened) to join. He resists briefly; then agrees with Vergil Grunch that he is being foolish, and within two weeks he is bellicose regarding the wickedness of Seneca Doane, the crimes of labor unions, and the perils of immigration. Babbitt also returns to the Boosters' Club, the church, and the Elks, and his father-in-law announces that their business is back to where it was before George's brief rebellion.

Lewis does, however, allow him one saving act. His son, Ted, has married the girl next door, much to the consternation of her parents. Furthermore, the boy has decided to skip college and work as a mechanic, and it is George F. Babbitt who tells him, "[d]on't be scared of the family. No, nor all of Zenith. Nor of yourself, the way I've been. Go ahead, old man! The world is yours!"

ARROWSMITH

First published: 1925
Type of work: Novel

An idealistic doctor finds his life's work in research.

In this novel, Lewis' protagonist, Martin Arrowsmith, is much more fully developed—more of a three-dimensional person—than are the characters in his earlier books. From the first, when he is shown as an adolescent, Martin makes mistakes; he is not always the perfect hero. He is, in fact, recognizably human.

The locale (Elk Mills, in the state of Winnemac) represents Lewis' Midwestern roots. There is the inevitable Main Street and the feeling of transition from rural life to that of a small town; there is also the alcoholic Doc Vickerson, who encourages the fourteen-year-old Martin to "study medicine, go to Zenith, and make money."

Martin goes to the state university as a medical student and has a professor, Dr. Max Gottlieb, who is to influence significantly the rest of his life. He also meets a number of other students who continue as characters throughout the novel. There is Ira Hinkley, the future medical missionary, Angus Duer, the future surgeon, and Clif Clawson, the practical joker, whose dismissal from medical school and subsequent appearance as an automobile salesman gives Lewis a fine chance to satirize hucksterism. At this point Martin also meets the love of his life, Leora Tozer, a young nursing student.

As Dr. Gottlieb's assistant, Martin is becoming very interested in the research area of medicine, but he makes a mistake, argues with Gottlieb, and after a night of drinking, tells Dean Silva that he will not apologize, so he is suspended from the university. With little sense of direction, and a lot of drinking, Martin actually becomes a hobo, but he finally heads west to Leora who has returned to her hometown at her parents' insistence. Her family opposes their marriage, but they elope, and the Tozers must accept it.

In the flush of graduation and a decision to set up practice in Wheatsylvania (Leora's hometown), Martin's devotion to research (and to Max Gottlieb) is temporarily forgotten. Max has been discharged from the hospital; his wife is ill, and the poor man is nearly at his wit's end when he is offered a position at a pharmaceutical firm, formerly a target of his scorn. From this time on, *Arrowsmith* deals largely with the commercial exploitation of scientific findings versus the need for pure research.

When Gottlieb refuses to turn his incomplete research into a saleable product, he is fired from Hunziker Pharmaceutical, but he finds a place at McGurk Institute almost immediately. Lewis criticizes the politics common at such institutions, based on Paul de Kruif's actual experience at the Rockefeller Institute.

Bored with his small-town practice, Martin obtains a position as second-in-command to the Director of Public Health, Dr. Almus Pickerbaugh, in Nautilus, Iowa, and becomes director himself after Pickerbaugh is elected to Congress, but this does not work out. Next, he obtains a position at Rouncefield Clinic in Chicago, through Angus Duer, and changes his goal of becoming a researcher to becoming a material success. He does qualify this new ambition by thinking that after he has made enough money, he will be able to have his own laboratory. Nevertheless, Lewis makes him very believable in his desire to be a monetary success rather than a man dedicated to pure science who is frustrated at every turn by those holding the purse strings.

A paper published by Martin reaches Gottlieb, who then invites him to McGurk, and the two are reconciled. All goes well despite the factions at the institute. Then the bombshell hits: Martin has been working tirelessly and has made a significant discovery. Those in power, anxious to enhance the reputation of the institute, want to make the research public at once. Finally, with Sondelius and Terry Wickett, Martin is able to work on an antidote for bubonic plague just when such a plague is breaking out in the West Indies. Sondelius, Martin, and Leora, who insists on going along, will represent the McGurk Institute, while Gottlieb has been made the director in New York.

Dr. Ira Hinkley, now a medical missionary in the West Indies, returns to the cast of the novel as he tries to thwart Martin's work by lying about Martin's days at Winnemac and by referring to the plague as "the wrath of God." Martin, however, continues his mission and succeeds, although both Sondelius and Leora die. Martin is devastated and returns to New York, little comforted by the success of his research. Max is no longer Director of McGurk, and once more there is a conflict between Martin and the new director who wants immediate publication to glorify the reputation of the institute.

In due time Martin decides to remarry, this time to a wealthy socialite, Joyce Lanyon, whom he had met briefly in the Islands. The marriage does not work out, however, despite their having a son. Joyce is not unsympathetic to his work, but she is not the ever-patient Leora, who truly understood that science was Martin's first love, his true passion.

Finally Martin decides to refuse the directorship at McGurk, to get a divorce from Joyce, and to defect to Terry Wickett and a simple life in the woods, dedicated to pure scientific research. It is the most romanticized ending of the four Lewis novels discussed, representing Lewis' rather naïve notion regarding man in a natural setting in the tradition of Huck Finn. In this same sense, it shows Martin as an eager adolescent akin to George Babbitt when he takes his vacation in the Maine woods with Paul, his one true friend.

ELMER GANTRY

First published: 1927
Type of work: Novel

A completely evil man uses evangelical religion as his road to undeserved success.

In this novel, Lewis' satire is unrelieved, beginning with his first description of Terwillinger College on the outskirts of Gritzmacher Springs, Kansas, where Elmer (nicknamed Hell-cat) Gantry is wasting his time and his mother's money pretending to get an education.

Elmer meets Judson Roberts, a preacher, and is beginning to consider a career as an evangelical minister, when he is pushed into the position of leading a crowd to exhort God. Since his original plan to become a lawyer would have required study, it is easy for him to change his vocational goal, but he needs to "get a Call." This he fakes, with the help of some whiskey, and he is on his way.

At Mizpah Theological Seminary, near Zenith, he meets Frank Shallard (one of the few decent characters in the novel), with whom he shares a part-time assignment at a small country church. Always extremely interested in sex, Elmer cannot resist seducing Lulu Bains, virginal daughter of the deacon, but when the girl begins to talk of marriage, Elmer devises a scheme to marry her off to Floyd Naylor, claiming her infidelity. For this, he is rewarded with a larger church in Monarch.

Unable to reach the deacon when he arrives, Elmer falls in with some salesmen, gets drunk, and forgets the Easter service completely. Summarily dismissed, and no longer a Reverend, he becomes a salesman himself for the next two years. Although he is quite successful and enjoys the freedom to drink and womanize, Elmer misses the adulation he had as a preacher so he becomes the assistant of an evangelist, Sharon Falconer, hoping to share the profits of her well-organized group.

Although Sharon remains "in charge," Elmer does well until Sharon is killed in the fire which destroys the new tabernacle they have built. Elmer becomes a Methodist, marries Cleo Benham, with an eye to promotion, and becomes a minister in Zenith, where he meets Frank Shallard again. An influential parishioner, T. J. Rigg, helps Elmer mount a phony anti-vice crusade, with publicity which results in standing-room-only crowds, but Elmer's greed is not satisfied. He wants a very rich parishioner to leave Frank's church for his; as a result of his plotting, Frank is branded an infidel, loses his pulpit, and eventually is taken for a 1920's style "ride" when he gives a lecture entitled "Are Fundamentalists Witch Hunters?" at the Zenith Charity Organization.

Elmer now has his new church and is accorded a doctorate of divinity; his services are being broadcast by radio. All should be well, but once more his lust gets him into trouble. He needs a new secretary, and the sexy Hettie Dowler seems an answer to his prayer. He gets rid of Lulu and begins an affair with Hettie. One evening, however, the two are interrupted by Hettie's husband, Oscar, who produces a gun and threatens suit for alienation of affections. He wants fifty-thousand dollars but will settle for ten thousand in cash. As Elmer turns back to Hettie, he realizes that she is in on the scam—for once, the great pretender seems to be the loser.

T. J. Riggs, however, comes through with a private detective who checks out the Dowlers so that they are glad to leave town with two hundred dollars, but not before they have signed a sworn statement describing Elmer as a Christian saint. He receives telegrams giving him a large church in New York and appointing him head of Napap, an organization formed to protect American morals. His congregation reassures him with a loud hallelujah, as he prays aloud: "Dear Lord, thy work is but begun! We shall yet make these United States a moral nation," as he eyes with appreciation the new member of the choir, "a girl with charming ankles and lively eyes." It is quite clear why *Elmer Gantry* infuriated churchmen of every denomination and their parishioners as well.

Summary

Although more than half a century has elapsed since Sinclair Lewis' major novels were published and there have been some marked changes in the style of popular novels, his books retain their place in American literature. Not only do they present a picture of an era, the 1920's, but they also make it uncomfortably obvious that in some unpleasant ways American society has not changed very much. Materialism and hucksterism still reign supreme. Prejudice has not been eliminated. Outward show is accepted in place of inward substance. Lewis' satirical style points up some serious faults, and the passage of time has done little to correct them.

Bibliography

Dooley, D. J. *The Art of Sinclair Lewis.* Lincoln: University of Nebraska Press, 1967.

Grebstein, Sheldon N. *Sinclair Lewis.* New York: Twayne, 1962.

Lewis, Grace H. *With Love from Gracie: Sinclair Lewis, 1912-1925.* New York: Harcourt Brace, 1956.

Light, Martin. *The Quixotic Vision of Sinclair Lewis.* West Lafayette, Ind.: Purdue University Press, 1975.

Lundquist, James. *Sinclair Lewis.* New York: McGraw-Hill, 1971.

Schorer, Mark. *Sinclair Lewis.* St. Paul: University of Minnesota Press, 1963.

____________, ed. *Sinclair Lewis: A Collection of Critical Essays.* Englewood Cliffs, N.J.: Prentice-Hall, 1962.

____________. *Sinclair Lewis: An American Life.* New York: McGraw-Hill, 1961.

Edythe M. McGovern

JACK LONDON

Born: San Francisco, California
January 12, 1876
Died: Glen Ellen, California
November 22, 1916

Principal Literary Achievement

Drawing on his own exciting life, London wrote fiction filled with high adventure that involved thoughtful, provocative reflections on the central, contemporary questions of philosophy.

Biography

Jack London was born on January 12, 1876, in San Francisco, California, the son of Flora Wellman and William Henry Chaney. Chaney, an astrologer and con man, had deserted his common-law wife as soon as he learned she was pregnant, which led Flora Wellman to attempt suicide. In September of 1876, she married a widower with two daughters, John London, who gave her son his name. The family was poor, made poorer by the mother's losing of money in get-rich-quick schemes, and was constantly moving between apartments and small ranches. Unable to put down roots, the child Jack was lonely. He worked hard and spent every spare moment reading dime novels and romances.

After completing grammar school in Oakland in 1891, he borrowed money and bought a sloop on which he engaged in oyster piracy. At fifteen he was a petty criminal, going out at night and raiding the beds where food companies kept their stock and drinking by day in waterfront saloons. He did well at first, but then his boat was burned by a rival and he decided to join the other side, the Fish Patrol, which had been established to guard the beds.

Soon his adventuring took a wider circuit; he sailed the North Pacific on a seal-hunting ship and then became a hobo, trekking across the United States with Coxey's army, a group of unemployed workers who were marching on Washington to demand jobs. This experience with the underprivileged converted London to socialism. Returning to Oakland in 1896, he completed high school and attended the University of California at Berkeley for two semesters. In the next year he was off again, this time joining the Yukon gold rush. Although unsuccessful in his search for monetary wealth, he had collected a wealth of material by the time of his return to California in 1898, which would bring him his first literary success.

Failing as a prospector, he was determined to make his living with words, and he began a ferocious regimen of pouring out essays, poetry, and stories with which he deluged every conceivable literary outlet. Soon he was making enough money to live on, writing mainly juvenile fiction, horror stories, and jokes—that is "hack work." In 1900, however, he achieved his first recognition and financial stability with the publication of a book of his Alaskan stories, *The Son of the Wolf*. In the next three years, he published three fictional works, culminating in *The Call of the Wild* (1903), the story of an Alaskan sled dog that brought him fortune and international acclaim.

It could be said that once he entered the public eye he gave it an eyeful. For one, there was his extravagant life-style, hardly becoming for a man who lectured for the Socialist Party. The first object of his conspicuous consumption was the grand yacht the *Snark*, which he constructed for a round-the-world cruise. This tour was dropped abruptly because of London's ill health, but he immediately began sinking his burgeoning income into another monstrosity, the Beauty Ranch in Sonoma Valley, California. Another factor that caught the public's attention was the author's flamboyance. He reported the Russo-Japanese War with great derring-do, scandalized the country by his marriage to a second wife shortly after divorcing his first, and aroused the public by his flaming speeches on class war. At the same time, he followed up his first best-seller with equally popular works. These included such novels of rousing adventure as *The Sea-Wolf* (1904) and *White Fang* (1906).

The wide range of interests he displayed in his earliest hack writing did not desert him, and in the sixteen years after his first success he was to compose in many genres, including futuristic political fiction (*The Iron Heel* in 1907), reportage (*The People of the Abyss* in 1903), and polemics (*John Barleycorn* in 1913).

By 1914, his health was failing. His mammoth expenses kept him writing at a furious pace; while during his South Sea voyages and war reporting he had contracted malaria, dysentery, pleurisy, yaws, and other diseases. His health worsened over the next few years, and matters were not helped by his refusal to slow down or by his eccentric enjoyment of the taste of raw meat. As the end neared, he was often in intense pain, which was alleviated by drugs. On the night of November 21, 1916, in an action that may or may not have been intentional, he injected himself with an overdose of morphine and was found near death in the morning. He died that evening.

Analysis

In the United States in the second half of the nineteenth century, fiction writers turned to Europe, and France in particular, for inspiration. Authors such as William Dean Howells, Hamlin Garland, and Frank Norris with one hand wrote essays on the validity of European writing practices and with the other composed their own stories and novels in the European realist or naturalist manner. Works such as Garland's *Main-Travelled Roads* (1891) or Norris' *McTeague* (1899) matched the Europeans in their ability to capture sordid surroundings and present controversial themes. What the Europeans had that the Americans did not, however, was a serious, adult reading public of significant proportions.

There was no place for an American Émile Zola, the savage French writer who raked his society over the coals in novel after novel. It was possible for Garland and Norris to turn out occasional hard-hitting works, but in order to earn a living they also had to lower their standards and turn to writing pot-boilers and sentimental stories.

Jack London, who came nearly a generation after these men, solved the problem of how to treat serious themes while making money by coming up with the realistic, philosophically oriented adventure tale. His life gave him an edge over those other authors in writing of adventure. Norris, for example, wrote a weak novel about Arctic exploration, but he had never been to the Far North. London, on the other hand, when he wrote, in *The Call of the Wild*, about prospectors and sharpers in gold-rush Alaska, was drawing on his own very real experiences. Yet he was also well read in the philosophy of the day, and this aided him in conceiving his stories as parables that tested and commented on contemporary thought.

The leading discussions of late nineteenth century social science were at the center of London's fiction; he was not intent on embodying these ideas uncritically, but rather on probing them for weaknesses. Questions about the effect of the environment on individual development and about the ability of the environment to screen out the best individuals for special positions were among the issues being debated. The biologist Charles Darwin's theory of evolution had been interpreted as implying that since an organism had to adapt to the ecological system in which it resided, man's free will was drastically limited. Naturalist writers such as Zola and his American followers wrote books in which vicious and villainous characters were shown to be products of unhealthy living conditions and heredity. The sociologist Herbert Spencer added a new twist to this pessimistic interpretation. Coining the term "survival of the fittest," he noted that every society had top places and that to reach those positions demanded willpower and perseverance. Though the conquerors of society's heights may have had to adapt themselves to the law of the jungle, they were magnificent successes when compared to the miserable failures that populate the lower ranks.

This Spencerian interpretation of Darwin dovetailed with American puritanism, which held that achievement in life corresponds with God's approval of one's righteousness, or, to put it in secularized terms, that success is testimony to one's virtue and abilities. This concept might certainly serve as a guiding star over London's own life: He had risen from being a street brawler to being one of the most celebrated writers of his time—certainly this proved that one could rise and triumph over one's natal circumstances. Yet, rather than wholeheartedly endorsing this idea, London repeatedly questioned its optimistic slant. In *The Sea-Wolf*, the ship's captain is a man of indomitable will, a leader, a physically strong man, and, on top of all that, an avid reader of profound books (particularly Spencer's). His superiority has raised him over other men, but it has had the fatal consequence of making him arrogant and friendless. In a novel that brings this theme even closer to home, *Martin Eden* (1909), a writer who has risen from obscurity to fame finds that his working-class viewpoint makes it impossible to associate with his new middle-class literary peers; moreover, his new learning isolates him from the type of people he grew up with and once could love. The fittest, in London's presentations, are so superior as to be unnatural.

A related sociological theme, developed particularly at the end of the century by American writers such as Brooks Adams, was the doctrine of racial hierarchy. This doctrine, particularly appropriate as a justification when the United States was beginning to acquire colonies, held that just as superior individuals rose to the top of a society, so superior races, such as the Anglo-Saxons, would naturally become the leaders and teachers of inferior races, such as the Eskimos. Again London accepted the theory but highlighted its tragic implications. In "In the Forests of the North" (1902), a lone white man survives an Arctic expedition and finds himself in a remote Indian village. He decides to throw in his lot with the tribe that has nurtured him, and, because of his natural superiority, which London explicitly attributes to his race, he can lead the tribe to victory over all the surrounding Eskimo tribes. Yet his superiority makes it impossible for him to communicate intimately with the people of the village and he lives with a tortured longing for his own kind.

A final important theme in London is the place of love in the world. London clearly sympathized with his superheroes, yet he seemed to see no hope for their integration into society unless it be through heart-humbling love. Again his thought chimed with contemporary speculation. Spencer argued that, although among savages strength and cunning set a man apart, in modern civilization it is a person's ability to sympathize widely that would take him or her to the top. Although in his major texts London did not show his strong men bowing to romance, it was an important secondary theme, becoming uppermost in minor novels such as *White Fang*. In this book a savage dog, who has been leading a wolf pack and who is subsequently caught and mistreated by a succession of masters, is obtained by a gentle Weedon Scott, "The Love-Master." Through all-enduring patience and caring, Scott converts the Arctic beast into a top-notch dog. In this case, a being has passed from barbarism to civilization without losing its superior ranking.

In every work discussed thus far except the last, London was setting forth a viewpoint that would not recommend him to a large audience. He was pronouncing negatively on the American credo of success at any price, for example, by showing that success leads to isolation and unhappiness. In compensation for this sobering message, London spun a whopping good yarn for his readers. One especially remarkable aspect of his narrative skills was the fashion in which he could transform metaphysical questions into dramatic tableaux. In *The Sea-Wolf*, for example, the captain, Wolf Larsen, is pointing out that men crave life above anything to the anemic intellectual Van Weyden, who has accidentally landed on his vessel. Van Weyden continues to maintain an idealistic position. Suddenly Larsen springs from his chair, grabs the intellectual by the throat, and nearly chokes him to death. After letting him up, Larsen asks him if he now gets the point. Through such maneuvers, London gave philosophical discussions the excitement of an adventure tale.

THE CALL OF THE WILD

First published: 1903
Type of work: Novel

A domesticated California farm dog is stolen and transported to Alaska, where his wild instincts gradually surface.

The Call of the Wild was London's first success, and it represented an imaginative recasting of strands of thought from Darwinism and literary naturalism. The general concept of the book is a clever play on themes generated by attacks on the theory of evolution. Religious writers ridiculed the evolutionists' idea that humans were the descendents of prehistoric apes and poured scorn on the concept that a being with a godlike soul shared traits with other members of the animal kingdom. Thinkers of this ilk lambasted writers such as Frank Norris, who in *McTeague* showed animal traits appearing in his characters when they were under stress.

London found a creative way to sidestep such objections while maintaining central evolutionary tenets. Rather than showing a man descending to animalistic behavior, he describes a dog making such a descent. Certainly a dog is already an animal, but in *The Call of the Wild*, through a series of misadventures, a pampered domestic dog is transformed into an Arctic wolf.

A central motor of this transformation is the influence of the environment. The dog protagonist, Buck, has adapted to life as a doted-on member of the family, but his life is imperiled by the Alaskan gold rush. Sled dogs are at a premium, and dognappers are scouring the country for hardy brutes. Buck is stolen and sold north to a government courier, Perrault, and learns to adapt to the hard life of pulling a dogsled through the snowy wastes.

His adaptation is eased by the revival of ancestral traits. As London notes, "not only did he learn by experience, but instincts long dead became alive. . . . [h]e remembered back to . . . the time the wild-dogs ranged in packs through the primeval forest." Such a note was often struck in Darwinian novels that described human behavior. In the already noted *McTeague*, the hero's wife, Trina, becomes increasingly miserly as characteristics of her German peasant forebears come to life. More startlingly, the hero, McTeague, when pursued by the police, resurrects lost animal behaviors, such as wonderfully keen hearing. The ethnic note is also sounded. Where writers describing humans noted the part that racial qualities played in the individual personality, London sees the same type of qualities accounting for Buck's growing superiority over the other dogs in the team: "His cunning was wolf cunning . . . his intelligence, shepherd intelligence and St. Bernard intelligence."

The novel is more than a vigorous endorsement of such biological themes; it is also a *Bildungsroman*, that is, a novel concerned with the education of the protagonist to the ways of the world. Bought by Perrault, Buck's main teachers are the seasoned sled dogs. He learns from them, for example, that he must not only "wolf" down his food ration to avoid having it stolen by other canines, but must try to rob others' portions to increase his prestige. He caps this stage of his education by killing the top dog and assuming his post.

These examples may suggest that a dog's life is all violence and competition, but, in fact, primitivism has two faces. London's unusual subject allows him to see virtues in a return to an aboriginal state that could not be found if humans were his subjects. When McTeague, to continue using Norris' novel as a counterpoint, becomes as wily as a hunted animal, there is little but degradation in his reversion to earlier animal patterns. When Buck recalls his ancestors' activities, however, there is the feeling that he is returning to a truer world. Life is hard there but authentic. The pampered house dog could never experience the joy of the hunt. Buck is "ranging at the head of the pack. . . . [in] an ecstasy that marks the summit of life."

The shift in perspective allows London to stand the typical ending of the Darwinian novel on its head. In Zola's *Le Bête humaine* (1890; *The Human Beast*, 1891), for example, the complete emergence of the protagonist's hereditary tendency to alcoholism leads to villainous actions. In London's novel, in sharp contrast, when Buck is at his most savage he is also most completely fulfilling his potential—utilizing his brain, muscles, and heart to the utmost.

After running a gamut of human masters, Buck is obtained by the kindly John Thornton, who allows him to wander in the woods, where he learns to hunt. One day he returns from an expedition to find Thornton killed by Indians; his last ties to humanity have been cut, so he gives in to the call of the wild. He ends the novel at the head of the a wolf pack, a legend to the Indians.

Such an upbeat ending was out of keeping with the general tenor of fiction that dealt with such themes, but it was appropriate for a work that had shifted the terrain of such writing from human to canine society. The optimistic but logically consistent presentation of how the law of the jungle could turn the protagonist from a civilized pet into a legend of the wilderness won readers who could not stomach the representation of similar themes in a human milieu.

THE SEA-WOLF

First Published: 1904
Type of work: Novel

A literary dilettante undergoes a rough education at the hands of a seagoing superman.

The plot of *The Sea-Wolf* was a popular one in the late nineteenth century; Rudyard Kipling, for example, had used it in *Captains Courageous* (1896). A snobbish upper-class weakling is forced to obey the commands of a harsh lower-class dictator and ends up greatly profiting by the experience. In London's novel, a literary gentleman, Humphrey Van Weyden, is washed off a San Francisco ferryboat and taken up by an outgoing seal hunter. The imperious captain, Wolf Larsen, has just lost a hand and decides to press the protesting Weyden into service as cabin boy for the long voyage.

An apter parallel for London's book than Kipling's novel may be found in Herman Melville's *Moby-Dick*. In both London's and Melville's novels, the center of attention is not the slowly maturing, sensitive narrator, but the superhuman ship's captain. In *Moby-Dick*, Captain Ahab is a monomanical, charismatic zealot, and the critical light thrown on him is also used to criticize basic premises of a then-current theoretical posture, Byronic Romanticism. In something of the same way, in *The Sea-Wolf* the judgment passed on Wolf Larsen, the dynamic, intelligent, yet brutal captain, also undercuts the materialism he expouses.

Larsen is contradictory. At first Van Weyden sees the ship's master as nothing more than an unfeeling hulk. He witnesses him tossing a dead body overboard without a proper burial ceremony and forcing his men to obey him through fear of his fists; however, as the trip progresses, he finds in the captain's cabin a well-stocked library of current literature, science, history, even grammar. At this discovery he says to himself about Larsen, "At once he became an enigma."

As it turns out, the captain's violence is rooted in a materialist metaphysics—and violent he is. When a crewman complains of an arrangement, Larsen and the first mate beat him senseless. When the cook does not keep the mess clean, he is dangled over the ship's side until a shark lops off his foot. Larsen's study of Darwin, Spencer, and other evolutionists has taught him that life, in his preferred phrase, "is like a yeast." It is a battle that goes to the strong, and, according to Larsen, every noble sentiment that Van Weyden defends is so much "bosh."

Furthermore, as if to corroborate the captain's doctrine, the ship is run on the law of the strong. The captain fights with the crew, terrorizing them—they futilely attempt a mutiny at one point—and almost every sailor plots vengeance against another for a real or imagined slight. Van Weyden himself is pushed around by the cook until, as if to confirm the captain's ideas, he employs threats to subdue his enemy, calmly sharpening the blade of a dirk until the cook is scared witless.

Yet though the captain's philosophy accounts rather well for the dog-eat-dog atmosphere on board ship, there are a number of fatal chinks in it. For one, it is a philosophy reserved for winners. It is small consolation for the sailors that the man beating them is their natural superior. Moreover, it is a philosophy of hopelessness. When the captain's debilitating headaches weaken him, his metaphysic offers him no solace, leaving him to a titanic despair. Larsen's superb fitness isolates him, and he is particularly unsuited for mixing with women. When the sealer picks up a shipwrecked young lady, Maud Brewster, Larsen treats her as roughly as he does his men and ends by trying to rape her.

As in most adventure tales, the actions and characters are exaggerated. The ship seems to undergo every catastrophe: losing its seal boats in a storm, a mutiny, pitched battle with a poaching sealer, and multiple desertions. Wolf Larsen is a larger-than-life but memorable creation, and it is to London's credit that he never softens the portrait. Though he is betrayed by his body, blind and half paralyzed, Larsen remains a staunch atheistic materialist. Even blind he tries to kill the narrator, Van Weyden. It begins to appear that materialism begets violence as the only way for the unbelieving soul to make a mark on a world that holds neither immortality nor lasting value.

London locates his final criticism of materialism in his depiction of Larsen's bodily dissolution. The captain's powerful will, trapped in a frame struck down in its prime, seems to be crying out for a way to continue. Although the arguments for immortality offered by Van Weyden are less than convincing, the book does leave a powerful impression that there must be something beyond the physical. Nevertheless, it is Wolf Larsen, a man so sincerely and devastatingly criticized, that fascinates the reader. Van Weyden, who gradually comes to accept a part of the captain's philosophy and learns how to be a good sailor, becoming a man in the process, is a much less interesting character.

Near the end of the novel, Van Weyden and Maud Brewster escape the ship and land on a desert island. A plodding Robinson Crusoe episode follows, which, without the presence of the captain, has little life in it. Happily, this section is brief: By a rather implausible coincidence, Larsen, abandoned in his blindness by the crew, lands on the same island. The story gathers excitement again as a cat-and-mouse game ensues between Van Weyden and the dying Larsen. In *The Sea-Wolf*, London finds that the savagery which he believes is relatively laudable in the canine world of Buck is much less palatable in human society.

MARTIN EDEN

First published: 1909
Type of work: Novel

A poor sailor sets out to turn himself into an intellectual and successful author to win a middle-class girl.

In *Martin Eden*, London turned away from writing science fiction and adventure tales to write a realistic study of a working-class writer's struggle to survive while educating himself. Many critics have called this book his masterpiece.

For all their verve and philosophical pungency, London's adventure novels lack the breadth and sympathetic observation found in serious realistic fiction. In *The Sea-Wolf*, to take one example, though there is a wealth of incident, the actions revolve around the three central characters; no broad social canvas is painted. The very complexity of the plot of *Martin Eden*, on the other hand, makes it necessary for the author to portray all of San Francisco society.

Martin Eden is an out-of-work sailor who is invited to the Morse home because he has helped one of the sons, who had been set upon by ruffians. In the home, he is enthralled by the college-student daughter, Ruth Morse, having never encountered such a vision of feminine purity before. Spurred by his growing affection, he determines to live by his brain rather than his back: He will be an author. While keeping contact with Ruth, he is forced to take handouts from his sister or work at casual labor when his money runs low and the rejection slips pile up. He moves through many sectors of society, from the upper-middle-class world of the Morses to the petit bourgeois world of his sister to the lower-class environs of his sailor friends to the sub-proletarian bowels where he seeks employment. A reader ends the book with an awareness of life as a whole in early twentieth century California.

Another drawback to London's more popular adventure yarns is that they seem to lack subtlety of observation, or, to put it another way, the scenes of dogsled travel or seal hunting described in this fiction are so out of the ordinary that their novelty overrides any question of their freshness. In *Martin Eden*, by contrast, London depicts typical everyday events with a brilliant eye for detail along with a fine sense of structure. The long opening scene, for example, in which the hero comes to his first Morse dinner party, moves back and forth narratively between the sailor's self-conscious gaucheries and Ruth Morse's alternating attraction and repulsion toward the stranger. Another beautifully rendered and observed scene occurs when Eden, after months of study and composition, attempts to rejoin his old mates for an evening of dancing and flirting. The failure of the attempt is poignantly pictured. As London concludes, "He was too far removed. Too many thousands of opened books yawned between them and him." Scenes such as these hit home with the sensitive reader in a way the scenes in his more fabulous stories cannot.

The core of the book concerns the struggles of a writer in the United States, struggles which can be divided into two phases. In the first, before the writer is recognized, everyone disregards him. Eden does not know the ropes, so the magazines reject or fleece him. What work he does sell is underpaid. His girlfriend, who started him on this course, tells him to get a regular job. The second phase starts when the writer becomes well known. Now everyone ignorantly lionizes him. Magazines beg for pieces they had previously rejected as obscene. His brother-in-law, who had despised him, now sheepishly comes to borrow money. Ruth, who had broken off their engagement because she believed a vituperative, false newspaper report about him, now comes back. His embittered conclusion is that genuine talent is never recognized for what it is. Although he has met a few discerning critics along the way, the vast majority merely follow the prevailing winds of fashion. This realization leads to Eden's suicide.

The fact that Eden has met some truly selfless critics and writers during phases of his life makes his chosen ending somewhat puzzling and unconvincing, as it is more pessimistic than the evidence warrants. The suicide, though, as is all of the book, is described with London's trademark vivacity.

London's adventure writing, whatever its limitations, did have positive value. This discipline taught him to write sentences that crackled with a crisp authority. He puts his finger on that trait in his own writing when he mentions the critics' growing appreciation of Eden's prose. "It had been discovered that he was a stylist, with meat under his style." To take one example from *Martin Eden*, this description of Eden's early failures: "Even his earliest efforts were not marked with the clumsiness of mediocrity. What characterized them was the clumsiness of too great strength." Stephen Crane or Ernest Hemingway, to whom London can be compared, could not produce such pithy, telling phrases.

Arguably London's most interesting innovation, following the lead of Kipling and Robert Louis Stevenson (though London introduced a more philosophical bent), was to use adventure tales to delve into the troubling questions of evolution and the environment's effect on human will. Yet to create his greatest novel, he had to step away from this type of fiction; in *Martin Eden*, he used a broader canvas to depict the adventure that is writing.

TO BUILD A FIRE

First published: 1908
Type of work: Short story

A prospector in the Yukon makes the mistake of setting out on a day's trek alone when the temperature is 75 degrees below zero.

London was not one to gloss over unpleasantness, and in "To Build a Fire" he described just how harsh the world can be to someone who disregards its laws. As the story opens, life seems benign enough. It is a still, clear day, and the unnamed protagonist has plenty of time to make the one-day walk to the camp where his friends wait. He is in fine fettle, alert and careful of his footing on the frozen riverbed. He has his dog for company. The only troubles are that it is fearfully cold—75 degrees below zero—and he is "without imagination."

From this seemingly slight situation, London crafts a tale of a universe where any step can be fatal, looking backward to the metaphysical despair of Stephen Crane and forward to the stoic code of Ernest Hemingway.

In Crane's short story "The Open Boat" (1897), a number of survivors of a sunken ship ride on a lifeboat in heavy seas. The fact that they may very well drown in sight of the shore underlines to them the indifference of the cosmos to men's undertakings. In London's tale, the omnipresent cold, though ready to sweep away human life, is simply part of the universe's thermodynamics. When the protagonist has gotten into a desperate plight, having fallen through the ice and wet his legs, the author emphasizes the larger picture: "The cold of space smote the unprotected tip of the planet, and he, being on that tip, received the full force of the blow." The largeness of the forces involved reduce his plight to insignificance.

In the works of Hemingway, such as *A Farewell to Arms* (1929) and *The Sun Also Rises* (1926), the author prescribes that the acknowledged indifference of the larger forces of reality be met by a stoic code of honor on the part of his characters.

Though London's protagonist, foolhardy in attempting the trip alone, lacks the judgment of Hemingway's ideal heroes, he does display admirable coolness in trying to build a fire to thaw out his legs, taking each difficulty in stride. When he finds, for example, that he can no longer work his numb fingers, he picks up wood with his two palms. Also, after an initial panic when he loses his fire, he resigns himself to death and musters whatever dignity he can, sitting down for the last time quietly.

The story is a short one (fifteen pages), and the compression works to magnify some of London's strengths while helping to diminish some of his weaknesses. His writing was often marred by purple passages, especially when discussing such charged topics as women or Anglo-Saxon superiority. In this piece, where the concentration is so tightly focused, his prose is always spare and telling. Each stroke of his pen underlines the tenuousness of life in the North or grimly describes the doomed man's survival strategies. London had another weakness—for all his experience in the Yukon, he often over-stretched his imagination and presented scenes that rang false. This was particularly true in his rendering of Indian life, a favorite subject of his and yet one he had never penetrated with any clarity, preferring clichés to anthropological understanding. The limited matter of this story, a man walking with his dog, meant that he never strayed from what he knew, and the tale has a raw authenticity. Finally, it should be noted that one of London's strengths was the ability to draw a landscape vividly. This skill was often downplayed, perhaps because long descriptions would have slowed the pace of his eventful narratives. In this piece, however, such descriptions come to the fore and serve as pointers to the theme of the piece: The seeming quiescence of the landscape he describes is undermined with pitfalls for the inexperienced.

As in *The Call of the Wild*, London draws attention to the importance of primitive instincts. In a surprising but appropriate manner, he contrasts the dog's intelligent intuitions to the man's wrongheaded reasoning. The dog "knew that it was no time for travelling. Its instinct told it a truer tale than was told to the man by the man's judgment." Its instinctive reactions, developed over generations in the Arctic, far outmatched the brain power of man, a recent visitor. As in other places, London finds a novel way to plump for primitivism.

Summary

Jack London developed what might be called the "thinking man's adventure story." Drawing on his own experiences as a sailor and gold prospector, he wrote rip-roaring sagas that went beyond being simple entertainments to broach speculative issues concerning evolution, free will, and the survival of primitive instincts in the civilized. His training as an action writer led him to rely on a pungent, direct prose that was a major asset in his non-genre novel, *Martin Eden*. In this triumphant work, he added the new strengths of breadth and keen observation to the skills he had already displayed in adventure stories.

Bibliography

Hedrick, Joan D. *Solitary Comrade: Jack London and His Work*. Chapel Hill: University of North Carolina Press, 1982.

Lundquist, James. *Jack London: Adventures, Ideas, and Fiction*. New York: Frederick Ungar, 1987.

Ownbey, Ray Wilson, ed. *Jack London: Essays in Criticism*. Santa Barbara, Calif.: Peregrine Smith, 1978.

Sherman, Joan R. *Jack London: A Reference Guide*. Boston: G. K. Hall, 1977.

Sinclair, Andrew. *Jack: A Biography of Jack London*. New York: Harper & Row, 1977.

Tavernier-Courbin, Jacqueline, ed. *Critical Essays on Jack London*. Boston: G. K. Hall, 1983.

Woodbridge, Hensley C., John London, and John H. Tweney, comps. *Jack London: A Bibliography*. Georgetown, Calif.: Talisman Press, 1966.

James Feast

HENRY WADSWORTH LONGFELLOW

Born: Portland, Maine
February 27, 1807
Died: Cambridge, Massachusetts
March 24, 1882

Principal Literary Achievement

Longfellow was one of the first to see the value of distinctly American myths as proper subjects for poetry; he also refined American poetry by his metrical skill and pure language.

Biography

Henry Wadsworth Longfellow was born into a well-to-do family in Portland, Maine, in 1807, a mere thirty years after the American Revolutionary War began. He entered Bowdoin College in Maine at the very early age of fourteen, and he studied the usual classical curriculum taken from British universities. He was graduated from Bowdoin in 1825, and he had made such an impression upon the faculty there that he was given a fellowship to go to Europe to study the modern languages to prepare himself for an appointment as a professor at Bowdoin. In 1829, he was appointed a professor of modern languages at Bowdoin and remained there for seven years. He was a successful and industrious teacher; he provided materials for his classes since there were no texts in the modern languages at the time. In 1831, Longfellow married Mary Potter, a fellow native of Portland. His success was marred by the death of his wife while traveling in Europe in 1835. The sunny poems of Longfellow, in fact, often mask private tragedies.

Longfellow's success at Bowdoin led to an appointment as professor of modern languages at Harvard College, which he began in 1835. Longfellow was writing poems at the same time. There was an obvious conflict between his duties as a professor and the demands of a career as a poet. He published *Ballads and Other Poems* in 1841; the first important poem by Longfellow was *Evangeline, a Tale of Acadie*, published in 1847. Suddenly, Longfellow made Americans see that their experience was as fit a subject for serious poetry as Greek myth or British history.

Evangeline is a narrative poem that tells the story of the expulsion of a group of settlers from Acadie (now Acadia) in Nova Scotia; it was popular with critics and readers alike and retained a place as a school text for American students until the 1960's. Longfellow married Fanny Appleton in 1843 and received the Craigie House in Cambridge as a wedding gift. The beautiful Victorian house is now a tourist attraction on Cambridge's historic Brattle Street.

In 1854, Longfellow resigned his professorship at Harvard to devote more time to poetry. In 1855, he published *The Song of Hiawatha*, another long narrative poem based on American legends. *Hiawatha* surveys the career of an American Indian hero, Hiawatha. Using as a structural model a European poem, the Finnish epic *The Kalevala*, he brought together a number of Indian tales into one unified book. His view of the American Indian, however, seems to have been constructed to please the taste of his audience. It has little of the violence and nobility others found in that people. The poem was immensely successful and was translated into many languages; Longfellow was becoming the model of the poet to most Americans.

The Courtship of Miles Standish (1858) is another long narrative poem on an American subject, the Pilgrims of Massachusetts. Personal relationships and marriage are the subject; it is a domestic poem, not a heroic one. It did re-create and make accessible another period of American history. Longfellow's great success as a poet was tarnished by the death of his wife, Fanny, in a fire at Craigie House in 1861. His last years, however, were serene. He received honorary degrees from the universities of Oxford and Cambridge in 1869. Between 1867 and 1869, he translated Dante's *La Divina Commedia* (c. 1320, *The Divine Comedy*), although he did not write many new or important poems. He died in Cambridge in 1882 and was honored as America's greatest poet.

Analysis

The major problem in analyzing Longfellow as a poet in the late twentieth century is disinterring what was once a great reputation. Longfellow was seen as a major American poet until the modernism of the twentieth century caught up with that reputation. The values of Longfellow's audience and time—metrical skill, the long narrative poem, and an abundance of sentiment—are not those of such modern poets as T. S. Eliot. He was judged, perhaps, too harshly and too unhistorically. Once can still recover some of Longfellow's poetry, although what one sees in it today may not be what the nineteenth century valued.

Longfellow's use of American myths and legends—and the way he altered them—remains important. There had been tales and novels in which American Indians appeared before those of Longfellow. Most prominently, there are the novels of James Fenimore Cooper; however, in those novels, the Indian is never the hero and never has a central position in the narrative. There is always a white man to lead or defeat the Indians, and the rites and ways of the Indian are seen as barbarous or passed over. Longfellow attempted to make the American Indian an epic hero on the scale of Achilles or Odysseus. He is, perhaps, less successful in his attempt to make

Evangeline into an epic heroine; she does not approach the heroes of Homer or Vergil. She is all too accepting of the fate that overcomes her. Finally, in *The Courtship of Miles Standish* (1858), he attempted to make the Puritan past of New England into a charming world where repression and the inculcation of dogma become a marriage triangle in which (in the Classical comic mode) an old man is forced to relinquish a young girl to one who is more fitting.

Longfellow's social goals seem very similar to those of the British Victorian poets. Longfellow's "Psalm of Life" proclaims: "Life is real! Life is earnest!/ And the grave is not its goal." This earnest striving to improve oneself and society is at the heart of many of his poems. Even Evangeline's tragedy is blotted out by a submission to a beneficent God who is working to make things better. There is a firm belief in progress. In addition, Longfellow portrays women in a very Victorian manner. They are pure and virginal, and their primary goal is to "follow" their male leader.

Longfellow's vision, in fact, was primarily domestic. The scenes between Evangeline and her father, Hiawatha and his mother, and Priscilla and John Alden all evoke the world of the parlor. He is not really interested in the wildness of the Indian or even the tyranny of the British in driving out the Acadians. One hears nothing of the dark worlds of Nathaniel Hawthorne and Herman Melville—or even Henry David Thoreau. In its place is the Angel of the House, the woman who is at the center of nearly all his works, who offers solace to all. One reason for his (once) nearly universal acceptance is his ability to present the sometimes violent American past as easily accessible and comforting. Rather than make the American past dark and mysterious, as other writers had, he attempted to make it familiar. His own sunny boyhood, very early success, and European sojourns may have led him to portray America in such a genteel manner.

EVANGELINE

First published: 1847
Type of work: Poem

The story of a woman who loses her Acadian home and her betrothed, whom she finds only at his death.

Evangeline had its origin in an anecdote. A South Boston man named Connolly urged Nathaniel Hawthorne to write the tale of a young woman who was exiled from Nova Scotia and searched for her lost love, only to find him a moment before his death. Hawthorne never picked up the subject, but Longfellow did. He believed that it was a wonderful tale of a woman's fidelity; it was a perfect subject for his gentle sensibility. He also used historical sources, so the basic tale and the historical frame were given to the poet.

Evangeline begins with a brief introduction in which Longfellow evokes the "forest primeval" that remains while the hearts "beneath it" have vanished. His poem has a "woman's devotion" as its epic theme and an Eden, "Acadie, home of the happy," as its beginning scene. The village of Grand Pre in the land of Acadie is a "fruitful valley" filled with happy peasants from Normandy. Evangeline, "the pride of the village," is a maiden of seventeen living with her aged farmer father, Benedict. Her life is a pastoral one; she helps the workers in the field and directs the household of her father.

The first scene in the poem is the visit of Basil the blacksmith and his son, Gabriel, to Benedict. Their purpose is to sign a contract of betrothal between Evangeline and Gabriel. The joyous occasion is threatened, however, by news of a British warship in the bay. Father LeBlanc believes that they are safe because they are "at peace." Basil, however, objects, saying that in this world "might is the right of the strongest!" The old notary reconciles these positions with a tale about a maid unjustly accused of stealing a necklace of pearls; as she is on the scaffold about to be hanged, a bolt of thunder reveals the "necklace of pearls interwoven" in a magpie's nest. The tale obviously mirrors that of *Evangeline*: An innocent girl is freed from her unjust oppression, although only at the end of a long trial.

The next day is one of feasting, especially in the house of Benedict, but this is broken by the arrival of British troops. The language changes from the soft descriptions of man and nature to legal language: "By his Majesty's orders . . . all your lands, and dwellings, and cattle of all kinds/ Forfeited be to the Crown." The settlers are to be "transported to other lands." In the rush to depart, Gabriel is separated from Evangeline. Evangeline has other problems, however, her father cannot bear the thought of being separated from his land and dies of age and sorrow.

The second part of the poem deals with Evangeline's search for Gabriel. She descends the established settlements of early America to the Mississippi and the bayous of Louisiana. She hears news of Gabriel, but she always seems to miss him. She has a guide, Father Felician, who attempts to assuage her sorrow and lead her to her beloved. Longfellow effectively conveys the mysteriousness of America at this time in the resonant names of places, rivers, and Indian tribes; the unusual words must have fascinated an audience of the mid-nineteenth century.

Evangeline does find Basil the blacksmith in Louisiana, but Gabriel "is only this day" departed. Basil is happy in Louisiana, since it is a more fertile land than Acadie and there is no winter; however, Evangeline yearns for Gabriel. Basil leads her into Indian country to search for Gabriel; they come upon a Shawnee maiden who leads them to the Mission of the Black Robe. The Shawnee maiden, after hearing the tale of Evangeline, tells her of Indian myths that mirror her tale. Longfellow uses the Indian tales as parallels and contrasts to Evangeline's tale; however, the fatalism of the Indian myths is very different from the Christian providence that dominates the main tale.

The priest at the mission tells Evangeline that Gabriel had been there six days before. He had departed, saying he would return to the mission. Evangeline decides to wait. When the seasons pass and he does not return, however, she goes in search of him in the "Michigan forests." Evangeline finds another refuge in a Moravian community and finally settles in Philadelphia, where the gentle Quakers are dominant. She becomes a Sister of Mercy, nursing the sick and comforting the dying. In the hospital, she notices a man dying of fever. Suddenly, the decrepit man assumes "once more the forms of [his] earlier manhood." She cries "Gabriel! O my beloved!" and he calls to his mind:

> Green Acadian meadows, with sylvan rivers among them,
> Village, and mountain, and woodlands; and walking under their shadow,
> As in the days of her youth, Evangeline rose in his vision.

While Evangeline has the power to convey Gabriel back to his earlier and happy life, however, she does not have the power to save him. He dies in her arms. Evangeline does not complain about this cruel trick of fate, but "meekly" accepts it: "Father, I thank thee!" Evangeline does find her beloved, even if it is at the moment of his death. Longfellow's world is one of affirmation, not doubt.

One reason that *Evangeline* is no longer popular is the passivity of the main character. She undergoes terrible trials but never seems to lose her optimism. The reader does not see any internal conflict, only a chain of accidents that separate the pair. Her affirmation at the seeming irony of discovering Gabriel on his deathbed rings hollow in the twentieth century.

THE JEWISH CEMETERY AT NEWPORT

First published: 1854
Type of work: Poem

A lament for a people who have been cast out and a nation that will never rise again.

"The Jewish Cemetery at Newport" is structured by a series of contrasts. The silent "Hebrews" in their graves are contrasted with the motion of the waves. Death, declare the mourners, "giveth Life that nevermore shall cease." The central contrast is the one between the living and the dead. The synagogue is closed and the living have gone, "but the dead remain,/ And not neglected; for a hand unseen,/ Scattering its bounty, like a summer rain,/ Still keeps their graves and their remembrance green." The dead seem to be especially blessed by that "unseen hand" of nature or God. Longfellow then traces the historical situation of the Jews, however, and no "unseen hand" has protected them from persecution.

Longfellow is very direct in assigning "Christian hate" as the cause of the persecution and dislocation of the Jews. He imaginatively captures the persecution in significant detail. He imagines their exile over the sea, "that desert desolate," and their lives in "narrow streets" and "mirk and mire." In another set of contrasts, the Jews "fed" upon the "bitter herbs of exile" and "slaked [their] thirst" with tears. In addition, they are "Taught in the school of patience to endure/ The life of anguish and the death of fire." The contrasts of the poem are resolved by reversing the position of past and future: "And all the great traditions of the Past/ They saw reflected in the coming time." Longfellow then uses an appropriate and powerful metaphor reversing past and present, the living and the dead.

> And thus forever with reverted look
> The mystic volume of the world they read,
> Spelling it backward, like a Hebrew book,
> Till life became a Legend of the Dead.

All the negative elements of the poem are contrasted with or overcome by their opposites. Death leads to life, and exile to knowledge.

The last stanza of the poem, however, reverses the patterns that have been established: "But ah! What once has been shall be no more!" The people of Israel may find life in death and endurance in exile, but the nation of Israel cannot. Its creation is described in a metaphor of birth. "The groaning earth in travail and in pain/ Brings forth its races, but does not restore,/ And the dead nations never rise again." A nation, in Longfellow's view, is bound by natural laws, while a people are free of such restraints (it is ironic that the nation of Israel was indeed to "rise again" in 1949). Longfellow overcame the prejudices of his time in imaginatively and sympathetically portraying the Jews, but in the last stanza, he becomes a man bound by his time and place by being unable to overcome ideas of the life cycle of a nation. Nevertheless, "The Jewish Cemetery at Newport" is a beautifully constructed and powerful poem.

HIAWATHA

First published: 1855
Type of work: Poem

The tale of an Indian hero and teacher who leaves a land that is soon to be transformed by the white man.

Longfellow gathered the material for *Hiawatha* from many sources, and his aim was to codify the various tales he read into a coherent mythology; he sought to introduce the white man to Indian mythology. It begins, as most mythologies do, with a god and his people, Gitche Manito, "the mighty/ He the Master of Life," brings the various tribes together to smoke the peace pipe. Gitche Manito will also send a prophet to the people "Who shall guide you and shall teach you,/ Who shall toil and suffer with you." This prophet, who sounds very much like Jesus, will bring prosperity if the people listen. The prophet is Hiawatha.

Section 2 of the poem shows the taming of nature, of the four winds—especially the West-Wind, who is to be Hiawatha's father. Hiawatha, after his mysterious conception (a common element in nearly all mythologies), lives with his grandmother, Nokomis, who teaches him about nature. In the fourth section of the poem, Hiawatha goes to see his father, the West-Wind. The West-Wind praises him and defines his mission in life:

> Go back to your home and people,
> Live among them, toil among them,
> Cleanse the earth from all that harms it,
> Clear the fishing grounds and rivers,
> Slay all monsters and magicians.

One of the most important contributions Hiawatha makes to his people comes after a long fast. Hiawatha is challenged by Mondamin, "a friend of man," to wrestle. The wrestling takes three days, and on the third day Hiawatha defeats, strips, and buries Mondamin. Soon after, shoots appear, then maize, the staple food of the people. Hiawatha does not go in search of great deeds so that he might win praise or honor; rather, he struggles to bring benefits to his people. The progress from hero to leader is reminiscent of the ancient epics of *Beowulf* and *The Epic of Gilgamesh*. Hiawatha has, as an epic hero should have, friends who embody lesser skills; Chibiabos is a musician, and Kwasind is "the strongest of all mortals." Hiawatha goes wooing, but once more it is not for his own pleasure but for the people. He will woo and marry Minnehaha, a Dacotah maiden, Nokomis describes the Dacotah as "very fierce" and says that "Often there is war between us." The wooing, therefore, has political and social benefits; a marriage will unite the warring Dacotah and Objibway tribes. Minnehaha is the only character in the poem invented by Longfellow, and she is another of his long-suffering and passive women. Her answer to Hiawatha's proposal is, "I will follow you, my husband!"

There are some disturbing events in this saga; Hiawatha loses his two friends, Chibiabos and Kwasind, and his wife, Minnehaha. His friends die in action, but Minnehaha dies in a famine; significantly, Hiawatha has no power to overcome this natural event. Her death, however, is seen as something of a blessing, since she will be carried to the "Islands of the Blessed" where there is no labor or suffering. Hiawatha had discovered the existence of these islands earlier in the poem, bringing consolation to the people—and to himself for the loss of his bride.

The next-to-last section of the poem deals with the coming of the white man. A canoe "Bigger than the Big-Sea Water,/ Broader than the Gitche-Gumee" appears. Hiawatha counsels peace: "Let us welcome, then, the strangers,/ Hail them as our friends and brothers,/ And the heart's right hand of friendship/ Give them when they come to see us." This vision of peace and brotherhood is, however, immediately obliterated by another vision. Hiawatha sees "our nation scattered" and the "remnants of the people" swept away "Like the withered leaves of Autumn." It is a poignant passage that reveals the historical fate of the American Indian and destroys the optimistic dream. Yet Longfellow does not assign any blame to whites for the destruction of the Indian way of life.

The last section of the poem shows Hiawatha's departure. He will not be there for the uprooting of the people he has served. Before departing, Hiawatha invites the "Black-Robes" and the Christian message they bring into his wigwam. The Christian message is then received and welcomed by the chiefs. (There is no hint of the historical martyrdom that was to come to so many Jesuits or of the lack of interest in and comprehension of the Christian message by the Indians.) After having completed his mission, Hiawatha departs in a birch-bark canoe in the sunset.

Hiawatha is one of Longfellow's most successful poems. It portrays the Indian with sympathy and some understanding. The meter of the poem is very noticeable. Longfellow rejected the long dactylic hexameters of *Evangeline* for a short unrhymed trochaic tetrameter. It has the effect of a chant and often fits the material perfectly. The hero of the poem, however, may be a little too noble, good, and unselfish. He has none of the human faults that make Beowulf and Gilgamesh, for example, so interesting. At times, he is more a Victorian gentleman bringing progress to "lesser breeds without the law" than an American Indian warrior.

THE COURTSHIP OF MILES STANDISH

First published: 1858
Type of work: Poem

A Puritan idyll in which an old warrior gives up his claim to a young girl to a more appropriate young scholar.

The Courtship of Miles Standish is another historical narrative poem; this time Longfellow turns to the Pilgrims of Plymouth Plantation for his material, and he once more softens the harshness of his subject and makes it accessible to his audience. The meter he chose for the poem is dactylic hexameter, but it has none of the monotony of *Evangeline*; it is very loosely structured and at times seems on the edge of prose. It also has none of the heroic treatment of *Evangeline* or *Hiawatha*. It is really a romantic drama, not an imitation of Greek or Finnish epic.

The poem begins with a description of Miles Standish as "strongly built and athletic,/ Broad in the shoulders, deep-chested, with muscles and sinews of iron." John Alden is not described in the same detail, but it is clear that he is the opposite of Miles Standish. Alden is no soldier but a "scholar"; Standish is a man of few words, while Alden is a closet poet hymning the name of Priscilla. The conflict of the tale is quickly brought out. Miles Standish has lost his wife and uses biblical authority rather than personal passion to justify his search for a new bride. She is to be Priscilla Mullins.

Standish does not have the words to woo a maiden, however, so he turns to John Alden. Alden's conflict is quickly resolved: "The name of friendship is sacred;/ What you demand in that name, I have not the power to deny you!" His divided feelings emerge, however, love contends with friendship, and he wonders if he must "relinquish" the joys of love. He resolves the dilemma be seeing his love as vanity; "I have worshipped too much the heart's desire and devices." Religious authority prevails.

Alden's delivery of Standish's proposal is surprisingly blunt. There is no poetic prologue or honeyed words, merely the facts of the case. "So I have come to you now, with an offer and proffer of marriage/ Made by a good man and true, Miles Standish the Captain of Plymouth." Priscilla replies directly: "Why does he not come himself, and take the trouble to woo me?" She is not the submissive Minnehaha or the dutiful Evangeline but an independent and witty woman. She takes the failure of Standish to woo her as a reason to reject him. She sees him as "old and rough" and one lacking in the basic elements of courtship: He will never win her.

Alden tries to make a case for Standish, but Priscilla is not interested in his virtues. Instead she give John hope and increases his conflict by uttering the famous words, "Why don't you speak for yourself, John?" Alden is filled with joy, yet downcast at his betrayal. He vows to depart from Plymouth and return to England on the Mayflower.

Standish is shocked and angered when he hears of Priscilla's rejection of his proposal and her encouragement of Alden's suit. More weighty matters demand his attention, however: How shall the Pilgrim settlers answer the Indians who have sent the "skin of a rattlesnake" as a challenge to war? The Elder of Plymouth counsels peace; Standish is adamant for war. "Truly the only tongue that is understood by a savage/ Must be the tongue of fire that speaks from the mouth of the cannon!" Standish consistently rejects language and translates words into military action. The next day, Alden's conflict over whether to sail for England or stay and woo Priscilla continues. He decides to stay but not to woo. Their relationship is redefined; he will be her friend. Priscilla defines the relationship with precision and candor. "Let us, then, be what we are, and speak what we think, and in all things/ Keep ourselves loyal to truth, and the sacred professions of friendship."

Standish goes to war and answers the words of the chief, Pecksuot, with action: He snatches Pecksuot's knife from him and kills him. Priscilla is not pleased by this valor but repelled by it. The poem's conflict is partially resolved when news comes that Standish has died in battle. Alden and Priscilla are free to marry, but the shadow of Standish still hovers over their relationship.

The denouement of the poem comes on the wedding day of Alden and Priscilla. After the service, the ghost of Standish appears to bless the marriage. "Mine is the same hot blood that leaped in the veins of Hugh Standish/ Sensitive, swift to resent, but as swift in atoning for error./ Never so much as now was Miles Standish the friend of John Alden!" Standish remains his old self, telling the people that he "had rather by far break into an Indian encampment,/ Than come again to a wedding to which he had not been invited." With his presence removed, the familiar landscape of Plymouth is transfigured into the "Garden of Eden."

The Courtship of Miles Standish is one of Longfellow's most successful poems.

The meter is not oppressive and the narrative is skillfully constructed; the biblical language elevates the romance without overwhelming it. The characters are also well conceived. Standish's gruff soldier in the role of a lover and his inability to use words is perfectly captured. Priscilla Mullins is a clever and imaginative creation, very different than the usual submissive female Longfellow usually portrays. Longfellow also removes some of the excessive solemnity of the Pilgrims and makes their world delightful and human.

Summary

Longfellow contributed much to American poetry. He showed that Americans had a marvelous and important history. He makes early America into a mythic land: The Indians, the Pilgrims, and the exiles from Nova Scotia are all given a treatment that had previously been reserved for Greek or Roman myth. Longfellow also opened American poetry to a variety of poetic meters and structures. Certain themes recur; Longfellow consistently portrays women as submissive and passive. He also suggests that there is progress in the world; the disaster of Evangeline or the dislocation of the Indians cannot drive out the optimism that things are getting better and man is becoming more civilized.

Bibliography

Arvin, Newton. *Longfellow: His Life and Work*. Boston: Little, Brown, 1962.

Bewley, Marius. "The Poetry of Longfellow." *Hudson Review* 16 (1963): 297-304.

Ferguson, Robert A. "Longfellow's Political Fears: Civic Authority and the Role of the Artist in Hiawatha and Miles Standish." *American Literature* 50 (1978): 187-215.

Hirsh, Edward L. *Henry Wadsworth Longfellow*. Minneapolis: University of Minnesota Press, 1964.

Wagenknecht, Edward. *Henry Wadsworth Longfellow: An American Humanist*. New York: Oxford University Press, 1966.

____________. *Henry Wadsworth Longfellow: His Poetry and Prose*. New York: Frederick Ungar, 1986.

____________. *Longfellow: A Full-Length Portrait*. New York: Longmans, Green, 1955.

Williams, Cecil B. *Henry Wadsworth Longfellow*. New York: Twayne, 1964.

James Sullivan

ROBERT LOWELL

Born: Boston, Massachusetts
March 2, 1917
Died: New York, New York
September 12, 1977

Principal Literary Achievement

Lowell revolutionized American poetry in the years after World War II with his confessional and political subject matter and the intensity of his language.

Biography

Robert Trail Spence Lowell, Jr., was born into the famous Lowell family of Boston. His father, however, was not a distinguished member of that family, being a commander in the United States Navy and later an unsuccessful businessman. His mother, who was the dominant figure in the family, was also a member of a famous New England family, the Winslows; her family had more money and more prestige at the time of Robert's birth, in fact, and she smothered her son with affection while denigrating her husband's incompetence. Lowell's memoir "91 Revere Street" in *Life Studies* (1959) shows a sensitive child caught in the perpetual conflict of his parents.

Lowell attended a fashionable prep school, St. Mark's, from 1930 to 1935 and Harvard University until 1937. He rebelled against his respectable parents in 1937 and left Harvard to pursue a possible career as a poet by going to live with the distinguished poet Allen Tate in Clarksville, Tennessee. In 1937, he entered Kenyon College to study with the poet John Crowe Ransom; he was graduated summa cum laude in 1940. Lowell also met such lifelong friends at Kenyon as Randall Jarrell and Peter Taylor. He often wrote about them in his later poetry. Lowell was attempting to become a modern American poet by absorbing the ideas and techniques of Tate and Ransom; both poets exemplified and supported the New Criticism. The New Criticism focused on the poem rather than the poet, and it used as models such seventeenth century poets as John Donne. A proper poem, in their view, was complex, with rich imagery, and filled with recondite allusions.

In 1940, Lowell married his first wife, the fiction writer Jean Stafford. The marriage was stormy. Each writer was producing significant work at the time, although she was more financially successful than he was. Another problem was Lowell's political beliefs. He became a conscientious objector in the early 1940's when he

learned about the bombing of the civilian population in Germany. In 1943, he was sentenced to a year in prison for refusing to be inducted into the military. He wrote a letter to Franklin Roosevelt stating his position, his "manic statement/ telling off the state and president." During this period, Lowell converted to Catholicism, which provided the subject matter for many of his early poems. He was later to reject Catholicism as the answer to his quest for a higher authority.

In 1944, Lowell's first book of poetry, *Land of Unlikeness*, was published. It was in the complex and allusive style that the New Critics favored, and the reviews, while not extensive, were favorable. The true breakthrough volume for Lowell was his next book of poetry, *Lord Weary's Castle*, published in 1946. It was an advance in style and technique, and, while it was still complex, it was much more forceful than the earlier book, especially such poems as "The Quaker Graveyard in Nantucket" and "After the Surprising Conversions." In 1947, *Lord Weary's Castle* was awarded the Pulitzer Prize for Poetry.

Although Lowell was recognized as an important American poet at this time, his life was troubled. He was subject to manic-depressive episodes and regularly had to spend brief periods in mental hospitals. The manic periods were especially disturbing because Lowell would claim that he was an all-powerful ruler and refuse the reasoned appeals of those closest to him. These episodes were usually accompanied by Lowell's acquiring a new girlfriend while he announced to whoever would listen that he meant to leave his wife. During one of these episodes he wrecked a car and seriously injured Jean Stafford. He divorced Jean Stafford in 1948 and married another writer, Elizabeth Hardwick, in 1949. In 1951, Lowell's third book of poetry was published; *The Mills of the Kavanaughs* is a series of dramatic monologues and is perhaps the least representative book he ever published. Critically, it was also one of the least successful.

The Beat poets of the 1950's and Lowell's turning to William Carlos Williams as a model (rather than the learned T. S. Eliot) led to a significant change in Lowell's style. In 1959, he published *Life Studies*, his most important book. *Life Studies* was nothing less than a revolution in American poetry. It included poems about his troubled relationship with his parents (who had died in the 1950's), his imprisonment for refusing induction into the military, and his confinement in mental institutions. It dealt with personal subjects—indeed, some believed that it was too personal. The style was no longer the complex style recommended by the New Critics but a simpler, much more direct and striking one. *Life Studies* won the National Book Award for 1959.

In 1964, he published *For the Union Dead*; most of the poems in the book were in the "confessional" mode of *Life Studies*, but there was one exception—the title poem. "For the Union Dead" is a political poem, not a confessional one. It contrasts the integrity and dedication of the nineteenth century Bostonians who fought for the liberation of blacks with the decadent and materialistic twentieth century. Appropriately, Lowell read the poem on the Boston Common at the Boston Arts Festival. Lowell's interest in politics is also reflected in the publication, also in 1964, of *The*

Old Glory; this is not a book of poems but dramatizations of Herman Melville's "Benito Cereno" (1856) and Nathaniel Hawthorne's "My Kinsman, Major Molineaux" (1832). It later had a successful run on the New York stage.

In 1967, Lowell published *Near the Ocean*, which, with the exception of "Waking Early Sunday Morning," is a forgettable book. In some passages Lowell attacks President Lyndon Johnson for his continuation of the Vietnam War; this clearly shows Lowell's continuing interest in power and American politics. In 1968, he campaigned for and became very friendly with Eugene McCarthy in an attempt to defeat Johnson and end the Vietnam War. He was becoming a public figure. In 1969, Lowell published *Notebook 1967-68* (later revised as *Notebook* (1970) and later still revised as *History* (1973) by excerpting the political poems). Some of the poems are about the private life of the poet, sometimes expressed in a very intimate manner, but the book also contains a number of poems on leaders and political subjects. Another innovation is that the poems are all written in a loose sonnet form.

In 1972, Lowell divorced Elizabeth Hardwick and married Caroline Blackwood. That divorce and the troubled and loving relationship between Lowell and Hardwick became the main subjects of *The Dolphin* (1973) and *For Lizzie and Harriet* (1973). Lowell even included letters from Elizabeth Hardwick in a nearly complete form in some poems. His last book of poems was *Day By Day* (1977); it dealt with the difficult marriage between Lowell and Caroline and their residence in England. He was visiting Elizabeth Hardwick and his daughter Harriet in 1977 when he had a heart attack; he died on September 12.

Analysis

Nearly all Lowell's poems have a richness of imagery, a wide range of references and allusions, and a density of syntax. His first two books stress religious themes and subjects. Such poems as "The Drunken Fisherman" and "Between the Porch and the Altar" clearly demonstrate his abiding religious concerns. They are difficult to unravel and do not easily yield themselves to the reader. Lowell was, as he often mentioned, trying to write poems in the manner of Hart Crane while under the critical influence of the New Critics. The last stanza of "The Drunken Fisherman" shows the richness and the difficulties of such poems.

> Is there no way to cast my hook
> Out of this dynamited brook?
> This Fisher's sons must cast about
> When shallow waters peter out.
> I will catch Christ with a greased worm,
> And when the Prince of Darkness stalks
> My bloodstream to its Stygian term . . .
> On water the Man-Fisher walks.

The poem is undoubtedly powerful, but it is not the best or most typical type of Lowell poem. Here he is trying to be another T. S. Eliot—writing learned and academic poetry with religious and mythic themes. He was not the equal of the Eliot of the *Four Quartets* (1943), however, and his natural bent lay elsewhere.

Life Studies led to the coinage of the term "confessional poet." The subjects of its poetry were Lowell's parents and grandparents, his bouts of madness, and his friends. The style is also freer and looser; in place of learned allusions there are ironic references to the misspelling of "Lowell" on his mother's coffin. In "Waking in the Blue," Lowell describes the inmates in McLeans Hospital for the " 'mentally ill.' " Lowell does not stand aloof but includes himself within the group of "thoroughbred mental cases." The last two lines convey Lowell's recognition of his state and make the reader a participant, not merely an observer: "We are all old-timers,/ each of us holds a locked razor." It is a direct and immensely moving poetry.

Lowell never ceased to write "confessional" poetry, but he expanded the range of his poetry by turning to political subjects. "For the Union Dead" is an indictment of modern life and leaders: There are no more Colonel Shaws to lead Negro infantry but only politicians who refuse to allow Negro children to attend school with whites. Lowell makes clear that twentieth century materialistic society has perverted once-noble values. A few years later, his politics became much more direct. In "Near the Ocean," for example, he portrays Lyndon Johnson "swimming nude, unbuttoned, sick/ of his ghost-written rhetoric!" Later, Lowell was a part of the march on Washington to stop the Vietnam War and wrote about his experience in a number of poems in *Notebook*. There are also studies of such leaders and power figures as Alexander the Great, Abraham Lincoln, and Adolf Hitler.

One aspect of Lowell's poetry that is often ignored by critics is the many elegies on and tributes to his friends and fellow poets. In *Life Studies*, there are poems on Ford Madox Ford, Delmore Schwartz, and Hart Crane. The finest ones, however, come from *Notebook*, especially the poem on Robert Frost. Lowell portrays Frost not as a genial New England sage but as a tortured man with "the great act laid on the shelf in mothballs." Lowell's Frost says at the end of the poem, "When I am too full of joy, I think/ how little good my health did anyone near me." There are poems on T. S. Eliot and Ezra Pound and a moving elegy to his friend, Randall Jarrell. Lowell was the greatest elegiac poet of his time, whether the subject was his family, his friends, fellow poets, or great men. "The Quaker Graveyard in Nantucket" and "My Last Afternoon with Uncle Devereux Winslow" are among the finest elegies in American literature.

The later books of Lowell show one surprising change; where before he had written in loose verse paragraphs and occasionally in stanzas, he now takes up the sonnet form. All the poems in *Notebook* and most of the other later books are written in a very idiosyncratic sonnet form. Lowell usually keeps to the sonnet's fourteen-line pattern but does not use rhyme or observe the usual Italian or English sonnet divisions. "Dolphin," for example, begins with a traditional quatrain but then does not continue the quatrain pattern; it breaks the meaning at the seventh line. The last section does, however, provide a counter-statement to those first seven lines which speak of being guided by a muse in the way that Racine was:

I have sat and listened to too many
words of the collaborating muse,
and plotted perhaps too freely with my life,
not avoiding injury to others,
not avoiding injury to myself—
to ask compassion . . . this book, half fiction,
an eelnet made by man for the eel fighting.

Then a very unconventional fifteenth line is added to complete the poem: "[M]y eyes have seen what my hand did." Some of Lowell's experiments with sonnet form seem casual and erratic, but "Dolphin" breathes a new life into the most fixed form in literature. Lowell was nevertheless worried that he had not successfully escaped the trap of that form. In an "Afterthought" to *Notebook* he said, "Even with this license, I fear I have failed to avoid the themes and gigantism of the sonnet."

MY LAST AFTERNOON WITH UNCLE DEVEREUX WINSLOW

First published: 1959
Type of work: Poem

A moving elegy on Robert Lowell's uncle and an analysis of the divisions in the Lowell and Winslow families.

"My Last Afternoon with Uncle Devereux Winslow" does not begin like an elegy, focusing instead on Lowell's childhood affection for his grandfather Winslow and his distance from his own parents. It begins, " 'I won't go with you. I want to stay with Grandpa!' " Grandfather Winslow's world was one of adventure and freedom. "the décor/ was manly, comfortable,/ overbearing, disproportioned." At his farm are photographs of silver mines and "pitchers of ice-tea,/ oranges, lemons, mints, and peppermints,/ and the jug of shandygaff." Most significant is the fact that "[n]o one had died there in my lifetime." The boy (young Lowell) is busy playing with a "pile of black earth" and one of "lime," an image of play and death that runs through the poem.

The pastoral innocence of the first part of the poem is swiftly challenged. The boy is now inappropriately dressed and is described as a "stuffed toucan/ with a bibulous, multicolored beak." There is a recognition of failure; Great Aunt Sara had once slaved away at perfecting her ability on the piano, only to fail to appear at the recital. She now plays on a "dummy" and "noiseless" piano. Uncle Devereux, however, is still as young as the posters and photographs that fill the cottage he is closing "for the winter." Suddenly, reality intrudes upon the stasis of old photographs: "My Uncle was dying at twenty-nine." Devereux resists the fact of death by sailing with his wife "for Europe on a last honeymoon" in a joyous affirmation of life. His parents are shocked at his seeming frivolity. The child has altered as well; he becomes an observer of bizarre and unfamilial behavior, an accomplice rather than an innocent child.

The last part of the poem contrasts Devereux's appearance with his fate. He appears to be "as brushed as Bayard, our riding horse," but he is "dying of the incurable Hodgkin's disease." The last image of the poem is of the boy mixing "earth and lime,/ a black pile and a white pile." He becomes a mythic figure sifting the sands of life and death; the innocent play of the earlier image of mixing earth and lime has become ominous. The last two lines have a child's simplicity and all the weight of fact: "Come winter,/ Uncle Devereux would blend to the one color."

"My Last Afternoon with Uncle Devereux Winslow" is an unusual elegy. It mourns the loss not only of a person but also of a hitherto unchanging and innocent world. Another change from the traditional elegy is that the main focus is the boy, not Uncle Devereux. His loss of innocence, his being cast out of an Edenic refuge, seems to be stressed much more than the actual death of Devereux Winslow. Lowell has expanded the usual range of the elegy to include the observer and a whole society.

SKUNK HOUR

First published: 1959
Type of work: Poem

A devastating analysis of the material and spiritual decay in modern life that contrasts to instinctual nature.

"Skunk Hour" is the last poem in *Life Studies*, and as such it was meant to sum up the themes and tone of the collection and suggest some sort of resolution. The first four stanzas portray a decayed Maine coastal town. The "hermit heiress" who should be a leader in the society isolates herself; her main activity is buying up houses near her to ensure her privacy and isolation: "[S]he buys up all/ the eyesores facing her shore,/ and lets them fall." She contributes to the decay rather than overcoming it by her wealth and position. In the third stanza, "our summer millionaire" has departed and "[t]he season's ill." The change is also suggested by an image: "A red fox stain covers Blue Hill." The last stanza in this sequence portrays a "fairy decorator" whose trendy and unsuccessful shop is filled with the tools (fishnets and orange cork) that were once used by fishermen. Since "there is no money in his work,/ he'd rather marry." Love and marriage have become commodities in a once fruitful and organic society that is now sunk in decay.

The next two stanzas shift from an analysis of the society to one person. He is the Lowell speaker, mad and in search of sexual experience. The setting is ominous: "One dark night," which is not merely the time of day but also an allusion to Saint John of the Cross's *Dark Night of the Soul*. The speaker's car climbs "the hill's skull" (a reference to Golgotha) to look for "love-cars." The cars lie "hull to hull" where "the graveyard shelves on the town." It is a wonderful image of mechanical sexuality amid the grotesque graveyard that overlooks the town. All that the speaker can do is declare, "My mind's not right." This section culminates with another declaration: "I myself am hell;/ nobody's here." The first line echoes John Milton's Satan in *Paradise Lost*, while the last line repeats the isolation and decay that began the poem.

Both society and the individual are sick and perverted; there seems to be no hope anywhere. The last two stanzas, however, turn the poem around. Suddenly a group of skunks appears marching down Main Street, strutting by the no longer life-giving "chalk-dray and spar spire/ of the Trinitarian Church." In the last stanza, the mad speaker of the second section of the poem watches as "a mother skunk with her column of kittens swills the garbage pail./ She jabs her wedge-head in a cup/ of sour cream, drops her ostrich tail,/ and will not scare." The skunks are a remarkable and very appropriate modern symbol. They do not redeem the society of the speaker, but they do provide an alternative. They live off the decay that was so noteworthy in the first section of the poem. In addition, they will not "scare" or give in to an overly morbid consciousness as the speaker so obviously does. The scene also shows a mother nurturing her "kittens," something that cannot be found in the decayed and isolated society.

"Skunk Hour" became one of Lowell's most popular poems. It perfectly captures the troubles of society and the individual while also offering a powerful and natural symbol that opposes both. Modern poetry can no longer draw on the traditional natural symbolism of centuries before. Lowell could not instantly evoke eagles or hawks in his poetry, and he had the genius to discover a modern symbolism.

FOR THE UNION DEAD

First published: 1960
Type of work: Poem

A contrast between the aristocratic code of the nineteenth century and modern materialism.

"For the Union Dead" is an unusually public poem; it was written for Lowell to deliver on the Boston Common before a large audience. It is also one of his finest poems. It begins with a childhood memory of the South Boston Aquarium, where his hand had "tingled/ to burst the bubbles/ drifting from the noses of the cowed, compliant fish." Now, however, the aquarium "stands in a Sahara of snow." The "broken windows are boarded" and the "airy tanks are dry." Lowell has found perfect images of emptiness and desolation in what was once a place of life-giving joy. Next he notices "the new barbed and galvanized/ fence on the Boston Common." Once a symbol of openness and community, the Common is now enclosed.

The only thriving elements are the parking spaces that "luxuriate like civic/ sandpiles in the heart of Boston." The construction of an "underworld garage" is shaking the famous seventeenth century Massachusetts Statehouse. The images are no longer of fish but have become "yellow dinosaur steamshovels." A mechanical and destructive world is replacing the traditional Puritan one. The only reminders of that heritage are the ironic "Puritan-pumpkin colored girders" that brace the "tingling Statehouse."

Lowell then shifts to imagery based on a statue and bas-relief of a Civil War hero, Colonel Shaw, a New Englander who led a regiment of free blacks in an attack on the fort at Charleston. The famous bas-relief of Colonel Shaw and his regiment has also been assaulted by the modern instruments of destruction and needs to be "propped by a plank splint." What the statue represents has also changed; no longer does Boston support the abolitionist cause or lead Negro infantry in a noble cause. Now, "[t]heir monument sticks like a fishbone/ in the city's throat." Colonel Shaw still possesses some of those older virtues: "He has an angry wrenlike vigilance,/ a greyhound's gentle tautness." Shaw's father had thought an appropriate monument would be "the ditch,/ where his son's body was thrown/ and lost with his 'niggers.' " Lowell then makes another contrast between the past and the present. The "ditch is nearer," and the only monument from the last war is an advertisement that "shows Hiroshima boiling/ over a Mosler Safe." War is no longer noble but has become mechanized and more destructive; advertisements replace the statues of Civil War heros.

Colonel Shaw awaits the "blessèd break" that will complete his cause, but instead "the drained faces of Negro school-children rise like balloons" as they attempt to enter an all-white school. The image of the "bubble" encloses the fish in the aquarium, Colonel Shaw, and the black children, but there is no "blessèd break." There is only a final and devastating symbol:

> Everywhere,
> giant finned cars nose forward like fish;
> a savage servility
> slides by on grease.

Once more, Lowell uses a mechanical symbol and opposes it to a natural one. No longer do aristocrats serve the republic; everyone is now mired in "servility" and a corrupt selfishness.

"For the Union Dead" is one of Lowell's finest poems; it brings together a number of image patterns and themes. The "fish" in the childhood reminiscence become "dinosaurs," then a "fishbone" that sticks in the city's throat, and finally "giant finned cars." The "bubbles" from those fish enclose (or imprison) the fish, Colonel Shaw, and the "Negro school-children"; all wait for the "blessèd break," but it has receded rather than come closer in twentieth century Boston. The poem also successfully blends the public with the private interests, something that Lowell did not always achieve.

WAKING EARLY SUNDAY MORNING

First published: 1967
Type of work: Poem

The poem portrays the desire of man for freedom and a natural life and how obstacles such as religion, politics, and man's own nature prevent it.

"Waking Early Sunday Morning" is the first section in the long poem called "Near the Ocean"; it attempts to find some relief or escape from man's disturbed, anxious, and apparently unnatural condition. It begins with that desire for an instinctual escape: "O to break loose, like the chinook/ salmon jumping and falling back." This leads to a childhood memory of freedom, "the unpolluted joy/ and criminal leisure of a boy." Such escapes are quickly closed, however, and the imagery shifts to the "sure of foot" and natural "vermin" in the walls of his house. In addition, dawn brings no renewal in this fallen world but only "business as usual in eclipse." Everything is stained or tarnished, so the speaker turns to religion, to the congregation at Sunday worship; however, that is no solution. Each day God recedes and "shines through a darker glass."

Having rejected the impossible instinctual life and the evasive spiritual one, he turns to another possibility: "O to break loose. All life's grandeur/ is something with a girl in summer." Love (or sex), however, has lost its power in a politically dominated world in which "earth licks its open sores" and man is "thinning out his kind." The last stanza reduces the escape to a plea for mercy.

> Pity the planet, all joy gone
> from this sweet volcanic cone;
> peace to our children when they fall
> in small war on the heels of small
> war—until the end of time
> to police the earth, a ghost
> orbiting forever lost
> in our monotonous sublime.

The Vietnam War and American foreign policy in general do not bring peace, only war upon war. Noble aims have become illusory, ghostlike, and all joy is gone from the planet. The image of man "orbiting forever lost" is frightening and unrelieved. Man's desire to be free is frustrated not only by his own nature but even more so by an environment of war and hostility.

THE NIHILIST AS HERO

First published: 1967
Type of work: Poem

A paradoxical analysis of the claims of stasis and change that Lowell refuses to resolve.

"The Nihilist as Hero" is a sonnet from *Notebook* and a poem that reveals much about Lowell as a poet and a man. The poem begins with a quote from poet Paul Valéry about sustaining a work of art beyond a single line. It is a vision of poetry as formal perfection. Lowell then announces a very different view of the nature of art: "I want words meat-hooked from the living steer." Such direct (confessional?) poetry is blocked, however, by the "metal log,/ beautiful unchanging fire of childhood/ betraying a monotony of vision." Life, too, is not based on stasis, but "by definition breeds on change"; however, change means only that "each season we scrap new cars and wars and women." It is an endless round of activity without hope or joy. The last lines of the sonnet bring the contrasts together. First, he states that when he is "ill or delicate,/ the pinched flame of my match turns unchanging green." The image of an illusionary stasis echoes the "tinfoil" flame of childhood. The last two lines complete the poem by balancing the two sides.

> A nihilist wants to live in the world as is,
> and yet gaze the everlasting hills to rubble.

There is no easy solution; one desires both reality and destruction, an unchanging art and a live one, stasis and continual activity. This does not mean that Lowell is a nihilist; he recognizes the claims of both sides and cannot find a way to synthesize them. Man is doomed to live with a dream of perfection in an imperfect world. It is a haunting conclusion to one of Lowell's most revealing poems.

Summary

Robert Lowell is perhaps the most important American poet of the last half of the twentieth century. He expanded the range and possibilities of poetry's subject matter with his confessional and political poems; no longer would poets have to write in the prescribed New Critical fashion. He also altered the way in which readers look at such traditional forms as the elegy and the sonnet. Lowell's style was also innovative. Those "words meat-hooked from the living steer" in his later poems showed that letters, diaries, advertisements could become forceful entities in poetry. Above all, Lowell's voice added an intensity and power to American poetry that had been lacking.

Bibliography

Axelrod, Steven Gould. *Robert Lowell: Life and Art*. Princeton, N.J.: Princeton University Press, 1978.

Bell, Vereen M. *Robert Lowell: Nihilist as Hero.* Cambridge, Mass.: Harvard University Press, 1983.

Cooper, Phillip. *The Autobiographical Myth of Robert Lowell*. Chapel Hill: University of North Carolina Press, 1970.

Cosgrave, Patrick. *The Public Poetry of Robert Lowell*. New York: Taplinger, 1972.

Hamilton, Ian. *Robert Lowell: A Biography.* New York: Random House, 1982.

Mazzaro, Jerome. *The Poetic Themes of Robert Lowell*. Ann Arbor: University of Michigan Press, 1965.

Parkinson, Thomas Francis, ed. *Robert Lowell: A Collection of Critical Essays.* Englewood Cliffs, N.J.: Prentice-Hall, 1968.

Perloff, Marjorie. *The Poetic Art of Robert Lowell*. Ithaca, N.Y.: Cornell University Press, 1973.

Rudman, Mark. *Robert Lowell: An Introduction to the Poetry.* New York: Columbia University Press, 1983.

Williamson, Alan. *Pity the Monsters.* New Haven, Conn.: Yale University Press, 1974.

James Sullivan

ALISON LURIE

Born: Chicago, Illinois
September 3, 1926

Principal Literary Achievement

Winner of the Pulitzer Prize in Fiction in 1985, Lurie's satirical novels of manners and academic behavior have brought her recognition as one of America's finest comic writers.

Biography

Alison Lurie was born in Chicago, Illinois, on September 3, 1926. She attended Radcliffe College, where she received an A.B. degree in 1947. The following year she married Jonathan Peale Bishop, Jr., who went on to become a professor of English at Cornell University. Before their divorce in 1985, the Bishops had three sons, John, Jeremy, and Joshua.

Lurie's first book was a privately printed memoir of a close friend, poet and playwright Violet Lang, but her first significant work of fiction was *Love and Friendship* (1962), a novel that contains the themes of domestic dissatisfaction and adultery that Lurie continued to explore in later work. Its principal character, Emily Stockwell Turner, is the prototype of Katherine Cattleman, Erica Tate, and the other unfulfilled, frustrated, middle-class American women who populate Lurie's narratives.

In addition to being a housewife and mother and working occasionally as a ghostwriter and librarian, Lurie continued to publish her novels, gaining more critical acclaim and a wider readership with each one: *The Nowhere City* (1965), *Imaginary Friends* (1967), and *Real People* (1969). Moreover, she began to garner fellowships and grants that helped further her career as a writer: Yaddo fellowships in 1963, 1964, and 1966 (Yaddo, an artist's colony, gave Lurie material for *Real People*); a Guggenheim grant in 1965-1966; and a Rockefeller Foundation grant in 1967-1968. Finally, in 1968 she joined the faculty of Cornell University, where she eventually became, like her husband, a professor of English, teaching fiction writing and children's literature. Cornell, too, became the fictional Corinth University of her later novels, and its faculty served as models for the well-educated, crisis-ridden academics that she places there.

It was her fifth novel, *The War Between the Tates* (1974), that earned Lurie an international reputation. Her most ambitious novel, the book captures the flavor of the early 1970's—its radical chic, comic conservatism, mindless rebellion, genera-

tion gaps, confused feminism, political marches, and private battles between the sexes. Nothing escapes Lurie's sharp tongue and witty intelligence, and the result is a mercilessly satiric attack on American middle-class values. It remains her best-known novel, and it was adapted as a television movie by NBC.

Her reputation secure, Lurie published three novels after *The War Between the Tates. Only Children* (1979) appeared to mixed reviews, but *Foreign Affairs* (1984) earned for Lurie the Pulitzer Prize in fiction, as well as an American Book Award nomination and a National Book Critics Circle Award nomination for best work of fiction. *The Truth About Lorin Jones* appeared in 1988. In addition, she began publishing children's fiction: *The Heavenly Zoo* (1980), *Clever Gretchen and Other Forgotten Folktales* (1980), and *Fabulous Beasts* (1981), stories that often privilege women in ways that traditional folk tales do not. In 1981, Lurie published a comprehensive history of clothing, *The Language of Clothes*, which argues for clothing as a communication system, a "language" that presents nonverbal information about people's occupations, interests, personalities, opinions, and tastes. The author employs photographs and illustrations, insights from literature, psychology, and sociology, and examples from her own experiences to inform this highly original work.

Alison Lurie became a member of the prestigious American Academy of Arts and Letters in 1989. In addition to teaching at Cornell in Ithaca, New York, she lives in London and Key West, Florida.

Analysis

Lurie has been compared to Jane Austen, Henry James, and Mary McCarthy (another satiric novelist who finds comic material in the American university), and to contemporaries such as Kurt Vonnegut, John Updike, Norman Mailer, and Philip Roth. Like Austen, she can be viewed as a novelist of "manners," a writer concerned primarily with the follies of highly sophisticated people who are often emotionally self-indulgent and insecure, caught between sense and sensibility, pride and prejudice. In fact, one of Austen's juvenile works is entitled *Love and Friendship*, the same title that Lurie used for her own first novel. Like James, Lurie is concerned not only with the manners and customs of Americans but also with their moral and psychological problems, with the "felt life" of the imagination as well as the realistic terrain of the social world. James was concerned with American character and often placed his Americans in European settings (or Europeans in American settings) to show them in stark contrast. In *Foreign Affairs*, Lurie employs James's "international theme" by sending her two principal Americans, Vinnie Miner and Fred Turner, to London, where American naïveté encounters European sophistication. Lurie's similarities to her contemporaries are more obvious. Like McCarthy in novels such as *The Groves of Academe*, Lurie finds comedy in academe; like Vonnegut, Roth, and others, her basic mode is satire.

Like many satirists throughout the history of literature, Lurie chooses sex, class, and religion as her targets. Adultery and sexual intrigues are common in her novels, and while such behavior always creates human complication, it is not at all clear that

Lurie condemns it. In fact, she refuses to judge sexual behavior at all. In *The Nowhere City,* Katherine Cattleman's affair with Dr. Isidore Einsam strengthens her, making her more self-assured as a woman, while in *The War Between the Tates,* Danielle Zimmern's affair with Dr. Bernard Kotelchuk weakens her, making her more dependent and turning her from an independent, intelligent woman into a frumpy housewife. Wendy Gahaghan and Cecile O'Connor, two of Lurie's younger women, both emerge from their sexual affairs with little emotional damage.

On the other hand, few of Lurie's men fare well from their sexual escapades. Paul Cattleman, after flings with a youthful hippie and an aging Hollywood starlet, slinks back East to a safe teaching job, a defeated man. Brian Tate, publicly humiliated by a group of radical feminists, is a victim of self-deceit, hypocrisy, and vanity. Einsam and Kotelchuk are little better than rapists, both forcing themselves on the women they want, but each ends up condemned to a lifetime of timid devotion to their women. Roger Zimmern, the narrator of *Imaginary Friends,* longs for Verena Roberts but flees from her when she becomes sexually aggressive; even worse, Sandy Finkelstein, the pathetic mystic who has worshipped Erica Tate for years, is unable to get an erection when she offers herself to him. In sum, Lurie's view of sex (and its concomitants, marriage and adultery) is essentially that of a social scientist. She is more concerned with its effects on individual lives than on its moral significance. Her characters are usually well-educated, upper-middle-class adults who are respectable, responsible, and conservative—just those Americans that one would expect to uphold virtues of family, marriage, and society. The power of sexual passion, ennui, or simply contradictory human nature proves too much for them, however, propelling them headlong into strange alliances and complicated sexual games. At their best, sexual encounters change the individuals involved by giving them self-knowledge they otherwise would not have gained.

Complicating matters further is Lurie's distinctly feminist view of marriage, children, and men. Her suburban, intelligent, middle-aged housewives have been left for younger women, have fallen victim to graying hair and sagging breasts, have been uprooted from friends and comfortable surroundings to follow their husband's career, or have witnessed their children grow from cherubic babyhood to monstrous adolescence. They have made their choices, chosen their men and their lives long ago (when they were inexperienced), and now that they have knowledge of themselves and their world, they have no choices to make. Their husbands are sexually bored, professionally frustrated, and emotionally restless. Such marriages as these stay together for the sake of what Lurie calls The Children. Typical of such children are the Tates' two teenagers, Jeffrey and Matilda, once known as "Jeffo" and "Muffy." Now growing into adulthood, they have become rude, abusive, profane, lazy, and selfish. They fight constantly, and both Erica and Brian Tate have come to despise them; to Erica, they are aliens who have taken over the bodies of the children she once loved. Lurie continually undermines the romantic notions of marriage and family that keep women from becoming fully developed, independent human beings. Women who spend their lives rearing children, she insists, might find those children growing into hateful monsters. Wives who devote their lives to the careers of their husbands might be left with no lives of their own if the husband leaves them for another woman, and women without men are subjected to the mindless stereotypes of society. Divorced women who take lovers such as Danielle Zimmern of *The War Between the Tates,* are categorized as sluts by society, while professional women who do not marry (Vinnie Miner of *Foreign Affairs*) are thought to be sexless spinsters.

Vinnie, in fact, is a good example of the realistic way that Lurie portrays women. A woman in her fifties who is not pretty by traditional American standards, Vinnie is juxtaposed to her English department colleague Fred Turner, a Hollywood-handsome young man. In London to do academic research, both have "foreign affairs," Vinnie with a somewhat loutish American tourist, Chuck Mumpson, and Turner with a famous British beauty and television actress, Lady Rosemary Radley. That Vinnie should have any affair whatsoever may seem surprising, for, as Lurie points out, society does not seem to expect physically unattractive women over fifty to have any sex life at all. Vinnie, however, though far from promiscuous, has been sexually active all her life, usually with male friends she has known for a long time. Sex, as she ponders at one point, has never been hard to attain, though love has been. (Sex, in fact, is not hard for any woman to attain, she concludes, if she sets her sights low enough.) Ironically, oafish Chuck Mumpson turns out to be a tender and sensitive lover, while the dazzlingly beautiful Rosemary is revealed as shallow, vain, incapable of love, and inwardly ugly. The beautiful and the handsome, like Fred and Rosemary, have just as much difficulty finding genuine love and affection as, by society's standards, the unattractive and no longer youthful.

Another favorite target of Lurie's satire is class, not only in the United States but, in *Foreign Affairs,* in England as well. Her upper-middle-class American academics range from uptight, conservative boors such as Don Dibble, who gets trapped in his office by a group of radical feminists in *The War Between the Tates,* to aspiring young professors such as Fred Turner, whose theatrical good looks make him suspect to his more conventional-looking male colleagues. Lurie's academics are pigeonholed in their sequestered world not only by whom they are sleeping with but also by how well they keep it hidden, by meaningless books and articles (and how well they are received by reviewers), and by the whimsical regard or disregard of their more powerful colleagues. Lurie has a wonderful eye for details of clothing, material possessions, and surroundings that typify middle-class American life. Her biting satire of southern California, *The Nowhere City,* captures the tacky architecture, labyrinthine freeways, twenty-four-hour "Joy Superdupermarkets," littered and smelly beaches, and voracious realty development that only a confirmed Easterner such as Lurie could describe with such gleeful malice. Gertrude Stein (another famous Radcliffe graduate) once said of Oakland, California, that there was "no there, there," and to Lurie, Los Angeles is a similar "nowhere" city: a stratified geographical area with a central valley thick with smog and poverty, topped by the private pools and hillside palaces of the tastelessly rich. Finally, there is the subclass of hippies, gurus, student groupies, and dropouts that appear frequently in Lurie's novels, not so much representing a class as a counterculture of the young and disenfranchised. Like Wendy Gahaghan and Ceci O'Connor, they live in "the now"—with no emotional commitment, no sense of responsibility, no ambition, and no hope. Small wonder that Wendy, at the end of *The War Between the Tates,* plans to go off with her latest casual lover to California, Lurie's favorite nowhere.

In *Imaginary Friends,* Lurie satirizes American religion, another favorite subject of traditional satirists. Reminiscent of both Sinclair Lewis's *Elmer Gantry* (1927) and Henry James's *The Bostonians* (1886, a satire not on religion, but on the feminist movement of his day), the novel explores a spiritualist group called the Truth Seekers, a group of lower-middle-class losers who are convinced they are in touch with a spiritual space traveler named Ro of Varna, who sends messages (via automatic writing) through a young woman in the group named Verena Roberts. The Seekers could be one of any number of similar groups throughout the United States, trying to find spiritual uplift for their pathetic and uneventful lives. The group is infiltrated by two sociologists from Corinth University who are out to prove a hypothesis about belief systems and find in the Seekers a perfect control group. As it turns out, the senior sociologist, Thomas McMann, is more lunatic than any of the Seekers (the novel also lampoons social scientists) and winds up in an asylum, believing that he himself is Ro of Varna. Both seekers and sociologists, Lurie tells us, get caught up in their own delusionary systems, irrational wishes, and distorted perceptions of reality—perhaps everyone does at one time or another—and who is to say that one form of delusion is better or worse than another?

Aside from the intelligence, social commentary, and sheer fun of Lurie's novels, many admire them simply for their artistry. Her carefully constructed novels often employ several voices and points of view, effortless shifts from present to past time, believable dialogue, and arresting images. Her prose is admirably lucid, concise, and direct, always perfectly suited to the narrative and subject. Her wit and use of irony are those of a highly sophisticated social novelist, and her illumination of the self-deceptions and disappointments of adult life reveal a novelist of serious intent for mature readers.

THE NOWHERE CITY

First published: 1965
Type of work: Novel

A young history professor and his wife encounter the cultural shock of Southern California.

The Nowhere City, Lurie's second published novel, is a somewhat malicious satire on California manners and customs, written from the point of view of someone who believes in the superiority of life in the eastern United States. In this early work, some of Lurie's dominant themes become evident: marital disharmony, the transformational effect of adultery, and the shabbiness of American middle-class culture.

The central characters are Paul and Katherine Cattleman, a young historian and his wife who have come to California from Harvard University, where Paul was completing work on his doctorate. Paul has taken a job with The Nutting Research Development Corporation, a large electronic firm in Los Angeles; his assignment is to write a history and description of the company's operations. To Paul, it is an ideal position: He will have time to write his dissertation and will be making twice the salary he would make as a young college instructor. Besides, he thinks of Los Angeles as an exciting and vital American frontier—the city of the future.

To his wife Katherine, however, Los Angeles is a nightmare. The smog irritates her sinuses, the people look weird and freakish, the weather is hot and uncomfortable, and the city seems plastic and unreal. She is even attacked by a buffalo while visiting a local zoo. Katherine's Los Angeles is a cheap, shoddy city of commercial exploitation, with desperate people seeking success, love, some hero to worship, or some beauty to ogle.

A subplot involves Hollywood starlet Glory Green and her husband, Dr. Isadore Einsam, a successful Beverly Hills psychiatrist. Lurie often casts dissimilar characters into her novels, comparing and contrasting their lives, and bringing them into unexpected relations with each other. In this novel, Katherine takes a job as a research assistant at UCLA, working for Einsam, and later, through Einsam, she becomes secretary to Glory Green. Paul, who has been having an affair with Cecile "Ceci" O'Connor, a coffee-shop waitress and California hippie, meets Glory when he goes to her Beverly Hills mansion to pick up his wife. Typical of Lurie's novels, too, the couples become sexually involved with each other. Katherine has an affair with "Iz" Einsam, while Paul has one with Glory. These brief encounters go nowhere (where else in a nowhere city?) and each goes back to the original spouse. Intellectual Iz goes back to Glory, the stereotypical dumb blonde, while neurotic Katherine returns to Paul, whose desire to be a California swinger is tempered by eastern common sense and propriety. At the end of the novel, he accepts a teaching job at Convers College, north of Boston, and flies off to what presumably will be a more responsible and satisfactory life.

Lurie's main thrust in this novel is to lampoon Southern California manners, morals, and life-styles. Paul, when he takes up with Ceci, becomes a ridiculous figure—a mature, well-educated man who dresses in paint-splattered chino pants, sweatshirt, and sandals, grows a beard, and hangs around espresso coffeehouses with Ceci. He even prides himself on getting busted by the police during a coffeehouse sweep for drug violators. Katherine, who hates Californians for their indifference and irresponsibility, goes Californian herself at the end of the novel, transforming from a neurotic, self-conscious, and somewhat plain young woman into a tanned, sexually flirtatious, and flashily dressed "Los Angeles type" who is indifferent to any responsibilities she might have as a wife. When Paul returns east, she remains behind.

Lurie has further fun with California freeways, buildings (homes shaped like pagodas, grocery stores like turkish baths, and restaurants like boats), art (vulgarly sensual nudes), self-indulgence (a billboard advertising coffee proclaims in huge red letters "Indulge Yourself"), and the state's seeming obsession with speed and the present, its apparent rejection of reason and the past. Children have names like Psyche, Astarte, and Freya, and Hollywood beauties such as Glory Green are beautiful only at a distance, for up close, as Paul notices, she is vulgar, freckled, and commonplace. Nothing in the Nowhere City is what it seems: Dashing Hollywood he-man Rory Gunn is gay, the Nutting Corporation (the name is suggestive) cares nothing for history and is even afraid that Paul Cattleman will find out some of the unsavory truth about its past, and Californians seem subject to what Lurie calls Watson's Law (named after a Boston mathematician), which states that the purpose of the economy is to expend as much time, money, and energy as possible without creating anything useful. That, in fact, seems precisely what has taken place in *The Nowhere City.* The activity of the characters has produced exactly nothing, and at the conclusion of the novel, they are right back where they started.

IMAGINARY FRIENDS

First published: 1967
Type of work: Novel

Two sociologists join a religious-spiritualist group called the Truth Seekers in order to write a sociological study of belief systems.

Imaginary Friends is unlike Lurie's other novels in that marriage, adultery, and the continuing war between the sexes, Lurie's most common themes, give way to other concerns. She does, however, continue to explore academic lives—in this case, an older sociology professor, Thomas McMann, and his younger colleague, Roger Zimmern—and she once again juxtaposes two kinds of culture; the simple, lower-middle-class Truth Seekers with the intellectual, well-bred, and sophisticated sociologists who come to study them. Lurie demonstrates that the rational beliefs and pretensions of intellectuals are often more monstrous than the seemingly lunatic beliefs of the uneducated, and that the most revered institutions of American life—colleges and churches, for example—are no more preferable to mystical cults and religious fringe groups, and often have fewer answers.

Lurie's interest in such things as spiritualism and automatic writing may have come from her friendship with poet James Merrill, whose long narrative poem *The Book of Ephraim* (1977) recounts twenty years of experience with seances and Ouija boards. The novel is, in fact, dedicated to Merrill and another Ouija board enthusiast, David Jackson. Like them, Lurie takes the supernatural seriously. Verena Roberts, a young Seeker through whom higher beings speak by way of automatic writing, often gives messages that are difficult to explain rationally, although McMann, the senior sociologist, is always ready with a glib explanation. At one point, for example, Zimmern (through Verena) receives a message from MAKES FAVOUR, SEE RIGHT ILLS, and O MAKE A VEIL HIGH, obvious puns on classic sociologists Max Weber, C. Wright Mills, and Nicolo Machiavelli, about whom Zimmern was thinking at the time. Moreover, Verena seems to have extra-sensory perception when it comes to such things as finding lost car keys: Zimmern's, she tells him correctly, had slipped down behind some furniture and were lying next to the wall. To Lurie, there are more things in heaven and earth than are dreamt of in sociology.

A more literary influence on *Imaginary Friends* is Henry James's novel *The Bostonians* (1886). In James's novel, principally concerned with the American women's movement of the late nineteenth century, Verena Tarrant is a young, charismatic public speaker who is an inspirational apostle of the feminist cause. In Lurie's novel, Verena Roberts is a similar inspirational apostle for the Truth Seekers. Both are the object of adoration by young men who wish them to renounce their passionate beliefs: Verena Tarrant is pursued by Basil Ransom, who, by muscular force, carries her off with him at the end; Verena Roberts, having been pursued by a tall, gawky boy named Ken (and worshipped from afar by narrator Roger Zimmern), finally gives up her beliefs, marries Ken, and goes off to Albuquerque, New Mexico. Both novels are about contemporary social movements (feminism in James's time, religious fundamentalism in Lurie's), and both novels contain conflicts between the natural, instinctive, naïve gifts of an idealistic young woman and the educated, neurotic, and insensitive demands of others who want her for personal gratification.

As Lurie's novel progresses, the story's narrator, Roger Zimmern, becomes aware of the increasing duplicity, neurotic behavior, and peculiarity of his senior colleague, Thomas McMann. Having gone to the home of the Seekers in Sophis (another suggestive name) to prove an academic theory that opposition and doubt unite rather than weaken a group such as the Seekers, McMann manipulates data to make the hypothesis come true. The Seekers have been in contact, by way of Verena's automatic writing, with a spiritual alien named Ro of Varna, and when Ro promises to appear physically at a certain date, McMann and Zimmern have an ideal test situation. What will happen to the group when Ro fails to materialize, as will surely happen? On the evening of his promised appearance (which, of course, does fail to happen), Ro sends a final message: "I am in Man on earth." This is interpreted by some of the Seekers to mean that Ro has become incarnate within McMann here on earth—an interpretation that McMann does not try to deny or dispel. Further, McMann assumes deific powers within the group when he takes it upon himself to "protect" Verena against the attempts of Ken to contact her, and, finally, when he chases Ken off the premises with a gun. The result is that Zimmern comes to realize that his colleague is mad, and McMann ends up in a mental asylum believing he is Ro of Varna.

Lurie's novel ultimately asks the reader to consider some very serious questions. Who is more self-deluded, those who believe in flying saucer saviors from the planet Varna or those who spend fruitless lifetimes studying them? Which of them live in the "real" world, those who believe that Varnians will deliver them the truth or those who believe the same from the high-level abstractions of the social sciences? Who do more harm, the Seekers with their weekly meetings of hymn singing, automatic writing, and nonsense about astral projection or McMann and Zimmern with their biased conclusions, their egomaniacal self-importance, their willingness to use others, and their questionable perception of reality? Lurie clearly comes down on the side of the Seekers. Ultimately, she forces one to question the ideals and attributes considered sacrosanct in American life—education, religion, science, society, and truth.

THE WAR BETWEEN THE TATES

First published: 1974
Type of work: Novel

The marriage of Erica and Brian Tate is a war between the sexes, not unlike actual battle with its victories, defeats, and victims.

The War Between the Tates, Lurie's best-known novel, is a wickedly humorous satire on marriage, infidelity, and American society. Lurie sets her narrative during the time of the Vietnam War, and early in the novel she develops an extended comparison between that disastrous American war and the typically American Tate marriage. Brian and Erica Tate, like the South Vietnamese, find that their territory, an upper-middle-class house on Jones Creek Road (near Corinth University), is being taken over by their teenage children, Jeffrey and Matilda, whom the Tates liken to North Vietnamese invaders. Like America's involvement in Vietnam, the conflict between the Tates and their children began as a police action and has steadily escalated into all-out deadly warfare. From the children's point of view, their parents are the American invaders—superior in experience and resources but deeply hypocritical. While the children want only independence and self-government, the parents refuse to negotiate, so the children retreat into the jungles of their upstairs rooms, coming out briefly for a guerrilla skirmish. Brian and Erica, on the other hand, regard themselves as democratic and freedom-loving people; never having officially declared themselves at war, they see their mission as a peace-keeping and advisory effort. Although they have won most of the brief, pitched battles, however, the parents know that, in the long run, they will never win the war. The separation of powers by which they have operated their marriage—Erica as the executive branch and Brian as the legislative and judicial—has utterly failed to suppress colonial revolt. The Tates' victories are now all negative ones; the best they can hope for is to contain the enemy within the existing combat zone.

Lurie's witty metaphor is carried throughout the novel (perhaps too much so, as some have criticized). Brian and Erica's separation is like the division in America itself. Erica, tired of her selfish, rude, and rebellious children, has given up the fight, while Brian finds her desertion disheartening and disloyal. Just as there was student unrest in the colleges during the early 1970's, so is there unrest at Corinth, where Brian teaches political science. Radical feminists, taking Brian's advice, protest the sexist remarks of Brian's department antagonist Don Dibble, and when things get out of hand, they invade Dibble's office. Attempting to help, Brian himself is taken hostage—becoming a prisoner of war. The novel concludes with a protest march on the Corinth campus, attended by most of the characters as well as an assortment of Maoists, gay activists, feminists, students, and local citizens. While the reader does not witness it, Lurie states that the group will eventually encounter violence at a bar called the Old Bavaria. This war has its victims, daily combats, withdrawals and retreats, and in the long run no one really wins.

The war that this novel is primarily about, however, is the war between the sexes. Brian, bored with Erica and suburban life, drifts into an affair with Wendy Gahaghan, a young graduate student in social psychology, while Erica, hurt by her husband's affair, attempts an affair of her own with Sandy Finkelstein, an old school friend who now goes by the name of Zed and manages a local metaphysical bookstore. Brian finds himself a victim of the generation gap; he disapproves of Wendy's use of marijuana, while she disapproves of his drinking alcohol. Her friends seem immature and shallow; Brian seems hopelessly uptight and square. When Wendy becomes pregnant with (possibly) Brian's baby, Brian urges abortion, while Wendy wants a lovechild. Erica, on the other hand, with a newly found freedom, finds herself a prisoner of sex. Finkelstein-Zed seems an intelligent, gentle, sensitive man (although an incredibly unattractive one), and she decides to give herself to him. Zed, however, proves impotent, and the affair is fruitless. Her friend Danielle Zimmern (who is divorced from Leonard Zimmern, brother of the Roger Zimmern who narrates *Imaginary Friends*) is an example of what Erica would have to look forward to after divorce. Having slept unhappily with various men, Danielle passively winds up with Dr. Bernie Kotelchuk, a loutish veterinarian who, after raping her, convinces her to marry him. In the war between the sexes, both Brian and Erica are defeated, and at the end of the novel they march together against the Vietnam War, imagining reconciliation. Yet, just as the war in southeast Asia divided the United States long after its end, so does the Tates' truce suggest that unity will be a long time coming.

The War Between the Tates is Alison Lurie at her best. The novel is carefully crafted, with the controlling metaphor of the war keeping the material well focused. Her main characters are sympathetic and genuine, and the details of the narrative capture with great accuracy the rebellious period of the early 1970's, a period of midlife crisis for the nation as well as for the Tates. The conflict between generations, between radical passions and conventional morality, between those who experimented with sex, drugs, and Eastern philosophy and those who believed in all the traditional American ideals and institutions—these are captured with irony and wit, and with an admirable detachment that avoids moralizing and sermons.

FOREIGN AFFAIRS

First published: 1984
Type of work: Novel

Two Corinth University professors travel to London, where they are confronted by experiences that alter their perceptions and values.

Foreign Affairs won the 1984 Pulitzer Prize in fiction and was nominated for both the American Book Award and National Book Critics Circle Award. Lurie juxtaposes American characters with British ones in order to explore national traits of both. "It's a complex fate to be an American," Henry James once said, and the complex fates of Lurie's two American academics in this novel are a good example.

In the opening chapter, Virginia "Vinnie" Miner, a small, plain, unmarried, fifty-four-year-old Corinth professor of children's literature, is traveling by plane to London, where she intends to do research on folk rhymes of schoolchildren. Feeling alone and having just read a bad review of her latest book, she visualizes herself traveling with an invisible dog named Fido, an imaginary manifestation of her self-pity. The worse she feels, the more Fido whines for attention, until he finally scrambles into her lap and goes to sleep. Seated next to her is American tourist Charles (Chuck) Mumpson, an engineer from Tulsa specializing in waste-disposal systems. Vinnie suffers his amiable conversation during the trip.

In the second chapter, the reader meets Vinnie's colleague Fred Turner, a strikingly handsome young man who is in London to do research on the eighteenth century poet and playwright John Gay, author of *The Beggar's Opera*. Turner, too, is lonely, having just separated from his wife Ruth and knowing no one in London except some graduate school friends and Vinnie, with whom he has had little contact at Corinth. Ripe for female companionship if not an affair, Turner takes up with Lady Rosemary Radley, a beautiful British television actress that he meets at a party. Equally lonely, Vinnie goes out with Mumpson, the waste-disposal specialist.

For the remainder of the novel, Lurie alternates chapters involving Vinnie and Turner, juxtaposing each one's British "affair" with the other's. Neither turns out happily. Mumpson, who seems to Vinnie's British friends like a comic American stereotype of the blustering tourist, dies of a heart attack while scouring the English countryside for traces of Mumpson family roots. Vinnie comes to realize, however, that he truly loved her and was an admirable human being. It was her blind Anglophilia, her tendency to become more snobbish and timid than the worst of the British, that prevented her from loving him completely. Vinnie, who has often had sex but never love, goes back home to Corinth knowing that at least once in her life, someone has loved her.

Turner is less fortunate. Gay, vivacious Rosemary turns out to be lecherous, ugly Mrs. Harris, a drunken, filthy cockney charwoman she dresses up as and pretends to be when she wants to keep Fred and others at a distance. An actress who has specialized in the role of an upperclass beauty, Rosemary plays that role in her public daily life, though her real self, the Mrs. Harris side, comes out when she is alone. More accurately, Rosemary does not seem to know who she is, Lady Radley or Mrs. Harris, and she consequently has lost touch with reality. Like many things in London, the Americans conclude, she is sophisticated and alluring on the surface but ugly and commonplace beneath.

In some ways, *Foreign Affairs* is like the fairy tales that Vinnie Miner (and Alison Lurie) teach and love. Vinnie, the ugly princess, is turned into a beloved beauty by Prince Charming (Charles) Mumpson, while Fred Turner, the handsome prince, falls in love with Rosemary, whose outward beauty hides the wicked witch within. Like those tales, fact and fancy intermingle (Vinnie's invisible dog Fido, for example), to raise troubling questions about illusion and reality. Contrary to the way things seems, the novel insists, true love, true goodness, and true beauty and ugliness exist, almost magically, beneath the surface of things.

Summary

Author Gore Vidal has called Alison Lurie the "Queen Herod of modern fiction," a reference to her capacity for slaying what seems most sacred to many people—marriage and the family, higher learning and intellect, and American life-styles and values. Yet, while she has an undeniable wit and savage irony in her novels, she also has a passion for truth, a generosity of spirit, and a reluctance to judge human conduct by any one set of restrictive standards.

Taken together, her eight novels constitute a major achievement of comic writing and detached observation of American life, and the artistry of her prose and carefully crafted narratives place her in the tradition of America's finest novelists.

Bibliography

Aldridge, John W. "How Good is Alison Lurie?" *Commentary* 59 (January, 1975): 79-81.

Helfland, Michael S. "The Dialectic of Self and Community in Alison Lurie's *The War Between the Tates*." *Perspectives on Contemporary Literature* 3, no. 2 (1977): 65-70.

Lurie, Alison. "Alison Lurie: An Interview." Interview by Liz Lear. *Key West Review* 1 (Spring, 1988): 42-52.

____________. "An Interview with Alison Lurie." Interview by David Jackson. *Shenandoah* 31, no. 4 (1980): 15-27.

Pearlman, Mickey, and Katherine Usher Henderson, eds. "Alison Lurie." In *Inter/View: Talks with America's Writing Women*. Lexington: University Press of Kentucky, 1990.

Kenneth Seib

MAGILL'S SURVEY OF AMERICAN LITERATURE

GLOSSARY

Absurdism: A philosophical attitude underlining the alienation that humans experience in what absurdists see as a universe devoid of meaning; literature of the absurd often purposely lacks logic, coherence, and intelligibility.

Act: One of the major divisions of a play or opera; the typical number of acts in a play ranges from one to four.

Agrarianism: A movement of the 1920's and 1930's in which John Crowe Ransom, Allen Tate, Robert Penn Warren, and other Southern writers championed the agrarian society of their region against the industrialized society of the North.

Allegory: A literary mode in which a second level of meaning (wherein characters, events, and settings represent abstractions) is encoded within the narrative.

Alliteration: The repetition of consonant sounds focused at the beginning of syllables, as in: "Large *m*annered *m*otions of his *m*ythy *m*ind."

Allusion: A reference to a historical event or to another literary text that adds dimension or meaning to a literary work.

Alter ego: A character's other self—sometimes a double, sometimes another side of the character's personality, sometimes a dear and constant companion.

Ambiguity: The capacity of language to sustain multiple meanings; ambiguity can add to both the richness and the concentration of literary language.

Angst: A pervasive feeling of anxiety and depression, often associated with the moral and spiritual uncertainties of the twentieth century.

Antagonist: The major character or force in opposition to the protagonist or hero.

Antihero: A fictional figure who tries to define himself and to establish his own codes, or a protagonist who simply lacks traditional heroic qualities.

Apostrophe: A poetic device in which the speaker addresses either someone not physically present or something not physically capable of hearing the words addressed.

Aside: A short passage generally spoken by one dramatic character in an undertone, or directed to the audience, so as not to be heard by the other characters onstage.

Assonance: A term for the association of words with identical vowel sounds but different consonants; "stars," "arms," and "park," for example, all contain identical "a" (and "ar") sounds.

Atmosphere: The general mood or tone of a work; it is often associated with setting, but can also be established by action or dialogue.

Autobiography: A form of nonfiction writing in which the author narrates events of his or her own life.

Avant-garde: A term describing works intended to expand the conventions of a genre through the experimental treatment of form and/or content.

Bardic voice: A passionate poetic voice modeled after that of a bard, or tribal poet/singer, who composed lyric or epic poetry to honor a chief or recite tribal history.

***Bildungsroman*:** Sometimes called the "novel of education," the *Bildungsroman* focuses on the growth of a young protagonist who is learning about the world and finding his place in life; typical examples are James Joyce's *A Portrait of the Artist as a Young Man* (1916) and Thomas Wolfe's *Look Homeward, Angel* (1929).

Biography: Nonfiction that details the events of a particular individual's life.

Black humor: A general term of modern origin that refers to a form of "sick humor" that is intended to produce laughter out of the morbid and the taboo.

Blank verse: Lines of unrhymed iambic pentameter; it is a poetic form that allows much flexibility, and it has been used since the Elizabethan era.

Caesura: A pause or break in a poem; it is most commonly indicated by a punctuation mark such as a comma, dash, semicolon, or period.

Canon: A generally accepted list of literary works; it may refer to works by a single author or works in a genre. The literary canon often refers to the texts that are thought to belong on university reading lists.

Catharsis: A term from Aristotle's *Poetics* referring to the purgation of the spectators' emotions of pity and fear as aroused by the actions of the tragic hero.

Character: A personage appearing in any literary or dramatic work.

Chorus: An individual or group sometimes used in drama to comment on the action; the chorus was used extensively in classical Greek drama.

Classicism: A literary stance or value system consciously based on classical Greek and Roman literature; it generally denotes a cluster of values including formal discipline, restrained expression, reverence for tradition, and an objective rather than a subjective orientation.

Climax: The moment in a work of fiction or drama at which the action reaches its highest intensity and is resolved.

Comedy: A lighter form of drama that aims chiefly to amuse and that ends happily; comedic forms range from physical (slapstick) humor to subtle intellectual humor.

Comedy of manners: A type of drama which treats humorously, and often satirically, the behavior within an artificial, highly sophisticated society.

Comic relief: A humorous incident or scene in an otherwise serious or tragic work intended to release the reader's or audience's tensions through laughter without detracting from the serious material.

Conceit: One type of metaphor, the conceit is used for comparisons which are highly intellectualized. When T. S. Eliot, for example, says that winding streets are like a tedious argument of insidious intent, there is no clear connection between the two, so the reader must apply abstract logic to fill in the missing links.

Confessional poetry: Autobiographical poetry in which personal revelation provides a basis for the intellectual or theoretical study of moral, religious, or aesthetic concerns.

Conflation: The fusion of variant readings of a text into a composite whole.

Conflict: The struggle that develops as a result of the opposition between the protagonist and another person, the natural world, society, or some force within the self.

Connotation: A type of meaning that depends on the associative meanings of a word beyond its formal definition. (*See also* Denotation.)

Conventions: All those devices of stylization, compression, and selection that constitute the necessary differences between art and life.

Counterplot: A secondary action coincident with the major action of a fictional or dramatic work. The counterplot is generally a reflection on or variation of the main action and is strongly integrated into the whole of the work.

Couplet: Any two succeeding lines of poetry that rhyme.

Cubism: In literature, a style of poetry, such as that of E. E. Cummings and Archibald MacLeish, which first fragments an experience, then rearranges its elements into some new artistic entity.

Dactyl: A metrical foot in which a stressed syllable is followed by two unstressed syllables; an example of a dactyllic line is "After the pangs of a desperate lover."

Deconstruction: An extremely influential contemporary school of criticism based on the works of the French philosopher Jacques Derrida. Deconstruction treats literary works as unconscious reflections of the myths of Western culture; the primary myth is that there is a meaningful world which language signifies or represents. The Deconstructionist critic is often concerned with showing how a literary text tacitly subverts the very assumptions or myths on which it ostensibly rests.

Denotation: The explicit, formal definition of a word, exclusive of its implications and emotional associations. (*See also* Connotation.)

Denouement: Originally French, this word literally means "unknotting" or "untying" and is another term for the catastrophe or resolution of a dramatic action, the solution or clarification of a plot.

Detective story: In the so-called "classic" detective story, the focus is on a crime solved by a detective through interpretation of evidence and clever reasoning. Many modern practitioners of the genre, however, have deemphasized the puzzle-like qualities, stressing instead characterization, theme, and other elements of mainstream fiction.

Determinism: The belief that a person's actions are essentially determined by biological and environmental factors, with free will playing a negligible role. (*See also* Naturalism.)

Deus ex machina: Latin, meaning "god out of a machine." In the Greek theater, it referred to the use of a god lowered by means of a mechanism onto the stage to untangle the plot or save the hero. It has come to signify any artificial device for the easy resolution of dramatic difficulties.

Dialogue: Speech exchanged between characters or even, in a looser sense, the thoughts of a single character.

Dime novel: A type of inexpensive book very popular in the late nineteenth century that told a formulaic tale of war, adventure, or romance.

Domestic tragedy: A serious and usually realistic play with lower-class or middle-class characters and milieu, typically dealing with personal or domestic concerns.

Donnée: From the French verb meaning "to give," the term refers to the premise or the given set of circumstances from which the plot will proceed.

Drama: Any work designed to be represented on a stage by actors. More specifically, the term has come to signify a play of a serious nature and intent which may end either happily (comedy) or unhappily (tragedy).

Dramatic irony: A form of irony that most typically occurs when the spoken lines of a character are perceived by the audience to have a double meaning or when the audience knows more about a situation than the character knows.

Dramatic monologue: A poem in which the narrator addresses a silent persona whose presence greatly influences what the narrator tells the reader.

***Dramatis personae*:** The characters in a play; often it refers to a printed list defining the characters and their relationships.

Dramaturgy: The composition of plays; the term is occasionally used to refer to the performance or acting of plays.

Dream vision: A poem presented as a dream in which the poet-dreamer envisions people and events that frequently have allegorical overtones.

Dualism: A theory that the universe is explicable in terms of two basic, conflicting entities, such as good and evil, mind and matter, or the physical and the spiritual.

Elegy: The elegy and pastoral elegy are distinguishable by their subject matter, not their form. The elegy is usually a long, rhymed, strophic poem whose subject is meditation upon death or a lamentable theme; the pastoral elegy uses a pastoral scene to sing of death or love.

Elizabethan: Of or referring to the reign of Queen Elizabeth I of England, lasting from 1558 to 1603, a period of important artistic achievements; William Shakespeare was an Elizabethan playwright.

End-stop: When a punctuated pause occurs at the end of a line of poetry, the line is said to be end-stopped.

Enjambment: When a line of poetry is not end-stopped and instead carries over to the next line, the line is said to be enjambed.

Epic: This term usually refers to a long narrative poem which presents the exploits of a central figure of high position; it is also used to designate a long novel that has the style or structure usually associated with an epic.

Epilogue: A closing section or speech at the end of a play or other literary work that makes some reflection on the preceding action.

Episodic narrative: A work that is held together primarily by a loose connection of self-sufficient episodes. Picaresque novels often have an episodic structure.

Epithalamion: A bridal song or poem, a genre deriving from the poets of antiquity.

Essay: A nonfiction work, usually short, that analyzes or interprets a particular subject or idea; it is often written from a personal point of view.

Existentialism: A philosophical and literary term for a group of attitudes surrounding the idea that existence precedes essence; according to Jean-Paul Sartre, "man is nothing else but what he makes himself." Existential literature exhibits an awareness of the absurdity of the universe and is preoccupied with the single ethical choice that determines the meaning of a person's existence.

Expressionism: A movement in the arts, especially in German painting, dominant in the decade following World War I; external reality is consciously distorted in order to portray the world as it is "viewed emotionally."

Fabulation: The act of lying to invent or tell a fable, sometimes used to designate the fable itself.

Fantastic: The fantastic has been defined as a genre that lies between the "uncanny" and the "marvelous." All three genres embody the familiar world but present an event that cannot be explained by the laws of the familiar world.

Farce: A play that evokes laughter through such low-comedy devices as physical humor, rough wit, and ridiculous and improbable situations and characters.

First person: A point of view in which the narrator of a story or poem addresses the reader directly, often using the pronoun "I," thereby allowing the reader direct access to the narrator's thoughts.

Flashback: A scene in a fictional or dramatic work depicting events that occurred at an earlier time.

Foot: A rhythmic unit of poetry consisting of two or three syllables grouped together; the most common foot in English is the iamb, composed of one unstressed syllable attached to one stressed syllable.

Foreshadowing: A device used to create suspense or dramatic irony by indicating through suggestion what will take place in the future.

Formalism: A school of literary criticism which particularly emphasizes the form of the work of art—that is, the type or genre to which it belongs.

Frame story: A story that provides a framework for another story (or stories) told within it.

Free verse: A poem that does not conform to such traditional conventions as meter or rhyme, and that does not establish any pattern within itself, is said to be a "free verse" poem.

Genre: A type or category of literature, such as tragedy, novel, memoir, poem, or essay; a genre has a particular set of conventions and expectations.

Genre fiction: Categories of popular fiction such as the mystery, the romance, and the Western; although the term can be used in a neutral sense, "genre fiction" is often used dismissively to refer to fiction in which the writer is bound by more or less rigid conventions.

Gothic novel: A form of fiction developed in the eighteenth century that focuses on horror and the supernatural.

Grotesque: Characterized by a breakup of the everyday world by mysterious forces, the form differs from fantasy in that the reader is not sure whether to react with humor or with horror.

Half rhyme. *See* Slant rhyme.

Hamartia. *See* Tragic flaw.

Harlem Renaissance: A flowering of black American writing, in all literary genres, in the 1930's and 1940's.

Hero/Heroine: The most important character in a drama or other literary work. Popularly, the term has come to refer to a character who possesses extraordinary prowess or virtue, but as a technical term it simply indicates the central participant in a dramatic action. (*See also* Protagonist.)

Heroic couplet: A pair of rhyming iambic pentameter lines traditionally used in epic poetry; a heroic couplet often serves as a self-contained witticism or pithy observation.

Historical novel: A novel that depicts past events, usually public in nature, and that features real as well as fictional people; the relationship between fiction and history in the form varies greatly depending on the author.

Hubris: Excessive pride, the characteristic in tragic heroes such as Oedipus, Doctor Faustus, and Macbeth that leads them to transgress moral codes or ignore warnings. (*See also* Tragic flaw.)

Humanism: A man-centered rather than god-centered view of the universe that usually stresses reason, restraint, and human values; in the Renaissance, humanism devoted itself to the revival of the life, thought, language, and literature of ancient Greece and Rome.

Hyperbole: The use of gross exaggeration for rhetorical effect, based upon the assumption that the reader will not respond to the exaggeration literally.

Iamb: The basic metric foot of the English language, the iamb associates one unstressed syllable with one stressed syllable. The line "So long as men can breathe or eyes can see" is composed of five iambs (a form called iambic pentameter).

Imagery: The simulation of sensory perception through figurative language; imagery can be controlled to create emotional or intellectual effects.

Imagism: A school of poetry prominent in Great Britain and North America between 1909 and 1918. The objectives of Imagism were accurate description, objective presentation, concentration and economy, new rhythms, freedom of choice in subject matter, and suggestion rather than explanation.

Interior monologue: The speech of a character designed to introduce the reader directly to the character's internal life; it differs from other monologues in that it attempts to reproduce thought before logical organization is imposed upon it.

Irony: An effect that occurs when a writer's or a character's real meaning is different from (and frequently opposite to) his or her apparent meaning. (*See also* Dramatic irony.)

Jazz Age: The 1920's, a period of prosperity, sweeping social change, frequent excess, and youthful rebellion, for which F. Scott Fitzgerald is the acknowledged spokesman.

***Künstlerroman*:** An apprenticeship novel in which the protagonist, a young artist, faces the conflicts of growing up and coming to understand the purpose of his life and art.

Leitmotif: The repetition in a work of literature of a word, phrase, or image which serves to establish the tone or otherwise unify the piece.

Line: A rhythmical unit within a poem between the foot and the poem's larger structural units; the words or feet in a line are usually in a single row.

Lyric poetry: Poetry that is generally short, adaptable to metrical variation, and personal in theme; it may explore deeply personal feelings about life.

Magical realism: Imaginary or fantastic scenes and occurrences presented in a meticulously realistic style.

Melodrama: A play in which characters are clearly either virtuous or evil and are pitted against one another in suspenseful, often sensational situations.

Memoir: A piece of autobiographical writing which emphasizes important events in which the author has participated and prominent people whom the author has known.

Metafiction: Fiction that manifests a reflexive tendency and shows a consciousness of itself as an artificial creation; such terms as "postmodernist fiction," "antifiction," and "surfiction" also refer to this type of fiction.

Metaphor: A figure of speech in which two different things are identified with each other, as in the T. S. Eliot line, "The whole earth is our hospital"; the term is also widely used to identify many kinds of analogies.

Metaphysical poetry: A type of poetry that stresses the intellectual over the emotional; it is marked by irony, paradox, and striking comparisons of dissimilar things, the latter frequently being farfetched to the point of eccentricity.

Meter: The rhythmic pattern of language when it is formed into lines of poetry; when the rhythm of language is organized and regulated so as to affect the meaning and emotional response to the words, the rhythm has been refined into meter.

Mise-en-scène: The staging of a drama, including scenery, costumes, movable furniture (properties), and, by extension, the positions (blocking) and gestures of the actors.

Mock-heroic style: A form of burlesque in which a trivial subject is absurdly elevated through use of the meter, diction, and familiar devices of the epic poem.

Modernism: An international movement in the arts which began in the early years of the twentieth century; modernism in general was characterized by its international idiom, by its interest in cultures distant in space or time, by its emphasis on formal experimentation, and by its sense of dislocation and radical change.

Monologue: An extended speech by one character in a drama. If the character is alone onstage, unheard by other characters, the monologue is more specifically referred to as a soliloquy.

Musical comedy: A theatrical form mingling song, dance, and spoken dialogue which was developed in the United States in the twentieth century; it was derived from vaudeville and operetta.

Myth: Anonymous traditional stories dealing with basic human concepts and fundamentally opposing principles; a myth is often constructed as a story that tells of supposedly historical events.

Narrator: The character who recounts the story in a work of fiction.

Naturalism: The application of the principles of scientific determinism to fiction. Although it usually refers more to the choice of subject matter than to technical conventions, conventions associated with the movement center on the author's attempt to be precise and objective in description and detail, regardless of whether the events described are sordid or shocking. (*See also* Determinism.)

Neoclassicism: The type of classicism that dominated English literature from the Restoration to the late eighteenth century. Modeling itself on the literature of ancient Greece and Rome, neoclassicism exalts the virtues of proportion, unity, harmony, grace, decorum, taste, manners, and restraint; it values realism and reason.

New Criticism: A reaction against the "old criticism" that either saw art as self-expression, applied extrinsic criteria of morality and value, or gave credence to the professed intentions of the author. The New Criticism regards a work of art as an autonomous object, a self-contained universe. It holds that a close reading of literary texts will reveal their meanings and the complexities of their verbal texture as well as the oppositions and tensions balanced in the text.

New journalism: Writing that largely abandons the traditional objectivity of journalism in order to express the subjective response of the observer.

Nonfiction novel: A novel such as Truman Capote's *In Cold Blood*, which, though taking actual people and events as its subject matter, uses fictional techniques to develop the narrative.

Novel: A long fictional form that is generally concerned with individual characterization and with presenting a social world and a detailed environment.

Novel of ideas: A novel in which the characters, plot, and dialogue serve to develop some controlling idea or to present the clash of ideas.

Novel of manners: The classic example of the form might be the novels of Jane Austen, wherein the customs and conventions of a social group of a particular time and place are realistically, and often satirically, portrayed.

Novella, novelle, nouvelle, novelette: These terms usually refer to that form of fiction which is said to be longer than a short story and shorter than a novel; "novella" is the term usually used to refer to American works in this genre.

Ode: A lyric poem that treats a unified subject with elevated emotion and seriousness of purpose, usually ending with a satisfactory resolution.

Old Criticism: Criticism predating the New Criticism and bringing extrinsic criteria to bear on the analysis of literature as authorial self-expression (Romanticism), critical self-expression (Impressionism), or work that is dependent upon moral or ethical absolutes (new humanism).

Omniscient narration: A godlike point of view from which the narrator sees all and knows everything there is to know about the story and its characters.

One-act play: A short, unified dramatic work, the one-act play is usually quite limited in number of characters and scene changes; the action often revolves around a single incident or event.

Opera: A complex combination of various art forms, opera is a form of dramatic entertainment consisting of a play set to music.

Original Sin: A concept of the innate depravity of man's nature resulting from Adam's sin and fall from grace.

Paradox: A statement that initially seems to be illogical or self-contradictory yet eventually proves to embody a complex truth.

Parataxis: The placing of clauses or phrases in a series without the use of coordinating or subordinating terms.

Pathos: The quality in a character that evokes pity or sorrow from the observer.

Pentameter: A line of poetry consisting of five recognizable rhythmic units called feet.

Picaresque novel: A form of fiction that involves a central rogue figure, or picaro, who usually tells his own story. The plot structure is normally episodic, and the episodes usually focus on how the picaro lives by his wits.

Plot: The sequence of the occurrence of events in a dramatic action. A plot may be unified around a single action, but it may also consist of a series of disconnected incidents; it is then referred to as "episodic."

Poem: A unified composition that uses the rhythms and sounds of language, as well as devices such as metaphor, to communicate emotions and experiences to the reader or hearer.

Point of view: The perspective from which a story is presented to the reader. In simplest terms, it refers to whether narration is first-person (directly addressed to the reader as if told by one involved in the narrative) or third-person (usually a more objective, distanced perspective).

Postmodernism: The term is loosely applied to various artistic movements which have followed so-called high modernism, represented by such giants as James Joyce and Pablo Picasso. The term is frequently applied to the works of writers (such as Thomas Pynchon and John Barth) who exhibit a self-conscious awareness of their predecessors as well as a reflexive treatment of fictional form.

Prose poem: A type of poem, usually less than a page in length, that appears on the page like prose; there is great stylistic and thematic variety within the genre.

Protagonist: Originally, in the Greek drama, the "first actor," who played the leading role. The term has come to signify the most important character in a drama or story. It is not unusual for there to be more than one protagonist in a work. (*See also* Hero/Heroine.)

Psychoanalytic theory: A tremendously influential theory of the unconscious developed by Sigmund Freud, it divides the human psyche into three components—the id, the ego, and the superego. In this theory, the psyche represses instinctual and sexual desires, and channels (sublimates) those desires into socially acceptable behavior.

Psychological novel: A form of fiction in which character, especially the inner life of characters, is the primary focus. The form has characterized much of the work of James Joyce, Virginia Woolf, and William Faulkner.

Psychological realism: A type of realism that tries to reproduce the complex psychological motivations behind human behavior; writers in the late nineteenth and early twentieth centuries were particularly influenced by Sigmund Freud's theories. (*See also* Psychoanalytic theory.)

Pun: A pun occurs when words which have similar pronunciations have entirely different meanings; a pun can establish a connection between two meanings or contexts that the reader would not ordinarily make. The result may be a striking connection or simply a humorously accidental connection.

Quatrain: Any four-line stanza is a quatrain; other than the couplet, the quatrain is the most common type of stanza.

Rationalism: A system of thought which seeks truth through the exercise of reason rather than by means of emotional response or revelation.

Realism: A literary technique in which the primary convention is to render an illusion of fidelity to external reality. Realism is often identified as the primary method of the novel form; the realist movement in the late nineteenth century coincided with the full development of the novel form.

Regional novel: Any novel in which the character of a given geographical region plays a decisive role; the Southern United States, for example, has fostered a strong regional tradition.

Representationalism: An approach to drama that seeks to create the illusion of reality onstage through realistic characters, situations, and settings.

Revue: A theatrical production, typically consisting of sketches, song, and dance, which often comments satirically upon personalities and events of the day; generally there is no plot involved.

Rhyme: A full rhyme comprises two or more words that have the same vowel sound and that end with the same consonant sound: "Hat" and "cat" is a full rhyme, as is "laughter" and "after." Rhyme is also used more broadly as a term for any correspondence in sound between syllables in poetry. (*See also* Slant rhyme.)

Rhyme scheme: Poems which establish a pattern of rhyme have a "rhyme scheme," designated by lowercase letters; the rhyme scheme of ottava rima, for example, is abababcc. Traditional stanza forms are categorized by their rhyme scheme and base meter.

Roman à clef: A fiction wherein actual persons, often celebrities of some sort, are thinly disguised.

Romance: The romance usually differs from the novel form in that the focus is on symbolic events and representational characters rather than on "as-if-real" characters and events. Character is often highly stylized, serving as a function of the plot.

Romantic comedy: A play in which love is the central motive of the dramatic action. The term often refers to plays of the Elizabethan period, such as William Shakespeare's *As You Like It* and *A Midsummer Night's Dream*, but it has also been applied to any modern work that contains similar features.

Romanticism: A widespread cultural movement in the late-eighteenth and early-nineteenth centuries, Romanticism is frequently contrasted with classicism. The term generally suggests primitivism, an interest in folklore, a reverence for nature, a fascination with the demoniac and the macabre, and an assertion of the preeminence of the imagination.

Satire: Satire employs the comedic devices of wit, irony, and exaggeration to expose and condemn human folly, vice, and stupidity.

Scene: In drama, a division of action within an act (some plays are divided only into scenes instead of acts). Sometimes scene division indicates a change of setting or locale; sometimes it simply indicates the entrances and exits of characters.

Science fiction: Fiction in which real or imagined scientific developments or certain givens (such as physical laws, psychological principles, or social conditions) form the basis of an imaginative projection, frequently into the future.

Sentimental novel: A form of fiction popular in the eighteenth century in which emotionalism and optimism are the primary characteristics. The best-known examples are Samuel Richardson's *Pamela* (1740-1741) and Oliver Goldsmith's *The Vicar of Wakefield* (1766).

Sentimentalism: A term used to describe any emotional response that is excessive and disproportionate to its impetus or occasion. It also refers to the eighteenth century idea that human beings are essentially benevolent, devoid of Original Sin and basic depravity.

Setting: The time and place in which the action of a literary work happens. The term also applies to the physical elements of a theatrical production, such as scenery and properties.

Short story: A concise work of fiction, shorter than a novella, that is usually more concerned with mood, effect, or a single event than with plot or extensive characterization.

Simile: Loosely defined, a simile is a type of metaphor which signals a comparison by the use of the words "like" or "as." Shakespeare's line, "My mistress' eyes are nothing like the sun," establishes a comparison between the woman's eyes and the sun, and is a simile.

Slant rhyme: A slant rhyme, or half rhyme, occurs when words with identical consonants but different vowel sounds are associated; "fall" and "well," and "table" and "bauble" are slant rhymes.

Slapstick: Low comedy in which physical action (such as a kick in the rear, tripping, and knocking over people or objects) evokes laughter.

Social realism: A type of realism in which the social and economic conditions in which characters live figure prominently in their situations, actions, and outlooks.

Soliloquy: An extended speech delivered by a character alone onstage, unheard by other characters. Soliloquy is a form of monologue, and it typically reveals the intimate thoughts and emotions of the speaker.

Sonnet: A traditional poetic form that is almost always composed of fourteen lines of rhymed iambic pentameter; a turning point usually divides the poem into two parts, with the first part presenting a situation and the second part reflecting on it.

Southern Gothic: A term applied to the scenes of decay, incest, madness, and violence often found in the fiction of William Faulkner, Erskine Caldwell, and other Southern writers.

Speaker: The voice which speaks the words of a poem—sometimes a fictional character in an invented situation, sometimes the author speaking directly to the reader, sometimes the author speaking from behind the disguise of a persona.

Stanza: When lines of poetry are meant to be taken as a unit, and the unit recurs throughout the poem, that unit is called a stanza; a four-line unit is one common stanza.

Stream of consciousness: The depiction of the thought processes of a character, insofar as this is possible, without any mediating structures. The metaphor of consciousness as a "stream" suggests a rush of thoughts and images governed by free association rather than by strictly rational development; the term is often used loosely as a synonym for interior monologue.

Stress: When more emphasis is placed on one syllable in a line of poetry than on another syllable, that syllable is said to be stressed.

Subplot: A secondary action coincident with the main action of a fictional or dramatic work. A subplot may be a reflection upon the main action, but it may also be largely unrelated. (*See also* Counterplot.)

Surrealism: An approach to literature and art that startlingly combines seemingly incompatible elements; surrealist writing usually has a bizarre, dreamlike, or nightmarish quality.

Symbol: A literary symbol is an image that stands for something else; it may evoke a cluster of meanings rather than a single specific meaning.

Symbolism: A literary movement encompassing the work of a group of French writers in the latter half of the nineteenth century, a group that included Charles Baudelaire, Stéphane Mallarmé, and Paul Verlaine. According to Symbolism, there is a mystical correspondence between the natural and spiritual worlds.

Syntax: A linguistic term used to describe the study of the ways in which words are arranged sequentially to produce grammatical units such as phrases, clauses, and sentences.

Tableau: A silent, stationary grouping of performers in a theatrical performance.

Terza rima: A rhyming three-line stanza form in which the middle line of one stanza rhymes with the first line of the following stanza.

Tetrameter: A line of poetry consisting of four recognizable rhythmic units called feet.

Theater of the absurd: The general name given to plays that express a basic belief that life is illogical, irrational, formless, and contradictory and that man is without meaning or purpose. This perspective often leads to the abandonment of traditional theatrical forms and coherent dialogue.

Theme: Loosely defined as what a literary work means. The theme of W. B. Yeats's poem "Sailing to Byzantium," for example, might be interpreted as the failure of man's attempt to isolate himself within the world of art.

Thespian: Another term for an actor; also, of or relating to the theater. The word derives from Thespis, by tradition the first actor of the Greek theater.

Third person: Third-person narration is related from a point of view more distant from the story than first-person narration; the narrator is not an identifiable "I" persona. A third-person point of view may be limited or omniscient ("all-knowing").

Three unities. *See* Unities.

Tone: Tone usually refers to the dominant mood of a work. (*See also* Atmosphere.)

Tragedy: A form of drama that is serious in action and intent and that involves disastrous events and death; classical Greek drama observed specific guidelines for tragedy, but the term is now sometimes applied to a range of dramatic or fictional situations.

Tragic flaw: Also known as hamartia, it is the weakness or error in judgment in a tragic hero or protagonist that causes the character's downfall; it may proceed from ignorance or a moral fault. Excessive pride (hubris) is one traditional tragic flaw.

Travel literature: Writing which emphasizes the author's subjective response to places visited, especially faraway, exotic, and culturally different locales.

Trimeter: A line of poetry consisting of three recognizable rhythmic units called feet.

Trochee: One of the most common feet in English poetry, the trochee associates one stressed syllable with one unstressed syllable, as in the line, "Double, double, toil and trouble."

Unities: A set of rules for proper dramatic construction formulated by European Renaissance drama critics and derived from classical Greek concepts: A play should have no scenes or subplots irrelevant to the central action, should not cover a period of more than twenty-four hours, and should not occur in more than one place.

Verisimilitude: The attempt to have the readers of a literary work believe that it conforms to reality rather than to its own laws.

Verse: A generic term for poetry; verse also refers in a narrower sense to poetry that is humorous or merely superficial, as in "greeting-card verse."

Verse paragraph: A division within a poem that is created by logic or syntax rather than by form; verse paragraphs are important for determining the movement of a poem and the logical association between ideas.

Victorian novel: Although the Victorian period extended from 1837 to 1901, the term "Victorian novel" does not include works from the later decades of Queen Victoria's reign. The term loosely refers to the sprawling works of novelists such as Charles Dickens and William Makepeace Thackeray, which are characterized by a broad social canvas.

Villanelle: The villanelle is a French verse form assimilated by English prosody. It is usually composed of nineteen lines divided into five tercets and a quatrain, rhyming aba, bba, aba, aba, abaa.

Well-made play: A type of play constructed according to a nineteenth century French formula; the plot often revolves around a secret (revealed at the end) known only to some of the characters. Misunderstanding, suspense, and coincidence are among the devices used.

Western novel: The Western novel is defined by a relatively predictable combination of conventions and recurring themes. These predictable elements, familiar from television and film Westerns, differentiate the Western from historical novels and other works which may be set in the Old West.

Worldview: Frequently rendered as the German *weltanschauung*, it is a comprehensive set of beliefs or assumptions by means of which one interprets what goes on in the world.

LIST OF AUTHORS

ABBEY, EDWARD, **1**-1
ADAMS, HENRY, **1**-10
AGEE, JAMES, **1**-22
ALBEE, EDWARD, **1**-30
ALCOTT, LOUISA MAY, **1**-41
ALGREN, NELSON, **1**-49
ANDERSON, SHERWOOD, **1**-61
ASHBERY, JOHN, **1**-69
AUCHINCLOSS, LOUIS, **1**-80

BACA, JIMMY SANTIAGO, **1**-94
BALDWIN, JAMES, **1**-101
BARAKA, AMIRI, **1**-113
BARNES, DJUNA, **1**-121
BARTH, JOHN, **1**-129
BARTHELME, DONALD, **1**-141
BEATTIE, ANN, **1**-151
BELLOW, SAUL, **1**-161
BERRY, WENDELL, **1**-175
BERRYMAN, JOHN, **1**-186
BIERCE, AMBROSE, **1**-200
BISHOP, ELIZABETH, **1**-207
BLY, ROBERT, **1**-216
BOWLES, PAUL, **1**-227
BOYLE, T. CORAGHESSAN, **1**-238
BRADBURY, RAY, **1**-246
BRADSTREET, ANNE, **1**-259
BRAUTIGAN, RICHARD, **1**-267
BRODKEY, HAROLD, **1**-279
BUKOWSKI, CHARLES, **1**-290

CAIN, JAMES M., **1**-302
CALDWELL, ERSKINE, **1**-311
CAPOTE, TRUMAN, **1**-319
CARVER, RAYMOND, **1**-332
CATHER, WILLA, **1**-343
CHANDLER, RAYMOND, **1**-354
CHEEVER, JOHN, **1**-366
CHOPIN, KATE, **1**-384
COOPER, JAMES FENIMORE, **1**-392
CORMIER, ROBERT, **1**-404
CRANE, HART, **2**-415
CRANE, STEPHEN, **2**-427
CREELEY, ROBERT, **2**-442
CUMMINGS, E. E., **2**-455

DELANY, SAMUEL R., **2**-466
DeLILLO, DON, **2**-474
DICK, PHILIP K., **2**-486
DICKEY, JAMES, **2**-498
DICKINSON, EMILY, **2**-509
DIDION, JOAN, **2**-528
DILLARD, ANNIE, **2**-539
DOCTOROW, E. L., **2**-550
DOS PASSOS, JOHN, **2**-561
DREISER, THEODORE, **2**-571
DUNBAR, PAUL LAURENCE, **2**-582
DUNCAN, ROBERT, **2**-589

ELIOT, T. S., **2**-602
ELLISON, RALPH, **2**-618
EMERSON, RALPH WALDO, **2**-627
ERDRICH, LOUISE, **2**-642

FARRELL, JAMES T., **2**-656
FAULKNER, WILLIAM, **2**-665
FITZGERALD, F. SCOTT, **2**-679
FRANKLIN, BENJAMIN, **2**-695
FRENEAU, PHILIP, **2**-703
FROST, ROBERT, **2**-713

GADDIS, WILLIAM, **2**-729
GARDNER, JOHN, **2**-741
GIBSON, WILLIAM, **2**-756
GINSBERG, ALLEN, **2**-764
GIOVANNI, NIKKI, **2**-777
GLASGOW, ELLEN, **2**-787
GORDON, MARY, **2**-798

HAMMETT, DASHIELL, **2**-810
HANSBERRY, LORRAINE, **2**-820
HARTE, BRET, **2**-829
HAWTHORNE, NATHANIEL, **3**-837
H. D., **3**-852
HEINLEIN, ROBERT A., **3**-863
HELLER, JOSEPH, **3**-878
HELLMAN, LILLIAN, **3**-886
HEMINGWAY, ERNEST, **3**-897
HERBERT, FRANK, **3**-913
HINTON, S. E., **3**-921
HOWELLS, WILLIAM DEAN, **3**-932
HUGHES, LANGSTON, **3**-943
HURSTON, ZORA NEALE, **3**-955

IRVING, JOHN, **3**-967
IRVING, WASHINGTON, **3**-980

JAMES, HENRY, **3**-989
JEFFERS, ROBINSON, **3**-1003
JEWETT, SARAH ORNE, **3**-1016

KEILLOR, GARRISON, **3**-1028
KENNEDY, WILLIAM, **3**-1039
KEROUAC, JACK, **3**-1050
KESEY, KEN, **3**-1059
KING, STEPHEN, **3**-1067
KINGSTON, MAXINE HONG, **3**-1082
KNOWLES, JOHN, **3**-1095

L'AMOUR, LOUIS, **3**-1103
LEE, HARPER, **3**-1113
LE GUIN, URSULA K., **3**-1120
LEWIS, SINCLAIR, **3**-1129
LONDON, JACK, **3**-1142
LONGFELLOW, HENRY WADSWORTH, **3**-1155
LOWELL, ROBERT, **3**-1166
LURIE, ALISON, **3**-1178

McCARTHY, CORMAC, **4**-1191
McCARTHY, MARY, **4**-1204
McCULLERS, CARSON, **4**-1215
MACDONALD, ROSS, **4**-1226
McGUANE, THOMAS, **4**-1239
McMURTRY, LARRY, **4**-1250
MAILER, NORMAN, **4**-1265
MALAMUD, BERNARD, **4**-1276
MAMET, DAVID, **4**-1291
MASTERS, EDGAR LEE, **4**-1302
MATTHIESSEN, PETER, **4**-1310
MELVILLE, HERMAN, **4**-1321
MERRILL, JAMES, **4**-1337
MICHENER, JAMES A., **4**-1348
MILLER, ARTHUR, **4**-1363
MILLER, HENRY, **4**-1374
MOMADAY, N. SCOTT, **4**-1383
MOORE, MARIANNE, **4**-1394
MORRIS, WRIGHT, **4**-1408
MORRISON, TONI, **4**-1422
MUKHERJEE, BHARATI, **4**-1435

NABOKOV, VLADIMIR, **4**-1448
NAYLOR, GLORIA, **4**-1463
NIN, ANAÏS, **4**-1473
NORRIS, FRANK, **4**-1485

OATES, JOYCE CAROL, **4**-1497
O'CONNOR, FLANNERY, **4**-1513
O'HARA, JOHN, **4**-1530
OLSEN, TILLIE, **5**-1543
OLSON, CHARLES, **5**-1555
O'NEILL, EUGENE, **5**-1567
OZICK, CYNTHIA, **5**-1583

PALEY, GRACE, **5**-1594
PERCY, WALKER, **5**-1606
PHILLIPS, JAYNE ANNE, **5**-1618
PLATH, SYLVIA, **5**-1626
POE, EDGAR ALLAN, **5**-1640
PORTER, KATHERINE ANNE, **5**-1655
PORTIS, CHARLES, **5**-1665
POTOK, CHAIM, **5**-1676
POUND, EZRA, **5**-1688
POWERS, J. F., **5**-1703
PRICE, REYNOLDS, **5**-1715
PYNCHON, THOMAS, **5**-1726

REED, ISHMAEL, **5**-1741
RICH, ADRIENNE, **5**-1753
RICHTER, CONRAD, **5**-1764
ROETHKE, THEODORE, **5**-1772
ROTH, PHILIP, **5**-1783

SALINGER, J. D., **5**-1798
SANDBURG, CARL, **5**-1809
SAROYAN, WILLIAM, **5**-1817
SHANGE, NTOZAKE, **5**-1829
SHEPARD, SAM, **5**-1841
SILKO, LESLIE MARMON, **5**-1854
SIMON, NEIL, **5**-1862
SNYDER, GARY, **5**-1873
STEINBECK, JOHN, **6**-1885
STEVENS, WALLACE, **6**-1900
STONE, ROBERT, **6**-1914
STOWE, HARRIET BEECHER, **6**-1926
SWARTHOUT, GLENDON, **6**-1932

THOREAU, HENRY DAVID, **6**-1942
TWAIN, MARK, **6**-1954
TYLER, ANNE, **6**-1972

UPDIKE, JOHN, **6**-1983

VIDAL, GORE, **6**-1998
VONNEGUT, KURT, JR., **6**-2009

WALKER, ALICE, **6**-2026
WARREN, ROBERT PENN, **6**-2038

LIST OF AUTHORS

WELTY, EUDORA, **6**-2050
WEST, NATHANAEL, **6**-2063
WHARTON, EDITH, **6**-2071
WHITMAN, WALT, **6**-2083
WIDEMAN, JOHN EDGAR, **6**-2100
WILBUR, RICHARD, **6**-2112
WILDER, THORNTON, **6**-2123
WILLIAMS, TENNESSEE, **6**-2135
WILLIAMS, WILLIAM CARLOS, **6**-2152
WOIWODE, LARRY, **6**-2168
WOLFE, THOMAS, **6**-2180
WOLFE, TOM, **6**-2194
WRIGHT, RICHARD, **6**-2203

ZINDEL, PAUL, **6**-2214